Lecture Notes in Computer Science 14529

The series Lecture Notes in Computer Science (LNCS), including its subseries Lecture Notes in Artificial Intelligence (LNAI) and Lecture Notes in Bioinformatics (LNBI), has established itself as a medium for the publication of new developments in computer science and information technology research, teaching, and education.

LNCS enjoys close cooperation with the computer science R & D community, the series counts many renowned academics among its volume editors and paper authors, and collaborates with prestigious societies. Its mission is to serve this international community by providing an invaluable service, mainly focused on the publication of conference and workshop proceedings and postproceedings. LNCS commenced publication in 1973.

Abderrahim Ait Wakrime ·
Guillermo Navarro-Arribas · Frédéric Cuppens ·
Nora Cuppens · Redouane Benaini
Editors

Risks and Security of Internet and Systems

18th International Conference, CRiSIS 2023
Rabat, Morocco, December 6–8, 2023
Revised Selected Papers

 Springer

Editors
Abderrahim Ait Wakrime (ID)
Computer Science Department, Faculty
of Sciences
Mohammed V University
Rabat, Morocco

Frédéric Cuppens
Polytechnique Montreal
Montréal, QC, Canada

Redouane Benaini
Computer Science Department, Faculty
of Sciences
Mohammed V University
Rabat, Morocco

Guillermo Navarro-Arribas (ID)
Universitat Autònoma de Barcelona
Bellaterra, Barcelona, Spain

Nora Cuppens (ID)
Polytechnique Montréal
Montréal, QC, Canada

ISSN 0302-9743   ISSN 1611-3349 (electronic)
Lecture Notes in Computer Science
ISBN 978-3-031-61230-5   ISBN 978-3-031-61231-2 (eBook)
https://doi.org/10.1007/978-3-031-61231-2

Preface

The 18th International Conference on Risks and Security of Internet and Systems was held during December 6–8, 2023 in Rabat, Morocco. The CRiSIS conference has been active for several years, continuing the tradition of successful conferences: Bourges (2005), Marrakech (2007), Tozeur (2008), Toulouse (2009), Montréal (2010), Timisoara (2011), Cork (2012), La Rochelle (2013), Trento (2014), Mytilene (2015), Roscoff (2016), Dinard (2017), Arcachon (2018), Hammamet (2019), Paris (2020), Ames (2021), and Sousse (2022).

The CRiSIS conference constitutes an open forum for the exchange of state-of-the-art knowledge on security issues in Internet-related applications, networks, and systems. This year's edition had a Program Committee composed of 33 members from the international community. We received 25 submissions from 10 countries around the world, of which 13 were accepted as regular papers complemented with 2 additional short papers. Accepted papers covered broad research areas on both theoretical and practical aspects. These papers include topics such as Machine Learning and Security, Security Approaches and Infrastructure, Security and Transportation Systems, and Blockchain and Distributed Ledger Technologies.

Papers were selected by the Program Committee based on their originality and contribution and which were supplemented by invited papers. The conference was completed, for the benefit of participants, by two outstanding keynotes given by Mohammad Hammoudeh (Aramco Cybersecurity Chair Professor, King Fahd University of Petroleum & Minerals, Saudi Arabia) and Samir Ouchani (CESI Engineering School and the Lineact CESI Laboratory in Aix-en-Provence, France), two industry talks given by Driss Raouh (Expert in Cybercrime at the International Criminal Court, the Hague, the Netherlands) and Housna Hamadet (Infoblox, Morocco), and two tutorials presented by Federico Ast (Kleros, France) and Zakaryae Boudi (Fevertokens, France).

We would like to thank everyone who helped at organizing the event, including all the members of the organizing committee, the general chairs, honorary chair, and publicity chairs of this year edition. Very special thanks go as well to all the CRiSIS 2023 Program Committee members, additional reviewers, and, most notably, all the authors who submitted papers, all session chairs, and all the conference attendees.

Finally, we want to acknowledge the support received from the industrial sponsors, Fevertokens, and Kleros, as well as the academic sponsors, Université Mohammed V, Faculté des Sciences in Rabat, and Universitat Autònoma de Barcelona (UAB).

We acknowledge support as well from projects PID2021-125962OB-C33, RED2022-134603-T, 2021-SGR-00643, and the Recovery, Transformation and Resilience Plan of the European Union (Next Generation) C062/23.

February 2024

Abderrahim Ait Wakrime
Guillermo Navarro-Arribas
Redouane Benaini
Frédéric Cuppens
Nora Cuppens

Organization

General Chairs

Redouane Benaini   Mohammed V University, Morocco
Frédéric Cuppens   Polytechnique Montreal, Canada
Nora Cuppens   Polytechnique Montreal, Canada

Program Committee Chairs

Abderrahim Ait Wakrime   Mohammed V University, Morocco
Guillermo Navarro-Arribas   Autonomous University of Barcelona, Spain

Publicity Chairs

Slim Kallel   University of Sfax, Tunisia
Khadija Slimani   LDR-ESIEA Paris, France

Program Committee

Abderrahim Ait Wakrime   Mohammed V University, Morocco
Saed Alrabaee   United Arab Emirates University, UAE
Esma Aïmeur   University of Montreal, Canada
Lotfi Ben Othmane   Iowa State University, USA
Redouane Benaini   Mohammed V University, Morocco
Jordi Castellà-Roca   Universitat Rovira i Virgili, Spain
Saoussen Cheikhrouhou   University of Sfax, Tunisia
Depeng Chen   Anhui University, China
Simon Collart-Dutilleul   Université Gustave Eiffel, France
Frédéric Cuppens   Polytechnique Montreal, Canada
Nora Cuppens   Polytechnique Montreal, Canada
Sabrina De Capitani di Vimercati   Università degli Studi di Milano, Italy
Joaquin Garcia-Alfaro   Institut Polytechnique de Paris, France
Ahmed Hadj Kacem   University of Sfax, Tunisia
Mohamed Jmaiel   University of Sfax, Tunisia
Slim Kallel   University of Sfax, Tunisia

Christos Kalloniatis	University of the Aegean, Greece
Sokratis Katsikas	Norwegian University of Science and Technology, Norway
Igor Kotenko	St. Petersburg Federal Research Center of the Russian Academy of Sciences, Russia
Evangelos Kranakis	Carleton University, Canada
Marc Lacoste	Orange Labs, France
Luigi Logrippo	Université du Quebec en Outaouais, Canada
Mohamed Mosbah	University of Bordeaux, France
Guillermo Navarro-Arribas	Autonomous University of Barcelona, Spain
Michael Rusinowitch	Loria, Inria Nancy, France
Khadija Sabiri	Fraunhofer Portugal AICOS, Portugal
Lingyun Situ	Nanjing University, China
Natalia Stakhanova	University of Saskatchewan, Canada
Ketil Stoelen	SINTEF, Norway
Vicenc Torra	Umea University, Sweden
Zouheir Trabelsi	United Arab Emirates University, UAE
Alexandre Viejo	Universitat Rovira i Virgili, Spain
Isabel Wagner	University of Basel, Switzerland
Junwei Zhou	Wuhan University of Technology, China

Organization Committee

Abderrahim Ait Wakrime	Mohammed V University, Morocco
Yassine Ouhammou	LIAS/ISAE-ENSMA, France
Khaoula Bouba	Mohammed V University, Morocco
Ahmed El-yahyaoui	Mohammed V University, Morocco
Ayoub Nfissi	Mohammed V University, Morocco

Additional Reviewers

Amal Abid
Faten Fakhfakh
Sameh Ben Aoun
Rawya Mars

Contents

Keynote Talks

A Review of the Progressive Odyssey of AI-Driven Intrusion Detection Within Embedded Systems

Aisha Alansari, Razan Alfaqeer, and Mohammad Hammoudeh[(✉)] [iD]

Department of Information and Computer Science, King Fahd University of
Petroleum and Minerals, Dhahran 31261, Saudi Arabia
{aisha.ansari,g202203760,m.hammoudeh}@kfupm.edu.sa

Abstract. Security of Embedded Systems (ES) has become a major
concern due to their growing usage in numerous industries. Their connectivity to the internet made them vulnerable to sophisticated cyber-
attacks. One of the most important strategies for strengthening their
security posture is using Intrusion Detection Systems (IDS). However,
the limited resources of ES make it difficult to utilize IDS. This paper
reviews the primary studies that contributed to developing IDS systems
applicable to ES. It examines the challenges of building such systems,
reports the current trends, and proposes future recommendations to
enhance the deployment of IDS in ES. The findings showed that most
studies currently employ machine and deep learning algorithms to build
IDS for ES. Although significant results were achieved, several gaps were
reported. The proposed frameworks did not investigate the security, privacy, and interpretability concerns of employing machine and deep learning. Moreover, a feasible framework to address all the ES resource constraints is lacking. Future recommendations include solutions to enhance
such models' security, privacy, and interoperability. Moreover, it includes
the employment of differential privacy, explainable artificial intelligence,
federated learning, and trusted executed environments.

Keywords: Embedded systems · Intrusion detection · Machine
learning

1 Introduction

In recent decades, numerous technological innovations have sought to improve
life. A standout among these advancements involved incorporating computing operations into a larger physical system, enabling predefined functionality,
named Embedded Systems (ES). ES is defined in many ways from various angles.
Vahid and Givargis [1] noted that providing a unified definition of ES is challenging due to its wide applications and the variety of technologies underlying its
implementation. However, they defined an ES as a computing system integrated
within a larger physical system to perform a specific, necessary function. It comprises a mix of software, hardware, and sometimes mechanical components. As

A. Ait Wakrime et al. (Eds.): CRiSIS 2023, LNCS 14529, pp. 3–16, 2024.
https://doi.org/10.1007/978-3-031-61231-2_1

a result, any computing system other than mainframes or general-purpose PCs is covered by the phrase [2].

Recently, ES was significantly expanded to be used in various sectors, such as power plants, vehicles, and mobile phone systems. Therefore, the security of ES is becoming a major concern due to their extensive use and exposure. ES face several security challenges due to their physical accessibility and unique operating environments [3]. They are particularly susceptible to specialized attacks, such as side-channel attacks [4]. These attacks include advanced methods, such as time and power analysis, to compromise security keys [5]. Moreover, ES have recently become widely connected to the Internet by incorporating them with networked and interconnected devices. Consequently, their vulnerability to cyber-attacks has escalated more than ever [6].

Identifying and designing precise security improvements is challenging due to numerous influencing factors, such as these systems' resource constraints [7]. Security features often impact other system aspects, such as timing. Improper handling of these aspects can lead to breaches of non-functional requirements, risking system failure [8]. For instance, selecting an encryption technique that performs complex computations can strain memory and energy, risking system functionality [10]. This arises from the nature of non-functional requirements like security, which cannot be considered in isolation. Accordingly, these challenges necessitate careful consideration in enhancing ES' cybersecurity measures [9].

In real-time ES, carefully choosing security mechanisms is crucial, especially in light of their strict temporal constraints. These systems must ensure that security measures do not impair operating efficiency since they are frequently used when delays might have serious repercussions [10]. Given the limited resources that ES have and the need for real-time threat detection and response, integrating Intrusion Detection Systems (IDS) is considered a crucial tactic for strengthening their security posture. It helps in the early detection of cyber threats, allowing for timely mitigation actions.

Much research has contributed to the development of smart IDS, achieving better network security. The attempt to develop an intelligent IDS using a Deep Neural Network (DNN) and unsupervised Machine Learning (ML) algorithms has shown encouraging results [11]. Moreover, in other studies, researchers have tried to enhance the performance of IDS by combining learning, case-based thinking, and interactive behavior. However, considering the limited processing power and energy resources of ES, those IDS solutions must be lightweight yet effective [12].

Accordingly, this paper aims to review and discuss the findings of the primary studies that built IDS for ES. It identifies the current trends in developing IDS in ES and outlines their limitations. Moreover, it proposes future directions to enhance the application of IDS in ES.

The research questions that this paper aims to answer are as follows:

- What are the most used techniques in developing IDS in ES?
- What are the approaches followed to address the resource constraints of ES while deploying IDS?

– What are the limitations of applying IDS in ES?
– What could be the possible future work directions to enhance the deployment of IDS in ES?

The rest of this paper is organized as follows: Sect. 2 presents background information on IDS used in ES. Section 3 presents the conducted literature and Sect. 4 describes the methodology for collecting relevant primary studies. Moreover, Sect. 5 analyzes the topic in terms of the key challenges, trends, and critiques, Sect. 6 outlines future recommendations, and Sect. 7 concludes the paper.

2 Background

ES are exposed to several security challenges that can compromise their integrity, availability, and confidentiality. This is due to its resource constraints. Some of the restrictions on ES that lead to security issues include low processing power. This limitation stops the system from executing sophisticated security programs. Limited power supply availability is another barrier, leaving ES with few power resources that could lead to exhaustion attacks. Additionally, the nature of ES functioning in an unregulated or hostile environment leaves them open to physical attacks. In this case, attackers can physically access the system and interfere by breaking sensors or peripherals or eavesdropping on the system bus [13].

In ES, the processors cannot efficiently implement advanced security mechanisms, such as data encryption, or incorporate complex secure platforms [14]. Furthermore, the Central Processing Unit (CPU) does not have sufficient hardware protection against logical and physical attacks [15]. Advanced CPUs can help prevent or mitigate various attacks. Still, these advanced processors are more expensive, and their use is usually limited to smart device cards or dedicated secure elements in SoCs [17]. Even if we assume that the processor performance has been optimized according to advanced encryption requirements, portable systems may face challenges. The high energy consumption required for such security measures often exceeds these systems' limited power capabilities [16].

The National Institute of Standards and Technology (NIST) defines IDS as monitoring occasions that occur within a network or computer system and examining them to look for indications of potential invasions [18]. IDS can potentially contribute to protecting ES against several attacks. IDS are categorized based on how rapidly they can deploy and identify threats. They have been divided into two distinct categories for deployment: host-based and network-based. In order to gather data on the host device's activities and identify any unusual or malicious activity in that device, a host-based IDS is installed within a local device. In contrast, a network-based IDS monitors and finds threats in traffic using specific methodologies. IDS uses two distinct detection mechanisms: anomaly-based and signature-based. The signature-based IDS performs pattern matching using some techniques to detect any abnormal activity. It matches the activities across the network system with the predefined attack signatures stored in the IDS database [19]. In other literature, the mechanisms are divided into four categories, namely anomaly detection, heuristic analysis, signature-based, rule-based, machine, and Deep Learning (DL) models.

To protect the system from malicious activities, monitoring procedures can be carried out using hardware or software. The use of the IDS security program comes after that of the firewall and antivirus software. As soon as a system malfunctions, the IDS modifies the network [21]. Along with detecting intrusions, the IDS records network activity within the system. When a host or network intrusion happens, the IDS notifies the system.

3   Review of Recent IDSs for ES

This section reviews the primary studies that developed IDS for ES. The review is arranged chronologically in each subsection according to the publication date. Table 1 summarizes the data collected from the reviewed primary studies.

3.1   Host-Based IDS

Kadar et al. [37] aimed to secure runtime program execution mix-critically ES by proposing a host-based IDS. The authors applied partitioning by using the Multiple Independent Layers of Security (MILS) architecture. Moreover, they defined the Host-based IDS service as a component of the separation kernel inside the architecture of a MILS system to separate it from possible adversaries. They first defined the way of executing the program formally. After that, they formulated the Host-based IDS around a substantial execution state description encompassing signals from software and hardware systems. In terms of recovery strategies, the proposed methodology is chosen from among four approaches based on trust and criticality levels. The approaches include the following: kill/reboot, isolate, migrate, and signal/log.

In another study, Liu et al. [35] aimed to address the scalability and efficiency shortcomings of host-based IDS. A two-tier host-based IDS framework was designed. The first tier is responsible for data collection, where an interface is installed in the embedded device. The second tier comprises a cloud-based analytics centre. Logistic Regression (LR) was trained to detect attacks, achieving an Area Under the Roc Curve (AUC) of 0.980 using 10-fold cross-validation. The results indicated that the proposed framework can automatically choose parameters that will lower latency and increase scalability. Although significant results were attained, the proposed framework was not tested on real-time streaming data from ES.

Martinez and Vogel-Heuser [32] proposed a host-based IDS for embedded industrial devices. The architecture design considered the capabilities and features of the industrial domain, as well as the system, device, and environmental characteristics. The authors evaluated their architecture by deploying it in a Programmable Logic Controller (PLC) hosting a Real-Time Operating System (RTOS). They claimed that their architecture is the first completely functional Host IDS installed and assessed on a PLC.

3.2   Network-Based IDS

Viegas et al. [39] introduced a feature selection strategy to determine the optimal trade-off between intrusion detection accuracy and system energy usage. With only a 0.9% decrease in accuracy, the authors' method was able to reduce energy use by up to 93%. In another study by Viegas et al. [38], the authors presented an anomaly-based technique for network intrusion detection in embedded devices. The suggested approach keeps the classifier reliable even in the event that the contents of network traffic fluctuate. Combining a few different classifiers with a novel rejection mechanism yields dependability. The suggested method is suitable for hardware implementation and energy efficiency. According to the results reported in this work, the feature extraction and packet capture modules utilize 58% and 37% of the energy consumed by their respective software counterparts, while the ML algorithms' hardware equivalents use 46% of that of their software counterparts.

Florencio et al. [34] employed Multilayer Perceptron (MLP) to build a real-time IDS. Experiments were conducted on an Arduino architecture to assess the MLP's performance. The results indicated a 95% confidence interval. Additionally, it was observed that there were no memory limitations, supporting the feasibility of an inexpensive IDS. However, the authors did not measure the energy used.

Furthermore, Khan et al. [36] proposed a unique framework to identify malicious behavior on ES using electromagnetic side-channel signals. The framework initially captures electromagnetic radiation from a secure reference device to create a pattern baseline. The framework then tracks the electromagnetic emissions from the target device. It records any deviation from the reference patterns as abnormal behavior. The target gadget is kept physically apart from the framework to avoid any adversarial attacks. The authors evaluated the performance of their framework by injecting ransomware, Distributed Denial of Service (DDoS), and code alteration. The findings show that the proposed framework can accurately detect various assaults from distances up to 3 m with an AUC of > 99.5% and 100% detection with less than 1% false positives.

More recently, Reyes et al. [33] proposed a hardware introspection-based anomaly detection framework. The framework uses ML algorithms to identify anomalous device behavior. The Joint Test Action Group (JTAG) interface was used to extract memory traces. After that, the authors formed an image representation of the extracted data and trained a Convolutional Neural Network (CNN) to detect abnormal behavior. The model achieved an accuracy of 98.7%. While both publications achieved noteworthy results, none of them used it in a real-time ES to guarantee the performance of their techniques.

Although significant efforts were made in the field of employing IDS in ES, IDS still face a challenge in detecting and preventing attacks in an effective way in ES. This is mainly due to the unique characteristics of ES. As far as we are aware, none of the frameworks that have been suggested can account for every resource constraint that ES have. For example, Florencio et al. [34] neglected to take energy efficiency into account in their focus on creating a cost-effective IDS.

Furthermore, the goal of Viegas et al. was to create an energy-efficient architecture without taking application costs into account. Accordingly, efforts must be directed at developing an IDS that considers all the resource limitations of ES. Moreover, as far as we are aware, none of the proposed frameworks considered investigating the security concerns of employing ML in IDS.

Table 1. Summary of preliminary studies

Research	Years	Data	Host based	Network based	Method	Result
[39]	2017	NIDS data set	–	✓	ML	Reduces energy use by up to 93%
[38]	2018	Intrusion dataset	–	✓	Anomaly-based with ML	Keeps the classifier reliable even in the event that the contents of network traffic fluctuate
[36]	2018	Signals	–	✓	IDEA framework	Detect various attacks from distances up to 3 m with an AUC of >99.5% and 100% detection with < 1% false positives
[34]	2018	NSL-KDD dataset	–	✓	MLP Networks	Achieves 95% confidence interval
[37]	2020	Signals	✓		MILS architecture	HIDs to secure runtime program execution mix-critically ES
[32]	2021	–	✓	–	IDS architecture	Completely functional Host-based IDS installed and assessed on a PLC
[35]	2021	ADFA-LD dataset	✓	–	ML pipeline	Automatically choose parameters to lower latency and increase scalability
[33]	2023	RAM data	–	✓	HIAD framework	Achieved an accuracy of 98.7%

4   Current State of IDS in ES

Network security is presently a major concern, according to several studies. IDS has been designed to safeguard network security. Various ML techniques, such as ensemble learning, have been utilized to improve IDS performance. There are two kinds of network attacks, namely, active attacks and passive attacks. In an active attack, the intruder sends out a command to disrupt network operations, whereas in a passive attack, the intruder intercepts data within the network. The dynamic nature of cyber attacks makes it impossible for the existing IDS to handle them, leading to several restrictions. According to Anchugam and Thangadurai [23], Ghorbani et al. [22], and Kumar et al. [20], the main causes of intrusion in a network are as follows: bad packets, encrypted packets, weak network identification and authentication, and protocol-based attacks.

The IDS contains four main components, namely: information source, feature selection, detection engine, and response. They work to identify attacks and generate a report in a pre-defined format [19]. Figure 1 shows how components are organized in IDS.

1. Data Collection: The evidence of any intrusion occasion is collected from the source comprehensively. Collecting all the information is costly, and the main challenge is collecting privileged information.
2. Feature Extraction: A set of features is maintained to categorize attacks and eliminate irrelevant or redundant features. A feature vector is then produced from the selected subset of attributes.
3. Detection Engine: Data is analyzed to detect intrusion events. The strength of this component is determined by its ability to detect all categories of attacks.
4. Response Engine: Determines how to respond and control the reaction mechanism after an intrusion activity is detected. The engine takes two types of response, either a passive or an active response. Passive response triggers an alert without responding to the source, whereas active response blocks the source for a pre-determined period.

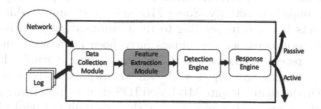

Fig. 1. General IDS architecture. Adapted from [19]

5 Key Challenges and Trends in IDS for ES

In host-based IDS, the information usually consists of data and logs generated by the host system. In contrast, network-based IDS rely on network traffic data. ES are limited by low data storage and processing power. Therefore, the amount of data collected, stored, and analyzed is restricted. Moreover, many ES require real-time or near real-time data processing for timely threat detection, posing a challenge given the limited computational resources. Operating in environments with limited network bandwidth affects data transfer for external analysis, especially when leveraging ML. Future trends focus on employing federated learning for collaborative, privacy-preserving data analysis across multiple ES without sharing raw data [24]. Moreover, other studies focus on minimizing data streams by using energy-efficient data processing techniques, such as pruning and quantization [25].

Network traffic produces a huge amount of high-dimensional data [26]. Such data may adversely affect the detection of IDS since there is redundant information in network traffic. The same is the case in host-based IDS. The detection process may be slowed down due to the significant processing complexity needed to handle this data, making it unusable in ES. Therefore, an effective way to deal with reducing the dimensions of the data must be proposed [27]. Imbalance class distribution is another challenging issue faced in this component. It causes the classifier to be biased towards the majority class, leading to the generation of many false alarms. Solutions have been designed to combat this problem, which are divided into two main categories: the data level and the algorithmic level. The first category focuses on altering the original data distribution, whereas the second category adjusts the algorithm to fit the minority group better. In the field of ML for anomaly detection, there has been a recent focus on the significance of feature selection and class imbalance. Its goals are to find the most valuable aspects and enhance the quality of the data. Nevertheless, there is a lack of research that demonstrates how crucial feature selection is for handling a high-dimensional class imbalance issue [19].

A number of researchers have put forward strategies and plans to increase the detection accuracy of IDS using ML classifiers. Enormous amounts of network traffic may be analyzed by ML algorithms, which can also spot complex patterns that point to malicious activity. Some ML-based IDS are capable of not just detecting threats but also responding to them automatically. Although several ML-based intrusion detection techniques have been introduced, most of them cannot identify recent, unknown attacks [29]. Some recent studies have focused on employing rejection techniques with ML algorithms to counteract evolving attacks [38]. Furthermore, despite ML-based IDS showing promising results, high computational resource requirements limit the possibility of deploying them in resource-constrained ES. Accordingly, some efforts were made to build a cost-effective and energy-efficient IDS to address this limitation, such as using Tiny-ML [25]. Scalability and latency are other challenges faced in detection engines. It is essential that detection engines can handle the growing data volume and resource constraints. Moreover, detection engines must process data in real-time or near real-time to effectively prevent or mitigate attacks. Consequently, current trends focus on proposing frameworks that can automatically choose parameters that lower latency and increase scalability.

The role of response engines is critical for threat mitigation in network-based and host-based IDS. Host-based IDS are limited by the response options compared to network IDS. Moreover, Host-based IDS finds it especially difficult to respond to attacks from legitimate users or compromised insider accounts. Network-based IDS is challenged by the ability to address threats in high-traffic environments without causing bottlenecks. Additionally, it is challenged by collaborating efficiently with other network security devices, such as routers or firewalls. As far as we are aware, not much research has been conducted on the problems with response engines in IDS that are used in ES. Future trends to improve response engines in host-based IDS must focus on integrating the host IDS in secure cloud environments with security tools for effective response. On the other hand, threat intelligence techniques could play a vital role in enhancing the response strategies against known and emerging threats in network-based IDS.

According to the conducted literature review, it is observed that the current trend is moving towards utilizing ML and DL algorithms in IDSs used in ES. Several studies employed different ML and DL algorithms while considering the resource constraints of ES. Significant efforts have been made to improve efficiency and cost-effectiveness. However, based on our knowledge, no proposed frameworks have fully met all constraints. Moreover, as far as we are aware, none of the previous studies discussed the new security vulnerabilities that may be introduced by ML and DL models. For example, an attacker can alter the ML model and generate inaccurate predictions if they manage to have access to it. This tampering can include poisoning the model during training (data poisoning) or manipulating input data to cause misclassification (adversarial attacks). In data poisoning, attackers inject malicious data into the training set, causing the model to learn incorrect patterns. Adversarial attacks involve subtly altered input data that leads the model to make wrong predictions while appearing normal to human observers. Another example is attackers can construct malicious activities that mimic normal behavior patterns. Accordingly, the system will fail to identify anomalous behaviors.

Furthermore, interpretability is another aspect that was not covered by the previous studies. Any ML models, especially DL models, lack transparency in their decision-making processes. This can help an attacker exploit the models and make it difficult to diagnose and rectify security breaches. Consequently, interpretability could contribute to enabling informed decision-making, effective responses, system refinement, compliance, and trust in the technology. For instance, a manufacturing facility monitors its production line with an IDS based on ML. In order to identify possible cyber-attacks, the IDS is made to analyze data from sensors and equipment. If the IDS triggers an alarm pointing to a potential cyber invasion from a conveyor belt system, but this system rarely shows deviations, interpretability can play a vital role. In this case, interpretability can aid in understanding the ML model's decision. The decision can be analyzed to determine whether it was based on historical data, specific sensor readings, etc. Interpretability can also help ensure the response's appropriateness. This is critical since if the alert is a false positive, an unnecessary shutdown could be costly. Thus, efforts should be directed at introducing explainable ML and DL models in this domain.

Data privacy is another issue that was not discussed in the literature [28]. Access to vast amounts of data, some containing private or sensitive information, is necessary for many ML models. This data may be compromised or exploited as part of the model's functioning or as a result of an exposure. For example, the models in driver-assistance systems collect vast amounts of data, including GPS location, camera footage, braking patterns, and more. Continuous data collection could lead to privacy concerns. Moreover, Lane-keeping and parking assistance cameras record video, which may capture sensitive locations or people. This may lead to personal data exposure, unauthorized data access, data misuse, and much more. Therefore, it is essential to introduce robust mitigation measures to enhance data privacy.

6   Research Gaps and Opportunities

One of the main challenges in the field of ES is the computational complexity. The emergence of TinyML made the implementation of ML algorithms on low-powered edge devices possible. It seems that TinyML can handle the demands of implementing ML algorithms in low-power edge devices, such as microcontrollers. This technique compresses an ML model into a small size after training it on the cloud. Later, on edge devices with limited resources, the compressed model is implemented [25]. However, some security concerns must be addressed to reduce the possibility of attacking such models. Securing the developed models by quantization technique is one way to improve the security of the models. Quantization hides the real values of the weights and parameters to prevent unauthorized users from uncovering the model's architecture. Quantization can also contribute to speeding up the inference process, which is essential for real-time IDSs. Moreover, it decreases power consumption, optimizes memory usage, and improves scalability [30].

In order to address the privacy issue, robust data retention and disposal policies must be developed. Data retention could include specifying retention duration based on different data types, outlining security measures for the retention period, and auditing the retained data. Similarly, data disposal policies could include defining secure disposal methods, identifying specific triggers for data disposal, and keeping a record of data disposal. Differential privacy is another useful technique for handling the privacy issue. One way is to include methods to introduce noise into the data in every embedded device at the time of collection. This makes sure that the details of the data are hidden even while the IDS is still able to identify patterns indicative of an attack. However, to guarantee that the IDS retains its efficacy in identifying threats while safeguarding data privacy, it is crucial to remember to adjust the noise level carefully. Moreover, differential privacy can be established when training ML models. This ensures that the model, even if exposed, does not reveal sensitive information about the data on which it was trained.

Explainable Artificial Intelligence (XAI) approaches, such as Local Interpretable Model-agnostic Explanations (LIME), might also be employed at this step to guarantee the reliability of the deployed model [31]. LIME provides local interpretability, which can aid in giving insights into debugging, quality assurance, model validation, and others. With the help of XAI, users and administrators may comprehend the reasoning behind an IDS's decision to flag an action as potentially dangerous. This understanding is crucial to building trust, especially in critical environments where ES are often deployed. Moreover, it helps administrators understand the reason behind an alert, determine the appropriate response, and enhance the model.

Another recommendation to enhance the development of IDS in ES is to use federated learning to overcome the issues of connecting with the cloud for training and storage purposes. Federated learning allows for dispersed training at the edge level and avoids sharing local data with servers. Keeping data local limits the risk of data breaches or leaks during transmission or central storage. Consequently, it could be vital in preserving privacy and reducing data transmission. Moreover, recently, embedded ML has extensively used Trusted Execution Environments (TEEs) to improve security and privacy. ML inference is carried out safely via TEEs. This is especially useful when sensitive data or models must be protected from outside attacks. Calculations are performed without revealing raw data to the public, and data is kept encrypted. Furthermore, TEEs provide safe over-the-air upgrades for embedded ML models and provide strong hardware security.

7 Conclusion

This paper reviewed the studies that developed IDS for ES. It was carried out using data from many research articles published in various journals and conferences between the years 2018 and 2023. It investigated current trends and challenges in the development of IDSs for ES, with a specific focus on the growing use of ML and DL algorithms. The main finding of this study showed that researchers are moving toward employing ML and DL to build IDS for ES. However, it is observed that there is a lack of frameworks that address all limited resources of ES while maintaining privacy, security, and interpretability. These findings highlight the necessity of enhancing IDS for ES through several recommendations discussed in this study. Future research should explore leveraging the latest technologies, such as TinyML, federated learning, and TEEs, to facilitate secure real-time data analysis. Moreover, to maintain privacy, security, and interoperability, it is recommended to introduce strong data retention and disposal policies, develop differential privacy techniques, and utilize XAI. It is believed that the discussed recommendations can play a vital role in improving the security of IDSs in ES.

References

1. Vahid, F., Givargis, T.D.: Embedded System Design: A Unified Hardware/Software Introduction. Wiley, New York (2001)
2. Papp, D., Ma, Z., Buttyan, L.: Embedded systems security: threats, vulnerabilities, and attack taxonomy. In: 2015 13th Annual Conference on Privacy, Security and Trust (PST), Izmir, Turkey, pp. 145-152 (2015)
3. Hammoudeh, M., Newman, R.: Information extraction from sensor networks using the Watershed transform algorithm. Inf. Fusion **22**, 39–49 (2015)

4. Ambrose, J.A., Ragel, R.G., Jayasinghe, D., Li, T., Parameswaran, S.: Side channel attacks in embedded systems: a tale of hostilities and deterrence. In: Sixteenth International Symposium on Quality Electronic Design, Santa Clara, CA, USA, pp. 452–459 (2015)
5. Azzedin, F., Albinali, H.: Security in Internet of Things: RPL attacks taxonomy. In: The 5th International Conference on Future Networks & Distributed Systems, pp. 820–825 (2021)
6. Azzedin, F., Alhejri, I.: A layered taxonomy of internet of things attacks. In: Proceedings of the 6th International Conference on Future Networks & Distributed Systems, pp. 631–636 (2022)
7. Epiphaniou, G., Pillai, P., Bottarelli, M., Al-Khateeb, H., Hammoudesh, M., Maple, C.: Electronic regulation of data sharing and processing using smart ledger technologies for supply-chain security. IEEE Trans. Eng. Manage. **67**(4), 1059–1073 (2020)
8. Benoudifa, O., Wakrime, A.A., Benaini, R.: Autonomous solution for controller placement problem of software-defined networking using MuZero based intelligent agents. J. King Saud Univ.-Comput. Inf. Sci. **35**(10), 101842 (2023)
9. Saadatmand, M., Cicchetti, A., Sjödin, M.: On generating security implementations from models of embedded systems. In: International Conference on Software Engineering Advances, Barcelona, Spain, (2011)
10. Cysneiros, L.M., do Prado Leite, J.C.S.: Nonfunctional requirements: from elicitation to conceptual models. IEEE Trans. Softw. Eng. **30**(5), 328–350 (2004)
11. Gala, Y., Vanjari, N., Doshi, D., Radhanpurwala, I.: AI based techniques for network-based intrusion detection system: a review. In: 2023 10th International Conference on Computing for Sustainable Global Development (INDIACom), New Delhi, India, pp. 1544–1551 (2023)
12. Sethi, K., Kumar, R., Prajapati, N., Bera, P.: A lightweight intrusion detection system using Benford's law and network flow size difference. In: 2020 International Conference on COMmunication Systems & NETworkS (COMSNETS), Bengaluru, India, pp. 1–6 (2020)
13. Carlin, A., Hammoudeh, M., Aldabbas, O.: Intrusion detection and countermeasure of virtual cloud systems-state of the art and current challenges. Int. J. Adv. Comput. Sci. Appl. **6**(6) (2015)
14. Lahbib, A., Ait Wakrime, A., Laouiti, A., Toumi, K., Martin, S.: An event-B based approach for formal modelling and verification of smart contracts. In: Advanced Information Networking and Applications: Proceedings of the 34th International Conference on Advanced Information Networking and Applications (AINA-2020), pp. 1303–1318 (2020)
15. Aloseel, A., He, H., Shaw, C., Khan, M.A.: Analytical review of cybersecurity for embedded systems. IEEE Access **9**, 961–982 (2021)
16. Bansod, G., Raval, N., Pisharoty, N.: Implementation of a new lightweight encryption design for embedded security. IEEE Trans. Inf. Forensics Secur. **10**(1), 142–151 (2015)
17. Koopman, P.: Embedded System Security. Computer **37**(7), 95–97 (2004)
18. National Institute of Standards and Technology. https://www.nist.gov/publications/intrusion-detection-systems
19. Binbusayyis, A., Vaiyapuri, T.: Comprehensive analysis and recommendation of feature evaluation measures for intrusion detection. Heliyon **6**(7), e04262 (2020)
20. Kumar, S., Gupta, S., Arora, S.: Research trends in network-based intrusion detection systems: a review. IEEE Access **9**, 157761–157779 (2021)

21. Aloseel, A., He, H., Shaw, C., Khan, M.A.: Analytical review of cybersecurity for embedded systems. IEEE Access **9**, 961–982 (2020)
22. Ghorbani, A.A., Lu, W., Tavallaee, M.: Network Intrusion Detection and Prevention: Concepts and Techniques. Springer Science & Business Media, 47 (2009). https://doi.org/10.1007/978-0-387-88771-5
23. Anchugam, C.V., Thangadurai, K.: Classification of network attacks and countermeasures of different attacks. In: Network Security Attacks and Countermeasures, pp. 115–156. IGI Global (2016)
24. Agrawal, S., et al.: Federated Learning for Intrusion Detection System: Concepts. Challenges and Future Directions, Computer Communications (2022)
25. Butt, M.A., Qayyum, A., Ali, H., Al-Fuqaha, A., Qadir, J.: Towards secure private and trustworthy human-centric embedded machine learning: an emotion-aware facial recognition case study. Comput. Secur. **125**, 103058 (2023)
26. Hammoudeh, M., Newman, R., Dennett, C., Mount, S., Aldabbas, O.: Map as a service: a framework for visualising and maximising information return from multi-modal wireless sensor networks. Sensors **15**(9), 22970–23003 (2015)
27. Balasaraswathi, V.R., Sugumaran, M., Hamid, Y.: Feature selection techniques for intrusion detection using non-bio-inspired and bio-inspired optimization algorithms. J. Commun. Inf. Netw. **2**, 107–119 (2017)
28. Walshe, M., Epiphaniou, G., Al-Khateeb, H., Hammoudeh, M., Katos, V., Dehghantanha, A.: Non-interactive zero knowledge proofs for the authentication of IoT devices in reduced connectivity environments. Ad Hoc Netw. **95**, 101988 (2019)
29. Liu, H., Lang, B.: Machine learning and deep learning methods for intrusion detection systems: a survey. Appl. Sci. **9**(20), 4396 (2019)
30. Sharmila, B.S., Nagapadma, R.: Quantized autoencoder (QAE) intrusion detection system for anomaly detection in resource-constrained IoT devices using RT-IoT2022 dataset. Cybersecurity **6**(1), 41 (2023)
31. Mahbooba, B., Timilsina, M., Sahal, R., Serrano, M.: Explainable artificial intelligence (XAI) to enhance trust management in intrusion detection systems using decision tree model. Complexity **2021**, 1–11 (2021)
32. Martinez, C.V., Vogel-Heuser, B.: A host intrusion detection system architecture for embedded industrial devices. J. Franklin Inst. **358**(1), 210–236 (2021)
33. Reyes, D.L., Perez-Pons, A., Dean, R.B.: Anomaly detection in embedded devices through hardware introspection. In: 2023 Silicon Valley Cybersecurity Conference (SVCC), pp. 1–7, IEEE, San Jose, CA, USA (2023)
34. de Almeida Florencio, F., Moreno, E.D., Macedo, H.T., de Britto Salgueiro, R.J.P., do Nascimento, F.B., Santos, F.A.O.: Intrusion detection via MLP neural network using an arduino embedded system. In: 2018 VIII Brazilian Symposium on Computing Systems Engineering (SBESC), pp. 190–195. IEEE, Salvador, Brazil (2018)
35. Liu, M., Xue, Z., He, X.: Two-tier intrusion detection framework for embedded systems. IEEE Consum. Electron. Mag. **10**(5), 102–108 (2020)
36. Khan, H.A., et al.: IDEA: intrusion detection through electromagnetic-signal analysis for critical embedded and cyber-physical systems. IEEE Trans. Dependable Secure Comput. **18**(3), 1150–1163 (2019)
37. Kadar, M., Tverdyshev, S., Fohler, G.: Towards host intrusion detection for embedded industrial systems. In: 2020 50th Annual IEEE-IFIP International Conference on Dependable Systems and Networks-Supplemental Volume (DSN-S), pp. 5–8. IEEE, Valencia, Spain (2020)

38. Viegas, E., Santin, A., Oliveira, L., Franca, A., Jasinski, R., Pedroni, V.: A reliable and energy-efficient classifier combination scheme for intrusion detection in embedded systems. Comput. Secur. **78**, 16–32 (2018)
39. Viegas, E.K., Santin, A.O., Oliveira, L.S.: Toward a reliable anomaly-based intrusion detection in real-world environments. Comput. Netw. **127**, 200–216 (2017)

Securing Autonomous Vehicles: Fundamentals, Challenges, and Perspectives

Samir Ouchani[✉]

CESI Lineact, Aix-en-Provence, France
souchani@esi.fr

Abstract. This work introduces a comprehensive methodology aimed at enhancing security and immunity in automotive networks, placing a primary focus on the detection, prediction, and forecasting of errors in autonomous vehicles. Conventional approaches to vehicle cybersecurity often struggle to keep pace with evolving threats and provide effective error detection mechanisms. Our proposed methodology seeks to bridge this gap by incorporating a hybrid approach that combines both model and data. This integration ensures the development of secure systems and facilitates real-time analysis of deployed systems, enabling the proactive prevention of errors and attacks based on collected data. The overarching goal is to leverage data to not only prevent attacks but also rectify errors within autonomous vehicles.

Keywords: Automotive Systems · Cybersecurity · Systems Immunity · Autonomous Vehicles · Attack Prevention · Error Correction

1 Introduction

Since the advent of Industry 2.0, road transport has witnessed substantial evolution, fostering rapid growth in the automotive market driven by intense competition. However, this growth has brought forth persistent concerns related to pollution and safety. Recognizing these challenges, the subsequent emergence of Industry 4.0 and now 5.0 has introduced transformative solutions, emphasizing the enhanced connectivity and autonomy of vehicles. Indeed, the evolution toward Industry 4.0 and Industry 5.0 signifies a paradigm shift in automotive technology, promising innovative approaches to address long-standing issues. The increased connectivity and autonomy aim to revolutionize the driving experience by ensuring safer journeys, optimizing road network utilization, and contributing to a cleaner environment. This evolution not only enhances the efficiency of road transport but also aligns with the broader goals of sustainable and reliable mobility [6].

In recent years, the automotive industry has faced an alarming surge in cyberattacks, emphasizing the critical necessity for robust cybersecurity measures.

A. Ait Wakrime et al. (Eds.): CRiSIS 2023, LNCS 14529, pp. 17–24, 2024.
https://doi.org/10.1007/978-3-031-61231-2_2

According to a report by Upstream Auto[1], the number of reported cyberattacks on vehicles has experienced a significant increase. In 2022 alone, automotive API attacks surged by a staggering 380%, constituting 12% of total incidents. This surge persisted despite original equipment manufacturers (OEMs) implementing advanced IT cybersecurity protections. These attacks bear profound implications for the safety and security of automotive systems. This disconcerting trend underscores the imperative for heightened cybersecurity measures throughout the automotive industry. Such measures are essential not only to protect the vehicles themselves but also to ensure the security of sensitive data and the well-being of their occupants.

In light of these alarming trends, this paper introduces a comprehensive methodology for enhancing security and immunity in automotive networks. The focus lies on developing robust mechanisms for the detection, prediction, and forecasting of errors within these networks. By integrating a hybrid approach between model and data, our methodology seeks to address evolving cybersecurity challenges, providing a framework for secure and resilient autonomous vehicles [7].

The subsequent sections detail the objectives of our proposed methodology, emphasizing the development of a dedicated modeling language, threat classification, security deployment standards, and the implementation of a flexible defense-in-depth mechanism. Furthermore, we delve into model-oriented risk analysis, error detection approaches, and the utilization of artificial intelligence for prevention and remediation. Our approach aims to contribute to the ongoing discourse on automotive cybersecurity, fostering not only safety but also the long-term security and immunity of autonomous vehicles.

2   Fundamentals

Autonomous Vehicles (AVs) incorporate various driving assistance mechanisms designed to aid the driver or assume control during specific tasks, such as *automatic parking*. These functionalities, as shown in Fig. 1 are enabled by onboard computers known as Electronic Control Units (ECUs), responsible for managing the car's functions. The integration of sensors and actuators distributed throughout the vehicle, tailored to specific tasks, facilitates these capabilities. To enhance control, ECUs exchange data through communication buses, forming an onboard-oriented network.

Nevertheless, the delegation of functions to software introduces heightened complexity and the potential for faults during both design and operation. Such faults can lead to failures with repercussions that may critically impact the vehicle's integrity and passenger safety. To address these concerns, the ISO 26262 standard offers methods for designing electrical and electronic systems that prioritize safety during operation. However, it is essential to note that these methods primarily focus on safety considerations and do not account for potential malicious interventions in embedded systems.

---

[1] https://upstream.auto/reports/global-automotive-cybersecurity-report/.

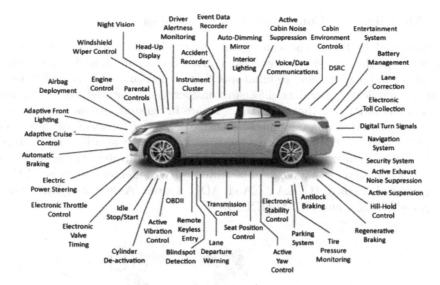

Fig. 1. Automatic Functions of an Autonomous Vehicle.

Like all computer systems, communication buses and ports constitute the primary attack surfaces within the onboard system network [8]. In the event of a successful attack, intruders can gain access to read, modify, and send messages on communication buses, potentially taking control of ECU operations. It is crucial to move beyond relying solely on preventive security measures and establish a comprehensive security policy for the entire system [5].

Merely implementing preventive security measures leaves the onboard system vulnerable. Therefore, it is imperative to identify specific actions and potential combinations of attacks [5,9]. Intrusion detection should not only focus on preventing attacks but also involve detecting security policy violations within the observed system. A safety mechanism designed for automobiles must remain effective throughout its development, deployment, and operation. Similarly, a security mechanism should be easily transferable across different architectures, ensuring that ECUs can operate autonomously and transparently for the user.

This article aims to establish intelligent mechanisms for enhancing the safety and immunity of automotive systems, primarily relying on formal methods and artificial intelligence techniques.

3   Challenges

The integration of autonomous vehicles into modern transportation systems has introduced a myriad of challenges at the intersection of modeling, communication, and security. This section delves into the multifaceted challenges faced by autonomous vehicles, exploring the intricacies of Electronic Control Units (ECUs), connectivity, and the imperative of ensuring security and safety in the dynamic landscape of automotive technology.

3.1   Modeling and Communication Challenges

As illustrated in Fig. 2, the concept of automotive networks encompasses a broader scope than merely the network of onboard computers. ECUs are crafted, akin to any onboard system, to fulfill specific requirements such as quality management, physical constraints, lifespan considerations, limited resources, and real-time operation. Furthermore, the software integrated into each car's ECU has undergone ad-hoc development. To cope with the intricacy of developed embedded systems, the automotive industry is shifting towards a more structured software development approach. This transition involves the adoption of model-based design methodologies like Automotive Modeling Language (AML), COmponent Language (COLA), EAST-ADL, Timing Augmented Description Language (TADL), and ICT MAENAD.

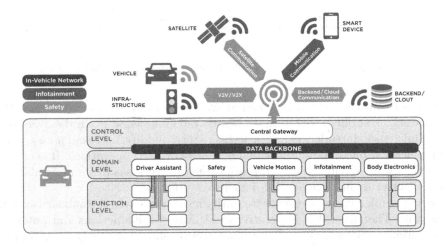

Fig. 2. Autonomous Vehicle Network.

Moreover, the integration of connectivity has empowered Advanced Driver Assistance Systems (ADAS) to provide intelligent functions, progressively automating various driving tasks. This connectivity has expanded through the implementation of vehicle cooperation, based on communication between nearby vehicles (V2V - Vehicle to Vehicle), and between a vehicle and fixed roadside infrastructure equipment (V2I - Vehicle to Infrastructure).

3.2   Security and Safety Challenges

On the safety front, ECUs bear the responsibility for potential critical malfunctions in vehicles, subject to the safety and security constraints outlined in ISO 26262. This standard establishes Automotive Safety Integrity Levels (ASIL) for each component of an onboard system, providing diverse design approaches and mechanisms to ensure the proper functioning of the system. Various attacks on embedded systems pose threats to owners, manufacturers, and even governments. Consequently, conducting a risk analysis associated with security and immunity incidents in automobiles enables the formulation of a more effective defense strategy based on identified needs.

To address this, Moody [4] introduced Safety Effect Levels of security threats (SELs) in the classification of ECUs, incorporating both safety and security aspects. This classification assesses the impact of specific attacks on the security of the onboard system. Additionally, efforts such as [3] aim to ensure the confidentiality of location data for mobile users through an architecture incorporating an epoch system, a labeled threat model, and a query measuring location sensitivity. Analyzing safety and security using a six-step method aligned with ISO 26262 and SAE J3061 standards, [2] further emphasizes the integration of these two critical aspects. The work of [10] illustrates the relationship between threats, attacks, vulnerabilities, and their impact on autonomous vehicles, while [1] presents an architecture designed to secure sensitive areas from potential suspicious activities of autonomous vehicles, employing recursive path navigation.

Regrettably, there is currently no standard providing an equivalent classification to ASIL that comprehensively addresses safety and immunity incidents. Given the paramount importance of vehicle safety, which directly affects lives, it is crucial to recognize that system malfunctions are not the sole consequences of attacks; attacks can also target data integrity and access, including data privacy. Consequently, safety in conjunction with security mechanisms designed for automotive systems must consider autonomy and compatibility, encompassing backward compatibility and interoperability. The aim is to make safety mechanisms as autonomous as possible, requiring the driver's attention only when necessary.

4   Perspectives

The goal of this work is to implement security and immunity measures in automotive networks, focusing specifically on the detection, prediction, and forecasting of errors within these networks. Considering the lifespan of a car and the frequency of updates, it is impractical to address attacks solely based on those known during the car's development. Therefore, there is a need to establish effective error detection against not only current but also future attacks, facilitating system updates. To safeguard against a diverse range of threats, a security policy should not rely solely on a single type of protective measure. Instead, it should employ mechanisms at various levels (software, systems, network, and environment) to ensure comprehensive protection.

Unfortunately, there is no standard describing the application of automotive safety policies or corresponding certifications. Given the relatively recent emergence of needs in terms of safety and immunity for automobiles, there is limited available data on the subject. To address these needs, we propose a hybrid approach that combines both model and data. This approach ensures the development of a secure system while concurrently analyzing the deployed system to prevent errors and attacks based on collected data. Our methodology supports the following steps.

1. **Development of a Standard Modeling Language:** Establishing a dedicated modeling language for autonomous vehicles, drawing upon existing languages and systems modeling standards (SysML, UML, OCL, etc.). This language is designed to streamline the precise representation and analysis of the intricate functionalities within the vehicle.

2. **Threat Classification:** Systematically classify threats that impact onboard systems in automobiles and the ECU network. This process involves the thorough identification and categorization of potential risks to enable the development of targeted security strategies. The overarching goal of the classification is to construct a taxonomy associating faults and errors with vulnerabilities, threats, attacks, and countermeasures.

3. **Security Deployment Standards:** Develop comprehensive standards for deploying security measures, employing a fusion of AI and formal methods to ensure consistent and effective implementation across automotive systems. This involves leveraging machine learning algorithms for anomaly detection, pattern recognition, and predictive analysis to proactively identify potential security threats. Formal methods, such as model checking and theorem proving, play a crucial role in rigorously verifying the correctness of security protocols and ensuring their resilience to potential vulnerabilities. By integrating AI and formal methods, the security deployment standards aim to establish a robust framework that evolves dynamically to adapt the emerging cyber threats while maintaining a high level of system integrity.

4. **Defense-in-Depth Mechanism:** Implementing a defense-in-depth and complementary defense mechanism involves deploying robust firewalls to monitor and filter network traffic, employing Intrusion Detection Systems (IDS) for detecting abnormal activities, utilizing strong encryption algorithms to secure communication channels, enforcing access control policies to limit system access, applying behavioral analysis techniques for identifying anomalous patterns, regularly updating software and firmware through security patching, and introducing redundancy and diversity in critical systems. This multi-layered security approach is designed to protect modern automobiles against intrusions by combining proactive measures such as access control and encryption with reactive measures like IDS and behavioral analysis. This mechanism is adaptable to various architectures, providing a dynamic and layered defense strategy to enhance overall system resilience.

5. **Model-Oriented Risk Analysis:** Adopting a model-oriented risk analysis approach based on formal methods is instrumental in systematically assessing and mitigating potential risks in automotive systems. This approach incorporates widely used techniques such as model checking, which rigorously verifies the correctness of system models, ensuring their adherence to specified safety and security requirements. By employing formal methods, the model-oriented risk analysis aims to provide a comprehensive understanding of the system's

vulnerabilities, threats, and potential consequences. This systematic approach enhances the development of targeted risk mitigation strategies, contributing to the overall safety and security of automotive systems.

6. **Error Detection Approach:** Deploying a data and model-oriented error detection approach, which integrates formal methods and artificial intelligence techniques, is pivotal for real-time error identification and rectification in automotive systems. The synergy between machine learning and theorem proving in this approach allows for a comprehensive and dynamic error detection process. By combining the pattern recognition capabilities of machine learning with the formal verification offered by theorem proving, the system can identify and rectify errors in real-time, contributing to the overall reliability and safety of automotive systems.

7. **AI-Based Prevention and Remediation:** Harnessing an AI-based prevention and remediation approach, especially leveraging advanced AI techniques, has proven highly effective in-depth on uncertain systems with large-scale data. This approach involves employing proactive measures to prevent potential security breaches and implementing efficient remediation strategies. Moreover, the AI-based approach includes remediation strategies that are adaptive and dynamic. By continuously learning from ongoing data, the system can evolve its response mechanisms, ensuring efficient and context-aware remediation of potential security incidents.

The integration of advanced AI techniques in prevention and remediation contributes to a robust and responsive security framework. This approach not only enhances the system's ability to thwart potential threats but also ensures a resilient and adaptive security posture against the evolving landscape of cyber threats in uncertain systems.

5   Conclusion

This paper has presented a forward-looking and comprehensive methodology aimed at addressing the evolving challenges in automotive cybersecurity. The transition from Industry 2.0 to the current Industry 5.0 has propelled the automotive market forward, introducing unprecedented connectivity and autonomy. While these advancements promise safer journeys, optimized road network utilization, and a cleaner environment, they also bring forth new security and immunity concerns. Our proposed methodology, embracing a hybrid approach between model and data, recognizes the impracticality of relying solely on known attacks during the development of autonomous vehicles. By setting objectives that encompass the development of a dedicated modeling language, the adoption of advanced and explainable AI techniques for prevention and remediation, and the integration of formal methods and a defense-in-depth mechanism, we have outlined a cohesive strategy to fortify automotive networks. This multi-layered approach addresses threats at various levels, contributing to the ongoing discourse on automotive cybersecurity and envisioning a future where autonomous vehicles embody safety principles and demonstrate resilience against evolving cyber threats.

As the automotive industry continues its trajectory towards enhanced connectivity and autonomy, the importance of robust cybersecurity measures cannot be overstated. Our proposed methodology serves as a foundational step towards creating a secure and immune environment for the next generation of autonomous vehicles, ushering in an era of safer, more reliable, and sustainable mobility.

References

1. Ayub, M.F., Ghawash, F., Shabbir, M.A., Kamran, M., Butt, F.A.: Next generation security and surveillance system using autonomous vehicles. In: 2018 Ubiquitous Positioning, Indoor Navigation and Location-Based Services (UPINLBS), pp. 1–5 (2018). https://doi.org/10.1109/UPINLBS.2018.8559744
2. Cui, J., Sabaliauskaite, G., Liew, L.S., Zhou, F., Zhang, B.: Collaborative analysis framework of safety and security for autonomous vehicles. IEEE Access **7**, 148672–148683 (2019)
3. Joy, J., Gerla, M.: Internet of vehicles and autonomous connected car - privacy and security issues. In: 2017 26th International Conference on Computer Communication and Networks (ICCCN), pp. 1–9 (2017).https://doi.org/10.1109/ICCCN.2017.8038391
4. Moody, J., Bailey, N., Zhao, J.: Public perceptions of autonomous vehicle safety: an international comparison. Saf. Sci. **121**, 634–650 (2020). https://doi.org/10.1016/j.ssci.2019.07.022
5. Ouchani, S.: A security policy hardening framework for socio-cyber-physical systems. J. Syst. Architect. **119**, 102259 (2021)
6. Ouchani, S.: Secure and Reliable Smart Cyber-Physical Systems (2022). https://tel.archives-ouvertes.fr/tel-04107896
7. Ouchani, S., Khaled, A.: Security assessment and hardening of autonomous vehicles. In: Garcia-Alfaro, J., Leneutre, J., Cuppens, N., Yaich, R. (eds.) CRiSIS 2020. LNCS, vol. 12528, pp. 365–375. Springer, Cham (2021). https://doi.org/10.1007/978-3-030-68887-5_24
8. Ouchani, S., Lenzini, G.: Generating attacks in SysML activity diagrams by detecting attack surfaces. J. Ambient. Intell. Humaniz. Comput. **6**, 361–373 (2015)
9. Ouchani, S., Mohamed, O.A., Debbabi, M., Pourzandi, M.: Verification of the correctness in composed UML behavioural diagrams. Softw. Eng. Res. Manag. Appl. **2010**, 163–177 (2010)
10. Plosz, S., Varga, P.: Security and safety risk analysis of vision guided autonomous vehicles. In: 2018 IEEE Industrial Cyber-Physical Systems (ICPS), pp. 193–198 (2018). https://doi.org/10.1109/ICPHYS.2018.8387658

Towards a B-Method Framework for Smart Contract Verification: The Case of ACTUS Financial Contracts

Zakaryae Boudi$^{(\boxtimes)}$ and Toub Mohamed

FeverTokens, 55 rue de la Boétie, 75008 Paris, France
{boudi,toub}@fevertokens.io
https://www.fevertokens.io

Abstract. The increasing use of advanced smart contract structures in finance necessitates rigor and scalability in ensuring their correctness. Traditional auditing methods fall short in providing comprehensive security, but formal verification offers a robust and scalable approach to constructing secure-by-design models and implementing smart contracts. In this paper, we introduce a B-method framework for modeling and verifying smart contracts based on the ACTUS standard for financial instruments. We start by converting ACTUS specifications into B-method constructs to bring a systematic approach to model, analyze, and verify financial contracts' implementations within the blockchain context.

Keywords: B-method · ACTUS standard · Smart Contracts · Formal Verification · Financial Instruments · Blockchain · Security

1 Introduction

Smart contracts have gained significant attention in recent years as a means of automating transactions and conveying ownership on blockchain platforms. They are digital contracts that self-execute when certain conditions are met, allowing for the automation of complex business processes and the elimination of intermediaries [3,8]. However, the complexity and potential for errors in smart contract code pose a significant challenge in ensuring their correct functionality [12,16]. Given the immutable and decentralized nature of blockchain, errors in smart contracts can have dire consequences, such as the loss of funds or inability to access assets.

In response to these challenges, we advocate for the use of formal verification techniques to mathematically substantiate the correctness of smart contracts. These methods enable the mathematical substantiation of a smart contract's correctness [4,7,10,11]. In software engineering, the B method is highly regarded [5], offering a formal specification language alongside tools for analyzing system behaviors and affirming key properties like safety and liveness [14]. Our selection of the B method is predicated on its comprehensive modeling capabilities, robust toolset, an active user community, and its proven track record in developing safety-critical software [1,13].

A. Ait Wakrime et al. (Eds.): CRiSIS 2023, LNCS 14529, pp. 25–32, 2024.
https://doi.org/10.1007/978-3-031-61231-2_3

This paper presents a novel methodology for the formal verification of smart contracts within the financial domain, specifically those based on the ACTUS standard for financial instruments. The ACTUS standard represents a holistic framework for algorithmically defining financial contracts using uniform data structures and deterministic functions [2]. Our approach includes the application of transformation rules for converting Actus specifications into B-method constructs to enable seamless and comprehensive formal verification process for any corresponding smart contract implementations.

The organization of this paper reflects the step-by-step approach taken to implement the B-method framework for modeling and verifying ACTUS-based financial contracts. We begin by introducing the challenges of scalability and standardization in smart contracts and the rationale behind FeverTokens' open-source Package-Oriented Framework in Sect. 2. Section 3 provides an overview of the ACTUS standard and its significance in representing financial contracts. Section 4 delves into the preliminary B-method framework for financial smart contracts, demonstrating the process of transforming ACTUS specifications into B-method structures.

2   Smart Contracts Scalability and the Rationale Behind the FeverTokens Open-Source Package-Oriented Framework

In the blockchain sphere, the scalability of smart contracts is a critical factor, especially as their complexity and applicability increase across various sectors. FeverTokens confronts this issue with its pioneering open-source Package-Oriented Framework, aimed at augmenting the scalability and flexibility of smart contracts [9]. This framework adopts a modular, package-oriented architecture, enabling developers to construct smart contracts as individual, updatable modules. This method enhances development efficiency and provides significant adaptability and scalability improvements.

The essence of the FeverTokens framework is its emphasis on functional scalability, allowing smart contracts to seamlessly integrate new functionalities while ensuring the integrity and security of the blockchain. Its open-source model promotes a collaborative development atmosphere, inviting community engagement and contributions, which fosters a robust and varied ecosystem of smart contract modules and encourages continuous innovation.

A key advantage of the framework is its capacity to facilitate advanced integration of established standards, particularly in the realm of financial instruments like ACTUS and Common Domain Model (CDM) by the ISDA [6]. The modular architecture of the framework is strategically designed to support the creation of libraries consisting of packages that correspond to specific standardized financial instruments. This feature is particularly beneficial for builders and institutions engaged in tokenization systems.

By aligning with standards like ACTUS and CDM, the framework ensures that the financial instruments modeled within it are compliant with global financial regulations and practices. This compliance is crucial for institutions looking to leverage blockchain technology for financial applications. The availability of these standardized packages within the framework not only simplifies the development process for builders but also enhances the reliability and interoperability of financial instruments across different platforms and systems. The modular approach, therefore, plays a pivotal role in bridging traditional financial models with the innovative capabilities of blockchain technology, offering a seamless and compliant pathway for the tokenization and management of financial assets.

Leveraging the Diamond standard (ERC-2535) [15], originally introduced by the Ethereum community as a solution to smart contract size limitations, the FeverTokens framework adds a substantial engineering layer to transform this standard into a tool for functional scalability. This enhancement standardizes facet and diamond structures within the framework, facilitating the seamless packaging and integration of modular smart contract components. This structure not only simplifies the management of smart contracts but also enables effective scaling in terms of version control, operational oversight, deployment, and upgrades. FeverTokens is actively developing infrastructure to efficiently manage these packages, addressing the challenges associated with scaling. The nature of this architecture underlines the importance of rigorous security verification processes. Given the increased frequency of updates and the inherent complexity of this system, verification efforts must be multi-dimensional, encompassing individual packages, the overall diamond structure, and governance aspects.

Traditional auditing methods, while reliable, become less feasible and more costly in this expanded scope. Consequently, automated formal verification mechanisms are crucial for ensuring safe-by-design development, enabling the framework to maintain robust security standards despite its scalability and modular complexity.

3   Overview of the Actus Standard and Financial Contracts

The ACTUS (Algorithmic Contract Types Unified Standards) standard is a pivotal development in the digital representation of financial contracts. Financial contracts, essentially legal agreements between parties for the exchange of future cash flows, are defined unambiguously through a set of contractual terms and logic. This clarity allows for their mathematical description and digital representation as machine-readable algorithms. The advent of distributed ledger and blockchain technologies, particularly the use of smart contracts, has opened up novel possibilities for these natively digital financial contracts.

Financial contracts typically follow established cash flow exchange patterns. Examples include bullet loan contracts with fixed principal payments and variable interest payment schedules, and amortizing loans where principal is paid back in portions. The ACTUS standard, through its taxonomy, organizes financial contracts based on their distinct cash flow patterns, covering a wide array of financial instruments like shares, options, swaps, and credit enhancements.

Table 1. Meta-structure of ACTUS financial contracts

Key Actus Element	Description
Contract Attributes	These represent the legal terms of a financial contract and define the exchange of cash flows
State Variables	These describe the state of a contract at a specific point in time. Examples include the outstanding Notional Principal and the applicable Nominal Interest Rate
Contract Events	These are scheduled or unscheduled events that occur at specific times during the contract's lifetime. They mark points where cash flows are exchanged or where the states of the contract are updated
State Transition Functions (STFs)	These define the transition of states from a pre-event state to a post-event state when a certain event occurs. STFs are specific to each event type and contract type
Payoff Functions (POFs)	These define how the cash flow for a certain event is derived from the current states and contract terms. Payoff Functions are specific to each event and contract type

The deterministic nature of these financial contracts is key. They define a set of rules and conditions under which, given any external variables, the cash flow obligations can be unambiguously determined. For example, in a fixed-rate loan, the obligations are explicitly defined, whereas in a variable rate loan, the rules for rate determination are set in advance, enabling clear derivation of future obligations. This deterministic approach forms the foundation of the ACTUS standard, providing a technology-agnostic, standardized description of financial contracts' cash flow obligations.

The integration of ACTUS with formal methods in the context of smart contracts offers numerous benefits. In the case of ACTUS-based smart contracts, they ensure that the contracts behave as intended, especially crucial given the financial implications and complex interactions involved. By using formal methods, developers can prove the correctness of these contracts against their specifications, thereby reducing the risk of errors and vulnerabilities. This approach is particularly beneficial in financial contexts and will play a crucial role in the safe and effective implementation of ACTUS standards in smart contracts.

4   A Preliminary B-Method Framework for Financial Smart Contracts Under the Actus Standard

In the ACTUS framework, financial contracts are defined using a meta-structure comprising several key elements: Contract Attributes, State Variables, Contract Events, State Transition Functions, and Payoff Functions (Table 1). The contribution of this paper lies in translating this complex meta-structure into a B-method project structure.

We encapsulate the ACTUS components within the B-method's formal constructs, facilitating not only the rigorous formalization of financial contracts but also ensuring their correctness and reliability through mathematical proof. Each ACTUS component –attributes, state variables, events, STFs, and POFs– is translated into a B-method construct, enabling a systematic and precise development of financial contracts (Fig. 1). Figure 1 reflects the mapping of the ACTUS specification onto a B-method structure where the Contract Attributes are implemented in the `contract_head` machine, while utility functions are implemented in separate modules (`utility.mch` and `env.mch`). The `contract_main` contains the key variables and operations that define the core functionality of the contract, with `contract_main_i` implementing the operations, encompassing the state transition and payoff logic.

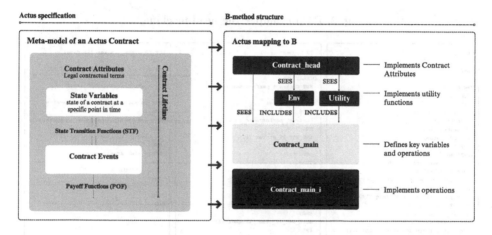

Fig. 1. Actus meta-model mapping to B-method structure.

In the context of formalizing financial contracts using the B-method, we set a head machine that serves as the cornerstone for this contract model, encapsulating the foundational constants and properties that govern the contract's behavior throughout its lifecycle (Fig. 2).

The head machine delineates a set of concrete constants –immutable parameters that define the financial contract's structure. The properties of the head machine establish the exact values for these constants, such as a notional amount of 100 units and an interest rate of 5%.

On the one hand, env machine within the B-method model functions as the dynamic context for the contract (Fig. 3). It sees the head machine constants, and it manages the stateful aspects of the contract's lifecycle. The OPERATIONS section defines actions that can be performed on the contract's state, such as updating the contract performance, setting payoff and state transition statuses,

```
MACHINE
    head
SETS
    Contract_Performance_States = {Performing, Delinquent, Default, Terminated, Matured};
    Event_states = {NA,missed,done}
CONCRETE_CONSTANTS
    NT,
    IPNR,
    MD,
    SD,
    PF_states,
    Year_convention
PROPERTIES
    NT = 100 &
    IPNR = 5 &
    MD = [01,09,2040] &
    SD = [01,09,2009] &
    PF_states = Contract_Performance_States &
    Year_convention = 365
END
```

Fig. 2. PAM example: the head machine.

```
MACHINE
  env
SEES
  head
VARIABLES
  Contract_performance,
  Date,
  IP_event_tracker,
  MD_event_tracker,
  IP_payment_tracker,
  STF_IP_status,
  POF_IP_status
INVARIANT
  Contract_performance : PF_states &
  Date : NATURAL &
  IP_event_tracker : seq(Event_states) &
  MD_event_tracker :seq(Event_states) &
  IP_payment_tracker : seq(seq(NATURAL)) &
  POF_IP_status : BOOL &
  STF_IP_status : BOOL
INITIALISATION
  Contract_performance := Performing ||
  Date := 1 ||
  IP_event_tracker := []||
  MD_event_tracker := [] ||
  ...
```

```
  IP_payment_tracker := [[0,0,0]] ||
  POF_IP_status := FALSE ||
  STF_IP_status := FALSE
OPERATIONS
  SET_Contract_performance (ii) =
  PRE
    ii : PF_states
  THEN
    Contract_performance := ii
  END;
  SET_POF_IP_status (ii) =
  PRE
    ii : BOOL
  THEN
    POF_IP_status := ii
  END;
  date <-- GET_Date =
  BEGIN
    date := Date
  END;
  BULK_SET_IP_event_tracker (ii) =
  PRE
    ii : seq(Event_states)
  THEN
    IP_event_tracker := ii
  END;
  ...
```

```
SET_IP_event_tracker (ii,date) =
PRE
  ii : Event_states & date : NATURAL1
THEN
  IP_event_tracker(date) := ii
END;
SET_IP_payment_tracker (ii,date) =
PRE
  ii : seq(NATURAL) & date : NATURAL1
THEN
  IP_payment_tracker(date) := ii
END;
MONTH_STEP_Eventdate =
PRE
  Date : NATURAL
THEN
  Date := Date + 1
END
END
```

Fig. 3. PAM example: excerpt of the env machine

and progressing the date to simulate the passage of time. On the other hand, the utility machine provides essential computational operations that serve various other components of the model. It acts as a library of functions that can be invoked to perform specific calculations needed for the contract's processing.

The main_i implementation refines the abstract main machine and serves as the executable part of the PAM contract within the B-method framework. It leverages the definitions and constants from the head machine and the dynamic behavior specified in the env machine, as well as the computational functions provided by the utility machine. The `main_i` operations collectively simulate the contract's progression through time, calculate payments, and track events, embodying the dynamic aspects of the contract's execution (Fig. 4).

```
IMPLEMENTATION main_i
REFINES main
SEES
  head
IMPORTS
  env, utility
CONCRETE_VARIABLES
  Nt,
  Accr,
  Schedule_AD
INVARIANT
  Nt : INTEGER &
  Accr : INTEGER &
  Schedule_AD : POW(INTEGER)
INITIALISATION
  Nt := NT;
  Accr := 0;
  Schedule_AD := {}
OPERATIONS
  IP_EVENT (state) =
    BEGIN
      VAR date IN
      date <-- GET_Date;
      SET_IP_event_tracker (state,date)
    END
  END;
  ...
```

```
Init_trackers =
  BEGIN
    VAR md,init_ip_event_tracker IN
    md <-- calculate_months(SD(3), SD(2),MD(3), MD(2));
    init_ip_event_tracker := {ee | ee : NATURAL1 & ee <= md}*{NA};
    BULK_SET_IP_event_tracker (init_ip_event_tracker)
  END
END;
Step =
  BEGIN
    VAR date IN
    date <-- GET_Date;
    IF date+1 : Schedule_AD
    THEN
      SET_IP_event_tracker(done,date+1);
      VAR md,dcf,ip IN
      md <-- calculate_months(SD(3), SD(2),MD(3), MD(2));
      dcf <-- calculate_day_count_fraction_ACT (date,md,Year_convention);
      ip := [Nt * IPNR * dcf(1),dcf(2), Nt * IPNR * dcf(3)];
      SET_IP_payment_tracker(ip,date+1)
      END;
      MONTH_STEP_Eventdate
    ELSE
      SET_IP_event_tracker(missed,date+1);
      SET_IP_payment_tracker([0,0,0],date+1);
      MONTH_STEP_Eventdate
    END
  END
END
END
```

Fig. 4. PAM example: excerpt of the `main_i` implementation

5   Conclusion and Perspectives

This paper has outlined a B-method framework tailored for the verification of smart contracts, with the ACTUS standard serving as a cornerstone for financial instruments. Looking ahead, we envision the application of this framework to the real case of Bond & Swap instruments, inviting both the financial industry and the research community to contribute to the evolution of this framework.

Future work will also include defining an approach for verifying Solidity implementations of ACTUS, exploring the potential for Solidity and bytecode generation directly from B models. This promises a seamless transition from model verification to practical deployment in the blockchain environment. The ultimate goal is to automate and certify the underlying methodology and tooling, ensuring a standard of excellence that facilitates safe-by-design development. By doing so, this work paves the way for robust financial instruments on the blockchain, marked by high levels of security and trust.

Acknowledgments. This research was supported by funding from the Casper Association and Bpifrance. We acknowledge their contributions, which have facilitated the foundational aspects of our study and set the stage for future developments.

References

1. Boudi, Z., Collart-Dutilleul, S., et al.: Safety critical software construction using CPN modeling and b method's proof. In: SESA 2014, Software Engineering and Systems Architecture, p. 4p (2014)
2. Brammertz, W., Mendelowitz, A.I.: From digital currencies to digital finance: the case for a smart financial contract standard. J. Risk Finance **19**(1), 76–92 (2018)
3. Britsiani, N.: Smart contracts: Legal aspects (2022). https://repository.ihu.edu.gr//xmlui/handle/11544/30033. Accepted 2022-09-30T08:47:30Z
4. Buchs, D., Klikovits, S., Linard, A.: Petri Nets: A Formal Language to Specify and Verify Concurrent Non-Deterministic Event Systems. Foundations of Multi-Paradigm Modelling for Cyber-Physical Systems, pp. 177–208 (2020)
5. Buchs, D., Klikovits, S., Linard, A.: Petri Nets: a formal language to specify and verify concurrent non-deterministic event systems. In: Foundations of Multi-Paradigm Modelling for Cyber-Physical Systems, pp. 177–208. Springer, Cham (2020). https://doi.org/10.1007/978-3-030-43946-0_7
6. Clack, C.D.: Design discussion on the ISDA common domain model. J. Digital Banking **3**(2), 165–187 (2018)
7. Colin, S., Mariano, G.: Coq, l'alpha et l'omega de la preuve pour B? (2009)
8. Cornelius, K.B.: Smart contracts as evidence: trust, records, and the future of decentralized transactions. In: Hunsinger, J., Allen, M.M., Klastrup, L. (eds.) Second International Handbook of Internet Research, pp. 627–646. Springer, Dordrecht (2020). https://doi.org/10.1007/978-94-024-1555-1_28
9. FeverTokens: FeverTokens' open-source Package-Oriented Framework (2023). https://github.com/FeverTokens/ft-package-oriented-framework. Accessed Dec 2023
10. Hansen, D., Leuschel, M.: Translating B to TLA+ for validation with TLC. Sci. Comput. Program. **131**, 109–125 (2016)
11. Jensen, K.: Coloured Petri Nets: Basic Concepts, Analysis Methods and Practical Use. Springer Science & Business Media (1996). https://doi.org/10.1007/978-3-662-03241-1
12. Khan, S.N., Loukil, F., Ghedira-Guegan, C., Benkhelifa, E., Bani-Hani, A.: Blockchain smart contracts: applications, challenges, and future trends. Peer-to-peer Netw. Appl. **14**, 2901–2925 (2021)
13. Lahbib, A., Ait Wakrime, A., Laouiti, A., Toumi, K., Martin, S.: An event-B based approach for formal modelling and verification of smart contracts. In: Barolli, L., Amato, F., Moscato, F., Enokido, T., Takizawa, M. (eds.) AINA 2020. AISC, vol. 1151, pp. 1303–1318. Springer, Cham (2020). https://doi.org/10.1007/978-3-030-44041-1_111
14. Treharne, H., Schneider, S.: How to drive a b machine. In: ZB 2000: Formal Specification and Development in Z and B: First International Conference of B and Z Users York, UK, August 29–September 2, 2000 Proceedings 1. pp. 188–208. Springer (2000)
15. Van Vulpen, P., Heijnen, H., Kroon, T., Mens, S., Jansen, S.: Decentralized Autonomous Organization Governance By Upgradeable Diamond Smart Contracts. SSRN 4634762 (2023)
16. Zou, W., et al.: Smart contract development: challenges and opportunities. IEEE Trans. Software Eng. **47**(10), 2084–2106 (2019)

Security and Transportation Systems

FERROMOBILE and Security for Low Moment of Traffic Level Crossing

Rim Brahim[1], Simon Collart-Dutilleul[1(✉)], Philippe Bon[1],
Pierre-Antoine Laharotte[2], and Nour-eddin El Faouzi[2]

[1] Univ Gustave Eiffel, COSYS-ESTAS, 59650 Villeneuve d'Ascq, France
{rim.brahim,simon.collart-dutilleul,philippe.bon}@univ-eiffel.fr
[2] Univ Lyon, Univ Gustave Eiffel, ENTPE, LICIT-Eco7, 69675 Lyon, France
{pierre-antoine.laharotte,nour-eddin.elfaouzi}@univ-eiffel.fr

Abstract. Level crossings (LCs) are critical components of railway networks and their safety is always at the centre of debate. Several accidents have occurred at level crossings due to non-compliance with road regulations, lack of visibility, behaviour of road users and many others. An innovative project called "Ferromobile" proposes a multi-modal, flexible, and electric vehicle capable of operating on both roads and rails. The main objectives of this project are to ensure flexibility, reconnect territories, promote carbon emission reduction, and maintain affordable costs.

In this paper, the Wireless Access in Vehicular Environments (WAVE) system is proposed as a solution to enhance safety at the LC. WAVE ensures connectivity through dedicated short-range communications (DSRC) between the "Ferromobile" and the infrastructure collecting data about the environment. To ensure the integrity, confidentiality, and authenticity of the exchanged information, the methodology may include encryption mechanisms to protect the data against intrusions that have already happened, inducing an accident involving tramways.

Keywords: Level Crossing · Ferromobile · WAVE · Encryption

1 Introduction

At the beginning stands the observation that even in rural areas, some roads were regularly congested, while the railway tracks remained surprisingly deserted. This led to the emergence of the "Ferromobile" project, which aims to use abandoned railway tracks to reduce road congestion and improve the quality of life for rural residents, offering them the convenience of comfortable travel. "Ferromobile" is a flexible electric vehicle capable of starting its journey on the road, transitioning onto the railway tracks, and then returning to the road. It operates at a speed of $70\,km/h^1$. It is a shared and collective public transport service.

---

[1] https://ferromobile.fr/actualites/insolite-un-vehicule-qui-roule-sur-la-route-mais-aussi-sur-les-rails-inaugure-pres-de-perpignan/.

A. Ait Wakrime et al. (Eds.): CRiSIS 2023, LNCS 14529, pp. 35–50, 2024.
https://doi.org/10.1007/978-3-031-61231-2_4

When the "Ferromobile" operates on railway tracks, it is autonomous. The question that arises is how to improve the safety of both road users and "Ferromobile" passengers at the LC?

Level crossings are places where railways and roads intersect at the same level. They are classified into 4 categories according to the ministerial decree of March 18, 1991 amended by decree no. 2019-525 of May 27, 2019[2]: Public LCs which are open to all road users are classified in the 1st category. They are equipped with barriers or half-barriers. They can be automated when the maximum speed of the trains is less or equal to 160 km/h, or else be monitored by agents authorized by the rail operator. In the 2nd category, there are public LCs which are crossed under the full responsibility of road users without the presence of barriers or half-barriers and without special surveillance by an agent authorized by the rail operator on lines at speed less or equal to 140 km/h. In the 3rd category we find the public LCs which can only be used by pedestrians and in the 4th category we find the private LCs, for private vehicles, pedestrians and/or shepherds.

The required safety equipment and surveillance measures for each LC depend on the intended use and characteristics of the railways and roads involved. On usual critical parameter is the moment of traffic which is demonstrated to be statistically linked with the number of accidents at LC [20]. The definition of the traffic moment is the multiplication of the number of cars per day and the number of trains per day at a given intersection.

The case we are dealing with is level crossings in the countryside, which are generally low-traffic and sometimes private. To manage the interaction between road users and the rail vehicle, it is necessary to study simple and economical solutions and above all to reduce the additional equipment at the LC.

To improve safety, Intelligent Transportation Systems (ITS) use both short-range communication networks and long-range cellular technologies. These technologies are valuable as they provide crucial safety information, such as alerts in case of nearby anomalies like construction, obstacles, locks, accidents, and others.

In this article, the WAVE protocol is selected as a data transmission solution for LCs in the countryside, which are sometimes private, that offers security and convenience in an ITS. In the considered use case, the ITS covers: the "Ferromobile" that ride on the railway track, as well as, depending on the category of LC, alternative users crossing the track, like shepherds, pedestrian, or agricultural vehicles. WAVE is a wireless communication system to enhance road user safety by facilitating information sharing among them through Dedicated Short-Range Communications (DSRC) [15]. The requirements of DSRC include maintaining real-time communication with low latency and high reliability [13]. Furthermore, it enables the deployment of decentralized traffic controllers, when the Roadside Units (RSU) supporting the communication are connected to local

---

[2] https://securite-ferroviaire.fr/reglementations/arrete-relatif-au-classement-la-reglementation-et-lequipement-des-passages-niveau.

sensors and equipped with embedded computational abilities to interpret data and automatically generate messages (hazard warnings, etc.) [2].

Indeed, a communication failure between a rail vehicle and the infrastructure can lead to serious risks. Without reliable information about the arrival of a rail vehicle, the LC may react inappropriately, thereby increasing the risk of severe accidents. Additionally, without critical information regarding the LC, the "Ferromobile" cannot respond appropriately. It is therefore essential to encrypt the messages exchanged between the rail vehicle and the LC to ensure the integrity and security of the wireless communication system.

To take an example, in 2008 [1], a 14-year-old boy who is an electronics enthusiast and an exemplary student, created a device similar to a TV remote control and used it to take control of the switching systems of public streetcars in the city of Lodz, Poland. As a result, four streetcars derailed and others applied emergency brakes, injuring passengers. Twelve people were injured. Although this attack was a prank as the teenager had told police[3], it is particularly significant as it represents the first cyber attack to have directly caused the injury. In many aspects, the "Ferromobile" system is similar to a tram system: it is a public transport where the infrastructure is not protected like the subway system. For this reason, it seems reasonable to implement protection against hacking even when it comes to level crossings in the countryside where the risks of accidents and collisions are lower compared to urban areas, but the risk of impact remains significant.. This protection remains at a very small cost in terms of money and computing time (being assimilated in the parameter "thinking time"). The country side low traffic lines are not a terrorist target like metro lines of Paris, as they have a little symbolic value.. However, since a prank has already led to serious consequences, this scenario should be reasonably considered. Message encryption is also considered in the following. To ensure the confidentiality of data generated by these connected objects, most Internet of Things (IoT) protocols incorporate cryptographic primitives into their specifications.

The evolution of classical encryption has given rise to a new type of encryption called lightweight encryption, specifically designed for IoT. This type of encryption is suitable for resource-constrained applications, meeting all the constraints of low-power computing applications, including energy consumption, data size, execution time, and more.

In the present paper, we further explore the feasibility and requirements to implement such a solution on the field through a deep analysis of feedback from the literature. The main specificity of the developed solution lies in the countryside requirements and constraints, i.e. restricted use of high-technologies and sensors (low-tech), compatibility between needs and resources, etc. We offer to consider a solution with an on-demand service request taking advantage only of communication technologies embedded into the "Ferromobile" vehicles. Some efforts are made in the feasibility analysis to ensure safe crossings and fit the requirements with the specificities of "Ferromobiles", which are lighter than usual trains and with specific braking distances.

---

[3] https://www.theregister.com/2008/01/11/tram_hack/.

The remainder of the paper is organized as follow. The second section introduces a description of the "Ferromobile" project. Then, the safe crossing solution for "Ferromobiles" designed for the countryside is developed, and a deep analysis of the feasibility is performed. The feasibility analysis explores the multiple dimensions: (i) the WAVE protocol technology that can be used for communication between the "Ferromobile" and the LC, (ii) the existing literature on braking distance calculation, and (iii) the cryptographic methodology for securing the information shared between the "Ferromobile" and the LC.

2   Objectives of the "Ferromobile" Project

In the 1930s, André Michelin developed a lightweight rail-car called the "Micheline" ("Fig. 1a")[4] that ran on rails and was designed to provide maximum comfort to its passengers. In revisiting this concept, an innovative project called "Ferromobile" ("Fig. 1b) has been proposed. The "Ferromobile" is an electric production vehicle from Peugeot that is capable of traveling on both roads and rails simultaneously. This car operates autonomously when on the railway tracks, allowing passengers to travel with ease without the need to drive.

(a) Micheline   (b) Ferromobile

Fig. 1. The Mechline of 1930 and the new project "Ferromobile".

To develop the entire system around the Railmobile, in 2021 the Society of Engineering Construction and Operation of the Ferromobile (SICEF) set up a collaboration between AKKODIS Technologies, Systra, Alstom, Gustave Eiffel University, Entropy, and the Occitanie region.

This project aims to reuse abandoned railroad tracks, which has several advantages. A de-carbonized mobility service will be available 24/7 in the territories, minimizing traffic and providing residents with safe and flexible travel options. It represents a cost-effective economic model suitable for low-traffic on small railway lines. The challenge is to bring back service where trains have disappeared.

The "Ferromobile" combines the best of the automobile and railway worlds. It has all the elements of passive safety (seat belts, airbags, etc.) and active

---

[4] https://ferromobile.fr/la-ferromobile/.

safety (Anti-lock Braking System (ABS), Emergency Brake Assistance (AFU), etc.). These systems ensure a safe journey from the first to the last mile.

This "Ferromobile" is a Peugeot series vehicle, an 8-seater public transport, traveling at 70km/h. Thanks to this speed and its mass, its stopping distance is more than 10 times shorter than that of trains. For a train traveling at 90 km/h, it takes 800 m to stop [17].

3 A Solution to Ensure Safe Crossing for "Ferromobiles"

This section details the global architecture and the technologies at stake to support our solution introduced to ensure safer crossing for "Ferromobiles".

In the subsequent sections, we provide an overview of the global architecture of the introduced system. Then, we explore the potential and feasibility of the described methodology according to two components: the use of the WAVE technologies to support data exchanges and the requirements

3.1 Overview of the Global Architecture

As mentioned earlier, our interest is the Level Crossings in the countryside, which receive low traffic and sometimes private flows. It is essential to monitor the crossing surface to identify potential hazards and improve the safety of road users(cars, pedestrians, and animals) as well as "Ferromobile" passengers.

However, in the countryside, alternative users crossing the "Ferromobile" tracks are expected to be sparse and epiphenomenon, which implies a high-level of risk *i.e.* even if the probability of risk is lower in rural areas due to lower occurrence compared to urban areas, the impact-risk remains significant. A careful attention need to be paid to monitor and manage the intersection during a short time period. To meet the requirements and as illustrated in Fig. 2, a pushbutton switch is used by alternative users to draw attention and trigger the safety system based on communication between the RoadSide Unit (connected to the pushbutton) and the "Ferromobile". Then, a secured communication protocols is applied. The system used to equip the LC can integrate the WAVE protocol as a solution for transmitting LC information to the "Ferromobile". This protocol enables efficient, reliable and interoperable transmission of information. This network enables the transfer of information for LC conditions, so that the "Ferromobile" can be warned immediately in the event of an obstacle on the track through broadcasted warning messages.

This message will be encrypted, broadcast through the Wave radio device and consulted by the "Ferromobile" (decryption and act accordingly). The warning message will continues to be broadcast until the shepherd presses an exit button to signal that the track is clear. This manual button has a light for feedback, when the ferromobile receive the message. See Fig. 2.

In summary, for this proposed system, the communication mode is divided into two types, demonstrating the effective integration of ITS

Fig. 2. Communication between infrastructure and "Ferromobile" through the WAVE protocol for LCs in the countryside.

- **Infrastructure-to-Vehicle (I2V) communication:** an alert message on the status of the LCs is provided from the level crossing to the autonomous vehicle (Ferromobile), making travel safer and more comfortable.
- **Vehicle-to-Infrastructure (V2I) communication:** this communication is visually confirmed by the lighting up of a light emitting diode to ensure effective reception of informations by the "Ferromobile".

Thus, V2V communication can take place when several "Ferromobiles" move one behind the other. When an alert message is triggered, the "Ferromobile" receives this message and acts accordingly, while the other railmobiles follow by slowing down or stopping. These "Ferromobiles" can communicate with each other through a local network.

An extended version could be considered for LCs on low-traffic urban areas, a communication system with a longer range than the Wave protocol is required. LC information can be detected by cameras, radars or other sensors. The use of two cameras can be envisaged: one to measure the upstream flow (flow priority level) and one to monitor the LC and detect dangerous situations. This enables the "Ferromobile" to react appropriately by adapting its speed or stopping to avoid a collision Fig. 3.

3.2   Wireless Communication Abilities and Contributions

WAVE Standardization Protocol: To interconnect machines, you need network cards, different types of cable (twisted pair, fiber optic, etc.), switches, and so on. This is a wired technology, i.e. cabling is required. In this type of communication, there are problems when stations are mobile, so wireless technologies are considered for data transmission with the critical agents that play a role in

Fig. 3. LCs on the outskirts of urban areas with low traffic levels.

a potential LC scenario of an accident [24]. Using a methodology proposed in the SELcat European project leads to a focus on the communication between the LC and the "Ferromobile". This methodology is not detailed in the current paper.

The IEEE 802.11p standard, also known as WAVE, is an amendment by the DSRC working group of the IEEE, focusing on wireless access in intelligent transportation systems. Based on the IEEE 802.11 standard, it can be considered as a mobile adaptation of Wi-Fi. Investigating the use of the WAVE protocol correspond to a strategy giving priority to the use of car industry technologies as there is no business model for dedicated technologies for LC for sheep crossing for example [8].

The primary objective of this technology is to enable wireless communication among vehicles and infrastructure, utilising the frequency band allocated to DSRC. For wireless communications in Intelligent Transportation Systems (ITS), a frequency band of 5.850 to 5.925 GHz has been allocated to the DSRC by the Federal Communications Commission (FCC) in the United States, and 5.875 to 5.905 GHz by the European Union [23]. Furthermore, this technology provides a transmission range of up to 1km, allowing efficient communication over longer distances between vehicles [7].

In April 2012 [2], a project called "PANsfer" was tested in collaboration with the French Institute of Science and Technology for Transport, Development, and Networks (IFSTTAR), the University of Technology of Belfort-Montbéliard (UTBM), École Centrale de Lille, and others[5].

Based on a statistical analysis of a database of accidents/incidents, in this article, the author developed three potential scenarios corresponding to the main causes of accidents (zigzagging, blockage due to congestion at the LC exit and obstruction on LC).

---

[5] https://www.youtube.com/watch?v=MiV41lW8kdk.

To improve safety, this project used a surveillance camera and the wireless communication system WAVE. The tests were conducted at a LC located in Mouzon, Ardennes. The objective of this project was to prevent collisions by informing vehicles of the presence of the LC and alerting them in case of abnormal behaviours observed on it.

Communication-Assisted Stopping Distance: The term "Stopping Distance" refers to the distance that a vehicle travels until it comes to a complete stop. This distance includes the time it takes for the driver or the vehicle's automated system to react to a problem and for the vehicle to decelerate fully after the brakes are applied. Stopping Distance can be divided into three categories that contribute to the total distance as described in "Fig. 4".

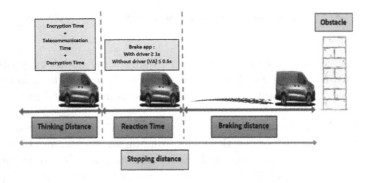

Fig. 4. Stopping Distance.

The categories of stopping distance are defined as follow:

- **Thinking Distance:** This refers to the distance a vehicle travels before the driver becomes aware of a problem. This concept of the state of the art is used to localize, in the functional architecture, the time used by the onboard computer to process information produced by the vehicle sensors or received through the network (for example from the LC). This elapsed time, includes the encryption, the telecommunication and the decryption delays. This duration finishes, when the system can take a decision.
- **Reaction Time:** This describes the time it takes for the driver to initiate a response to the encountered problem, such as applying the brakes. In the case of low-traffic LC with "Ferromobile", there is no Human Driver, but an automated one controlled by a computer. Obviously, the computer's reaction time is expected to be shorter than the human driver's one.
- **Braking Distance:** This is the distance the vehicle travels after the driver has responded, such as engaging the brakes, before the vehicle comes to a full stop.

On July 1, 2018[6],[7], the measure number 5 of the Interministerial Committee for Road Safety (CISR) came into effect. This measure reduces the speed limit from 90 to 80 km/h on two-way roads without a central separator. The objective of this measure was to save lives by reducing the number of severe accidents on these roads.

To highlight the importance of this measure, Road Safety produced a film titled "13 Meters.." This experiment was conducted by engineers from UTAC CERAM, experts, and specialists in testing and evaluations. It details an emergency braking situation and demonstrates that a reduction of just 10 km/h can result in gaining 13 m during braking, which makes a significant difference in terms of stopping distance and accident consequences.

In this experiment, they showed that in the case of emergency braking:

- For a car traveling at 80 km/h, it would have covered 57 m before coming to a complete stop.
- For a car traveling at 90 km/h, it would cover 70 m before coming to a stop.

Since our "Ferromobile" travels at a speed of 70 km/h, we can conclude that its stopping distance in case of an emergency is approximately "43 m".

Furthermore, in [13], the author discussed two equations for calculating the stopping distance. The two equations yield the same result when the car travels below 113 km/h. Using the simplest equation.
The stopping distance is formulated in Eq. 1:

$$D_S(m) = D_R + D_B \tag{1}$$

With:

- D_R : The thinking distance:

$$D_R(m) = V * T_R \tag{2}$$

V: Velocity / T_R: reaction time
In our case the thinking distance is:

$$D_R(m) = V * (T_R + T_E + T_T + T_D) \tag{3}$$

T_E : Encryption time / T_T : Telecommunication time / T_D : Decryption time

- D_B : The braking distance. For a vehicle traveling at speeds below 113 km/h, the braking distance is as follows:

---

[6] https://www.interieur.gouv.fr/Archives/Archives-des-communiques-de-presse/
2018-Communiques/Mise-en-aeuvre-des-decisions-du-CISR-du-9-janvier-2018-
concernant-les-pietons-et-l-alcool.
[7] https://www.securite-routiere.gouv.fr/les-medias/nos-campagnes-de-
communication/13-metres.

$$D_B(m) = \frac{V^2}{2g\mu} \tag{4}$$

g: Gravity $(9.81\,\text{m/s}^2)$ /μ: coefficient of friction (usually around 0.8)

Generally, the reaction time T_R is about 1 s. However, this delay can be extended due to challenging traffic conditions such as night, fog, or rain, as well as the physical condition of the driver, such as fatigue, illness, or alcohol consumption.

All these issues do not have to be faced in the context of the "Ferromobile" project, as the vehicle is driverless. All the direct safety consequences must be eliminated from the safety analysis.

In terms of safety, autonomous vehicles (AVs) should outperform human drivers, since they adopt a more predictable and responsible driving system, and also have a shorter reaction time than humans (less than or equal to 0.5 s [19]).

Regarding the thinking time and reaction time in the context of automated vehicles, they are expected to remain short and at minimal values with respect to the ones observed for Human Drivers. They will be much faster due to the automated system.

Before investigating deeper the selected technology performances, a big upper approximation corresponding to a thinking time and reaction time of 1 s is used. Please note that the telecommunication time reach a few tens of milliseconds plus the encryption and decryption time of a few micro or nanoseconds plus the reaction time less than or equal to 0.5 s.

The Fig. 5 illustrates the relationship between stopping distance and velocity.

As shown in Fig. 5, the stopping distance for a car travelling at 70 km/h is approximately "43.25 m".

It is necessary to take into consideration that the friction between the tires and the rails is different from the friction between the tires and the road surface. On the rails, the tires have to adapt to a smooth metal surface. Therefore, the sliding of tires on the rails is generally higher than on the road, resulting in a longer braking distance on the rails than on the road. There is a working team focusing of this particular aspects, but at the moment the road braking distance are used as a reference, assuming that they are an underestimated approximation.

In addition, it is necessary to take into consideration that the alert message can be sent and the "Ferromobile" is not yet within the scope of the Wave protocol (range of 1km). As already mentioned, the message will be repeated until the railroad track becomes clear (until a button is pressed at the exit). The frequency of the periodic alert message sending produce a time which must be added to the thinking time and the reaction time in order to be able to stop.

Actually, assuming all the preliminary approximations that we have made, the stopping distance including thinking time, reaction time and stopping distance is equal to 43.25 m. This is more than 20 times less than the WAVE telecommunication distance of 1 km. Since the WAVE protocol allows for signal

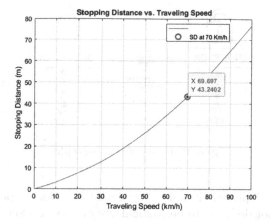

Fig. 5. Stopping distance as a function of speed

transmission at a distance of 1 km, we can conclude that the "Ferromobile" has enough time to come to a complete stop before a collision occurs at the LC.

3.3 Cryptography

Given that a 14-year-old was able to control the switching systems of public streetcars, it is likely that the basic Wave short-range communication system would be vulnerable to attack. Based on cryptographic algorithms available in the literature and simulation results for Brahim's master's thesis [6], the execution time for the encryption and decryption process of some micro or nanoseconds [22] is acceptable with the previously mentioned assumption (1 s for: thinking time and reaction time).

Nowadays, in the context of vehicular environments, security requirements such as confidentiality, integrity, non-repudiation, availability, authenticity, reliability, and many others, are of paramount importance due to the recent increase in cyber-attacks.

In the realm of the IoT, the extensive inter-connectivity of devices and the abundance of data being transmitted wirelessly, creates a susceptibility to various forms of attacks. To counteract this, cryptographic algorithms are used to provide the confidentiality of information and maintain its integrity.

"Cryptography" consists of transforming clear information into unintelligible information so that it can only be read by authorised individuals using a key, as described in Fig. 6.

The small size, constrained computational capacity, limited memory, and power resources of devices, make it challenging to employ resource-intensive traditional cryptographic algorithms for ensuring data security.

Unfortunately, traditional cryptographic techniques can cause problems in the context of embedded applications as they can be too slow, bulky, and energy-consuming. The Advanced Encryption Standard algorithm (AES) for example,

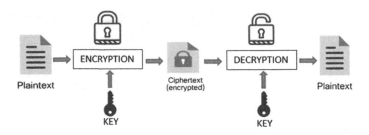

Fig. 6. Principle of cryptography.

is an excellent and preferred choice for almost all block cipher applications. However, it was not designed to be particularly efficient on low-power platforms such as those dedicated to IoT devices [5,18].

Recently, research has mainly focused on improving cryptographic algorithms in order to achieve an optimal balance between security, speed, energy consumption, and cost. The development and implementation of lightweight block cipher (LWC) algorithms are very important in wireless sensor networks (WSN) [21].

Encryption algorithms are separated into two main categories, symmetric and asymmetric algorithms.

Asymmetric encryption is so called because two different keys are used each time. A public key to encrypt the message and a private key for the decryption process. Among these algorithms, we mention: Rivest Shamir Adleman (RSA), Diffie Hellman, Digital Signature Algorithm (DSA) and Elliptical Curve Cryptography (ECC) [9].

In symmetric encryption, also known as secret key algorithms, the sender and receiver use the same secret key for both encryption and decryption processes. It includes hash functions, stream cipher and block cipher.

- **Hash functions**, example: The MD5 and SHA-1 algorithms.
- **Stream ciphers**: Among these algorithms, RC4 [3] is used as WIFI encryption algorithm, E0 algorithm [16] is used in Bluetooth protocol to secure communication and protect transmission, the A5/1 algorithm is used in most countries of the world to ensure confidentiality of conversations on GSM mobile phones and protect communications from eavesdropping [4] ...
- **Block ciphers**: There are different types of block ciphers based on their inner structure. Feistel networks, Substitution Permutation Networks (SPNs), AddRotate-XOR (ARX), NLFSR-based and hybrid. The algorithms based on Feistel network schemes and SPNs network schemes are the two most widely-used families [11]. Example: PRESENT, PRINCE, LED, SIMON, PICOLO, RECTANGLE, TWINE...

To ensure IoT devices, Three lightweight cryptographic algorithms have been implemented in Brahim's thesis [6]: SIMECK, SIMON and LED in a monoprocessor architecture as three cryptographic instructions extension. The table in Fig. 7, extracted from Brahim's works [6], shows that the SIMECK and SIMON algorithms have an execution time of 440 ns, while the LED algorithm has an execution time of 1920 ns. These execution times are almost negligible compared to our total approximation of 1 s time (thinking and reaction times). The same technology was used in [10], implementing the "PRESENT" and "PRINCE" algorithms as two instructions of lightweight cryptographic. These two proposed block cipher algorithms are characterized by high performance, They exhibit high throughputs, as well as good efficiency while maintaining moderate power consumption and dissipation. Consequently, such a technology could be used to ensure message security and respond to real-time and field requirements of our proposed system.

	FPGA	Data path/ bit	Key size/ bit	Slices number	Flip Flops number	LUTs number	Execution time (ns)	Maximum frequency (MHZ)	Throughput (Mbps)	Efficiency (Mbps/slices)
SIMECK	Spartan6 (Xc6s16 -3)	32	128	206	199	308	440	220.466	320.677	1.556
	Virtex7 (Xc7vx3 30t-3)			200	197	304		613.242	891.988	4.459
SIMON	Spartan6 (Xc6s16 -3)	32	128	206	199	346	440	236.867	344.534	1.672
	Virtex7 (Xc7vx3 30t-3)			202	199	309		576.777	838.948	4.153
LED	Spartan6 (Xc6s16 -3)	32	128	154	146	326	1920	251.27	83.921	0.544
	Virtex7 (Xc7vx3 30t-3)			144	144	323		564.685	250.971	1.742

Fig. 7. Table showing the results of implementing SIMECK, SIMON and LED architectures on two Spartan 6 and Virtex 7 platforms.

Moreover, chaos-based encryption has become popular among researchers due to its high efficiency in data protection. For data security, Jalolouli et al. [12] developed two lightweight chaos-based stream ciphers for devices with limited energy and time resources, such as those for IoT. Korba's thesis [14] aimed at designing new chaos maps (3D Cubic-Sine and 2D Cubic-Cat chaotic maps) for the security of images transmitted over the physical layer of wireless multimedia sensor networks.

Such approaches could be used to refine the process and improve the communication efficiency between infrastructure and the "Ferromobiles".

4   Conclusion and Perspectives

Level crossings are a particularly vulnerable link in the railway infrastructure. Numerous accidents occurred at this kind of intersection, resulting in life loss, serious injuries, major property damage, and more. Consequently, at LCs, it is essential to avoid collisions and ensure the safety of road users and rail vehicle passengers. For each type of LC, equipment and safety solutions differ. The "Ferromobile" project is designed to be deployed in rural areas and small towns, where there are LCs in the countryside that are sometimes private, as well as LCs in low-traffic urban peripheries. We, therefore, need simpler, less expensive, and above all, resource-parsimonious solutions to control LC. To sum it up, the LC technological package can be achieved without major investment in hardware and software development.

To improve safety, this article proposes the WAVE protocol as a communication solution between the infrastructure and the "Ferromobile" for LCs in the countryside. This wireless communication network offers significant safety benefits. It enables the transfer of information concerning LC status, thus warning the "Ferromobile" at an opportune moment. This enables it to react appropriately, adapting its speed or stopping to avoid a collision. The warning message can be broadcast up to a distance of 1 km, which is sufficient for a "Ferromobile" traveling at 70 km/h to brake in an emergency. A failure in communication between the LC and the vehicle can lead to dramatic or unacceptable consequences. To ensure the security of shared data, this paper proposes the use of LWC methodology and chaotic system-based encryption. These measures are designed to guarantee the confidentiality, integrity and authenticity of the information shared between the infrastructure and the "Ferromobile". Let us recall to mind that the execution times remain compliant with the global stopping distance of the current paper, even using the various considered technologies of encryption. Consequently, the main architectural assumptions are validated by the preliminary studies of the present paper:

- A low automation LC sending a safety message to the "Ferromobile" increase the safety.
- The use of the WAVE protocol is compatible with the stopping distance.
- The global safety assumptions are preserved by the use of an encrypted WAVE telecommunication mean, where encryption is used to protect the installation from a security point of view.

The aim of future work is to develop complete systems for each type of level crossing. For level crossings in the countryside, which are sometimes private, the combination of the WAVE protocol with the equipment on LCs, will open up new prospects for more efficient management of LC, reducing the risk of collisions and improving the flow of rail traffic. For level crossings on the outskirts of low-traffic urban areas, a longer range communication system than the Wave protocol is required and security solutions differ. It exists a norm managing the links between security and operational safety. This was typically the case, when in 2008 a teenager corrupted the control of the interlocking of a tram in Poland.

A systematic review of this normative context with regard to the targeted application on low-traffic LCs will be performed. In addition, providing the best safety services, taking into account the availability of different telecommunication services depending on the location of the LCs, will require an in-depth analysis of the system which has yet to be carried out.

Acknowledgment. The "Ferromobile" project is granted by ADEME in the "France 2030 program" (grant number 2282D0215-F).

References

1. Applegate, S.D.: The dawn of kinetic cyber. In: 2013 5th International Conference on Cyber Conflict (CYCON 2013), pp. 1–15. IEEE (2013)
2. Bahloul, K., Defossez, F., Ghazel, M., Collart-Dutilleul, S.: Adding technological solutions for safety improvement at level crossings: a functional specification. Procedia. Soc. Behav. Sci. **48**, 1375–1384 (2012)
3. Berbain, C.: Analyse et conception d'algorithmes de chiffrement à flot. Ph.D. thesis, Paris 7 (2007)
4. Berzati, A.: Analyse cryptographique des altérations d'algorithmes. Ph.D. thesis, Université de Versailles-Saint Quentin en Yvelines (2010)
5. Bogdanov, A., et al.: PRESENT: an ultra-lightweight block cipher. In: Paillier, P., Verbauwhede, I. (eds.) CHES 2007. LNCS, vol. 4727, pp. 450–466. Springer, Heidelberg (2007). https://doi.org/10.1007/978-3-540-74735-2_31
6. Brahim, R.: Implémentation d'un algorithme léger sur une architecture monoprocesseur pour l'internet des objets (IoT). master thesis, Monastir scientific university (2021)
7. Dar, K., Bakhouya, M., Gaber, J., Wack, M., Lorenz, P.: Wireless communication technologies for its applications [topics in automotive networking]. IEEE Commun. Mag. **48**(5), 156–162 (2010)
8. Dutilleul, S.C., Bon, P., Hamidi, H.: A railway norms application for small traffic railway lines autonomous vehicle. In: 2023 7th IEEE/IFAC International Conference on Control, Automation and Diagnosis (2023)
9. Dutta, I.K., Ghosh, B., Bayoumi, M.: Lightweight cryptography for internet of insecure things: a survey. In: 2019 IEEE 9th Annual Computing and Communication Workshop and Conference (CCWC), pp. 0475–0481. IEEE (2019)
10. El Hadj Youssef, W., Abdelli, A., Dridi, F., Brahim, R., Machhout, M., et al.: An efficient lightweight cryptographic instructions set extension for IoT device security. Secur. Commun. Netw. **2022**(2), 1–17 (2022)
11. Hatzivasilis, G., Fysarakis, K., Papaefstathiou, I., Manifavas, C.: A review of lightweight block ciphers. J. Cryptogr. Eng. **8**, 141–184 (2018)
12. Jallouli, O., Chetto, M., El Assad, S.: Lightweight stream ciphers based on chaos for time and energy constrained IoT applications. In: 2022 11th Mediterranean Conference on Embedded Computing (MECO), pp. 1–5. IEEE (2022)
13. Knowles Flanagan, S., Tang, Z., He, J., Yusoff, I.: Investigating and modeling of cooperative vehicle-to-vehicle safety stopping distance. Future Internet **13**(3), 68 (2021)
14. Korba, K.A.: La Sécurité des Réseaux de Capteurs sans fil Multimédia par des Systèmes Chaotiques. Ph.D. thesis, Université 08 mai 45 Guelma (Algérie) (2022)

15. Kumar, P., Ali, K.B.: Intelligent traffic system using vehicle to vehicle (v2v) & vehicle to infrastructure (v2i) communication based on wireless access in vehicular environments (wave) std. In: 2022 10th International Conference on Reliability, Infocom Technologies and Optimization (Trends and Future Directions)(ICRITO), pp. 1–5. IEEE (2022)
16. Lu, Y., Vaudenay, S.: Faster correlation attack on Bluetooth keystream generator E0. In: Franklin, M. (ed.) CRYPTO 2004. LNCS, vol. 3152, pp. 407–425. Springer, Heidelberg (2004). https://doi.org/10.1007/978-3-540-28628-8_25
17. Mervent, P.: La question de la sécurité routière et de la sécurité ferroviaire aux passages à niveau. Les Notes du CREOGN **69** (2022)
18. Mohammad, H.M., Abdullah, A.A.: Enhancement process of AES: a lightweight cryptography algorithm-AES for constrained devices. TELKOMNIKA (Telecommunication Computing Electronics and Control) **20**(3), 551–560 (2022)
19. Patel, R., Levin, M.W., Boyles, S.D.: Effects of autonomous vehicle behavior on arterial and freeway networks. Transp. Res. Rec. **2561**(1), 9–17 (2016)
20. Prosser, I.: Level Crossings: A Guide for Managers, Designers and Operators. Tech. rep, Office of Rail and Road (ORR) (December (2011)
21. Radosavljević, N., Babić, D.: Power consumption analysis model in wireless sensor network for different topology protocols and lightweight cryptographic algorithms. J. Internet Technol. **22**(1), 71–80 (2021)
22. Tawalbeh, L.A., Tawalbeh, H.: Lightweight crypto and security. Security and Privacy in Cyber-Physical Systems: Foundations, Principles and Applications, pp. 243–261 (2017)
23. Wong, R., White, J., Gill, S., Tayeb, S.: Virtual traffic light implementation on a roadside unit over 802.11 p wireless access in vehicular environments. Sensors **22**(20), 7699 (2022)
24. Öörni, R., Collart-Dutilleul, S., Khoudour, L., Heddebaut, M.: Use of fixed and wireless communication technologies in LC safety application. In: Proceeding of 2nd SELCAT Safer European Level Crossing Appraisal and Technology Workshop, pp. 161–162. Les collections de l'INRETS, INRETS (Nov 2007)

Improvement and Evaluation of Resilience of Adaptive Cruise Control Against Spoofing Attacks Using Intrusion Detection System

Mubark Jedh[1]($\boxtimes$), Lotfi ben Othmane[2], and Arun K. Somani[1]

[1] Iowa State University, Ames, IA, USA
mjedh@iastate.edu
[2] University of North Texas, Denton, TX, USA

Abstract. The Adaptive Cruise Control (ACC) system automatically adjusts the vehicle speed to maintain a safe distance between the vehicle and the lead (ahead) vehicle. The controller's decision to accelerate or decelerate is computed using the target speed of the vehicle and the difference between the vehicle's distance to the lead vehicle and the safe distance from that vehicle. Spoofing the vehicle speed communicated through the Controller Area Network (CAN) of the vehicle impacts negatively the capability of the ACC (Proportional-Integral-Derivative variant) to prevent crashes with the lead vehicle. The paper reports about extending the ACC with a real-time Intrusion Detection System (IDS) capable of detecting speed spoofing attacks with reasonable response time and detection rate, and simulating the proposed extension using the CARLA simulation platform. The results of the simulation are: (1) spoofing the vehicle speed can foil the ACC to falsely accelerate, causing accidents, and (2) extending ACC with ML-based IDS to trigger the brakes when an accident is imminent may mitigate the problem. The findings suggest exploring the capabilities of ML-based IDS to support the resilience mechanisms in mitigating cyber-attacks on vehicles.

1 Introduction

The Adaptive Cruise Control (ACC) is an advanced cruise control system that automatically adjusts the vehicle speed to maintain a safe distance between the (ego) vehicle and the lead (ahead) vehicle. The objective of the ACC system is to make the ego vehicle travels at the driver's specified speed as long as it travels at a safe distance from the lead vehicle. The ACC-equipped vehicle uses radar sensors to measure the distance to the lead vehicle, as depicted by Fig. 1, to take proper actions (acceleration or deceleration) in order to keep a safe distance from the lead vehicle.[1] Winner et al., for example, designed an ACC control module that uses a range sensor to measure the distance between the vehicle and the

---

[1] The lead vehicle is driving in the same lane as the ego vehicle.

A. Ait Wakrime et al. (Eds.): CRiSIS 2023, LNCS 14529, pp. 51–66, 2024.
https://doi.org/10.1007/978-3-031-61231-2_5

lead vehicle [1].[2] The first commercial system in use was a lidar-based distance detection system Debonair Mitsubishi, which is available since 1992.

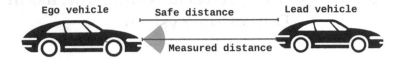

Fig. 1. Visualisation of the Adaptive Cruise Control (ACC). It shows that the sensor measured distance is smaller than the safe distance.

The promises of Adaptive Cruise Control (ACC) systems in terms of driver comforts and safety assurance encouraged researchers to experiment with the feasibility and impact of cyber-attack on ACC systems. The experiments showed that forcing the ACC to use the wrong information about the distance between the vehicle and the lead vehicle leads to the wrong acceleration/deceleration decision, which leads to accidents. The falsification of the safe distance was achieved using two techniques: (1) forcing the distance sensor (e.g., LIDAR or front Camera) to report wrong information to the ACC [3,4], and (2) manipulating the distance between the vehicle and the lead vehicle communicated by the distance sensor to the ACC through the CAN Bus [5,6]. The proposed solutions

Table 1. Strategy for resilience.

ID	Technique	Addressed security aspect	Description	Ref.
1	Recursive Least square	No Security	Online parameter estimation of distance gap by optimizing the root mean squared error (RMSE) between simulated space gap data and recorded space gap data.	[7,8]
2	Recursive Least square	Challenge response authentication	A RLS is used to estimate the spoofed sensor measurement.	[9]
3	Extended Kalman filter	Yes, through estimation	Estimating the velocity of the vehicle in the local reference system	[10,11]
4	Kalman filter	No Security	Estimating the velocity of the vehicle in the local reference system and concurrently the absolute position	[10]
5	Particle filter	No Security	Online parameter estimation of ACC	[8]
6	Model Predictive Controller	Yes, through estimation	Applies the linear model of the system, disturbance, and noise models to estimate the state of the control system and also anticipate the system's future outputs	[5]

---

[2] Cooperative Adaptive Cruise Control (CACC) uses, in addition, to the ego vehicle's speed and distance to the lead vehicle (which are used by ACC), information about the speed and location of close-by vehicles to better regulate its speed [2].

focus on communicating the wrong distance between the vehicles to the ACC by, e.g., using time-varying sampling of the distance between the two vehicles [6] or Model Predictive Controller (MPC) system [5].

The ACC uses the vehicle's speed, besides the distance between the vehicle and the lead vehicle, in computing the acceleration/deceleration control decision. Forcing the ACC to use the wrong vehicle speed could also potentially lead to the wrong acceleration/deceleration decision, which leads to accidents. Hoque et al. analysed the effect of spoofing speed on ACC and proposed using GPS signals to identify attacks on ACC. First, GPS signals are highly susceptible to spoofing and jamming attack, thereby the solution introduces high-risk security concerns [12]. Second, the paper does not propose changes to ACC controller to address the issue, which we do in this work.

This paper proposes extending the ACC system with a real-time IDS to detect cyber-attacks on the vehicle and to trigger the brakes when spoofing of the vehicle speed is detected. We implemented the solution into CARLA simulator [13] considering the performance of a real-time IDS implemented in our previous research [14–16]. The solution is assessed using the following scenarios: (1) simulate the ego vehicle trailing the lead vehicle and using an ACC to avoid crashes; (2) simulate the ego vehicle trailing the lead vehicle while using the ACC to avoid crashes, and spoofing the speed of the ego vehicle; and (3) simulate the ego vehicle trailing a lead vehicle, spoof the speed of the ego vehicle, and use an ACC extended with a simulated real-time IDS [15].

The contributions of the paper are:

- Demonstrate that spoofing the speed of the vehicle can mislead the ACC to compute the wrong safety distance with the lead vehicles, leading to potential crashes.
- Extend the ACC (Proportional-Integral-Derivative (PID) variant [17]) with a real-time IDS to force cold brake when spoofing of the vehicle speed is detected addresses the problem.

The results suggest that using the vehicle's IDS by proactively monitoring the CAN bus will improve the resilience of the ACC system to cyber-attacks.

The paper is organized as follows: Sect. 2 gives an overview of related works; Sect. 3 describes the proposed ACC extension with real-time IDS; Sect. 4 describes and analyses the results of simulating the proposed extension; and Sect. 5 concludes the paper.

2   Related Work

This section describes related work on cyber-attacks on ACC systems and cyber-resilience of ACC systems.

2.1   Cyber-Attacks on Adaptive Cruise Control

Several researchers investigated the security of LiDAR, especially spoofing the LiDAR signal. For instance, Harris [4] developed an attack on LiDAR laser that makes the vehicle wrongly believe that there is a large object in front of it, preventing it from moving by overwhelming the LiDAR sensor [4]. Coa et al. spoofed obstacles, leading the LiDAR-based perception to believe it is close to the object [3]. Also, Rad et al. [18] and Jagielski et al. [19] showed that sensor spoofing against RADAR and LIDAR impacts the efficiency of the ACC and CACC leading to potential discomfort of the passenger and safety hazard including accidents. Farivar et al. [5] proposed a covert attack on ACC that manipulate radar sensor input, which leads the ACC to decrease the safe distance, causing crashes. The authors developed an IDS for such attacks and corrected the system using MPC system. Moreover, Sun et al. demonstrated a spoofing attack against a LiDAR sensor, effectively tricking the system into perceiving an obstacle in its path by transmitting laser signals to the victim's LiDAR [20]. Their result showed that attackers can achieve 80% mean success rate on all LiDAR target models. Petit et al. [21] showed the efficacy of the Lidar relay attacks and spoofing attacks using a cheap transceiver.

The proposed solutions to such attack include the physical chall-enge-response authentication (PyCRA) technique, which was developed by Shoukry et al. [22] to enhance the cyber-resilience of sensors to attacks. PyCRA assumes that an attacker cannot detect a challenge immediately due to its hardware and signal processing latency. Given that, PyCRA detects an attack signal that continues to be higher than a noise threshold during a challenging period using the Chi-square method. PyCRA turns off sensors that have been attacked, providing an authentication mechanism that not only detects malicious attacks but provides resilience against them.

The ACC system uses the speed and distance sensors information to compute the desired acceleration to maintain a safe distance from the lead vehicle. The system is integrated as an embedded system into the CAN Bus, which is known to be vulnerable to cyber-attacks exploiting the lack of secure communication between the Electronic Control Units (ECUs) communicating through the bus [23]. Heijeden et al. [24] showed that controllers are vulnerable to jamming or Denial of Service (DoS) and message injection attacks and proposed quantifying the impact of attacks on vehicle controllers system. Furthermore, Tianxiang et al. [6] studied the stability of the ACC system subject to DoS by performing real-time DoS attacks on the ACC system at various time steps and studying the time it takes the ACC system to return to the closed-loop system. They found that under DoS attacks, the ACC system behaves as an open-loop system, and the speed errors increase.

2.2 Cyber-Resilience of Adaptive Cruise Control

Several authors investigated different aspects of ACC resilience to cyber-attacks. Table 1 summarizes the main proposed techniques. Oh et al. proposed using a sliding mode observer to detect sensor faults in the case of cyber-attacks on the acceleration sensor and radar [25]. Abdollahi et al. also proposed using a sliding mode observer to detect DoS attack and estimate correction [26]. Fiu et al. proposed a technique to estimate the position of a vehicle under GPS

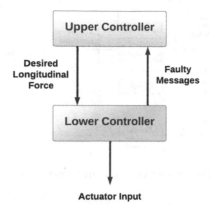

Fig. 2. Controllers composing the Adaptive Cruise Control System.

spoofing and LIDAR replay attacks [11]. In addition, Liu proposed the use of an extended Kalman filter to fuse sensor measurements to estimate a vehicle's position and designed a Cumulative Sum (CUSUM) detector based on the residual of Extended Kalman Filter (EKF) to monitor the inconsistency [11]. When detecting that the sensor is under cyber-attack, EKF is reconfigured to estimate the correct position of a vehicle [11].

Each of the resilience methods discussed above proposes new formulations of the controllers to mitigate specific attacks such as DoS, which limit their adaptation in practice. Also, given that the algorithms/formulation are public, the attackers should be able to design attacks that avoid the protection–much like avoiding the failure-detection capabilities of existing controllers. This paper proposes delegating detecting cyber-attacks to IDS and extending the ACC controller to use IDS to mitigate such cyber-attacks. This allows having a robust and generic solution for cyber-attacks for ACC systems.

3   Extending Adaptive Cruise Control with ML-Based Intrusion Detection System

The negative impact of spoofing distance sensors on the efficiency of ACC started to be known, and the community started developing ACC models resilient to cyber-attacks on these sensors and the distance data communicated through the CAN bus. These models do not consider spoofing the vehicle speed, also used by the ACC system. This paper proposes a generic solution to the ineffective resilience of ACC to cyber-attacks, focusing on spoofing vehicle speed. This section describes the proposed solution.

3.1   Overview of the Adaptive Cruise Control

The primary goal of the ACC is to maintain a safe distance from the lead vehicle, that is, keeping the difference between the current distance from the lead

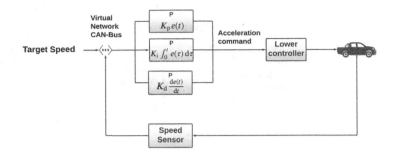

Fig. 3. Components of the Proportional-Integral-Derivative (PID) Controller model.

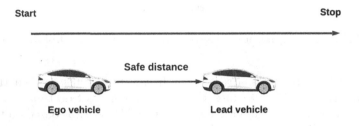

Fig. 4. The Ego vehicle uses an ACC while following the lead vehicle, which allows it to keep a safe distance.

vehicle and the safe distance, as shown by Fig. 4, formulated using Eq. 1, higher than zero. The The Safe Stopping Distance (SSD), or simply the safe distance, determines how far the vehicle travels before it comes to a complete stop and avoids collision with the lead vehicle, as is formulated using Eq. 2 [27].

$$D = D_c - SSD \tag{1}$$

$$SSD = 0.278 \times t \times v + \frac{v^2}{254 \times f + g} \tag{2}$$

where SSD is the stopping distance in meters, t is the perception-reaction time in seconds (it is 2.5 s for most drivers), v is the speed of the car in km/h, g is the slope of the road, and f is the coefficient of friction between the tires and the road. The ego vehicle avoids collision while moving by stopping immediately when the SSD is less than its current distance from the lead vehicle.

The ACC system uses two controllers as depicted by Fig. 2: an upper-level controller and a lower-level controller. The lower-level controller determines the throttle and brake while the upper-level controller determines the desired longitudinal acceleration to attain the desired spacing and constant speed [17]. Different dynamic responses that implement the two-levels ACC system have been proposed including PID controllers [17], Linear Quadratic Regulator control (LQR) [28], Sliding Mode Control [29], Fuzzy Logic Control [30], and Model

Predictive Controller (MPC) [5]. We use in this paper the PID model because it is widely used in many systems to reach the stability status.

$$e(t) = S_t(t) - S_c(t) \tag{3}$$

Figure 3 depicts the overall PID-based ACC system [17]. The PID controller adjusts the acceleration and deceleration commands to minimize the error computed using Eq. 3, which measures the difference between the target speed of the vehicle (S_t) and its current speed (S_c) as measured by the speed sensor [17]. The speed error is used to compute the control signal $u(t)$, shown in Fig. 3, using Eq. 4, which uses three constants:

- K_p – proportional gain of the action to the error,
- K_i – integral gain to reduce the steady-state errors through low-frequency compensation by an integrator,
- K_d – derivative gain to improve the transient response through high-frequency compensation by a differential.

$$u(t) = K_{\mathrm{p}}e(t) + K_{\mathrm{i}} \int_0^t e(t)\,\mathrm{dt} + K_{\mathrm{d}}\frac{\mathrm{d}e(t)}{\mathrm{dt}} \quad [17] \tag{4}$$

Increasing the K_p value helps the vehicle reaching the target speed more quickly, but tends to exceed its target and overshoot. The K_d term affects the decrease of the overshoot. The K_i value affects the capability to limit the steady error and prevent oscillatory. Adjusting the gains of the K_p, K_d, and K_i allows to achieve a satisfactory overall response.

3.2   Architecture of the Extended Adaptive Cruise Control

Resilience has been an effective active solution for vehicle controllers, providing robust capabilities for vehicles to reduce errors and detect failures during vehicle operation. Resilience mechanisms trust the sensors to provide measurements and consider the random outliers as errors. Cyber-attacks mislead the controllers by spoofing the sensor measurements. A resilient controller should enhance the system's performance during an attack.

IDS has been proposed as a solution, although passive, to mitigate cyber-attacks on vehicles [31,32]. It detects intrusion that results in compromised system components in the ACC system (e.g., sensors and controllers output) and reports the anomaly to combat the malicious attackers. ACC cannot report an intrusion detected by the IDS to a remote security expert or even the driver and wait for their decision while possibly getting closer to the lead vehicle.

The ACC must use a correct, safe distance to work properly. We propose to extend the ACC with a vehicle IDS that allows detecting the vehicle's speed spoofing with reasonable efficacy. The ACC has two options to mitigate detected cyber-attacks: (1) trigger cold brake and (2) get the correct speed using another approach, including predicting it using machine learning models. We use option one in this paper as it allows us to evaluate the solution more easily (Fig. 5).

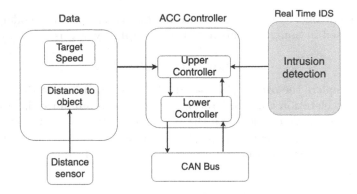

Fig. 5. Architecture design simulation setup for scenario three

Table 2. The performance of the IDS in the simulated scenario [16].

Factor	Parameter
Dataset	Simulated real-time
Network	Simulated CAN bus
Detection rate	0.97%
Detection latency	152 ms
Response time	1026 ms

Figure 7 shows the architecture of the proposed extended ACC, called from now on ACC-IDS, that uses a real-time IDS to detect attacks [16], in addition to the driver-specified target speed, the distance to the lead vehicle, and the vehicle speed (used to compute the safe distance).[3] Real-time IDS for cars monitors the CAN bus of the vehicle and detects message injections that spoof, for example, the speed sensor using, e.g., machine learning techniques.

Figure 6 shows the flowchart of the proposed ACC-IDS. It shows that the messages read from the CAN bus of the vehicle are processed by the IDS component and also used to check whether the vehicle maintains a safe distance from the lead vehicle. The ACC-IDS applies an emergency brake when either the distance to the object is less than the SSD or an intrusion is detected.

The ACC-IDS can be effective only if the IDS provides high accuracy in detecting messages injections[4] and low response time sufficient for the upper and lower controllers to adjust the vehicle's speed and avoid an accident. There is currently no real-time IDS for connected vehicles to use in evaluating the solution. To assess the solution, we use the performance measures of a real-time IDS that we have proposed and simulated [15,16] using data collected

---

[3] Let's assume that spoofing the road's slope and the friction coefficient between the tires and the road may not have an important impact on the safe stopping distance.

[4] Messages are injected as spoofing of a given ECU.

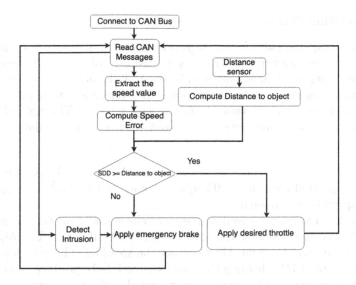

Fig. 6. Flowchart of the proposed extended ACC, called ACC-IDS. The IDS components are marked with the gray color.

from a moving vehicle under malicious speed reading message injections [14]. Table 2 provides the performance measurement of the real-time IDS deployed on a Raspberry Pi in a simulated environment [16]. Notably, the response time of the IDS is 1.026 s, which is lower than the driver's reaction time of 2.5 s.

4 Evaluation of the ACC-IDS Using CARLA Simulation

We evaluate the ACC-IDS solution using the simulation method and CARLA simulation environment tool.

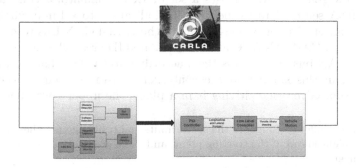

Fig. 7. Architecture for simulation setup

4.1 Simulation Setup

In the simulation, the position of the ego vehicle and lead vehicle is set in defined coordinates at the start point with a safe distance of 30 m. The ego vehicle detects the positions of neighboring vehicles and obstacles in real time.[5] The PID controllers compute both the steering and acceleration/braking commands in order to achieve a safe distance from the lead vehicle.[6] The ego vehicle uses obstacle detection and safe distance to avoid crashes. The simulated scenarios are:

1. Scenario 1 - Ego vehicle drives at target speed of 25 km/h and lead vehicle drives at speed of 0 km/h to 30 km/h and back to 0 km/h.[7] The ego vehicle sensor speed is not spoofed
2. Scenario 2 - The target speed of the ego vehicle and lead vehicle are set to 60 km/h. The ego vehicle sensor speed is spoofed to 10km/h. The ACC of the ego vehicle does not use an IDS to detect the spoofing. The attack interval is fixed at a rate of 75%, leading the controller to falsely produce more throttle force than sufficient. The scenario is repeated with the target speed of the ego vehicle and lead vehicle is set to 90 km/h.
3. Scenario 3 - The target speed of the ego vehicle and lead vehicle is set to 60 km/h. The ego vehicle sensor speed is spoofed to 10km/h. The ACC of the ego vehicle uses the real-time IDS to detect the spoofing. The parameters of the IDS are provided by Table 2. The scenario is repeated with the target speed of the ego vehicle and lead vehicle is set to 90 km/h.

We note that we also simulated the three scenarios with the target speed of the ego vehicle and lead vehicle is set to 40 km/h [33]. The results are omitted as it provides less insight as setting target speed of 60 km/h and 90 km/h.

We designed our simulation scenario using the CARLA simulator [13]. The proposed evaluation framework, including the structure of the simulation, is shown in Fig. 7. Data from the sensors are obtained by connecting to the CARLA server. We used Town04 and Town05 given by the CARLA simulator to model both vehicles' routes. CARLA uses a set of ECUs emulators. Our simulation sends CARLA sensor data as messages periodically into a Linux virtual CAN bus. It also injects "spoofed" messages into the virtual CAN Bus to mislead the moving vehicle. CARLA's ACC and the simulated IDS read the ECUs data from the virtual CAN bus and process them according to the flowchart of Fig. 6.

We used in this simulation the controller' constants used by the default CARLA setup. Given that driving is in a plane, the upper controller uses two

---

[5] The vehicle is allowed to ignore the speed limits and traffic lights. The stop destination is straight ahead of the starting point, and there are no dynamic objects in the environment.

[6] It is assumed that the lower-level controller applies controller output synchronously, which makes the vehicle accelerate or decelerate exactly with the desired acceleration.

[7] The speed of the lead vehicle is read from a CAN bus log dataset of a moving vehicle [14].

Table 3. Summary of the simulated scenarios. The ego vehicle uses PID-based ACC for all the scenarios.

Scenario	Target speed of ego vehicle	Target speed of lead	Attack type	Use of IDS	Crashes
1	25 km/h	extracted from the CAN Bus	no spoofing	No	No
2	60 and 90 km/h	60, and 90 km/h	spoofing of speed sensor	No	yes
3	60 and 90 km/h	60, and 90 km/h	spoofing of speed sensor	yes	No

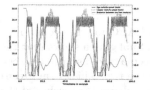 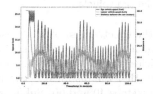 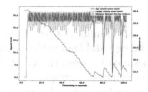

(a) The ego vehicle mimics a car driving at speed increasing from 0 km/h to 30 km/h and decreasing to 0km/h again. The ECUs of the vehicle are not spoofed.

(b) The ego vehicle uses the CAN bus log of moving vehicle while the RPM reading is being spoofed.

(c) The ego vehicle uses CAN log of moving vehicle while speed reading is being spoofed.

Fig. 8. Simulation results of the effectiveness of PID-based ACC for the scenario 1 - The ego vehicle drives at target speed of 25 km/h and the lead vehicle drives at varying speed values. The figure shows that the distance between the two vehicles (in green) oscillates to keep a safe distance between the vehicles and avoid crashes. The used CAN Bus log is available in [14] (Color figure online).

controllers: (1) a longitudinal controller and (2) a latitude controller. We used $K_p = 1.0$, $K_d = 0$, $K_i = 0.7$, and $dt = 0.05$ for the longitudinal controller and $K_p = 1.98$, $K_d = 0.20$, $K_i = 0.07$, and $dt = 0.05$. for the lateral controller. We implemented and deployed the simulation in accelerated computing AWS instances with 12 core processors, 200 GB of memory, and 8 GB of dedicated Nivida GPU running with a 64-bit Ubuntu 18.04.3 LTS.

4.2   Result and Analysis of the Simulation Experiments

This subsection reports about the results of the simulation scenarios (Table 3).

Results of Simulating Scenario 1. In this scenario, we simulate an ego vehicle driving at target speed of 25 km /h and a lead vehicle driving at speed of 0 km/h to 30 km/h and back to 0 km/h. We used a dataset [14] of a CAN Bus log of a moving car to mimic driving at speed of 0 km/h to 30 km/h and back to 0 km.

Figure 8 plots the speed of the ego vehicle, lead vehicle and the distance between the two vehicles as time progresses. The speed of the ego vehicle in

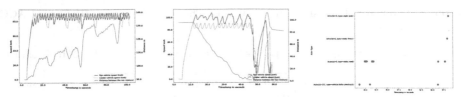

(a) Simulation of normal driving of the ego and lead vehicle.

(b) Simulation of normal driving of the lead vehicle and spoofing of the speed of the ego vehicle.

(c) Collision frequency of the ego vehicle for the case of spoofing of the speed values.

Fig. 9. Simulation results of the effectiveness of PID-based ACC for the scenario 2 - The ego and lead vehicles drive at target speed of 90 km/h. Subfigure a shows that the distance between the two vehicles (in green) oscillates to keep a safe distance between the vehicles. Subfigure b shows that the distance between the two vehicles (in green) gets to low values between time steps 40 and 60. Subfigure c shows the crashes of the two vehicles. (Color figure online)

subfigure 8a is read from the log of a vehicle driving at speed increasing from 0 km/h to 30 km/h and back to 0 km/h again. The speed of the ego vehicle in subfigure 8b is read from the log of a vehicle driving at speed increasing from 0 km/h to 13 km/h and back to 0 km/h again, while the RPM reading is being spoofed. The speed of the ego vehicle in subfigure 8c is read from the log of a vehicle driving at speed increasing from 0 km/h to 13 km/h and back to 0 km/h again, while the speed reading is being spoofed.

The figure shows that the distance between the two vehicles (in green) oscillates to keep a safe distance between the vehicles. The ego vehicle accelerates and decelerates according to a command issued by the PID controller Eq. 4. The distance between the two vehicles decreases multiple times but the ego vehicle applies emergency brakes or decreases the speed to avoid crashing into the lead vehicle. The spoofed RPM and speed datasets didn't cause the ego vehicle to crash into the lead vehicle. The figure shows that the PID-based ACC succeeds in this scenario to regulate the speed of the ego vehicle to avoid crashes.

Results of Simulating Scenario 2. In this scenario, we simulate an ego vehicle driving at target speed of 90 km/h and a lead vehicle driving at speed of 90 km/h. In addition, the speed sensor of the ego vehicle is spoofed to 10 km/h. Figure 9 plots the speed of the ego vehicle, lead vehicle and the distance between the two vehicles as time progresses. Subfigure a shows that the distance between the two vehicles (in green) oscillates to keep a safe distance between the vehicles. Subfigure b shows that the distance between the two vehicles (in green) gets to low values between time steps 40 and 60. Subfigure c shows the crashes of the two vehicles. The figure shows that PID-based ACC succeed to regulate the speed of the ego vehicle in normal driving condition but fails to do so when the speed

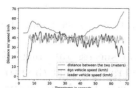 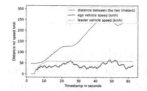 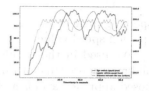

(a) The ego vehicle speed is 40 km/h.

(b) The ego vehicle speed is 60 km/h

(c) The ego vehicle speed is 90 km/h

Fig. 10. Resilience response of ego vehicle while using the ACC-IDS. The figure shows that ACC-IDS reacts to messages injections correctly and avoids the crashes.

sensor is spoofed. The experiments was repeated for speed target of 40 km/h and 60 km/m with the same observation.[8]

Results of Simulating Scenario 3. In this scenario, we simulate an ego vehicle driving at target speed of 90 km/h and a lead vehicle driving at speed of 90 km/h. In addition, the speed sensor of the ego vehicle is spoofed to 10 km/h and acts following a uniform distribution with probability of injection of spoofed message of 0.75. We changed the PID-based ACC controller to use a flag returned by the IDS. The ACC initiates cold brake when an attack is returned by the IDS and applies the default behavior otherwise.

Figure 10c shows the speed and distance of the ego vehicle and lead vehicle. The IDS was simulated with a success rate of 0.97% and a response time of 149 ms as a single process with no threads. furthermore, Fig. 10c shows the distance between the ego and the lead vehicle increases drastically as the ego vehicle continues to apply the emergency brake to avoid crashing with the lead vehicle.

4.3   Impacts and Limitations of the Study

These simulation results demonstrate that extending ACC with ML-based real-time IDS would allow for mitigating cyber-attacks. The simulation covers three cases: (1) vehicles drive at 40 km/h, and the spoofed speed is 5 km/h, (2) vehicles drive at 60 km/h, and the spoofed speed is 10 km/h, and (3) vehicles drive at 90 km/h, and the spoofed speed is 10 km/h. The three scenarios show that spoofing the speed of the Ego vehicle misleads the ACC to accelerate, which causes accidents and that the ACC-IDS responds to the attacks and avoids accidents.

The simulation of the three scenarios with the target speed of the ego vehicle and lead vehicle is set to 40 km/h shows that spoofing the speed of an ACC-equipped ego vehicle driving at a speed of 40 km/h causes accidents when the spoofed value is 5 km/h and does not cause accidents when the value is 10 km/h [33]. We observe also that spoofing the speed of an ACC-equipped ego vehicle with a value of 10 km/h does not cause accidents when the speed of the vehicle is 40 km/h but causes an accident when the speed of the vehicle is 60 km/h or 90 km/h. Thus, the ACC-equipped vehicle fails to mitigate speed

---

[8] Interested reader may consult reference [33].

spoofing attacks based on the combination of the Ego vehicle's speed and the spoofed speed value.

We used in the simulation study a spoofing detection success rate of 97% and a response time of 1.026 s for the IDS. These parameters show that the proposed approach avoids accidents for the three simulated scenarios. An extensive simulation that varies the speed of the vehicle, the values of the spoofed speed, the IDS's success rate to detect injection, and the IDS's response time should be performed to set the boundaries of success of ACC-IDS in mitigating message injection.

The current simulation is centered on specific speed values, simulating the detection rate of attacks through a random process. Additional simulations will be conducted to evaluate a wider range of speeds and acceleration/deceleration rates to determine the reliability of the proposed solution. Furthermore, further research is required to assess the method's reliability in real-time attack mitigation and ensuring safe driving with the extended ACC. This assessment can be accomplished using formal proof systems, such as the B-method [34].

5 Conclusion

Newer vehicles include ACCs that regulate the vehicle's speed for driver comfort and accident avoidance. Spoofing the vehicle speed communicated through the CAN bus of the vehicle can mislead the ACC to accelerate and crash the vehicle with the lead vehicle. The paper proposes extending the ACC with a real-time IDS capable of detecting speed spoofing attacks with reasonable response time, and detection rate. The CARLA simulation shows that the proposed extended ACC, called ACC-IDS, mitigates speed spoofing attacks as the ML-based IDS triggers the brakes when an accident is imminent. The findings suggest exploring the integration of real-time IDS into the resilience mechanisms to mitigate cyber-attacks on vehicles instead of using the estimation approach.

References

1. Winner, H., Witte, S., Uhler, W., Lichtenberg, B.: Adaptive cruise control system aspects and development trends. In: International Congress and Exposition, SAE International (1996)
2. Sardesai, S., Ulybyshev, D., ben Othmane, L., Bhargava, B.: Impacts of security attacks on the effectiveness of collaborative adaptive cruise control mechanism. In: 2018 IEEE International Smart Cities Conference (ISC2), pp. 1–5 (2018)
3. Cao, Y., et al.: Adversarial sensor attack on lidar-based perception in autonomous driving. In: Proceedings of the 2019 ACM SIGSAC Conference on Computer and Communications Security, CCS '19, (New York, NY, USA), pp. 2267–2281, Association for Computing Machinery (2019)
4. Harris, M.: Researcher hacks self-driving car sensors (2015)
5. Farivar, F., Sayad Haghighi, M., Jolfaei, A., Wen, S.: On the security of networked control systems in smart vehicle and its adaptive cruise control. IEEE Trans. Intell. Transp. Syst. **22**(6), 3824–3831 (2021)

6. Tianxiang, Q., Defeng, H., Liangye, L., Xiulan, S.: Adaptive cruise control of vehicles subject to denial-of-service. In: 2017 32nd Youth Academic Annual Conference of Chinese Association of Automation (YAC), pp. 382–386 (2017)
7. Wang, Y., Gunter, G., Work, D.B.: Online parameter estimation of adaptive cruise control models with delays and lags. In: 2020 IEEE 23rd International Conference on Intelligent Transportation Systems (ITSC), pp. 1–6 (2020)
8. Wang, Y., Gunter, G., Nice, M., Monache, M.L.D., Work, D.B.: Online parameter estimation methods for adaptive cruise control systems. IEEE Trans. Intell. Veh. **6**(2), 288–298 (2021)
9. Dutta, R.G., et al.: Estimation of safe sensor measurements of autonomous system under attack. In: Proceedings of the 54th Annual Design Automation Conference 2017, DAC '17, (New York, NY, USA), Association for Computing Machinery (2017)
10. Bersani, M., Vignati, M., Mentasti, S., Arrigoni, S., Cheli, F.: Vehicle state estimation based on kalman filters. In: 2019 AEIT International Conference of Electrical and Electronic Technologies for Automotive (AEIT AUTOMOTIVE), pp. 1–6 (2019)
11. Liu, Q., Mo, Y., Mo, X., Lv, C., Mihankhah, E., Wang, D.: Secure pose estimation for autonomous vehicles under cyber attacks. In: 2019 IEEE Intelligent Vehicles Symposium (IV), pp. 1583–1588 (2019)
12. Hoque, M.A., Hasan, R.: Exposing adaptive cruise control in advanced driving assistance systems. In: 2022 IEEE 8th World Forum on Internet of Things (WF-IoT), pp. 1–6 (2022)
13. Dosovitskiy, A., Ros, G., Codevilla, F., Lopez, A., Koltun, V.: CARLA: an open urban driving simulator. In: Proceedings of the 1st Annual Conference on Robot Learning, pp. 1–16 (2017)
14. Ben Othmane, L., Dhulipala, L., Abdelkhalek, M., Multari, N., Govindarasu, M.: On the performance of detecting injection of fabricated messages into the can bus. IEEE Trans. Dependable Secure Comput. **19**, 468–481 (2022)
15. Jedh, M., Ben Othmane, L., Ahmed, N., Bhargava, B.: Detection of message injection attacks onto the can bus using similarities of successive messages-sequence graphs. IEEE Trans. Inf. Forensics Secur. **16**, 4133–4146 (2021)
16. Jedh, M.B., Lee, J.K., Othmane, L.B.: Evaluation of the architecture alternatives for real-time intrusion detection systems for connected vehicles. In: Proceedings of the IEEE International Conference on Software Quality, Reliability, and Security, (Guangzhou, China) (2022)
17. Rajamani, R.: Vehicle dynamics and control. Springer Science & Business Media (2011). https://doi.org/10.1007/978-1-4614-1433-9
18. Rad, S.A., Tamizi, M.G., Azmoun, M., Masouleh, M.T., Kalhor, A.: Experimental study on robust adaptive control with insufficient excitation of a 3-DOF spherical parallel robot for stabilization purposes. Mech. Mach. Theory **153**, 104026 (2020)
19. Jagielski, M., Jones, N., Lin, C.-W., Nita-Rotaru, C., Shiraishi, S.: Threat detection for collaborative adaptive cruise control in connected cars. In: Proceedings of the 11th ACM Conference on Security & Privacy in Wireless and Mobile Networks, pp. 184–189 (2018)
20. Sun, J., Cao, Y., Chen, Q.A., Mao, Z.M.: Towards robust lidar-based perception in autonomous driving: General black-box adversarial sensor attack and countermeasures (2020)
21. Petit, J., Stottelaar, B., Feiri, M., Kargl, F.: Remote attacks on automated vehicles sensors: experiments on camera and lidar. Black Hat Europe **11**(2015), 995 (2015)

22. Shoukry, Y., Martin, P.D., Yona, Y., Diggavi, S.N., Srivastava, M.B.: PyCRA: physical challenge-response authentication for active sensors under spoofing attacks. In: Proceedings of the 22nd ACM SIGSAC Conference on Computer and Communications Security (2015)

23. Othmane, L.B., Weffers, H., Mohamad, M.M., Wolf, M.: A survey of security and privacy in connected vehicles. In: Benhaddou, D., Al-Fuqaha, A. (eds.) Wireless Sensor and Mobile Ad-Hoc Networks, pp. 217–247. Springer, New York (2015). https://doi.org/10.1007/978-1-4939-2468-4_10

24. van der Heijden, R., Lukaseder, T., Kargl, F.: Analyzing attacks on cooperative adaptive cruise control (CACC). In: 2017 IEEE Vehicular Networking Conference (VNC), pp. 45–52 (2017)

25. Oh, K., Park, S., Lee, J., Yi, K.: Functional perspective-based probabilistic fault detection and diagnostic algorithm for autonomous vehicle using longitudinal kinematic model. Microsyst. Technol. **24**(11), 4527–4537 (2018)

26. Abdollahi Biron, Z., Dey, S., Pisu, P.: Real-time detection and estimation of denial of service attack in connected vehicle systems. IEEE Trans. Intell. Transp. Syst. **19**(12), 3893–3902 (2018)

27. A. A. of State Highway and T. Officials., Policy on geometric design of highways and streets with 2013) (2011)

28. Jiang, Y., Cai, L., Jin, X.: Optimization of adaptive cruise control system controller: using linear quadratic gaussian based on genetic algorithm (2019)

29. Ganji, B., Kouzani, A.Z., Khoo, S.Y., Nasir, M.: A sliding-mode-control-based adaptive cruise controller. In: 11th IEEE International Conference on Control and Automation (ICCA), pp. 394–397 (2014)

30. Ko, S.-J., Lee, J.-J.: Fuzzy logic based adaptive cruise control with guaranteed string stability. In: 2007 International Conference on Control, Automation and Systems, pp. 15–20 (2007)

31. Young, C., Zambreno, J., Olufowobi, H., Bloom, G.: Survey of automotive controller area network intrusion detection systems. IEEE Design Test **36**(6), 48–55 (2019)

32. Wu, W., et al.: A survey of intrusion detection for in-vehicle networks. IEEE Trans. Intell. Transp. Syst. **21**(3), 919–933 (2020)

33. Jedh, M.: Attacks detection and cyber resilience: securing in-vehicle controller area network. PhD thesis, Iowa State University (2023)

34. Gruteser, J., Geleßus, D., Leuschel, M., Roßbach, J., Vu, F.: A formal model of train control with AI-based obstacle detection. In: Milius, B., Collart-Dutilleul, S., Lecomte, T. (eds.) Reliability, Safety, and Security of Railway Systems. Modelling, Analysis, Verification, and Certification. RSSRail 2023. LNCS, vol. 14198. Springer, Cham (2023). https://doi.org/10.1007/978-3-031-43366-5_8

A New Efficient PUF-Based Mutual Authentication Scheme for Drones

Edoukou Berenger Ayebie[(✉)] (iD), Karam Bou-chaaya, and Helmi Rais

Expleo France, 3 avenue des près, 78180 Montigny-le-Bretonneux, France
{edoukou-berenger.ayebie,karam.bou-chaaya,helmi.rais}@expleogroup.com

Abstract. This paper proposes a new lightweight mutual authentication scheme for drones that is based on a Physical Unclonable Function (PUF) which uses type-III pairing friendly elliptic curves, and cryptographic accumulators. The use of a PUF in this scheme helps to avoid the risk of drone cloning. Additionally, the use of elliptic curves allows for a lightweight mutual authentication scheme that satisfies many security requirements, such as secrecy and forward secrecy. Furthermore, this paper allows direct mutual authentication between drones. The cryptographic accumulator accumulates the entire drone identity database into a single element, which reduces the amount of data that needs to be stored on a drone. Moreover, the proposed scheme is, in the worst case, equivalent to the most recent PUF-based mutual authentication schemes for drones in terms of communication data. Moreover, this paper give an implementation of the proposed scheme.

Keywords: Mutual Authentication · Physically Unclonable Function (PUF) · Elliptic Curve Cryptography · Cryptographic Accumulator · Drone

1 Introduction

With the increasing use of drones for domestic purposes [16, 23, 24], standards for drone safety have emerged like ISO 21384 which provides general requirements for the operation and use of unmanned aircraft systems or ANSI/UL 3030, which provides safety requirements for unmanned aerial systems, including performance, reliability, and quality. For instance, in the case of a swarm of drones collaborating to accomplish a task in an urban environment (e.g. search and rescue mission, mapping), the introduction of a malicious drone could compromise collaboration or even harm physical objects and people on the ground by sending erroneous data to the Ground Controller (GS) and other drones. To remedy this, one of the most effective actions is to implement a mutual authentication protocol for drone-to-drone and drone to control center communication channels. However, drones are devices with limited resources [15], making it not feasible for the standard drone to store a large database for self-authentication of other drones. To address this limitation, papers proposed to use the control center as a relay for mutual authentication between two drones. This approach requires proximity to the control center [3, 12]. The second most commonly used approach is to divide the drone swarm into several groups and define a master drone with many resources that can serve as a relay between the standard drones [25]. Nerveless, in the event of a master drone failure, collaboration between drones will be compromised. Even with an authentication protocol, if a malicious entity clones a drone, it can self-authenticate with the malicious drone and compromise collaboration. Despite using a mutual authentication scheme, if an adversary manages to clone a drone belonging to the system, the adversary can still infect other drones and compromise the collaboration. Hence, Physical Unclonable Functions (PUF) can be used.

A PUF is a device used in hardware security to generate a unique response for a given challenge. The principal property of this device is that two devices with the same production process will generate different responses for a same challenge. This paper uses PUF to ensure the physical security of the proposed protocol. Another big issue that drives current approach to use the control center as a relay for mutual authentication between two drones. Also, they divide the drone swarm into several groups and define a master drone with many resources that can serve as a relay between the standard drones. This limitation prevents the implementation of databases within drones. Consequently, this paper proposes, for the first time as far we know, to use cryptographic accumulators. The cryptographic accumulator notion was first introduced by Benaloh and De Mare [10] in 1993. It is defined as a cryptographic primitive that allows for the accumulation of a finite set of elements into a single value called the Accumulated Value (a public value). Thus, for each element, it is possible to generate a short membership proof called a Witness, which attests to the element's belonging to the set. For a cryptographic accumulator to be secure, it should not be possible to find a valid witness for an element not belonging to the set.

To overcome all the limitation, this paper proposes a new lightweight mutual authentication scheme between a drone and the control center as well as between two drones. By using cryptographic accumulators and PUF, the proposed scheme does not require intermediaries for mutual authentication between two drones, and is resistant to many attacks like desynchronizing attack and replay attak. This technique minimizes the storage efficiency and make it constant regardless the number of drones. Additionally, this paper provides two security analyses: A formal security analysis based on the Real-Or-Random model [1] and an informal Security Analysis that discusses security properties. Finally, we implement the proposed mutual authentication scheme.

The reminder of this paper is organized as follow: Sect. 2 reviews related works. Section 3 recalls mandatory preliminaries and definitions for the well understanding of the paper. Section 4 details scheme proposed scheme. Section 5 makes a focus on the security analysis. Section 6 highlight the implementation and some practical results. Finally, Sect. 7 conclude the paper and discuss future research directions.

2   Related Work

In 2020, A lightweight mutual authentication scheme for drones called PARTH was proposed by T. Alladi et al. [2]. The PARTH protocol was developed to establish two unique session keys, protect identities, and achieve mutual authentication in surveillance areas. The protocol considered three layers of distinct network entities: the GS, mini drones with limited resources, and powerful intermediate leader drones acting as relay network nodes. The authentication process between the GS and the leader drone took place in the first stage, while the second stage was related to the authentication between the leader drone and a mini drone. The performance of the PARTH protocol was evaluated in terms of computing cost, latency, and resistance to known threats, and was found to be capable of countering drone tampering, replay, man-in-the-middle, and impersonation attacks, despite the absence of keys stored onboard the drones.

Later, P. Gope and B. Sikdar proposed a simple key agreement scheme to preserve privacy and handle authentication in MEC-enabled IoD while avoiding use of volatile memory [13]. her scheme is resistant to invasive and non-invasive attacks, while using minimal resources with PUFs and hash functions. In their paper, P. Gope and B. Sikdar are tested their scheme on a vulnerable IoD and the results show superior performance in terms of total authentication time for varying number of UAVs. Moreover In [3], an authentication protocol called SecAuthUAV was developed by Alladi et all using PUFs to improve mutual authentication in UAV-to-GS and inter-UAV connections while minimizing communication, computation, and storage requirements. But this mutual authentication process inter-UAV need the GS as intermediary device.

Always in the same year, C. Pu and Y. Li proposed an energy-efficient and computation-efficient mutual authentication protocol for secure UAV-to-GS communication links named PCAP [21]. It used a PUF unit and a chaotic system for non-linear behavior to generate a unique secret session key. Later in 2021, P. Gope et al. proposed a combination of radio frequency identity (RFID) technology and PUFs for efficient recognition and tracking of UAVs [12]. Specifically, for military use, to authenticate UAVs for secure operation in a certain airspace. An interrogator scans the tags to verify credentials while UAVs use a weak SRAM PUF for device-intrinsic fingerprint generation. Their proposed combine low computational complexity and security based on Ouafi and Phan's security model [20].

In addition, P. Mall et al. proposed CoMSeC++ [17], a lightweight and PUF-based authentication protocol with hash functions. This protocol enabled secure wireless connectivity between the sensors and the cloud via the UAV and included five separate phases.

Moreover, an identity security authentication protocol, called Optimized Identity Authentication Protocol (ODIAP), for the Internet of Drones (IoD) was presented by Y. Lei et al. in [14]. It aims to prevent impersonation and replay attacks in an energy-efficient way. The protocol includes three phases and considers four network entities. ODIAP uses the Chinese residual theorem to optimize computing resources at UAV nodes and assigns complex computation tasks to server nodes. It was verified using ProVerif-based tools and shown to ensure adequate security.

In the same year, an authentication protocol that uses PUFs was developed by G. Bansal and B. Sikdar in [6] to address physical security challenges in monitoring, surveillance, and disaster management applications with UAV swarms and multiple stationary and trusted base stations (BSs). It uses a spanning tree algorithm to simultaneously authenticate multiple UAVs with unique PUFs while protecting against DoS, replay attacks, man-in-the-middle attacks, impersonation attacks, and node-tampering attacks. The protocol can handle dynamic multi-hop propagation scenarios with varying mobility and topology.

Thereafter, in [4], a mutual authentication protocol called Drone-MAP was proposed by T. Alladi et al. for 5G UAV-aided backhaul networks to protect against common security attacks. It aims to establish secure sessions and meet confidentiality and untraceability requirements for communication between a single BS and multiple UAVs. The protocol uses PUFs to generate unique secret keys, eliminating the need for storing sensitive data. Security analysis and performance results were provided using a Raspberry Pi 3B to demonstrate the benefits of Drone-MAP in terms of computation time.

Later in [5], G. Bansal and B. Sikdar proposed an authentication protocol for UAV-BS communications that uses the K-Means clustering algorithm and the efficiency of PUF chips. Their paper considers a dynamic UAV position, then it allows the formation of several groups corresponding to different distances between UAVs and base stations using the clustering algorithm. The security or their proposed is ensued by the integration of an PUF-based digital fingerprinting on each UAV to perform the identification procedure via CRP check.

Recently in 2022, L. Zhang et al. proposed in [25] an efficient two-stage authentication and key agreement protocol for UAV-enabled networks. Each network layer was associated with a specific entity, such as member drones, head drones, or the trusted GS. The protocol used PUF chips embedded in UAVs to protect privacy and produce two session keys in one session, using only hash and XOR operations to reduce computation and energy consumption. The key agreement provided confidentiality and integrity between member drones and head drones, as well as between head drones and GS. The protocol was simulated using various tools to test its security against different types of attacks, and the results showed its feasibility and efficacy in terms of function properties, computing and communication cost.

All of the scheme proposed above [2,4–6,12,14,17,21,25] need to use the control center as a relay or to divide the drone swarm into several groups and define a master drone with many resources that can serve as a relay between the standard drones for mutual authentication drone-to-drone. That require the proximity of the control center. In addition to proposing a lightweight mutual authentication scheme, the proposed uses cryptographic accumulators to reduce the size of stored data. This improvement will thus enable mutual drone-to-drone authentication without the need to go through the control center or through an intermediary drone with a large memory. Table 1, which compares the characteristics of the proposed scheme with other existing schemes. This table indicates that all the schemes are equivalent in terms of security, as they ensure the following security properties. First, resilience to Resynchronization Attacks, which refers to the ability of the schemes to withstand attempts to force synchronization between the communication parties. Second, replay attack resistance ensures that the schemes can detect and prevent replay attacks, where an attacker intercepts and maliciously retransmits previously valid messages to gain unauthorized access or deceive the system. Additionally, anonymity ensures that the identities of the communicating parties remain hidden or protected, while untraceability refers to the inability to trace the flow of communication or activities back to the original source. Withal, physical attack resistance ensures that even if an adversary gains physical access to the device, they are unable to obtain any confidential information. Moreover, mutual authentication ensures that both parties involved in the communication can verify each other's identities, and secrecy guarantees that unauthorized parties cannot access or decipher the content of the messages or transactions. Furthermore, forward secrecy guarantees that even if the long-term secret keys used in the scheme are compromised in the future, past communications remain secure. However, the proposed scheme stands out from the rest as it enables direct drone-to-drone authentication without any intermediary involved.

Table 1. Comparison of security requirements

	[25]	[6]	[17]	[14]	this scheme
Physical Attacks	Y	Y	Y	Y	Y
Untraceability	N	N	N	Y	Y
Mutual authentication	Y	Y	Y	Y	Y
Desynchronizing attack	Y	Y	Y	Y	Y
Replay attack	Y	Y	Y	Y	Y
Forward secrecy	Y	Y	Y	Y	Y
Direct Drone-Drone	N	N	N	N	Y

3 Preliminaries

In this section, we define the key terms used in this our study. Now we recall from [22] the cryptographic accumulator used in our proposal. Due to recent progress in discrete logarithm computations, which weakens the security of efficient implementable elliptic curves provided with a Type-I pairing, Giuseppe Vitto and Alex Biryukov use a Type-III pairing.

Physical Unclonable Function. PUFs are hardware-based security primitives that exploit the inherent variations in physical structures and manufacturing processes to generate unique, non-reproducible responses. These responses serve as digital fingerprints, enabling the authentication of a physical device without relying on stored secrets or pre-shared keys. PUFs exhibit desirable properties such as uniqueness, randomness, and robustness against various attacks, including invasive and non-invasive techniques. Different types of PUFs have been proposed and studied in the literature, including silicon PUFs (SPUFs), ring oscillator PUFs (RO-PUFs), and arbiter PUFs (APUFs). Each type leverages specific physical phenomena, such as delay variations or circuit mismatch, to generate unique responses. The choice of PUF type depends on factors such as the target application, desired security level, and available resources. Because they are suitable for cryptographic and key establishment protocols [19], This paper uses RO-PUFs. Figure 1 depicts a RO-PUF circuit consisting of multiple identical delay loops called ring oscillators. Each ring oscillator oscillates at a slightly different frequency due to manufacturing variation. By selecting specific pairs of oscillators and comparing their frequencies, output bits are generated. These output bits vary between chips and are equally likely to be one or zero when random variations dominate. Duplicating ring oscillators ensures their identical layout, eliminating the need for careful layout and routing. The circuit can generate $\frac{N(N-1)}{2}$ bits from pairwise comparisons, but the entropy is lower due to correlation between these bits. The maximum entropy can be derived based on the number of oscillators N, assuming pairwise comparisons and equally likely orderings.

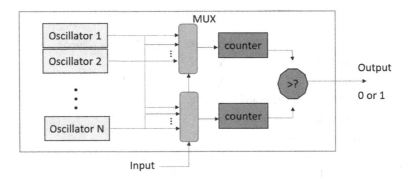

Fig. 1. Ring oscillator based PUF circuit

Bilinear Group Generation. Given a security parameter 1^λ, generate over a prime order finite field $\mathbb{F}_q$ an elliptic curve $E(\mathbb{F}_q)$ with embedding degree k which has an efficiently computable non-degenerate bilinear map $e : G_1 \times G_2 \to G_T$ such that

- G_1 is a subgroup of $E(\mathbb{F}_q)$.
- Letting d be the cardinality of the automorphisms group of $E(\mathbb{F}_q)$, G_2 is a subgroup of $\tilde{E}(\mathbb{F}_{q^{k/d}})$ which is the unique degree-d twist of E over $\mathbb{F}_{q^{k/d}}$.
- G_T is a subgroup of $\left(\mathbb{F}_{q^k}\right)^\star$.
- $|G_1| = |G_2| = |G_T| = p$ is prime.
- $P, \tilde{P}, e(P, \tilde{P})$ are generators of G_1, G_2, G_T, respectively.

– There are no efficiently computable isomorphisms between $G1$ and $G2$.

Then denote as $\mathbb{G} = \left(p, G_1, G_2, G_T, P, \tilde{P}, e\right)$ the resulting bilinear group.

Accumulator Parameters. Uniformly sample an $\alpha \in \mathbb{Z}_p$ and consider $\mathcal{ACC} = \mathbb{Z}_p \backslash \{\alpha\}$ as the domain of accumulatable elements. The bilinear group $\mathbb{G}$, and the point $\tilde{Q} = \alpha\tilde{P}$ are the accumulator public parameters and are available to all accumulator users, while α is the accumulator secret parameter and is known only to the Accumulator Manager.

Accumulator Initialization. Select a set $\mathcal{Y}_V \subset \mathcal{ACC}$ and let the accumulated value be $V = \left(\prod_{y \in \mathcal{Y}_V}(y + \alpha)\right)P$. the set $\mathcal{Y}_V$ is keep secret.

Membership Witness. Let V be the accumulated value and y an element in $\mathcal{ACC}$. Then w_y is a membership witness for y with respect to the accumulator value if $C = \frac{1}{y+\alpha}V$ and $w_y = C$. The Accumulator Manager issues the membership witness w_y to a user associated to the element y, in order to permit him to prove that y is accumulated into V.

Witness Verification. A membership witness $w_y = C$ for an element $y \in \mathcal{ACC}$ is valid if and only if $e\left(C, y\tilde{P} + \tilde{Q}\right) = e\left(V, \tilde{P}\right)$.

Now we recall some elliptic curves difficult problems.

Problem 1 (Elliptic curve discrete logarithm problem [18]*).* Let P be a point of an elliptic curve $E(\mathbb{F}_q)$ over a finite $\mathbb{F}_q$ of prime field q. Let a be an element of $\mathbb{F}_q$. Given the points P and aP, the elliptic curve discrete logarithm problem is use to find a.

Problem 2 (Decision elliptic curve Diffie-Hellman problem [11]*).* Let P be a point of an elliptic curve $E(\mathbb{F}_q)$ over a finite $\mathbb{F}_q$ of prime field q. Let a, b and c be elements of $\mathbb{F}_q$. Given the points aP, bP and cP, elliptic curve Diffie-Hellman problem is use to decide if c is a random element of $\mathbb{F}_q$ or if c is equal to ab.

Note that, Problem 1 was proved to be hard by Menezes *et al.* in [18]. And Problem 2 was proved to be difficult by Dan Boneh in [11].

4   The Proposed Scheme

This section describes the proposed authentication protocol.

4.1   System Model

Network Model. The system presented in this paper (Fig. 2) consists of two main entities: the drones and the control center. In this system, although limited in resources, the drones can authenticate and communicate directly with each other and with the control center. Thus, during a mission far from the control center, the drones can authenticate each other and establish session keys, enabling them to communicate securely. After the initial phase described in this paper, called the initialization phase, there is no distinction between the entities, and they are referred to as devices. Each device is composed of the following components:

- A True Random Number Generator (TRNG)
- A Hash Function h
- A Physically Unclonable Function (PUF)

Adversary Model. In our system model, the devices primarily use public network-based communication. Consequently, there is a possibility of various attacks by a wide range of adversaries. In this paper, we consider the security and privacy threats presented in Table 1.

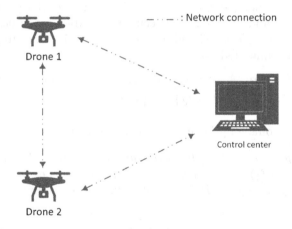

Fig. 2. Network Model

4.2   Description of the Proposed Scheme

This protocol regroups three main cryptographic objects which are elliptic curves, cryptographic accumulators, and PUFs with well-defined roles. Here the combination of elliptic curves and cryptographic accumulators is the key to obtain a protocol that requires less storage space while demanding less computational power. It is also worth noting that the use of PUFs allows to avoid cloning the device used and also allows us to store elements in the form of challenge-response. At the end of the authentication process between two devices, a session key is generated.

Let $\mathbb{G} = \left(p, G_1, G_2, G_T, P, \tilde{P}, e \right)$ be a bilinear group and let $\alpha \in \mathbb{Z}_p^*$, $\mathcal{ACC} = \mathbb{Z}_p^* \backslash \{\alpha\}$, and the point $\tilde{Q} = \alpha \tilde{P}$ be the parameters of an cryptographic accumulator as described in Sect. 2.

Initialization. During the initialization phase, all connections between the control center and the device is secure and safe. The control center sets Y_V to empty.

In this step, for each device d_i, $i \in U \subset \mathbb{N}$, the control center takes the following actions:

1. The control center randomly chooses a unique element id_i in $\mathcal{ACC}$ and computes $m_i = PUF_i(id_i) \mod p$, where PUF_i is the PUF operation for device d_i. If $m_i \notin Y_V$, the control center store m_i in Y_V else the control center chooses another id_i.
2. The control center randomly chooses $\beta_i' \in \mathcal{ACC}$, computes $\beta_i = \alpha - PUF_i(\beta_i') \mod p$ and generates the accumulated value V of the set $Y_V = \{m_i\}_{i \in U}$.
3. The control center stores in each device d_i the tuple: $id_i, \beta_i, \beta_i', V, p, P, \tilde{P}, \tilde{Q}, e$.

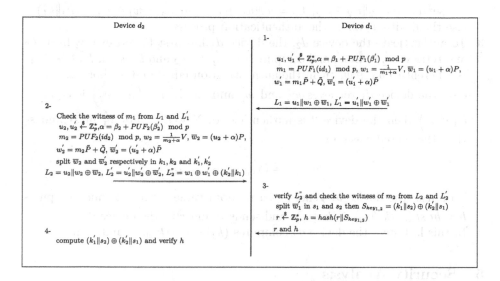

Fig. 3. The proposed scheme

Authentication. In the following, the authentication process illustrated in Fig. 3 is performed between two devices d_1 and d_2. This process is executed in four steps and generate a shared key at the end.

1. The device d_1 generates random values u_1 and u_1' from $\mathbb{Z}_p^\star$ and computes:
   - $\alpha = \beta_1 + PUF_1(\beta_1') \mod p$, $m_1 = PUF_1(id_1) \mod p$
   - $w_1 = \frac{1}{m_1+\alpha}V$ which is equivalent to compute the witness of m_1 using the cryptographic accumulator, $\overline{w}_1 = (u_1 + \alpha)P$
   - $w_1' = m_1\tilde{P} + \tilde{Q}$, $\overline{w}_1' = (u_1' + \alpha)\tilde{P}$.
   and send $L_1 = u_1 \| w_1 \oplus \overline{w}_1$, $L_1' = u_1' \| w_1' \oplus \overline{w}_1'$ to the device d_2. Were $\|$ denote the concatenation.
2. To authenticate the device d_1, the device d_2 has to do the following steps:
   - computes $\alpha = \beta_2 + PUF_2(\beta_2') \mod p$, retrieves u_1 from L_1 and retrieves u_1' from L_1'

– computes $\overline{w}_1$ and retrieves w_1
– computes $\overline{w}_1'$ and retrieves w_1'

Now the device d_2 checks if $e\left(w_1, w_1'\right)$ is equal to $e\left(V, \tilde{P}\right)$, which is equivalent to verify the witness of m_1 using the cryptographic accumulator. Then the device d_1 is partially authenticated and the device d_2 does the following steps:

– generates a random values u_2 and u_2' from $\mathbb{Z}_p^*$
– computes $w_2 = \frac{1}{m_2+\alpha}V$, $\overline{w}_2 = (u_2 + \alpha)P$, $w_2' = m_2\tilde{P} + \tilde{Q}$ and $\overline{w}_2' = (u_2' + \alpha)\tilde{P}$
– split $\overline{w}_2$ and $\overline{w}_2'$ respectively in k_1, k_2 and k_1', k_2' such that $\overline{w}_2 = k_1\|k_2$ and $\overline{w}_2' = k_1'\|k_2'$
– send $L_2 = u_2\|w_2 \oplus \overline{w}_2$, $L_2' = u_2'\|w_2' \oplus \overline{w}_2'$ and $L_2'' = w_1 \oplus w_1' \oplus (k_2'\|k_1)$

else the device d_2 abort the authentication process.

3. To authenticate the device d_2, the device d_1 has first to retrieve u_2 from L_2 and retrieve u_2' from L_2' and compute $\overline{w}_2, \overline{w}_2', k_1, k_2$ and k_1', k_2'. if $L_2'' \oplus (k_2'\|k_1)$ is different to $w_1 \oplus w_1'$ then, the authentication failed and is aborted.

else, the device d_1 retrieves w_2 and w_2' and checks if $e\left(w_2, w_2'\right)$ is equal to $e\left(V, \tilde{P}\right)$ then the device 2 is authenticated. Now d_1 splits $\overline{w}_1'$ in s_1 and s_2 then the shared session key is

$$S_{key_{1,2}} = (k_1'\|s_2) \oplus (k_2'\|s_1)$$

To finish, the device d_1 generates a random value r from $\mathbb{Z}_p^*$ and computes $h = hash(r\|(k_1'\|s_2) \oplus (k_2'\|s_1))$ and sends h and r to the device d_2

4. In this last step, the device d_2 computes $(k_1'\|s_2) \oplus (k_2'\|s_1)$ and verifies h.

5   Security Analysis

In this section, we study the security of the proposed scheme. This paper provides two security analysis: A formal security analysis based on the Real-Or-Random model [1] and an informal Security Analysis which consist in a discussion on the paper's security properties. let n be the number of bit needed to encoded an element of $\mathbb{Z}_p$ i.e. $n = \log_2(p)$ and let k be the number of bit needed to encoded an element of $\mathbb{G}_1$.

5.1   Privacy Model

In [1] Abdalla *et al.* proposed the Real-Or-Random model is commonly used to measure the indistinguishability of session keys. This model adversary can run the following queries:

Execute(d_1,d_2,i) This query allows the adversary $\mathcal{A}$ to get access to a honest execution of the protocol between the devices d_1 and d_2 at the ith session.

Send(d, M) This query allows the adversary $\mathcal{A}$ to send a message M of its choice to an instance of the device d and then receive response from d. d_1 and d_2 at the ith session.

Reveal(d) In this query the adversary $\mathcal{A}$ obtains the session key S_{key} established between the device d and its partner using this query.

Corrupt(d) This query allows $\mathcal{A}$ to learn the stored secrets of the device d.

Test(d) In this query, the adversary $\mathcal{A}$ requests d for session key S_{key} and receives a probabilistic output based on an hidden bit c: (i) if S_{key} is fresh and $c = 1$, d returns S_{key}, (ii) if S_{key} is fresh and $c = 0$, d delivers a random number, and (iii) otherwise d delivers null.

5.2 Formal Security Analysis

We first define the collision resistant cryptographic one-way hash function and Uncloneability of a PUF function as follows.

Definition 1 (Uncloneability of a PUF function). *Let f representing the PUF function as $f : \mathbb{F}_2^{\ell_1} \to \mathbb{F}_2^{\ell_2}$, where for a given input of length ℓ_1 the PUF outputs an arbitary string of length ℓ_2. Let $\mathcal{A}$ be an adversary against the Uncloneability of the PUF, $\mathcal{A}$ interact with the PUF using the following phases.*

Phase 1 *For a given challenges C', the adversary $\mathcal{A}$ obtains the PUF outputs C'. Next, $\mathcal{A}$ pick another challenge C that has not been queried before.*

Phase 2 *Here, the adversary $\mathcal{A}$ can query the PUF for any challenge expected the challenge C. Finally, the adversary $\mathcal{A}$ outputs its guess R" for the response R to C.*

We say that the adversary $\mathcal{A}$ has successfully break the Uncloneability if R" $= R$. Therefore, the advantage $Adv_{\mathcal{A}}^{PUF}$ of $\mathcal{A}$ in breaking the Uncloneability of the PUF is:

$$Adv_{\mathcal{A}}^{PUF} = Pr[R" = R]$$

where the probability of an event X is $Pr[X]$,

Definition 2 (collision resistant cryptographic one-way hash function). *A collision resistant cryptographic one-way hash function is a functions $h : Y \to Z$ where Y and Z are sets of values, with the following properties:*

1. *The function $h(\cdot)$ is computable in polynomial time.*
2. *The probability to have a colision on $h(\cdot)$ is less than ϵ, where ϵ is an arbitrary small number.*

Now, we study the sementic security of the proposed scheme in Theorem 1.

Theorem 1. *Let $\mathcal{A}$ be a polynomial time adversary running in time t against the protocol. Then, the advantage of $\mathcal{A}$ in breaking the semantic security of the proposed scheme can be represented as follows:*

$$Adv_{\mathcal{A}}^{SEM} \leq 2Adv_{\mathcal{A}}^{ECDL} + \frac{2^{n_h}!}{(2^{n_h} - q_h)!} \times \frac{1}{2^{n_h \cdot q_h - 1}} + \frac{2^{n_f}!}{(2^{n_f} - q_f)!} \times \frac{1}{2^{n_f \cdot q_f - 1}}.$$

where $Adv_{\mathcal{A}}^{ECDL}$, q_h, n_h, q_f and n_f denote respectively the advantage of $\mathcal{A}$ against the ECDL problem (Problem 1), the number of hash, the length of the hash function output, the number of PUF queries and the length of the PUF function output.

Proof. This proof uses a succession of experiments $\mathcal{E}_i$ for an integer $i \in [0, 4]$ where the goal of the adversary $\mathcal{A}$ is to guess the value of the bit c in the *Test* query presented in Part 5.1. Let $Succ_{\mathcal{A}}^{\mathcal{E}_i}$ and $Pr[Succ_{\mathcal{A}}^{\mathcal{E}_i}]$ be respectively, the event that $\mathcal{A}$ guesses the good value of the bit c in Experiment $\mathcal{E}_i$ and the probability that the event $Succ_{\mathcal{A}}^{\mathcal{E}_i}$ may occurs.

Experiment $\mathcal{E}_0$. This is the original experiment described by the *Test* query where the adversary $\mathcal{A}$ attack the semantic security of the proposed scheme. Since the bit c was randomly chosen, the advantage $Adv_{\mathcal{A}}^{SEM}$ in this experiment is null. Then, we can write:

$$Adv_{\mathcal{A}}^{SEM} = \left| 2Pr[Succ_{\mathcal{A}}^{\mathcal{E}_0}] - 1 \right| \tag{1}$$

where, for a number x, $|x|$ is the absolute value of x.

Experiment $\mathcal{E}_1$. In this experiment, the adversary $\mathcal{A}$ acts like an eavesdropper that intercept the communication. Then, the adversary $\mathcal{A}$ gets $T_\eta = \{L_*^{(\eta)}, L_*^{'(\eta)}, L_i^{(\eta)}, L_i^{'(\eta)}, L_i^{''(\eta)}, r^{(\eta)}, h^{(\eta)}\}$ that represent the ηth communication transcript between d_* and d_i. Under this experiment, the adversary $\mathcal{A}$ calls the *Execute, Reveal* and *Test* queries. In this paper, the generation of the session key S_{key} uses α an m that are the responses of the PUF function. Then, an adversary of type eavesdropping learns nothing else than the adversary presented in Experiment $\mathcal{E}_0$. Therefore, we can write:

$$Pr[Succ_{\mathcal{A}}^{\mathcal{E}_1}] = Pr[Succ_{\mathcal{A}}^{\mathcal{E}_0}] \tag{2}$$

Experiment $\mathcal{E}_2$. In this experiment, the adversary $\mathcal{A}$ has to find a collision on the hash function by using q_h hash queries, where q_h is a non-null positive integer. As in Experiment $\mathcal{E}_0$ the adversary $\mathcal{A}$ learns nothing about the shared secret key S_{key} by using *Send* query. Thus, from the birthday paradox attack on the hash function, we can write:

$$\left| Pr[Succ_{\mathcal{A}}^{\mathcal{E}_1}] - Pr[Succ_{\mathcal{A}}^{\mathcal{E}_2}] \right| \leq \frac{2^{n_h}!}{(2^{n_h} - q_h)!} \times \frac{1}{2^{n_h \cdot q_h}} \tag{3}$$

Experiment $\mathcal{E}_3$. This experiment is the same as Experiment $\mathcal{E}_2$ but here $\mathcal{A}$ also tries to attack the Uncloneability of the PUF function described in Definition 1. Thus, the adversary $\mathcal{A}$ uses q_f challenge-response queries to the PUF function and simulate the *Send* query, where q_f is a non-null positive integer. In this paper the PUF used is Uncloneable, then we can write:

$$\left| Pr[Succ_{\mathcal{A}}^{\mathcal{E}_2}] - Pr[Succ_{\mathcal{A}}^{\mathcal{E}_3}] \right| \leq \frac{2^{n_f}!}{(2^{n_f} - q_f)!} \times \frac{1}{2^{n_f \cdot q_f}} \tag{4}$$

Experiment $\mathcal{E}_4$. This experiment is the same as Experiment $\mathcal{E}_3$ but here $\mathcal{A}$ also simulates the *Corrupt* query. Thus, the adversary $\mathcal{A}$ can obtain $id_i, \beta_i, \beta'_i, V, p, P, \tilde{P}, \tilde{Q}$ and e stored in the device d_i. In this scheme, an device does not store a secret in its memory. Hence, the adversary $\mathcal{A}$ learns nothing more about the session key S_{key} compared to Experiment $\mathcal{E}_3$. Now, the adversary $\mathcal{A}$ tries to get all sensitives information like α, $m_\star$ and m_i from the ηth communication transcript $T_\eta = \{L_\star^{(\eta)}, L_\star^{'(\eta)}, L_i^{(\eta)}, L_i^{'(\eta)}, L_i^{''(\eta)}, r^{(\eta)}, h^{(\eta)}\}$ between the devices $d_\star$ and d_i which is equivalent to solve the ECDL problem (Problem 1). Then, we can write :

$$\left| Pr[Succ_{\mathcal{A}}^{\mathcal{E}_3}] - Pr[Succ_{\mathcal{A}}^{\mathcal{E}_4}] \right| \leq Adv_{\mathcal{A}}^{ECDL} \tag{5}$$

where $Adv_{\mathcal{A}}^{ECDL}$ denote the advantage of $\mathcal{A}$ against the ECDL problem (Problem 1).

At the end, the adversary $\mathcal{A}$ tries to guess le value of c engaged im the *Test* query. Therefore,

$$Pr[Succ_{\mathcal{A}}^{\mathcal{E}_4}] = \frac{1}{2}. \tag{6}$$

From Eqs. (1), (2) and (5) we get:

$$\frac{1}{2} Adv_{\mathcal{A}}^{SEM} = \left| Pr[Succ_{\mathcal{A}}^{\mathcal{E}_0}] - \frac{1}{2} \right|$$

$$= \left| Pr[Succ_{\mathcal{A}}^{\mathcal{E}_1}] - \frac{1}{2} \right|$$

$$= \left| Pr[Succ_{\mathcal{A}}^{\mathcal{E}_1}] - Pr[Succ_{\mathcal{A}}^{\mathcal{E}_3}] \right|.$$

Thereafter, using the triangular inequality with (4), (5) and (6) we have the following:

$$\frac{1}{2} Adv_{\mathcal{A}}^{SEM} = \left| Pr[Succ_{\mathcal{A}}^{\mathcal{E}_1}] - Pr[Succ_{\mathcal{A}}^{\mathcal{E}_3}] \right|$$

$$\leq \left| Pr[Succ_{\mathcal{A}}^{\mathcal{E}_1}] - Pr[Succ_{\mathcal{A}}^{\mathcal{E}_2}] \right| + \left| Pr[Succ_{\mathcal{A}}^{\mathcal{E}_2}] - Pr[Succ_{\mathcal{A}}^{\mathcal{E}_3}] \right|$$

$$+ \left| Pr[Succ_{\mathcal{A}}^{\mathcal{E}_3}] - Pr[Succ_{\mathcal{A}}^{\mathcal{E}_4}] \right|.$$

Finally, we get:

$$Adv_{\mathcal{A}}^{SEM} \leq 2Adv_{\mathcal{A}}^{ECDL} + \frac{2^{n_h}!}{(2^{n_h} - q_h)!} \times \frac{1}{2^{n_h \cdot q_h - 1}} + \frac{2^{n_f}!}{(2^{n_f} - q_f)!} \times \frac{1}{2^{n_f \cdot q_f - 1}}.$$

$\square$

5.3 Informal Security Analysis

In this section, we presents a discussion on a security properties of the scheme presented in this paper.

Secrecy. In this protocol the identity of a device d_i is represented by $m_i \in \mathbb{Z}_p^\star$. In all steps of the proposed, m_i is always masked using the elliptic curve scalar multiplication before to be sent. Then to break the secrecy of the proposed, an adversary $\mathcal{A}$ have to solve the logarithm discrete problem (Problem 1) which is difficult or guess m_i. This event may occur with a probability of $\frac{1}{2^n}$.

Forward Secrecy. Let $\mathcal{A}$ an adversary that can have access to a device $d_\star$ i.e. $\mathcal{A}$ can get $id_\star, \beta_\star, \beta_\star' \ V, p, P, \tilde{P}, \tilde{Q}, e$. We say that the adversary $\mathcal{A}$ can break the forward secrecy of the proposed if $\mathcal{A}$ can compromise the confidentiality of the previous communications between $d_\star$ and another device d_i. That means that $\mathcal{A}$ can retrieve m_i or the session key $S_{key_{\star,i}}$.

Let $T_\eta = \{L_\star^{(\eta)}, L_\star^{'(\eta)}, L_i^{(\eta)}, L_i^{'(\eta)}, L_i^{''(\eta)}, r^{(\eta)}, h^{(\eta)}\}$ be the ηth communication transcript between $d_\star$ and d_i. Since the adversary $\mathcal{A}$ have access to $d_\star$ memory he can get $id_\star, \beta_\star, V, p, P, \tilde{P}, \tilde{Q}, e$. Then, the adversary $\mathcal{A}$ can retrieve m_i or $m_\star$ from $L_\star^{(\eta)}, L_\star^{'(\eta)}, L_i^{(\eta)}, L_i^{'(\eta)}, L_i^{''(\eta)}, h^{(\eta)}$ and $id_\star$ imply that $\mathcal{A}$ can resolve the discrete logarithm problem (Problem 1) or can guess the correct value of m_i or $m_\star$ that event may occur with a probability of $\frac{1}{2^{n-1}}$. In the same time, the adversary $\mathcal{A}$ get the session key $S_{key_{\star,i}}^{(\eta)}$ imply that $\mathcal{A}$ can resolve the discrete logarithm problem (Problem 1) to get the m_i, $m_\star$ and α values or can guess the correct value of m_i, $m_\star$ and α or $S_{key_{\star,i}}^{(\eta)}$ that event may occur with a probability of $\frac{1}{2^k} + \frac{1}{2^{3n}}$.

De-synchronized Attack. In this attack, the adversary $\mathcal{A}$ tries to make unsuccessful the future authentication session by modify or interrupt the communication data between two devices in the current session. The adversary $\mathcal{A}$ actions in the current session will stop the protocol execution. However since the proposed does not update any internal state, it will have a normal execution in the next session.

Mutual Authentication. To break the mutual authentication property of the proposed, the adversary $\mathcal{A}$ has to impersonate a devices d_i or d_j during an authentication process. Let n_1, n_2, n_3, n_4, n_5 be a positive integers. To perform the attack, the adversary $\mathcal{A}$ first execute the learning phase to finish with the challenge phase as follow.

Learning: In this phase, $\mathcal{A}$ observes the protocol running n_1 times, interacts n_2 times with the device d_i and interacts n_3 times with the device d_j.

Challenge: In this phase, $\mathcal{A}$ tries to impersonate n_4 times the device d_i and n_5 times the device d_j.

Let $\mathcal{E}_1$ be the event where $\mathcal{A}$ successfully impersonate the device d_i which means that $\mathcal{A}$ guesses the device d_i identity ($m_i \in \mathbb{Z}_p$) or retrieves it from L_i, L_i', L_j'' and h in one of the n_5 sections during the challenge phase or solves the discrete logarithm problem (Problem 1). Thus $\mathcal{E}_1$ may occur with a negligible probability of $\frac{n_5}{2^{n-1}}$. Now let $\mathcal{E}_2$ be the event where $\mathcal{A}$ successfully impersonates the device d_j. Witch mean that $\mathcal{A}$ guesses the device d_j's identity ($m_j \in \mathbb{Z}_p$) or retrieves it from L_j, L_j', L_j'' and h in one of the n_4 sections during the challenge phase or solves the discrete logarithm problem (Problem 1). Thus $\mathcal{E}_2$ may occur with a negligible probability of $\frac{n_4}{2^{n-1}}$.

Security Against Physical Attacks. In the proposed scheme, the device does not store any secret keys in its memory. This design ensures that even if an adversary $\mathcal{A}$ physically seizes the device, they will be unable to extract any secrets from the device's memory. Furthermore, if the adversary $\mathcal{A}$ attempts to tamper with the device's hardware, the behavior of the PUF will be altered, preventing the generation of the intended response. Consequently, another device will be capable of detecting authentication attempts made by the tampered device, thus safeguarding against physical attacks. Moreover, since PUFs possess the property of uncloneability, adversary $\mathcal{A}$ cannot replicate the PUFs associated with the device.

Untraceability. Considering two devices d_b, with $b \in 0, 1$, the objective of an adversary $\mathcal{A}$ against the Untraceability is to determine which of these devices, d_b, authenticates itself with another device $d_\star$ by correctly guessing the value of b. Despite having access to the transcriptions $\{L_\star, L'_\star, L_b, L'_b, L''_b, r, h\}$ of the communication between device d_b and device $d_\star$, constructing a distinguisher capable of accurately guessing the value of b is tantamount to developing an algorithm that can solve the Decision elliptic curve Diffie-Hellman problem (Problem 2).

6   Practical Results and Comparison

This section evaluates the performance of the proposed scheme in term of memory usage, computational cost and execution time.

Memory Usage and Computational Cost. Let n, k_1, and k_2 represent the number of bits required to store an element of $\mathbb{Z}_p$, $\mathbb{G}_1$, and $\mathbb{G}_2$, respectively. The required storage for a drone is then $4n + 2k_1 + 2k_2$ bits. One of the peculiarities of the scheme is that this quantity remains fixed regardless of the number of devices in the system and thus depends only on the chosen elliptic curve. To implement the protocol and depending on the security level that we want to ensure for the discrete logarithm problem (Problem 1), we have the possibility to chose between the following two pairing friendly curves: BLS12-381 [8] for a 126 bits security level and BN158 [9] for a 80 bits security level. For BLS12-381, we obtain $n = 256$; $k_1 = 384$ and $k_2 = 768$, which gives a required storage of 3328 bits. Regarding the data exchanged during an authentication, it is a question of $6n + 3k_1 + 2k_2 + \ell$, where ℓ is the size of the hash function. This gives a total of 4224 bits of exchanged data for the proposed implementation in this paper. Also, note that the scheme proposed in this paper generates a shared data of k_1 bits and 341 bits for the proposed implementation. For BN158, we obtain $n = 80$; $k_1 = 158$ and $k_2 = 316$, which gives a required storage of 1346 bits. This gives also a total of 1746 bits of exchanged data for the proposed implementation in this paper. Also, note that, for this curve, the scheme proposed in this paper generates a shared data of k_1 bits and 158 bits for the proposed implementation.

Table 2. Comparison of communication cost depending on the security level (in bit). Where n_d is the number of drones.

	Total Comm	Security Level
Zhang *et al.* [25]	2688	80
Bansal *et al.* [6]	4000	80
Mall *et al.* [17]	1568	80
Lei *et al.* [14]	$n_d \times 320$	80
Proposed scheme	1746	80
	4224	126

Table 2 compares the proposed scheme in this paper with recent PUF-based authentication schemes regarding the amount of data exchanged during an authentication session. It is worth noting that, except for [17], the scheme proposed in this paper uses less data for communication. In fact, for a security of 80 bits, the proposed scheme saves respectively 56% and 35% in terms of communication data compared to the protocols proposed in [6,25]. As for scheme [14], the proposed scheme in this paper becomes efficient when the number of devices used is equal to or greater than 5.

Finally, during an authentication session, a device performs five (5) exclusive or (Xor), three (3) modular additions in $\mathbb{Z}_p$ (Add), one (1) modular inversion in $\mathbb{Z}_p$ (Inv), two (2) scalar multiplications in $\mathbb{G}_1$ and $\mathbb{G}_2$ (MultSG1, MultSG2), one (1) point addition in $\mathbb{G}_2$ (AddG2), and one (1) evaluation of the pairing function $e(.,.)$ (Pair), which gives

$$1Pair + 2MultSG1 + 2MultSG2 + 1AddG2 + 1Inv + 4Add + 5Xor.$$

Implementation. To assess the feasibility of the proposed PUF-based Mutual Authentication Scheme, we implement the protocol on a laptop with a 1.8 GHz CPU and 4 GB of RAM running Ubuntu 18.04 as a virtual machine. The Relic Toolkit [7] implemented in C language was used for the pairing-friendly elliptic curve. Table 3 shows the results in terms of execution time using the BLS12-381 [8] elliptic curve, which ensures a 126 bits security. This table presents the time required to initialize and authenticate devices on a drone for varying numbers of devices. The table has three columns: "number of devices", "initialization time (ms)", and "authentication time (ms)". Each row represents a different number of devices, and the corresponding initialization and authentication times are provided in milliseconds. The table indicates that as the number of devices increases, the initialization time increases, while the authentication time appears to remain relatively constant across all rows, with times ranging from 4.062726 ms for 20 devices to 4.077623 ms for 10000 devices.

Table 3. Initialization and Authentication execution Time for Different Numbers of Devices

nb of devices	init time (ms)	authentication time (ms)
20	0.842964	4.062726
100	0.966706	4.074717
500	1.559311	4.075866
1000	2.313118	4.071018
10000	15.748394	4.077623

7   Conclusion

This paper proposes a new lightweight PUF-based mutual authentication scheme for drones. The proposed scheme fulfills all security requirements based on the hardness of the logarithm discrete problem (Problem 1) for elliptic curves. This scheme efficiently enables drone-to-drone authentication without the need for a control center as an intermediary or the use of a master drone. Additionally, by utilizing cryptographic accumulators, the proposed scheme is either equivalent to or saves at least 35% in terms of communication data compared to the most recent PUF-based mutual authentication scheme for drones. Finally, this paper demonstrates the feasibility of the proposed scheme by providing an implementation. In future work, it would be interesting to enhance the proposed protocol by allowing drones to dynamically join and leave the swarm.

References

1. Abdalla, M., Fouque, P.-A., Pointcheval, D.: Password-based authenticated key exchange in the three-party setting. In: Vaudenay, S. (ed.) PKC 2005. LNCS, vol. 3386, pp. 65–84. Springer, Heidelberg (2005). https://doi.org/10.1007/978-3-540-30580-4_6
2. Alladi, T., Chamola, V., Kumar, N.: PARTH: a two-stage lightweight mutual authentication protocol for UAV surveillance networks. Comput. Commun. **160**, 81–90 (2020)
3. Alladi, T., Bansal, G., Chamola, V., Guizani, M.: SecAuthUAV: a novel authentication scheme for UAV-ground station and UAV-UAV communication. IEEE Trans. Veh. Technol. **69**(12), 15068–15077 (2020)
4. Alladi, T., Venkatesh, V., Chamola, V., Chaturvedi, N.: Drone-MAP: a novel authentication scheme for drone-assisted 5G networks. In: IEEE INFOCOM, pp. 1–6 (2021)
5. Bansal, G., Sikdar, B.: Location aware clustering: scalable authentication protocol for UAV swarms. IEEE Network. Lett. **3**(4), 177–180 (2021)
6. Bansal, G., Sikdar, B.: S-maps: scalable mutual authentication protocol for dynamic UAV swarms. IEEE Trans. Veh. Technol. **70**(11), 12088–12100 (2021)
7. Barbulescu, R., Gaudry, P., Joux, A., Thomé, E., Vercauteren, F.: The RELIC toolkit (2014). https://github.com/relic-toolkit/relic

8. Barreto, P.S.L.M., Lynn, B., Scott, M.: Constructing elliptic curves with prescribed embedding degrees. In: Cimato, S., Persiano, G., Galdi, C. (eds.) SCN 2002. LNCS, vol. 2576, pp. 257–267. Springer, Heidelberg (2003). https://doi.org/10.1007/3-540-36413-7_19

9. Barreto, P.S.L.M., Naehrig, M.: Pairing-friendly elliptic curves of prime order. In: Preneel, B., Tavares, S. (eds.) SAC 2005. LNCS, vol. 3897, pp. 319–331. Springer, Heidelberg (2006). https://doi.org/10.1007/11693383_22

10. Benaloh, J., de Mare, M.: One-way accumulators: a decentralized alternative to digital signatures. In: Helleseth, T. (ed.) EUROCRYPT 1993. LNCS, vol. 765, pp. 274–285. Springer, Heidelberg (1994). https://doi.org/10.1007/3-540-48285-7_24

11. Boneh, D.: The decision Diffie-Hellman problem. In: Buhler, J.P. (ed.) ANTS 1998. LNCS, vol. 1423, pp. 48–63. Springer, Heidelberg (1998). https://doi.org/10.1007/BFb0054851

12. Gope, P., Millwood, O., Saxena, N.: A provably secure authentication scheme for RFID-enabled UAV applications. Comput. Commun. **166**, 19–25 (2021)

13. Gope, P., Sikdar, B.: An efficient privacy-preserving authenticated key agreement scheme for edge-assisted internet of drones. IEEE Trans. Veh. Technol. **69**(11), 13621–13630 (2020)

14. Lei, Y., Zeng, L., Li, Y.X., Wang, M.X., Qin, H.: A lightweight authentication protocol for UAV networks based on security and computational resource optimization. IEEE Access **9**, 53769–53785 (2021)

15. Li, T., et al.: Lightweight security authentication mechanism towards UAV networks. In: NaNA 2019, Daegu, Korea (South), October 10-13, pp. 379–384. IEEE (2019)

16. Liang, H., Seo, S.: UAV low-altitude remote sensing inspection system using a small target detection network for helmet wear detection. Remote. Sens. **15**(1), 196 (2023)

17. Mall, P., Amin, R., Obaidat, M.S., Hsiao, K.F.: CoMSeC++: PUF-based secured light-weight mutual authentication protocol for drone-enabled WSN. Comput. Netw. **199**, 108476 (2021)

18. Menezes, A., Okamoto, T., Vanstone, S.A.: Reducing elliptic curve logarithms to logarithms in a finite field. IEEE Trans. Inf. Theory **39**(5), 1639–1646 (1993)

19. Ning, H., Farha, F., Ullah, A., Mao, L.: Physical unclonable function: architectures, applications and challenges for dependable security. IET Circ. Devices Syst. **14**(4), 407–424 (2020)

20. Ouafi, K., Phan, R.C.W.: Privacy of recent RFID authentication protocols. In: Chen, L., Mu, Y., Susilo, W. (eds.) Information Security Practice and Experience, pp. 263–277. Springer, Berlin Heidelberg, Berlin, Heidelberg (2008)

21. Pu, C., Li, Y.: Lightweight authentication protocol for unmanned aerial vehicles using physical unclonable function and chaotic system. In: LANMAN, pp. 1–6 (2020)

22. Vitto, G., Biryukov, A.: Dynamic universal accumulator with batch update over bilinear groups. Cryptology ePrint Archive, Paper 2020/777 (2020)

23. Xu, Z., Chen, B., Zhan, X., Xiu, Y., Suzuki, C., Shimada, K.: A vision-based autonomous UAV inspection framework for unknown tunnel construction sites with dynamic obstacles. CoRR **abs/2301.08422** (2023)

24. Xue, G., Li, Y., Wang, Z.: Vessel-UAV collaborative optimization for the offshore oil and gas pipelines inspection. Int. J. Fuzzy Syst. **25**(1), 382–394 (2023)

25. Zhang, L., Xu, J., Obaidat, M.S., Li, X., Vijayakumar, P.: A PUF-based lightweight authentication and key agreement protocol for smart UAV networks. IET Commun. **16**(10), 1142–1159 (2022)

Formalizing for Proving the System Safety of the Software Component for a Small Sized Guided Transport System

Amine Hamidi, Simon Collart-Dutilleul$^{(\boxtimes)}$, and Philippe Bon

Univ Gustave Eiffel, COSYS-ESTAS, 59650 Villeneuve d'Ascq, France
{amine.hamidi,simon.collart-dutilleul,philippe.bon}@univ-eiffel.fr

Abstract. This paper focuses on the design and analysis of a safe software component respecting the signalling system of railway applications, specifically addressing the challenges related to ensuring safe train movements. The proposed system incorporates hybrid aspects, combining discrete and continuous behaviours, to effectively manage train operations. The Rodin platform and the Why3 prover are considered to provide formal verification and validation of the system's correctness. The approach refers to existing norms, like subset 125 and industrial feed backs for formal proofs of safety properties in the metro area. Nevertheless, as the considered 8 vehicles seats autonomous guided systems running on tires, the dynamic this less than two tones cyber physical system could be quite different. As a consequence, holding the exact equation must be performed to check the consistency of common assumptions.

The Why3 prover is integrated into the development process, allowing for the verification of system properties and the generation of proof obligations. This enhances the assurance of the system's correctness and compliance with safety requirements.

The combination of the Rodin platform, which supports the formal modeling and analysis of hybrid systems, and the Why3 prover, which provides powerful reasoning capabilities, offers a comprehensive approach to the design and verification of complex signalling systems in railway applications. The proposed methodology contributes aims to insure safety by comparing industrial approach consistency with industrial feedbacks and norms.

Keywords: Signalling system · System hybrid · Rodin · Why3 · Traction/brake control

1 Introduction

To guide the design of existing autonomous rail transport adapted to the specific environment of low-traffic lines, it makes sense to draw on existing standards, tools and methodologies, and to specify the necessary adjustments [11]. A standard ATO (Automatic Train Operation) over ETCS (European Train Control System) system enables automatic train control on GoA2 (Grade of Automation). The system includes the Technical Specifications for Interoperability - Train Control. ATO over ETCS will therefore be the EU (European Union) solution for automated driving, enabling interoperability of components. In order for our system to achieve GoA2, we are faced with a problem: the braking curves rely on real numbers to accurately represent the braking performance of trains. However, to ensure formality and verifiability of our system, we need to adopt the B method, This method is widely recognized and validated by experts in the railway domain. It relies on the use of integers and formal operations to guarantee the accuracy and rigor of specifications and proofs. By utilizing the B method, we can develop formal models and specifications that accurately capture the behavior and properties of the railway system, facilitating the validation and verification of its compliance with safety requirements. By incorporating integers and formal operations into our development approach, we ensure a reliable, robust system that adheres to industry standards.

This presents a challenge in reconciling the precision of real-number-based braking curves with the formality requirement of our B-method-based system using integers. It is essential to find a solution that combines these two aspects.

One possible approach is to approximate the real braking curves using integers while maintaining a sufficient level of precision to ensure the safety of railway operations. This approximation can be based on mathematical modeling and analysis techniques to determine integer values that closely approximate the real values of the braking curves.

It is important to note that this approximation of the braking curves may result in a slight loss of precision compared to the real values. However, this can be compensated for by employing a more conservative analysis approach and incorporating additional safety margins in the system design.

In conclusion, to achieve GoA2 while maintaining the formality of the system, we need to find a solution that allows us to approximate the real braking curves using integers. This will enable us to benefit from the advantages of the B method while ensuring the safety of railway operations.

This article focuses on designing and overseeing an independent and secure railway system using a hybrid modeling approach based on Event-B methodology. The different sections of the paper are organised as follows: the second section present the main autonomous control challenges, the third section explains the safety contribution of the signaling system. This leads to the specification of hybrid system modelling using B method. Existing works dealing with physical components are considered and there application to train ATO is discussed. The last section provides some conclusions and describes long term and short term prospects.

2 Autonomous Train Control

Implementing autonomous train control on existing railway networks requires using various technologies. To minimize costs, it is preferable to avoid modifying the existing infrastructure, including track-side signalling equipment [10]. Managing this design specification in a certified framework, may allow to generate software component directly from a formally proved specification [13]. In this case, the produces software is proved to be without programming error. A discussion and a use case discussing the global safety impact concerning railway software is presented By Bougacha [3]. A wider presentation was developed by Thierry Lecomte during the Isola 2022 Conference [14].

In line with the recommendations of the Federal Railroad Administration of the U.S. Department of Transportation [22], a sensor platform integrating multiple technologies is proposed to identify objects of interest (OOI) and conditions of interest (COI). This platform aims to detect obstacles, landmarks for improved position calculation, train stations, and other relevant factors. Perception of the immediate train environment is crucial for accurate navigation, as it ensures compliance with signalling equipment and prevents collisions with obstacles, including other trains, objects, and animals. Achieving this requires the use of different sensing techniques and technologies, such as radar, laser, time-of-flight cameras, and infrared cameras. By employing various wavelengths or physical principles, the platform can avoid false information and adapt to different environmental conditions.

Weather conditions directly impact the reliability and precision of perceived information, which can significantly affect the representation of the observed scene. Factors like precipitation, snow, humidity, high light levels, mist, and dust can influence the quality of data. For instance, occlusions in the optical system may obscure obstacles, while a low sun position on the horizon can cause sensor saturation, hindering the detection of important signals.

In summary, implementing autonomous train control requires a sensor platform that combines multiple technologies to ensure accurate perception of the train's environment. The platform must be capable of detecting objects and conditions of interest while accounting for diverse environmental factors. By carefully selecting sensing techniques and considering the impact of weather conditions, the system can enhance safety and efficiency in railway operations [16].

3 Railway Signalling Systems

Railway signalling systems exhibit both discrete and continuous behaviors, making them complex to model accurately. Hybrid models offer a more comprehensive approach to capturing the dynamics of these systems, allowing for a higher level of safety assurance.

In the context of heterogeneous signalling systems, where communication plays a crucial role, the precision and reliability of onboard systems in rolling stock are of utmost importance. These hybrid systems are responsible for calculating and controlling train movement, ensuring safe and efficient operations.

The proposed development method and the general signalling model provide a robust framework for modeling and reasoning about the hybrid nature of heterogeneous signalling systems. This framework allows for the formal development of Event-B models that capture the dynamic aspects of both discrete and continuous elements in railway signalling systems [18].

Using the Event-B formalism, the development process ensures a systematic and rigorous approach to designing and verifying the behavior of the signalling systems. It allows for the identification and mitigation of potential hazards and the validation of safety requirements.

Overall, the formal development of Event-B models for dynamic discrete and continuous railway signalling systems contributes to enhancing the understanding and design of complex signalling systems. It enables engineers and researchers to analyze system behaviors, identify potential vulnerabilities, and improve system safety and reliability.

3.1   Danger Related to Train Movements

One of the fundamental imperatives of railway safety is that the system must prevent trains from colliding. Figure 1 illustrates the various dangerous events in the collision section of this diagram, divided into four cases.

It is crucial to develop and analyse these cases in order to implement appropriate measures and devices to effectively prevent train collisions.

1. **head-on collision** on a one-way road. As both trains are on the same track, the only way to avoid a collision is to brake to a stop. This scenario is very difficult when both trains are in motion, as the two speeds reduce the distance between them. In the event of collision, the two kinetic energies physically add up, with serious consequences.
2. **both vehicles are travelling in the same direction.** A safety distance has to be maintained between the two train for avoiding collision. One technical solution is to control that the two trains do not belong to the same zone. An efficient technique is to keep an empty zone between two trains.
3. Even when the two vehicles are travelling in different lanes but some safety limit must be fulfilled otherwise the physical dimensions of trains makes that they touch each other.

In the derailment section, there are 3 cases;

1. the general case of derailment.
2. derailment on a bend. derailment may happen in case of over speed. For this reason, ERTMS provides an ATP (Automatic Train Protection) monitoring train speeds.
3. to take another route, it takes the route it was following.

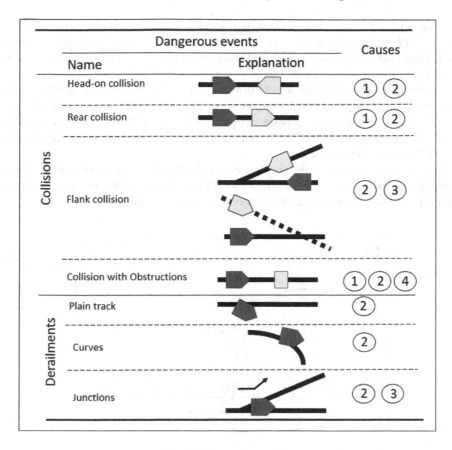

Fig. 1. Dangerous events

The objective is to ensure the safety of public transportation by connecting and arranging switches and signals in a manner that prevents hazardous situations from occurring.

A GoA2 system will respect the signalling, but in the context of the subset 125 there is a driver checking the normal conditions and managing hazards.

Among other hazards, collisions with an obstacle that lay on the track must be considered. A particular case is a collision with a wild beast.

3.2 The Protective Safety Distance in an ATP System

In the given scenario, the distance S0 represents the ATP system's protection distance. Many factors, such as train speed, control method, braking system variability, ATP system response time, and wheel-rail adhesion in different conditions, influence the accuracy of braking. Mathematically, these factors can be considered as variables in a multi-variable function.

The optimal protection distance is a significant consideration when designing an ATP system. It aims to provide enough space between trains to ensure operational safety. In this case, train B must come to a stop before point T while train A is already stopped.

However, in practice, the actual braking curve of train B may exhibit variations and errors, represented by curves C' or C" and actual stopping points T0' or T0". Delta S1 represents a positive error, while delta S2 represents a negative error. These errors highlight the importance of the safety protection distance in an ATP system (see Fig. 2).

Insufficient protection distance poses a risk of collision between train B and train A. Negative errors occur when the ATP system applies braking, but the train fails to stop precisely at the intended stopping point [19].

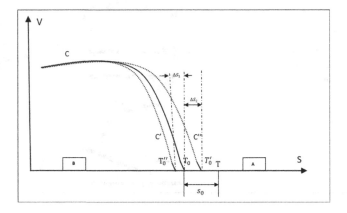

Fig. 2. The protective safety distance in an ATP system

Therefore, ensuring braking accuracy and maintaining an adequate safety protection distance are vital in the design and operation of an ATP system to guarantee the safety of railway operations.

4   Hybrid System Modeling with Event-B

A theoretical extension process has been developed and implemented as a Rodin platform plug-in [7], enabling users to expand the language. Through this theory extension approach, new theories can be defined, encompassing data types, operators, and proof rules, and their correctness can be proven by fulfilling the generated proof obligations.

The theory of real numbers holds particular significance in reasoning about hybrid systems' properties. This work builds upon the dense theory of real numbers originally developed by Abrial and Butler [6], and subsequently extended by Dupont et al. [9] to support the theory of continuous functions and ordinary differential equations (see Fig. 3).

```
THEORY
TYPE PARAMETERS E, F
DATA TYPES
   DE(F)
CONSTRUCTORS
   ode(fun : P(R × F × F), initial : F, initialArg : R)
OPERATORS
   solutionOf < predicate > (D_R : P(R), η : D_R → F, eq : DE(F))
   Solvable < predicate > (D_R : P(R), eq : DE(F))
DIRECT DEFINITION
   ∃x · x ∈ (D_R → F) ∧ solutionOf(D_R, x, eq)
   ⋮
END
```

Fig. 3. Differential equation theory

When dealing with a hybrid system, it is necessary to incorporate both discrete and continuous concepts. While Event-B inherently supports discrete parts, the same cannot be said for continuous aspects [18].

4.1   Event-B Modeling of Hybrid Train Dynamics

The mathematical model commences by deriving a precise differential equation for acceleration, obtained from fundamental principles of physics and models related to rolling bodies.

$$
\begin{cases}
F_{net} &= m \cdot a \vdash a = \frac{F_{net}}{m} \vdash a = \frac{f_{eng.} - R_{tot.}}{m} \\[2mm]
R_{tot.}(t) &= a + b \cdot v(t) + c \cdot v(t)^2 \\[2mm]
\dot{v}(t) &= \frac{f(t) - (a + b \cdot v(t) + c \cdot v(t)^2)}{m} \\[2mm]
\dot{p}(t) &= v(t)
\end{cases}
$$

Fig. 4. Mathematical differential equation theory

The control over the train's engine power, whether by a driver or an automated train operation system, is limited to influencing the acceleration. According to Newton's second law, acceleration is directly proportional to the net force, which, in this case, is the tractive force generated by the engine. The total tractive force is determined by the difference between the tractive force and the resistance force, which opposes the motion and includes mechanical and air resistances. This resistance can be mathematically expressed as a second-order polynomial equation, with fixed parameters and the train's speed as variables [18] (see Fig. 4).

In terms of train speed control, the system receives updates of the end of movement authority (EoA) from the communication centre. The speed controller is designed to assess its distance to the EoA and determine, based on the current speed and acceleration, whether it can come to a stop before reaching the EoA. Typically, a complex algorithm is used for calculating the stopping distance within the onboard computer. However, in our train model, we simplify this algorithm by employing a stopping distance function (StopDist) that takes the current acceleration and speed as inputs and provides an estimation of the required distance to stop.

4.2   Potential Solutions

In the context of our work, our approach is based on utilizing an existing specification to design a component responsible for respecting closed signals and preventing any excessive speed. This component plays a crucial role in the system's safety. To operate effectively, it relies on data originating from subsets 130 and 39.

Specifically, our objective is to leverage this existing specification to create a control component that continuously monitors adherence to closed signals and speed limits. To achieve this, it actively utilizes information sourced from subsets 130 and 39. These data are essential to enable the component to make real-time decisions and respond accordingly, ensuring the safety and compliance of the railway transport system. According to the author knowledge there are no alternative solution for implementing this strategy in the state of the art. A clear methodological innovation is proposed, but it leads to a scientific and technological deadlock relative to continues variables.

In the context of a braking system, both real and integer numbers can be used to represent different quantities such as speed, distance, time, etc. Real numbers provide a more precise and continuous representation of these quantities, while integer numbers are used for discrete measurements or countable quantities.

Regarding conic approximation, it is a method used to approximate real values by using intervals or upper and lower bounds. This approach can be used to model uncertainties or error margins in the braking system.

As for Rodin and Why3, they are tools that can be used for formal specification, modeling, and verification of systems. Rodin is specifically designed for the Event-B method, while Why3 is an automatic theorem prover that can be used with various specification languages, including Event-B. These tools can be used to analyse and verify properties of the braking system, including aspects related to real and integer numbers, as well as the necessary approximations to model the system accurately and reliably.

Using Rodin as a Basis for System Analysis: The Event-B method, in conjunction with the Rodin environment, provides a robust approach to formal system development. Proofs and theoretical extensions help ensure the accuracy and verifiability of the model, while Rodin's features streamline the development and verification process. This makes it a valuable tool for the development of critical systems.

A specific Rodin plugin, allows to both export and accept external solutions [9]. In the Rodin environment, we need to specify our system in the form of formal models using the B method. These models can be used to represent the behaviour, properties and constraints of our system. Once we have specified our system in Rodin, we need to use the Rodin plugin to perform various verification activities, such as checking model consistency, proving properties specified using the B method, or generating code from the formal model. However, it is also possible to export our formal model from Rodin to other tools or specification languages that offer specific verification features. For example, we can export our model to an external model-checking tool or theorem prover for further verification of the system. Once we have obtained the verification results from these external tools, we can use the Rodin plugin to import the resolutions or verification results into our Rodin model. This allows us to integrate specialised tools or additional verification techniques into our formal verification process. We can exploit the specific capabilities of these tools to reinforce confidence in our formal system and obtain additional guarantees of its correctness and conformity to specified properties.

Using WHY3 for Real Variables: Why3 is an environment dedicated to formal verification that supports different logic and provers.

To export Rodin's proof obligations to Why3, we'll take the following steps:

- Generating proof obligations in Rodin: Using Rodin's functionalities, we will formally specify our system and generate the corresponding proof obligations. These proof obligations are logical assertions that must be proven to guarantee the correctness of the system.
- Exporting proof obligations: using the Rodin plugin to export proof obligations in Why3 format. The plugin must support this Why3 export functionality.
- Import into Why3: by importing proof bonds exported from Rodin. Why3 supports various input formats, including that used by Rodin.
- Resolving proof obligations in Why3: Once the proof obligations have been imported into Why3, Why3's functionalities can be used to resolve these proofs.

By exporting the proof obligations generated in Rodin to Why3, we'll use Why3's features and provers to resolve these proofs, thus strengthening the formal verification of our system.

5 Managing Uncertainties of a Real Cyber Physical System

Taking account the feed-back coming from the experience of modelling adn analysing the line 7 of the metro New-York by a collaboration between the RATP and Clearsy societies [15], a methodology based on industrial experience is detailed.

The modelling approach use refinement mechanisms of the B method to abstract the subsystems by keeping only the security related properties. In this paper, imprecision comes from the odometer using a coding wheel. Metro wheels coupled to the odometer, can spin when accelerating or slip when braking. When you read a beacon on the ground, its position is exact (depends on the precision with which it was placed on the track initially). These two mechanisms are used to provide the position information. By using beacons, upper-bound of the imprecision is provided.

Another source of imprecision comes from the approximation of the real values, in the mathematical sense of the word, by an interval defined by their nearest integer.

This approximation is commonly used for Communications-based train control (CBTC) metro systems to simplify calculations and graphical representations of railway tracks [8] It provides a reasonable level of accuracy while streamlining the modelling of train trajectories, track curves, and signal positions. Moreover, using integer values, the system model can be fully proved using the atelier B. This tool is certified as T2 by the corresponding transport authority. By utilising the conical approximation, railway systems can benefit from improved efficiency and simplified analysis. However, it is important to note that the conic approximation may not offer the highest level of precision compared to other methods.

In the present paper, the 8 places vehicles is weighting much less than a train line or a metro a line. Moreover, the considered vehicle is running on rubber tires. As a consequence, the main hypothesis while being plausible, must be systematically checked. Modelling with exact real values may be performed in order to verify that the common industrial assumptions still stand. For example, using the Rodin plugin allowing the use of a Why3 solver for specific proof obligation discharging can be considered [1]. Some other framework like a plugin of the atelier B [5], and other complementary solver like Isabelle [4] may be considered too.

These tools ensure the consistency and correctness of the system by generating and satisfying proof obligations, thereby ensuring its reliability and compliance with specifications.

If the classical assumption are proved to be correct, than a methodology based on the atelier B and the use of neighbour integers will be correct. In this case, the main challenge will be safety requirement tracing using a formal approach [3].

5.1   Traction/Brake Control

In the ATO system, the traction/brake control takes on the role of the driver in the C-DAS system by determining appropriate commands for each mode. Instead of providing advice, supervisory information is displayed. The control can be implemented in various ways, with regime-based approaches defining specific actions for different regimes. The cruising regime is particularly intricate and requires an algorithm to adjust traction and brake commands based on train and track resistance. This algorithm aims to minimize deviations from the optimal speed profile and triggers trajectory recalculation if needed. In situations where the train cannot stay within the designated Journey Profile (JP), the Train Management System (TMS) generates adjusted time targets for the ATO-Trackside (ATO-TS) subsystem. This ensures that the train adheres to the planned trajectory within the JP [21].

5.2   Previous Step Towards Implementation

The transition from a human driver to an automatic system results in a change in the capabilities of the driving agent. This change necessitates configuration modifications both on the track-side and on the on-board systems, utilising the communication means offered by Subset 126. In this subsection, a comprehensive overview of the associated architecture is provided through the use of SysML block definition diagrams [12]. The paper provides a detailed presentation of the system architecture by describing the state machine of each block, which defines their behaviour, as well as sequence diagrams that illustrate the interaction between components at each level. However, the final layer and its corresponding sequence diagrams are not included in the paper. The system architecture for modeling the GoA2 ATO over ETCS is decomposed into four levels, as depicted in the Fig. 5. The lower level of the system consists of the autopilot and ATP. This level represents the control software of the train. The autopilot is a proprietary software component that is not specified in the standards. On the other hand, the ATP component is derived directly from the subset 26 curves, taking into account uncertainties in position measurements caused by the odometer and sliding effects [20]. The dynamic behavior of the autopilot must fulfilled the specification extracted from the subset 125. The OnBoard component must be in a relevant state before engaging ATO mode, whereas in the same time the track states has to be able to transmit the needed data. The interaction between the Track and Onboard automation of the train is depicted in the sequence diagram shown in Fig. 6. The train receives a specified length for which it is authorized to proceed. As the train covers this distance, it reaches the EOA (End of Authority) and is required to come to a stop. It remains stationary until it receives a new MA (Movement Authority) that grants a new authorization to proceed for a specific distance.

In the final layer of the architecture, the ETCS system is divided into ATP and Autopilot components. However, since there is no longer a driver present,

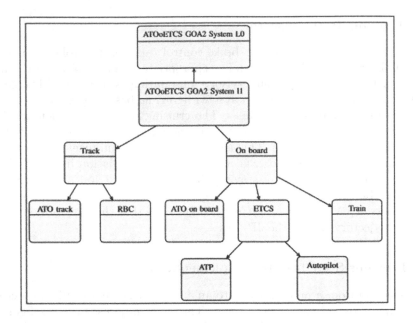

Fig. 5. Architecture model

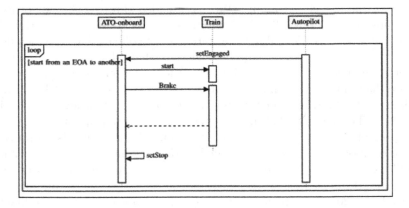

Fig. 6. Level 2 sequence diagram for the sub-case "perform travel running ATO"

the DMI (Driver-Machine Interface) no longer holds any significance. The functionalities previously performed by the driver are now assumed by the Autopilot component. This section has focused on modeling and analysis specifically tailored to the requirements of Subset 125, with a simplified approach for the case of "bus driver-less trains". The ATP component, which plays a critical role in ensuring system safety, has not been extensively discussed as it is situated at a lower level in the architecture.

Nonetheless, the main challenges associated with ATP validation are addressed in the subsequent discussion, as it has historically encountered technical deadlocks that could potentially be resolved through the use of formal methods [10].

In order to give a flavor of the on going software development, a code is provided under the following link[1]. The corresponding scientific analysis can be consulted in [3] where the proof obligations are totally automatically proved.

This code correspond to a particular implementation of the subset 125 for freight trains [2]. In this model, grade of automation is 2, as there is still a driver, but the ferromobile application is driver-less. As a consequence, the driver tasks of the subset 125 are allocated to the Autopilot component as shown in Fig. 5. As a consequence, if one want to reuse the code in the context of ferromobile, the "Driver" variable should be replaced by "Autopilot". In this analysis we use two different components taking the place of the driver:

- ATO in charge of respecting limitations, it can be implemented in the framework of the subset 125. The subset 125 is a norm for main railway lines, but in the considered application the functional specification can used as a reference for a safety demonstration.
- Autopilot is in charge of handling hazardous events and transient modes. Actually, it is supposed to take the role of the driver when a GOA2 system is used. However, some of the driver action cannot be performed by a train software component and some other agent will have to take the responsability of specific missions?

6   Conclusion

Integrating hybrid elements into the signalling system, which combines discrete and continuous behaviours, allows a more realistic and accurate representation of how the system operates. This enables the consideration of factors such as speed, acceleration, braking distance, and other relevant parameters to ensure precise control of train movements.

One solution can be, using the Rodin integrated development environment (IDE) and the Why3 prover which provides powerful tools for formally modeling, to formally verify, and validate the signalling system.

Using the mentioned tooled methodology, it is possible to model and verify the functioning of these control systems, for the sake of proving safety.

This may significantly contributes to the safety approach by checking the consistency of the usual industrial assumptions which with the same requirements, but quite different vehicles. When the similarity of the results is not demonstrated, the Event B Rodin (or other exact methodology) must be used. A transformation of the Event B of the Rodin tool into the B system of the atelier B will be needed, as we needed a certified tool chain for code generation. This transformation is actually a part of the targetted code generation and it

---

[1] https://github.com/RacemBougacha/ATO-over-ETCS.git.

has to be proved. For further work, building a systematic proved transformation using the EB4EB framework that proves transformation within Rodin is considered [17]. Moreover, critical use cases, corresponding to the studied low traffic line with small autonomous vehicle will demonstrate the approach and illustrate the efficiency of the tooled chain. As an example, the need to never stop on a bridge, including the potential occurrence of mechanical failures is a scenario that will be demonstrated [10].

Acknowledgement. The Ferromoblile project is granted by ADEME in France 2030 program (grant number 2282D0215-F).

References

1. Aït-Ameur, Y., Bogomolov, S., Dupont, G., Iliasov, A., Romanovsky, A.B., Stankaitis, P.: A refinement-based formal development of cyber-physical railway signalling systems. Formal Aspects Comput. **35**(1), 3:1 (2023). https://doi.org/10.1145/3524052
2. Bon, P., Collart-Dutilleul, S., Bougacha, R.: Ato over etcs: a system analysis for freight trains. Comput. Railways XVIII: Railway Eng. Des. Oper. **213**, 37 (2022)
3. Bougacha, R., Laleau, R., Bon, P., Collart-Dutilleul, S., Ben Ayed, R.: Modeling train systems: from high-level architecture graphical models to formal specifications. In: Kallel, S., Jmaiel, M., Zulkernine, M., Hadj Kacem, A., Cuppens, F., Cuppens, N. (eds.) CRiSIS 2022. LNCS, vol. 13857, pp. 153–168. Springer, Cham (2023). https://doi.org/10.1007/978-3-031-31108-6_12
4. Brucker, A.D., Wolff, B.: Isabelle/DOF: design and implementation. In: Ölveczky, P.C., Salaün, G. (eds.) SEFM 2019. LNCS, vol. 11724, pp. 275–292. Springer, Cham (2019). https://doi.org/10.1007/978-3-030-30446-1_15
5. Burdy, L., Déharbe, D., Prun, É.: Interfacing automatic proof agents in atelier B: introducing "IAPA". In: Proceedings of the Third Workshop on Formal Integrated Development Environment, F-IDE@FM 2016, Limassol, Cyprus, November 8, 2016. EPTCS, vol. 240, pp. 82–90 (2016). https://doi.org/10.4204/EPTCS.240.6
6. Butler, M.J., Abrial, J., Banach, R.: Modelling and refining hybrid systems in event-b and rodin. In: From Action Systems to Distributed Systems - The Refinement Approach, pp. 29–42. Chapman and Hall/CRC (2016). https://doi.org/10.1201/b20053-5
7. Butler, M., Maamria, I.: Practical theory extension in event-B. In: Liu, Z., Woodcock, J., Zhu, H. (eds.) Theories of Programming and Formal Methods. LNCS, vol. 8051, pp. 67–81. Springer, Heidelberg (2013). https://doi.org/10.1007/978-3-642-39698-4_5
8. Comptier, M., Déharbe, D., Perez, J.M., Mussat, L., Thibaut, P., Sabatier, D.: Safety analysis of a CBTC system: a rigorous approach with event-b. In: Fantechi, A., Lecomte, T., Romanovsky, A. (eds.) Reliability, Safety, and Security of Railway Systems. LNCS, vol. 10598, pp. 148–159. Springer, Cham (2017). https://doi.org/10.1007/978-3-319-68499-4_10
9. Dupont, G., Ameur, Y.A., Pantel, M., Singh, N.K.: Proof-based approach to hybrid systems development: Dynamic logic and event-b. In: Fantechi, A., Lecomte, T., Romanovsky, A. (eds.) ABZ 2018. LNCS, vol. 10817, pp. 155–170. Springer, Cham (2018). https://doi.org/10.1007/978-3-319-91271-4_11

10. Dutilleul, S.C., Bon, P., Hamidi, A.: A railway norms application for small traffic railway lines autonomous vehicle. In: 2023 7th IEEE/IFAC International Conference on Control, Automation and Diagnosis, pp. 1–6 (2023). https://doi.org/10.1109/ICCAD57653.2023.10152328

11. Fantechi, A.: The role of formal methods in software development for railway applications. In: Software Design and Development: Concepts, Methodologies, Tools, and Applications, pp. 1103–1118. IGI Global (2014)

12. Holt, J., Perry, S., of Engineering, I., Technology: SysML for Systems Engineering. Computing and Networks Series, Institution of Engineering and Technology (2008). https://books.google.fr/books?id=OEKtufR7spYC

13. Lecomte, T.: Programming the CLEARSY safety platform with B. In: Raschke, A., Méry, D., Houdek, F. (eds.) ABZ 2020. LNCS, vol. 12071, pp. 124–138. Springer, Cham (2020). https://doi.org/10.1007/978-3-030-48077-6_9

14. Lecomte, T.: Safe and secure architecture using diverse formal methods. In: Margaria, T., Steffen, B. (eds.) ISoLA 2022, Part IV. LNCS, vol. 13704, pp. 321–333. Springer, Cham (2022). https://doi.org/10.1007/978-3-031-19762-8_24

15. Mussat, L., Sabatier, D.: Modeling modelling and proof of safety of railway transportation systems. In: 19 Congrés de Maitrise des Risques et sureté de Fonctionnement- Dijon 21-23 octobre 2014, pp. 1–5. Springer (2014)

16. Peleska, J., Haxthausen, A.E., Lecomte, T.: Standardisation considerations for autonomous train control. In: Margaria, T., Steffen, B. (eds.) ISoLA 2022, Part IV. LNCS, vol. 13704, pp. 286–307. Springer, Cham (2022). https://doi.org/10.1007/978-3-031-19762-8_22

17. Riviere, P., Singh, N.K., Aït-Ameur, Y., Dupont, G.: Standalone event-b models analysis relying on the EB4EB meta-theory. In: Glässer, U., Creissac Campos, J., Méry, D., Palanque, P. (eds.) ABZ 2023. LNCS, vol. 14010, pp. 193–211. Springer, Cham (2023). https://doi.org/10.1007/978-3-031-33163-3_15

18. Stankaitis, P.: A Formal Methodology for Engineering Heterogeneous Railway Signalling Systems. Ph.D. thesis, Newcastle University (2021)

19. Sun, P.: Ingénierie de modèle pour la sécurité des systèmes critiques ferroviaires. Ph.D. thesis, École centrale de Lille (2015)

20. Subset 26: "system requirements specification". Std, UNISIG (2016). https://www.era.europa.eu/content/set-specifications-3-etcs-b3-r2-gsm-r-b1_en

21. Wang, Z., Quaglietta, E., Bartholomeus, M.G.P., Goverde, R.M.P.: Assessment of architectures for automatic train operation driving functions. J. Rail Transp. Plan. Manag. **24**, 100352 (2022). https://doi.org/10.1016/j.jrtpm.2022.100352

22. Withers, J., Stoehr, N., et al.: Automated train operations (ATO) safety and sensor development [research results]. Technical report, United States. Department of Transportation. Federal Railroad Administration ... (2020)

Blockchain and Distributed Ledger Technologies

Smart Contracts for a Secure and Privacy-Preserving Smart Grid

Joan Ferré-Queralt[✉][iD], Jordi Castellà-Roca[iD], and Alexandre Viejo[iD]

Departament d'Enginyeria Informàtica i Matemàtiques, Universitat Rovira i Virgili,
UNESCO Chair in Data Privacy, CYBERCAT-Center for Cybersecurity Research of
Catalonia, Av. Països Catalans 26, 43007 Tarragona, Catalonia, Spain
{joan.ferreq,jordi.castella,alexandre.viejo}@urv.cat

Abstract. The current energy landscape faces challenges such as escalating demand, rising prices, and the depletion of traditional energy sources. Existing electricity grids face significant limitations and vulnerabilities and the society would clearly benefit from the adoption of a new energy model that integrates locally-generated renewable energy. In order to achieve that, the use of the smart grid has been proposed as a way to modernize and optimize energy distribution. Generally, current works in the literature that study this area fail to effectively address the security and privacy threats that smart grids and their users may face while participating in the system. Moreover, those proposals that consider the privacy of the users do not prevent them from performing fraudulent actions while they hide in the anonymity. As a result of that, in this work, we propose a new smart grid system which uses blockchain technology and smart contracts as core components. The new scheme takes into account the privacy of the users and the availability and security of the system; while still offering measures to identify and take punitive actions against misbehaving users.

Keywords: Smart grid · Smart contracts · Security · Privacy

1 Introduction

In order to ensure the energy needs of a country, it is of paramount importance to find a balance between supply and demand. Traditionally, the energy supply has been carried out by the deployment of power plants that consume fossil fuels (i.e., coal, natural gas, etc.) or nuclear fuel. Those solutions have significant shortcomings such as the large expenses involved in the construction and maintenance of all the required infrastructure, the greenhouse gas emissions, pollution, nuclear waste, etc. Therefore, it might be beneficial to move towards another main source of energy. In recent years, the cost of renewable energy sources, such as wind and solar, has fallen significantly, making them more competitive and leading the European Union towards a more sustainable and decarbonized electricity sector. However, the adoption of renewable energy has not been increasing at a

A. Ait Wakrime et al. (Eds.): CRiSIS 2023, LNCS 14529, pp. 103–118, 2024.
https://doi.org/10.1007/978-3-031-61231-2_8

sufficient pace[1] This is due in part to the challenges of transitioning away from fossil fuels, as renewable sources may not be as reliable, available and efficient as traditional ones [20].

One way to potentially improving the availability and efficiency of the energy distribution system is to locate energy producers closer to consumers. This can help to reduce the cost and loss of distributing energy over long distances. The use of distributed renewable energy technologies, like solar panels, also opens up the possibility of local, decentralized production and consumption of electricity [8]. In this way, some households are currently using distributed energy resource (DER) systems, like solar panels, to generate and consume their own electricity. If these homes produce more energy than they need, they can sell the excess back to the main grid. However, the price at which this excess energy can be sold is often not attractive enough to sell due to certain impositions or taxes that may be applied by governments or electric utility companies.

In the light of the above, it can be concluded that the society would clearly benefit from the adoption of a new energy model that helps to meet the growing demand by incorporating decentralized and locally-generated renewable energy. In order to achieve that, the use of the *smart grid*, which has been proposed as a way to modernize and optimize energy distribution [6], can play a key role by properly encouraging those DER-equipped households to offer their surplus power to the main grid.

1.1   Related Work

In the recent years, there have been lots of studies about different implementations of a smart grid system, each of those focusing on different aspects of it. In this work, we focus on those implementations that consider the trading of electricity between prosumers.

The first definition of a smart grid was made in [4], which made a first list of requirements that this new energy model should have. Later on, in [17], they discussed some different communication standards for the smart grid, all of which were focused on the traditional centralized structure of the main grid. However, a centralized structure in a smart grid is considered to have several security issues such as a Denial of Service attack, as explained in [3]. Some of those security concerns could be avoided using a distributed system, avoiding the single point of failure problem [14].

One of the first distributed-based solutions was introduced in [13]. The authors of this work proposed the use of an energy currency based on the blockchain technology proposed in [15]. This proposal paved the way for the use of the blockchain as the base for the new grid and the integration of smart contracts. In this way, numerous works have been conducted on this topic, including those proposed in [1,2,10,12,13], which present various blockchain architectures for implementing a smart grid.

---

[1] IEA: Wholesale energy costs made simple, https://www.edfenergy.com.

At this point, it is important to note that all the aforementioned solutions employ a blockchain that uses the *Proof-of-Work* consensus mechanism. This method has been proved to be highly energy-intensive, as it requires substantial computing resources to verify transactions [5]. Such energy consumption is a major drawback that disqualifies them from being integrated in a real smart grid setting. It is, therefore, imperative to explore alternative consensus mechanisms that can minimize energy consumption while maintaining the integrity and security of the system.

Other works such as [9,10], and [18] have explored the introduction of the blockchain technology into energy systems, but those proposals put little focus on the concealment of users' identities, which we consider as anonymity or their energy consumption patterns, which we consider as privacy. This situation, as a result, directly jeopardizes the privacy and anonymity of the users. It is essential to address these privacy concerns when designing blockchain-based energy systems to ensure that the data shared on the network is secure and not susceptible to malicious attacks. A lack of privacy measures can lead to various issues, such as unauthorized access to sensitive information or profiling of user behavior [21].

In response to that, other proposals such as [7,11] and [19] have emerged recently. In this way, the solutions presented in [11] and [7] take into account the anonymity of the users, however they do not verify whether the production or consumption claimed by the users is truly the one being specified. As a result, a dishonest user could potentially submit a fake energy production record, which can mislead the system and other users, leading to undesirable outcomes. On the other hand, [19] uses a reputation system to punish those users who misbehave. However, in this scheme no one possesses the relationship between the smart grid accounts and real identity of the users and, hence, it is not capable of effectively applying coercing measures to the misbehaving user.

1.2   Contribution and Plan of This Paper

This work proposes a new energy trading system based on a smart grid that empowers users to both consume and produce electricity using distributed energy resources. The new system improves the current literature by taking into account the privacy of the users and the availability and security of the system; while still offering measures to identify and take punitive actions against misbehaving users. These features are achieved by means of the blockchain technology and the use of smart contracts.

Our smart grid system monitors the electricity consumption of every user, allowing for precise calculations of individual prosumers' total debts. Moreover, it facilitates seamless electricity trading among geographically proximate prosumers, providing the added flexibility of borrowing from or contributing to the main grid when necessary, whether due to a deficit or surplus.

The rest of the paper is organized as follows. Section 2 presents the system's architecture and offers an overview of how the new scheme works. Section 3 gives specific details about the system components and steps. Section 4 studies how the new solution deals with security and privacy threats. Finally, Sect. 5 provides the conclusions and presents some lines of future work.

2   Architecture and System Overview

2.1   General Architecture

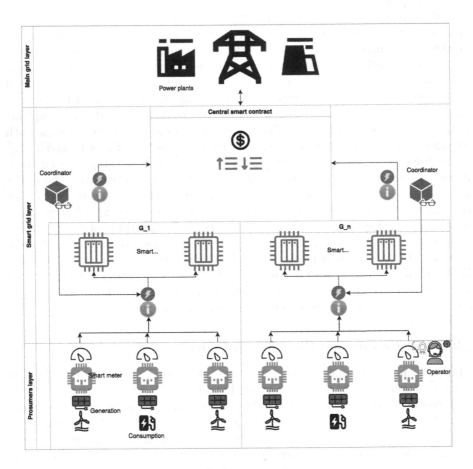

Fig. 1. Architecture scheme

The proposed architecture is depicted in Fig. 1. It consists of three main layers: *prosumers layer*, *smart grid layer*, and *main grid layer*. The following actors/components are involved:

– Smart meters (SM_i): devices who keep track of a prosumer's usage of energy (production and consumption).

- Prosumers: each system user that at a certain time can both produce and consume energy, depending on the balance between the production and consumption that prosumer can be: a *Consumer* (C_i) if she consumes more energy than produced; or a *Producer* (P_i) if she produces more energy than consumed. Each prosumer owns a smart meter and can have consumption, production facilities or both in their household.
- Main grid (MG): connects the main energy sources to the smart grid and is in charge of electricity distribution. Is the one in charge of energy consumption prediction and providing the extra electricity needed.
- Smart grid: keeps transactions between prosumers and between prosumers and the main grid. Also coordinates all payments.
- Coordinators (Co_i): responsible for verifying user's transactions, they own the smart meters used by the prosumers and, hence, they can verify that the prosumers are not lying about their consumption/production amounts. Also, if a prosumer fails to pay, the coordinator may take the necessary measures, although those are outside the scope of this proposal.
- Operators (O_i): are tasked with registering prosumers on the smart grid layer, connecting them, and giving them the authorization to send messages with the relevant trading information to their respective groups. They connect the prosumers to the smart grid physically (wiring) and digitally (giving them the necessary permissions).

The *prosumer layer* is composed of several groups of prosumers who are geographically close to each other. In these groups, they trade electricity among themselves to increase efficiency.

The *smart grid layer* is located between the prosumers layer and the main grid layer. This layer also has a coordinator for each group of prosumers, each coordinator verifies their group members transactions. This layer has the information of the energy usage of each group, which means that, in case a prosumer group needs more electricity or has a surplus, the smart grid layer communicates with the main grid level to buy or sell that electricity. In order to obtain that information, it records all transactions between prosumers in each group with the energy usage information.

Finally, the *main grid layer* is the system as we know of it today. It is composed of the main electrical companies with their bulk electricity generators and also control the distribution of energy.

2.2 Overview of the Proposal

The four main steps of the envisaged system are: *Initialization, Price calculation, Energy trading,* and *Debt liquidation.*

In the *Initialization* step, prosumers (i.e., consumers and producers) should register to the operators and they must be authorized to interact with the smart grid infrastructure.

The *Price calculation* step starts the day before energy trading, with a prediction of energy usage, which is already in use in most energy markets and its development is out of the scope of this work. That's when the main grid estimates the demand and communicates with the main electricity producers. The producers are ranked based on their prices, with the most expensive determining the trading price for electricity in each time slot. This is done in resemblance as in most parts of the EU [16]. In this proposal, the price is determined in different time slots of the day.

The *Energy trading* step consists of the communication between the prosumers' smart meters with the smart grid layer. In particular, the user's electricity usage and transactions is monitored by a smart meter located at their home. This device periodically stores the electricity production/consumption information to the smart grid layer via transactions on the blockchain, allowing to track the user's electricity usage so that the debt of the user can be calculated with the amount of energy produced/consumed and the price in each time slot. The smart grid infrastructure monitors the energy needs of each group and can request additional electricity from the main grid or sell any surplus energy back to it. To facilitate these transactions, the main grid is treated as an additional prosumer in the system. Prosumers' transactions are verified by the coordinators. These entities own the smart meters located at the prosumers' homes and they act as trusted third parties (TTPs).

Finally, in the *Debt liquidation* step, the smart grid collects all of user's transactions and assigns each of them a debt to be paid (to them if they're producers of from them if they're consumers). This debt is communicated to the consumers and, once it's paid, the corresponding amount is distributed to the producers. This way, there's no direct interaction between each consumer and producer.

3   The Proposed System in Detail

This section first explains the blockchain-based smart contracts which are the core components of the proposed solution. After that, it details the four main steps: *Initialization, Price calculation, Energy trading,* and *Debt liquidation.*

3.1   Main Smart Contract

The main smart contract (SC_{MG}) is the first component to be deployed. This contract acts as an intermediary between each prosumer group (G) and the main grid.

Its initial task is to obtain and store the necessary information about each main grid producer (MG_P) so they can communicate their energy production capacity and price of production. To achieve this, each MG_P creates a blockchain account and registers it with the main SC. The SC then verifies the provided information and stores the address of each MG_P. Using the information provided by each MG_P and the knowledge possessed by the main grid (MG), the SC_{MG} can calculate the price of electricity at any given time of the day. In addition to that, the SC_{MG} needs the addresses of all the other SC so that they can communicate any missing or surplus energy in each group.

The MG_P keeps track of all transactions between each SC and the MG. Once a prosumer group needs energy from the MG or is willing to sell a surplus, the SC_{MG} registers the transaction with the quantity of energy and the price. This procedure is similar to the one followed between prosumers in each SC.

The SC_{MG} consists of a class which holds:

- *Date*: Date of the trading day of the SM_{MG}
- *Producer identities*: Public keys of MG_P which can interact with the SC_{MG} and sell electricity to the MG.
- *Coordinator identities*: Public keys of Co which can register SC into the SC_{MG}
- *Main Grid Authority*: Public key of the owner of the SC_{MG}.
- *Expected electricity consumption*: The predicted electricity consumption by the MG for the following day.
- *Production capacity*: List of the production capacity of the different MG_P and its price, divided by time slots.
- *Prices*: List of the price of electricity in each time slot.
- *Group smart contracts*: Addresses of all the SC that can interact with the SC_{MG} and sell or buy energy from the MG.
- *Transactions*: List of all transactions made between the MG and the SC. Each transaction contains the amount sold/bought and its price.
- *Debts*: List of all debts from each SC and the MG.
- *Time slot*: Number of the current time slot. -1 before the trading and 24 when it's over.
- *Trading flag*: Boolean which is "True" when the trading in the MG_{SC} is available.
- *Producers flag*: Boolean which is "True" when MG_P are able to be registered into the MG_{SC} and make an offer.
- *Smart Contracts flag*: Boolean which is "True" when the SC are able to be registered into the MG_{SC}.

When a new SC_{MG} is deployed, the MG must provide the following arguments: i) *Date of the trading day*; ii) *Expected energy consumption*. By default, *Trading flag* is set to "False" and *Producers flag* is set to "True", *Time slot* is set to -1.

Once the SC_{MG} is deployed, the different actors can interact with it with the following methods:

- *newProducer*() method can only be called by the MG authority when the *Producers flag* is set to "True". It introduces a new MG_P which will be able to sell electricity in the trading day. The producer is added to *identities*.
- *newSC*() method can only be called by the Co when *Smart Contracts Flag* is set to "True". It registers all SC that will be able to communicate the need or surplus of electricity of each group. The new SC is added to *Group Smart Contracts*.

- *addOffer()* method which can be called by MG_P when *Producers flag* is set to "True". It communicates the available production and its price at a certain time slot. The offer is added to *Production capacity*.
- *beginAuction()* method called by the MG which, once all MG_P have registered and added their offers or the time limit has come, it determines the electricity price for each time slot. It sets *Producers Flag* to "False".
- *beginTrading()* method called by the MG when the trading day starts. It sets *Smart Contracts Flag* to "False" and *Trading Flag* to "True". It also communicates all the SC that the trading begins.
- *changeTime()* method called by MG, it increases *Time slot* by 1.
- *buyElectricity()* and *sellElectricity()* methods are called by the SC during the trading day, when *Trading flag* is set to "True". SC communicate the needed electricity or the surplus that has to be bought/sold to the MG. Both the amount and the price is stored in *Transactions*.
- *calculateDebts()* method called by the MG once the trading has ended. From all the registered transactions, it calculates the debt each SC and the MG has. Every debt is stored in *Debts*. It sets *Trading Flag* to "False". It also calls the method *calculateDebts()* from each SC.
- *payElectricity()* method called by each SC which has a debt with the MG. The SC_{MG} distributes the funds to the corresponding sellers (MG_P or other SC).
- *getDebt()* method is called by any actor and, if it exists, it returns the debt that she has to pay.

3.2   Group Smart Contracts

After deploying the SC_{MG}, the next step is to deploy the SCs. Each prosumer group (G) has several SCs that are responsible for tracking the energy usage and price for each user (U) within the G. Each group has its own SC in order to incentivize first local electricity trading. Furthermore, each group has several SC in order to increase the privacy of the users by dividing their real electricity usage into different values.

To ensure that each U can send Tx to their respective SC, they must be registered in the SC. It possesses a table which contains the necessary information to authorize each user. Additionally, the SC must register with the SC_{MG} in order to receive information on the price at which electricity is sold during each time slot. It is worth mentioning that the authorization tables within each SC must be kept up to date. For example, if a new U joins the group or an existing U leaves, the table must be updated accordingly. This ensures that only authorized Tx are recorded and that the energy usage and billing remain accurate. Moreover, each SC must possess the identity of the coordinator (Co) of the group. The coordinator is the only authority that can verify the Tx from each U.

Once the SCs have been deployed and authorized, they can start collecting the Tx made by each U within the group. This data is important for ensuring fair and accurate billing according to the energy usage within the group.

SCs can communicate with the SC_{MG}. For example, if one group has a surplus of energy, they can communicate with the SC_{MG} which can communicate with another group that needs more energy and sell their surplus.

Each SC consists of a class which holds:

- *Main smart contract*: Address of the SC_{MG} in which the SC is registered.
- *Date*: Date of the trading day of the SC.
- *Coordinator*: Public key of the SC's Co.
- *User Identities*: Public keys of all U of SC's G. Those users are able to sell/buy electricity.
- *Operator Identities*: Public key of operators who can register new U into the SC.
- *Prices*: List of the price of electricity in each time slot.
- *Transactions*: List of all transactions made between U. Each transaction contains the amount sold/bought and its price.
- *Debts*: List of all debts from each U.
- *Time slot*: Number of the current time slot. -1 before the trading and 24 when it's over.
- *Trading flag*: Boolean which is "True" when the trading in the SC is available.

When the SC is deployed, the Co must provide the following arguments: i) *Date of the trading day*; ii) *Main smart contract address*. By default, *Trading flag* is set to "False", *Time slot* is set to -1.

Once the SC is deployed, the different actors can interact with it with the following methods:

- *newOperator()* method called by the Co which adds a new O public key which will be able to register U.
- *newUser()* method called by the O which adds a new U which will be able to sell/buy electricity.
- *beginTrading()* method called by the SC_{MG} which sets the *Trading flag* to "True" and also communicates all prices.
- *buyElectricity()* and *sellElectricity()* methods are called by U during the trading day once every time slot, only when *Trading flag* is set to "True". U communicates the consumed or produced electricity to be bought/sold to others U. Both the amount and the price of the time slot is stored in *Transactions*.
- *verifyTransaction()* method is called by Co when, at the end of each time slot, the Co verifies each U transaction.
- *calculateDebts()* method is called by the SC_{MG} once the trading day has ended. From all the registered transactions, it calculates the debt each U has.
- *payElectricity()* method called by each U which has a debt with the G. The SC distributes the funds to the corresponding sellers (SC_{MG} or other U).
- *changeTime()* method called by Co, it increases *Time slot* by 1. It also calculates the surplus energy or the needed energy that the G has had in the previous time slot and communicates it to the SC_{MG}.
- *getDebt()* method is called by any actor and, if it exists, it returns the debt that she has to pay.

3.3 Initialization

During the initialization stage some tasks must be performed by the Main Grid (MG), Operators (O), Coordinators (Co), and Users (U). These tasks for each entity are next detailed:

- The MG authority performs the following steps:
  1. Deploys the SC_{MG}, with the corresponding arguments explained in the previous section.
  2. Communicates the SC_{MG} address to the Co and MG_P.
  3. Registers MG_P to the SC_{MG} using *newProducer()*.
- The Co of each group performs the following steps:
  1. Deploys each SC, with the corresponding arguments explained in the previous section.
  2. Communicates each SC address to the SC_{MG} using *newSC()*.
  3. Registers O to the SC using *newOperator()*.
- Each O performs the following steps:
  1. Installs a sealed smart meter SM_k at U_k's domicile.
  2. Connects SM_k to U_k generation and consumption's electricity line in order for SM_k to read U_k's electricity usage information.
  3. Connects SM_k to Co_k in order for Co_k to validate SM_k information.
- Each U registers to the system by following the next steps:
  1. U is given a blockchain account and a private key and uses a Key Derivation Function to create n key pairs/addresses. The private keys are stored in a secure storage in which only U has access.
  2. U communicates every public key to the O, as well as their identification via a secure and private communication system.
  3. O registers U into each SC using the *newUser()* function and a group signature scheme.
  4. O communicates U information to Co in order for the Co to be able to identify the U.
  5. O sends U each SC address.

Users of the smart grid need to have a wallet address to interact with the smart grid It also serves as a form of identification and verification, allowing other users and smart contracts to confirm the user's identity.

The user registration process is a crucial aspect of any smart grid system, as it ensures that only authorized individuals are able to access and perform transactions within the network. In this particular smart grid system, the registration of users is managed by the operators through the use of smart contracts. These contracts provide a secure and reliable mechanism for verifying the identity of users and controlling their access to the network. During the registration process, users are required to provide certain information such as their name, contact information, and other relevant details. This information is then stored by the coordinator, and it's linked to the user's blockchain address in a private storage. Once a user is registered, the smart contract assigns them a unique identifier or address, which is used to track their transactions within the network. This address is also used to authorize their access to the network, ensuring that only authorized users are able to perform transactions.

3.4   Price Calculation

1. All available P send their offer to the SC_{MG} using *addOffer()*.
2. When the deadline comes, MG authority ends the bidding time using *begin-Auction()*.
3. SC_{MG} does the following:
   (a) In each time slot, it sorts the offers from the cheapest to the most expensive one.
   (b) Selects the n cheapest MG_P in each time slot so that the expected electricity consumption meets with the production.
   (c) The price in that time slot is the one from the most expensive MG_P offer from the n selected.

3.5   Energy Trading

1. The MG authority sends the method *beginTrading()* to the SC_{MG} when the trading day starts (Fig. 2).
2. When the SC_{MG} receives the order, it also sends the method to all the SC.
3. In order for a U/SM to communicate the consumption/production of energy in order to sell or buy it, they have to go through the following steps:

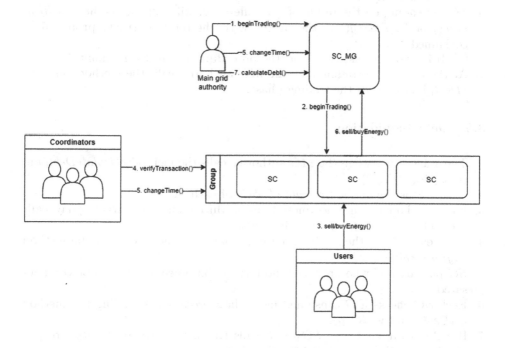

Fig. 2. Energy trading

(a) Every n amount of time, at least once in every time slot, SM checks if the electricity usage is positive or negative. Depending on the result, it will use the method $sellEnergy()$ or $buyEnergy()$, but the procedure is the same.

(b) The energy usage is divided into m transactions.

(c) From k SC the G possesses, m SC are selected to receive each, one of the m transactions.

(d) Each SC, when it receives the transaction, it adds it to the *Transactions* list with the current price of electricity. However, it's still marked as unverified.

4. Before the end of the time slot, Co must verify U's transactions in order for them to be traded successfully. To do so, it follows the next steps:

(a) During the time slot, it stores the energy usage information from each U of the G.

(b) It checks the *Transactions* list and for each transaction it's able to verify, it sends the method $verifyTransaction()$ with the transaction ID to the SC_{MG}.

(c) SC_{MG} marks the transaction as verified.

5. Co now communicates the end of the current time slot to the SC. MG authority does the same with the SC_{MG}. They both use the method $changeTime()$.

(a) SC calculate the difference between the total electricity produced and consumed by G.

6. SC depending on the result of the difference, will call the methods $sellEnergy()$ or $buyEnergy()$ in the SC_{MG} with the total electricity produced or consumed.

(a) If it's not the last time slot, the procedure returns to the point 3.

7. At the end of the trading day, the MG authority calls the method $calculateDebt()$ which ends the trading phase.

3.6   Debt Liquidation

1. The stage starts when the MG authority calls the method $calculateDebt()$ in the SC_{MG} (Fig. 3).

2. SC_{MG} calls the method $calculateDebt()$ of each SC.

3. Each U who has consumed more than produced during the trading day, calls the method $getDebt()$ from their G SCs.

4. Once each C has their debt, they must pay it to each SC with the method $payElectricity()$.

5. SC pays each U who produced more than consumed and has to be compensated.

6. Each SC checks if G consumed more than produced by calling the method $getDebt()$ in the SC_{MG}.

7. If SC owes funds to the SC_{MG}, it calls the method $payElectricity()$ to pay the MG for the extra electricity the G needed.

8. Finally, SC_{MG} pays every MG_P for the energy produced, ending the third and final stage.

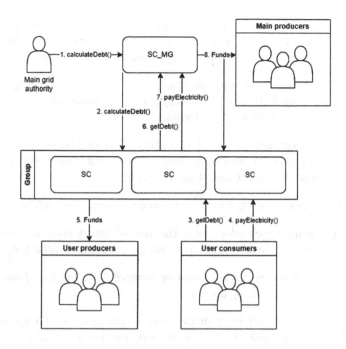

Fig. 3. Debt liquidation

4 Dealing with Security and Privacy Threats

This section studies the set of security and privacy claims that the new scheme fulfills.

Claim 1. *The system can detect unauthorized modifications or tampering of data.*

Proof. The immutability of transactions within a blockchain ensures the integrity and authenticity of each transaction, eliminating the possibility of double-spending. Given a secure and functioning blockchain, modifications or tampering of the ledger are not possible.

Claim 2. *Modified messages from producers and the smart grid layer are prevented from participating in the system.*

Proof. The system is secure due to the use of blockchain, which ensures that only legitimate transactions are allowed. This is due to the digital signature that each transaction possesses, if someone tried to modify a sent message to the smart contract, the signature would no longer be valid.

Claim 3. *The proposed system maintains high availability and is able to function without interruption.*

Proof. The proposed system provides high availability by leveraging the use of a blockchain with enough working nodes. The decentralized nature of the blockchain provides availability, providing constant and reliable access to data.

Claim 4. *The proposed system effectively restrict access to only authorized users preventing unauthorized individuals from performing protected actions and accessing protected resources and functions.*

Proof. The smart contract verifies the identity of users who sign every transaction. Then, it authorizes transactions only for registered users, maintaining the authorization requisites in the smart grid system.

Claim 5. *Users cannot deny having performed a particular action or Tx.*

Proof. The blockchain technology and the use of smart contracts ensure that transactions are traceable and tamper-proof, providing non-repudiation.

Claim 6. *Energy usage patterns cannot be derived from the Tx of the SC, even when having access to some of the Tx.*

Proof. Users are registered in multiple smart contracts in the group using a unique address in each one. In this way, only partial information about each user is available in each contract and those addresses cannot be linked by an external observer.

Claim 7. *The identity of a user and other personal information is not visible within the system.*

Proof. The link between each U's address and their true identity is only known by the Co which is assumed to be a TTP. Blockchain transactions do not uniquely identify users and they do not contain any personal information, only the partial energy usage. The link between the users and the operators that registered them is hidden behind the use of group signatures for operators. Operators use this method to generate a digital signature on behalf of the group of operators, hence, hiding the specific signing operator within the group and still validating the signature. Moreover, to further enhance user anonymity, users should periodically update their addresses.

Claim 8. *The proposed system uses coordinators to verify the messages sent by prosumers and to identify the misbehaving ones.*

Proof. Coordinators verify each prosumer's message to ensure that all transactions are free from any fraudulent activity such as double spending. Moreover, they can see all the transactions made by a certain U and evaluate whether they are fraudulent or not. Then, they can identify that U.

5   Conclusions and Future Work

This work has proposed a new energy trading system that serves as a bridge between the traditional grid and a smart grid, addressing the challenges associated with increasing demand, rising prices, and the limited availability of renewable energy sources.

The new scheme empowers users to both consume and produce electricity using distributed energy resources and it improves the current literature by taking into account the privacy of the users and the availability and security of the system; while still offering measures to identify and take punitive actions against misbehaving users.

As future work, we plan to implement this solution in lightweight devices (as real smart meters are assumed to be) and perform a deep study of its functionality, deployability (i.e., the economical and energetic cost of using smart contracts should be reasonable), and resiliency against security attacks.

Acknowledgments and Disclaimer. This research is supported by the project "HERMES" funded by INCIBE and the European Union NextGenerationEU/PRTR, by project PID2021-125962OB-C32 "SECURING/DATA" funded by MCIN/AEI/10.13039/501100011033/FEDER, UE, and by the grant 2021SGR 00115 from the Government of Catalonia.

References

1. Agung, A.A.G., Handayani, R.: Blockchain for smart grid. J. King Saud Univ. Comput. Inf. Sci. **34**(3), 666–675 (2022)
2. Aitzhan, N.Z., Svetinovic, D.: Security and privacy in decentralized energy trading through multi-signatures, blockchain and anonymous messaging streams. IEEE Trans. Dependable Secure Comput. **15**(5), 840–852 (2018)
3. Bhat, K., Sundarraj, V., Sinha, S., Kaul, A.: IEEE cyber security for the smart grid. IEEE Cyber Security for the Smart Grid, pp. 1–122 (2013)
4. Congress, U.: Energy independence and security act of 2007. Public Law **2**, 110–140 (2007)
5. de Vries, A.: Bitcoin's energy consumption is underestimated: a market dynamics approach. Energy Res. Soc. Sci. **70**, 101721 (2020)
6. Fang, X., Misra, S., Xue, G., Yang, D.: Smart grid - the new and improved power grid: a survey. IEEE Commun. Surv. Tutor. **14**(4), 944–980 (2012)
7. Guan, Z., et al.: Privacy-preserving and efficient aggregation based on blockchain for power grid communications in smart communities. IEEE Commun. Mag. **56**(7), 82–88 (2018)
8. Hoffacker, M.K., Hernandez, R.R.: Local energy: spatial proximity of energy providers to their power resources. Front. Sustain. **1** (2020)
9. Hou, J., Wang, H., Liu, P.: Applying the blockchain technology to promote the development of distributed photovoltaic in china. Int. J. Energy Res. **42**(6), 2050–2069 (2018)
10. Kang, J., Yu, R., Huang, X., Maharjan, S., Zhang, Y., Hossain, E.: Enabling localized peer-to-peer electricity trading among plug-in hybrid electric vehicles using consortium blockchains. IEEE Trans. Industr. Inf. **13**(6), 3154–3164 (2017)

11. Khalid, R., Javaid, N., Almogren, A., Javed, M.U., Javaid, S., Zuair, M.: A blockchain-based load balancing in decentralized hybrid p2p energy trading market in smart grid. IEEE Access **8**, 47047–47062 (2020)
12. Mengelkamp, E., Notheisen, B., Beer, C., Dauer, D., Weinhardt, C.: A blockchain-based smart grid: towards sustainable local energy markets. Comput. Sci.-Res. Dev. **33**, 207–214 (2018)
13. Mihaylov, M., Jurado, S., Avellana, N., Van Moffaert, K., de Abril, I.M., Nowé, A.: Nrgcoin: virtual currency for trading of renewable energy in smart grids. In: 11th International Conference on the European Energy Market (EEM14), pp. 1–6 (2014)
14. Mollah, M.B., et al.: Blockchain for future smart grid: a comprehensive survey. IEEE Internet Things J. **8**(1), 18–43 (2021)
15. Nakamoto, S.: Bitcoin whitepaper (2008). https://bitcoin.org/bitcoin.pdf-(: 17.07. 2019)
16. PETCU, I.: How are EU electricity prices formed and why have they soared? (2022). https://www.eurelectric.org/in-detail/electricity_prices_explained/
17. Reddy, K., Kumar, M., Mallick, T., Sharon, H., Lokeswaran, S.: A review of integration, control, communication and metering (ICCM) of renewable energy based smart grid. Renew. Sustain. Energy Rev. **38**, 180–192 (2014)
18. Samuel, O., Javaid, N.: A secure blockchain-based demurrage mechanism for energy trading in smart communities. Int. J. Energy Res. **45**(1), 297–315 (2021)
19. Samuel, O., Javaid, N.: Garlichain: a privacy preserving system for smart grid consumers using blockchain. Int. J. Energy Res. **46**(15), 21643–21659 (2022)
20. Stram, B.N.: Key challenges to expanding renewable energy. Energy Policy **96**, 728–734 (2016)
21. Zhuang, P., Zamir, T., Liang, H.: Blockchain for cybersecurity in smart grid: a comprehensive survey. IEEE Trans. Industr. Inf. **17**(1), 3–19 (2021)

EHRVault: A Secure, Patient-Centric, Privacy-Preserving and Blockchain-Based Platform for EHR Management

Marwa Chaieb$^{(\boxtimes)}$ (iD), Karam Bou-Chaaya, and Helmi Rais

Cybersecurity R&D Department, Expleo Group, Paris, France
{marwa.chaieb,karam.bou-chaaya,helmi.rais}@expleogroup.com

Abstract. The use of Electronic Health Records (EHRs) is becoming more common in the healthcare industry due to their potential to improve patient care and streamline medical workflows. However, EHRs are vulnerable to security breaches and data manipulation, which can have severe consequences for patient privacy and safety. Blockchain technology has shown promise in addressing the challenges of secure and trustworthy EHR management. In this paper, we propose a Blockchain-based platform for EHR management, considering the requirements and challenges of the healthcare industry. Called *EHRVault*, our platform incorporates various advanced security features. It is based on Hyperledger Fabric as a permissioned Blockchain and InterPlanetary File System (IPFS) as a distributed storage layer to ensure data availability, integrity, transparency, and auditability. Additionally, we use AES-256 to encrypt EHR and Crystal Kyber for exchanging encryption keys, making it resistant to quantum attacks. To ensure privacy, we also integrate an anonymization layer. EHRVault is patient-centric, interoperable, and compliant with various Protect Health Information (PHI) standards and regulations. Finally, we demonstrate that it is a trustworthy and secure platform that provides confidentiality, integrity, transparency, auditability, privacy, authentication, authorization, and availability.

Keywords: EHR management · Blockchain technology · Distributed Storage · Patient-centric · Health data privacy · Anonymization technique · Post-quantum cryptography · PHI standards and regulations

1 Introduction

The healthcare industry has been undergoing a significant transformation over the past few years due to the increasing use of Electronic Healthcare Records (EHRs) and other digital health technologies. This transformation has brought many benefits to the industry, including improved patient care, reduced costs, and enhanced data security. However, the rise of these technologies has also brought many challenges, including the vulnerability of EHRs to cyber attacks.

© The Author(s), under exclusive license to Springer Nature Switzerland AG 2024
A. Ait Wakrime et al. (Eds.): CRiSIS 2023, LNCS 14529, pp. 119–140, 2024.
https://doi.org/10.1007/978-3-031-61231-2_9

Recent attacks, such as the WannaCry[1] ransomware attack in 2017, the Trinity Health Data Breach in 2020[2] and the ransomware attack on the André-Mignot Hospital of the Versailles Hospital Center in 2022[3], have highlighted the significant risks posed by cyber attacks to healthcare organizations. These attacks not only compromise sensitive patient data but also disrupt healthcare services, causing significant financial and reputational damage to healthcare organizations. The adoption of EHRs has also raised concerns regarding data privacy, interoperability, and access control. Medical records contain highly sensitive patient data, including medical history, medications, and lab results. The unauthorized access or manipulation of this data can lead to serious consequences, including misdiagnosis, delayed treatment, and medical identity theft. One of the main issues with EHRs is the centralized storage and architecture of traditional systems. Centralized storage systems create a single point of failure, making the data vulnerable to cyber attacks. Moreover, traditional EHR systems are often siloed, making it difficult to share patient data between different healthcare providers and organizations.

Blockchain technology has emerged as a potential solution to address the challenges facing the healthcare industry. Blockchain can provide a decentralized, secure, and transparent platform for storing and sharing patient data. By using cryptography and distributed ledger technology, Blockchain can ensure the following properties: *(1) Security:* it provides a highly secure and tamper-resistant method of storing data. This ensures that patient data is protected from unauthorized access, tampering, or other malicious activities; *(2) Transparency and auditability:* it allows for a transparent and auditable system of data management. Each transaction in a Blockchain is recorded and can be traced back to its source, which makes it easier to verify the authenticity and integrity of the data. This also enables auditors to easily verify the transactions and keeps the healthcare institutions in compliance with Protected Health Information (PHI) regulations and standards; *(3) Access Control:* it allows patients to control their own data. Patients can grant access to their EHRs to specific individuals or organizations, and they can revoke that access at any time; *(4) Interoperability:* it facilitates interoperability between different EHR systems by creating a shared network of data that can be accessed and updated by different providers and organizations; *(5) Efficiency:* it helps streamline administrative processes related to EHRs, such as managing patient consent, tracking data access, and ensuring data accuracy. This can help reduce administrative costs and improve overall efficiency in healthcare systems.

However, the implementation of Blockchain-based platforms for EHR management requires compliance with standards and regulations to ensure the privacy and security of patient data. *The Health Insurance Portability and*

---

[1] https://www.cloudflare.com/learning/security/ransomware/wannacry-ransomware/.

[2] https://www.upguard.com/blog/biggest-data-breaches-in-healthcare.

[3] https://www.france24.com/en/france/20221205-french-hospital-suspends-operations-after-cyber-attacks.

Accountability Act (HIPAA)[4] *, General Data Protection Regulation (GDPR)*[5] *, California Consumer Privacy Act (CCPA)*[6] *, ISO/IEC 27001*[7] *, and Privacy by Design (PbD)* [8] are examples of regulations and standards that healthcare organizations must comply with to protect patient data.

In this paper, we discuss the potential of Blockchain technology to revolution-ize EHR management and explore the security requirements necessary for the successful implementation of Blockchain-based platforms in healthcare. Then, we propose a fully distributed platform for EHR management, based on Hyper-ledger Fabric Blockchain [1], InterPlanetary File System (IPFS) [3] and a set of cryptographic primitives. The proposed platform is secure, patient-centric and compliant with the different PHI standards and regulations. Our contributions can be summarized as follows:

1. We provide an overview of the following privacy standards and regulations of healthcare data: HIPAA, GDPR, CCPA, ISO/IEC 27001 and PbD. Then, we define a list of the specific security requirements commonly imposed by the presented regulations and standards on health data. The provided list is used to assess the security of our proposed platform, as well as the security of other existing systems.
2. We explore the literature to present a comparative performance evaluation of several permissioned Blockchain platforms, which are: Hyperledger Fabric [1], Ethereum [7], Parity [28], Quorum [9], Corda [6], Hyperledger Iroha [25] and Hyperledger Sawtooth [15]. Based on this study, we choose the most perfor-mant Blockchain to implement our proposed system.
3. We design a fully distributed system for EHR storing and sharing, based on Blockchain technology and a distributed storage layer. Called *EHRVault*, our proposed platform is patient-centric and ensures health data privacy, accuracy and interoperability. It improves health data auditability and is compliant with the different privacy standards and regulations.
4. We assess the security of our scheme against the list of security requirements, that we define, and prove that we ensure trust and security and preserve patient privacy.

The rest of the paper is organized as follows: in the next section, we study a set of existing Blockchain-based platforms for EHR management. In Sect. 3, we present the different technologies and cryptographic primitives used in our pro-tocol. Section 4 presents a detailed description of EHRVault platform. In Sect. 5, we discuss the security of our proposed platform as well as the different sys-tems presented in the related work section. Section 6 is a conclusion and a set of perspectives.

---

[4] https://www.hhs.gov/hipaa/for-professionals/privacy/laws-regulations/index.html.
[5] https://eur-lex.europa.eu/legal-content/EN/TXT/?uri=celex%3A32016R0679.
[6] https://leginfo.legislature.ca.gov/faces/billTextClient.xhtml?
    bill_id=201720180AB375.
[7] https://www.iso.org/standard/54534.html.

2   Related Work

In this section, we give an overview of some recently proposed Blockchain-based platforms for healthcare data management. We evaluate these systems against the list of security requirements, defined in Sect. 3. This evaluation is summarized in Table 2.

MedicalChain: [8,9] It is a commercial solution that has been proposed in 2018, by the company of the same name. It offers two main functionalities: telemedicine consultations and health data marketplace control. Founders claim to offer a user-focused EHR management. However, patients' medical records are stored in a centralized data store, limiting their control over their data. They also claim that MedicalChain is GDPR and HIPAA compliant, although details are not provided. Authors mention that health data is anonymized before being shared. Medicalchain utilizes a dual Blockchain system, with one managing authorization of access to health records, using Hyperledger Fabric, and the other serving as the foundation for integrated applications and services through an ERC20 token on Ethereum.

PharmaLedger: [10] It is a 3-year project supported by the Horizon 2020 program. It is a collaboration between 29 partners from the pharmaceutical industry, academia, and technology companies, and it focuses on several use cases, including supply chain management, clinical trials, and health data management. The platform is composed of separate Blockchain for each use case and organizes these Blockchains in a naming system Called Blockchain Domain Naming System (BDNS), provided by the Open Data Sharing Unit [26]. OpenDSU storage is a content addressable storage. It encrypts everything by default. In addition, it provides a concept called KeySSI to manage secret data sharing. The main drawback of this solution is the centralized data storage. In fact, it uses cloud-based storage, controlled by the healthcare actors (such as hospitals). Thus, the patient does not have a full control on his/her medical records.

Ancile [12]*:* It is a Blockchain-based platform for EHR management claimed to preserve health data privacy. However, authors do not include any anonymization technique in their platform. Ancile is not patient centric. In fact, healthcare providers' nodes are responsible for the maintenance of the Blockchain. In addition, data are stored in a centralized way, in the providers' data bases. Ancile uses a collection of six smart contracts to govern transactions and access to electronic medical records. Patients can monitor who has permission to access their private information and grant transfer permissions to other nodes. The platform uses a common data format to ensure interoperability between different healthcare providers. Authors did not specify the specific data standard used by

---

[8] https://medicalchain.com/en/.
[9] https://medicalchain.com/Medicalchain-Whitepaper-EN.pdf.
[10] https://pharmaledger.eu/.

Ancile, but it is likely that they would use one of the existing healthcare data standards, such as HL7 FHIR or openEHR.

MedChain [13]: It is based on Ancile [12] schema and uses the same smart contracts and cryptographic primitives. However, it introduces a new incentive mechanism and integrates it with the Proof of Authority consensus algorithm. The new incentive mechanism selects nodes with less degrees as block creators, while those with higher degrees act as voters responsible for validating new nodes. The block creator is rewarded with an incentive that is added to their degree, reducing the probability of them recreating the next block. To validate new nodes, voters ensure that the requested role is suitable and that the node is a legitimate health provider or third party.

MedRec [2]: Built on top of Ethereum, the system is designed to integrate with existing local data storage solutions used by healthcare providers. It provides a mapping mechanism that links a patient's existing identification to their Ethereum address. This is done through a Registrar Contract. The system also includes a Patient-Provider Relationship Contract that defines the access permissions and data pointers between two nodes in the system. A Summary Contract then maintains a list of references to all previous and current engagements between a patient and their healthcare providers. MedRec incentivizes medical stakeholders such as researchers and public health authorities to participate in the network as Blockchain miners. It provides two incentivization models: the Ethereum model that rewards miners with Ethers, and a new model that grants miners access to aggregate and anonymized data as rewards. Authors do not precise the standardized data code for EHR but they mention that they have designed the system with flexibility to support open standards for health data exchange (such as FHIR and other flavors of HL7).

MediBchain [19]: Based on a permissioned Blockchain as a data store, the platform keeps only encrypted data without being anonymized. The proposed system unfolds in the following steps: *(1)* after being registered, the patient authenticates him/herself by sending his/her ID and PWD to the Registration Unit; *(2)* After being successfully authenticated, *(3)* the patient locally encrypts his/her private health data, using Elliptic Curve Cryptography (ECC), and *(4)* sends it to the Blockchain via the Private Accessible Unit; *(5)* In return, the patient gets the transaction id (denoted U_{ID}), which is used to access his/her data. To request a patient's EHR, *(6)*the data receiver starts by performing the steps *(1) & (2)*. *(7)* Then, he interacts with the PAU by sending the U_{ID} to retrieve the corresponding health data. *(9)* Finally, the Private Accessible Unit gets the private data from the Blockchain and returns it to the data receiver. In this paper, authors did not specify the used Blockchain platform.

3   Preliminaries

In this section, we start by presenting different PHI standards and regulations and providing a summary of the specific security requirements commonly imposed by those regulations. Then, we present Blockchain technology and a set of permissioned Blockchain platforms and give a comparative performance evaluation of the studied Blockchains. Finally, we give an overview of the Inter-Planetary File System (IPFS) and data anonymization techniques as well as the set of cryptographic primitives used in our proposed system.

3.1 PHI Standards and Regulations

Due to its sensitive nature, medical data must be safeguarded and managed through stringent security measures that prevent unauthorized access, use, disclosure, or destruction. To ensure compliance, various standards and regulations have been established for protecting healthcare data: *(1) Health Insurance Portability and Accountability Act (HIPAA):* It is a US federal law enacted in 1996 that establishes national standards for protecting the privacy and security of personal health information. The law applies to all healthcare providers, plans, and clearinghouses that transmit PHI electronically. HIPAA includes several key provisions related to the privacy and security of PHI; *(2) General Data Protection Regulation (GDPR):* It is a european data protection law that applies to any organization, regardless of its location, that processes the personal data of EU residents. It establishes strict rules on how organizations must handle personal data, including how it is collected, processed, stored, and shared. Under the GDPR, individuals have the right to access, edit, erase and export their data. Organizations that process personal data must obtain explicit consent from individuals for each specific use of their data. They must also implement appropriate technical and organizational measures to protect personal data from unauthorized access, disclosure, alteration, or destruction; *(3) California Consumer Privacy Act (CCPA):* It is a California state law enacted in 2018 that provides California residents with certain rights over their personal information collected by businesses, including the right to know what personal information is being collected, the right to delete their personal information, the right to opt-out of the sale of their personal information to third parties and the non-discrimination; *(4) ISO/IEC 27001:* It is an international standard that outlines best practices for information security management systems (ISMS). It provides a systematic approach for managing sensitive information, such as health data, and ensures that appropriate security controls are in place to protect confidentiality, integrity, and availability of information. ISO/IEC 27001 outlines a set of requirements for establishing, implementing, maintaining, and continually improving an ISMS, including risk assessment and management, information security policies, access control, business continuity planning and Compliance with applicable legal, regulatory, and contractual requirements related to the protection of health data; *(5) Privacy by Design (PbD):* It is a concept that refers to the integration of privacy and data protection considerations into every stage of the development process, including the design, implementation, and operation of systems that process health data.

3.2 Security Requirements for Health Data Management

Using the presented standards and regulations as a guide, we have compiled a list of specific security requirements that are commonly applicable to health data. This list includes: *(1) Confidentiality:* Health data must be kept confidential and only accessed by authorized personnel with a need to know. This includes requirements for access controls, and data encryption. *(2) Integrity:* Health data must be protected from unauthorized alteration or destruction. *(3) Accuracy:* Health data must be accurate and complete, reflecting the most up-to-date information available. *(4) Privacy:* Health data must be protected from unauthorized disclosure. This includes measures such as data masking or de-identification to prevent the identification of individuals from the data. *(5) Authentication:* Access to health data must be authenticated ensuring that only authorized users can access it. *(6) Authorization:* Access to health data must be authorized based on the roles and responsibilities of personnel. This Includes the principle of least privilege, which limits access to only the necessary data for a given role. *(7) Availability:* Health data must be available to authorized personnel when needed. *(8) Auditability/Traceability:* Health data must be auditable to track access and changes to the data. *(9) Transparency:* Health data must be collected, used and shared in a transparent way. *(10) Patient-centric data management:* Health data must be managed by and under the control of patients. This includes the right to access their data, the right to rectification, erasure, and restrict processing. *(11) Interoperability:* Health data must be stored following a standardized data code. *(12) Explicit Consent:* Health data must be collected and processed with the consent of the individuals to whom it pertains. This requires informed consent procedures.

3.3 Blockchain Technology

Blockchain is a distributed ledger technology that provides a secure and transparent way to record transactions and store data. A Blockchain consists of a network of nodes that work together to maintain a shared database of transactions. Each transaction is verified and recorded by multiple nodes on the network, and once confirmed, it becomes a part of a block of transactions. Each block is then linked to the previous block, creating a chain of blocks, hence the term Blockchain. One of the main advantages of Blockchain technology is its decentralized nature. The distributed network of nodes eliminates the need for a central authority to validate transactions, making it more secure and resistant to tampering. Another advantage is its transparency, which allows all participants to view the transactions on the Blockchain, promoting accountability and trust. Blockchain technology offers several advantages for managing electronic health records, including security, privacy, efficiency, interoperability and auditability. For our proposed platform, we opt for a permissioned Blockchain. In such a Blockchain, access to the network is restricted to a limited number of authorized participants. This approach allows for greater control and privacy, as well as faster transaction processing times.

To evaluate the performance of permissioned Blockchains for EHR management, we conducted a comprehensive review of existing literature [14, 18, 21] and [29]) and analyzed factors such as throughput and latency for a set of permissioned Blockchain platforms, including Hyperledger Fabric [1], Ethereum [7], Parity [28], Quorum [9], Corda [6], Hyperledger Iroha [25] and Hyperledger Sawtooth [15].

Due to space limitation, we only present the summary of the comparative performance analysis of the cited Blockchain platforms in Table 1.

Based on this comparative study, we design our system using Hyperledger Fabric Blockchain, since the experimental observations show that this platform is performing better than the other private platforms due to its simple, efficient and modular architecture.

Table 1. Summary of Performance Evaluation; Where *Fbc: Fabric* and *Eth: Ethereum*.

Paper	Blockchain platforms	Latency	Throughput
[14]	Fbc v0.6, Eth v1.4.18 & Parity v1.6	Eth < Fbc < Parity	Fbc > Eth > Parity
[21]	Fbc v0.6 & Eth 1.5.8	Fbc < Eth	Fbc > Eth
[18]	Fbc, Eth, Quorum & Corda 4.3 & 4.5	Fbc < Corda < Quorum < Eth	Fbc > Corda > Quorum > Eth
[29]	Fbc v1.4.0, Iroha v1.0.0-rc5 & Sawtooth v1.0.5	Fabric < Iroha < Sawtooth	Fbc > Iroha > Sawtooth

3.4 IPFS

IPFS [3] is a protocol and network designed to create a decentralized and distributed system for storing and sharing files. Unlike traditional client-server file systems, IPFS is based on a peer-to-peer (P2P) network architecture that allows users to access files from multiple nodes in the network rather than from a centralized server. It uses a content-addressed system that assigns a unique cryptographic hash to each file, enabling efficient retrieval and verification of data. When a user uploads a file to the IPFS network, it is broken down into smaller chunks and stored across multiple nodes. When another user requests the file, its IPFS node retrieves the chunks from various nodes on the network and assembles them into the complete file. IPFS has a layered architecture. At the core, there is the Content-Addressed File System (CAFS), which stores content using a cryptographic hash of its contents as the unique identifier. On top of the CAFS, IPFS has several other layers, including the distributed hash table (DHT), the peer-to-peer (P2P) network layer, and the Merkle Directed Acyclic Graph (DAG) layer. The DHT is responsible for managing a distributed database of peers and content hashes. The P2P network layer provides connectivity between nodes in the network, allowing content to be shared and retrieved from other nodes. Finally, the DAG layer enables the creation of data structures that can represent complex data models, such as directories or file systems.

3.5   Anonymization Technique

The protection of health data is crucial due to its highly sensitive nature and the personal information it contains, which can be vulnerable to privacy breaches. Anonymization techniques are commonly employed to safeguard health data privacy, since they aim to sever the connection between the data and the individual it pertains to, while still maintaining the data's usefulness. To anonymize EHRs, our platform uses *Anonympy*[11], which is a general data anonymization library written in python for images, PDFs and tabular data. To anonymize images, Anonympy uses blurring technique. Image blurring is employed to obfuscate identifiable visual information, such as patient photographs or sensitive medical images, by applying blurring algorithms that reduce the level of detail while maintaining the overall context. This technique helps prevent the identification of individuals based on visual characteristics while ensuring the integrity of the underlying data. Additionally, the platform employs black boxes for PDF files, which involve placing opaque black boxes over sections of text or images containing sensitive information within PDF documents. These black boxes effectively conceal the sensitive content from unauthorized access or unintended exposure, allowing authorized users to view and work with the document while protecting patient privacy.

3.6   Cryptographic Primitives

To ensure health data confidentiality, EHRVault combines both symmetric and asymmetric encryption techniques. The symmetric encryption is used to encrypt the anonymized EHRs. For this, we use the Advanced Encryption Standard (AES) [10,11] with 256 bit key size. AES was developed and has been standardized by NIST as FIPS 197[12], and it is used in many applications, including data storage. The asymmetric encryption is used to share the secret key used to encrypt an EHR, when granting access to a new user. For this, we use Crystal Kyber cryptosystem [5], which is post-quantum and based on the hardness of the Learning With Errors (LWE) problem [22]. The rise of quantum computing poses a significant threat to traditional cryptographic systems such as RSA [23] and ECC [17]. These widely used encryption algorithms rely on the difficulty of certain mathematical problems such as integer factorization and discrete logarithm problem, which can be efficiently solved by quantum computers using Shor's algorithm [24]. Recognizing this vulnerability, NIST initiated a competition in 2016 to identify quantum-resistant cryptographic algorithms for future adoption. The NIST competition attracted numerous submissions from the global cryptographic community, including various lattice-based, code-based, multivariate, and hash-based schemes. NIST announced the winners in 2022, and among them was Crystal Kyber, a post-quantum secure key encapsulation mechanism (KEM). Crystal Kyber demonstrated post-quantum security properties, computational efficiency, and a solid mathematical foundation, making it

---

[11] https://pypi.org/project/anonympy/.

[12] https://nvlpubs.nist.gov/nistpubs/FIPS/NIST.FIPS.197.pdf.

a promising choice for securing sensitive data in the era of quantum computing. The cryptosystem unfolds in the following steps:

- **Key Generation:** Implemented in Algorithm 4. It returns a key pair (PK, SK).

Algorithm 4 $KyberKeyGen$

OUTPUT: (PK, SK)
1:    $R_q \leftarrow \mathbb{Z}_q/(X^n + 1)$
1:    $s \leftarrow$ random polynomial from R_q
2:    $A \leftarrow$ random matrix from R_q^{k*l}
3:    $e \leftarrow \chi$; with χ a noise distribution on R_q
4:    $t \leftarrow A * s + e$
5:    $PK \leftarrow (A, t)$
6:    $SK \leftarrow s$
4:    return(PK, SK)

- **Encryption:** Implemented in Algorithm 5. It takes as input the public key PK and the message to encrypt m and returns the ciphertext (u, v). We mention here that m is a bit (0 or 1).
- **Decryption:** Implemented in Algorithm 6. It takes as input the encrypted message (u, v) as well as the secret key SK and returns the plaintext m.

Algorithm 5 $KyberEncryption$

INPUT: PK, m
OUTPUT: (u, v)
1:    $r \leftarrow$ random polynomial from R_q
2:    $e \leftarrow \chi$; with χ a noise distribution on R_q
4:    $(u, v) \leftarrow r * PK + e + m$
5:    return(u, v)

Algorithm 6 $KyberDecryption$

INPUT: $SK, (u, v)$
OUTPUT: m
1:    $m + e \leftarrow v - u * SK$
2:    if ($(m + e) \in \,] - q/4, q/4[$)
3:        $m \leftarrow 0$
4:    else
5:        $m \leftarrow (q - 1)/2$
4:    return(m)

---

4   EHRVault Platform Description

EHRVault is a fully distributed platform for EHR storage and management. It has a modular architecture and designed to be secure and compliant with PHI standards. We assume that our platform is trusted and does not reveal sensitive information to unauthorized parties. In this section, we present the architecture of the proposed solution and detail its different functionalities.

4.1   Architecture

As illustrated by Fig. 1, EHRVault platform consists of the following five main layers:

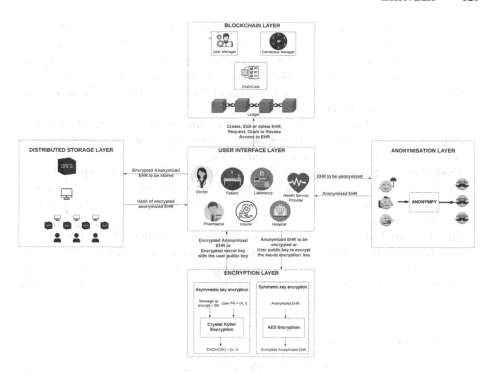

Fig. 1. EHRVault Platform Architecture.

- **User Interface Layer:** It provides a user-friendly interface for healthcare providers and patients to access and manage EHR data. The different interfaces allow healthcare providers to access patient data securely and empower patients to control and manage the access to their data.
- **Anonymization Layer:** It is responsible for anonymizing sensitive data in the EHR, which includes personal health information. This layer ensures that sensitive data is anonymized before being stored on the distributed storage layer, providing an additional layer of privacy protection. Our platform further enhances privacy by offering varying levels of anonymization, depending on the user's role and access requirements. Healthcare providers with direct patient care responsibilities may have access to partially anonymized data, where personally identifiable information is replaced with pseudonyms or unique identifiers. This allows healthcare providers to view and work with patient records while protecting their identities. In contrast, researchers and insurers accessing the platform are typically granted access to fully anonymized datasets, where identifying information is extensively blurred. Also, patients may not want to give access to parts of their records to clinicians, so they have the possibility to mask these parts.
- **Encryption Layer:** It is responsible for providing a secure mechanism to protect the confidentiality of the medical records stored in the system, by encrypting them using a combination of symmetric and asymmetric key

encryption. The symmetric encryption technique is used to encrypt the medical records themselves, using AES with a key length of 256 bits. For asymmetric encryption, we use the Crystal Kyber algorithm, which is a secure and efficient post-quantum encryption scheme. This algorithm is used to securely share the symmetric encryption key with authorized parties, such as doctors, health service providers and insurers.

The encryption layer constitutes a critical component of the EHRVault system, as it provides an additional layer of security to protect sensitive data from unauthorized access or malicious attacks.

- **Distributed Storage Layer:** It is based on IPFS and is responsible for storing the medical record data in a decentralized manner. This layer ensures that the medical data is available even if some of the nodes in the network are offline or compromised.
- **Blockchain Layer:** It is built on the top of Hyperledger Fabric Blockchain. It is responsible for recording all EHR transactions in a tamper-evident and immutable ledger. The network also includes a ChainCode layer that manage the execution of EHR-related transactions, which are: access control, consent management and data sharing.

4.2   System Functionalities

Figure 2 illustrates the different functionalities and access control mechanism provided by EHRVault platform, per actor.

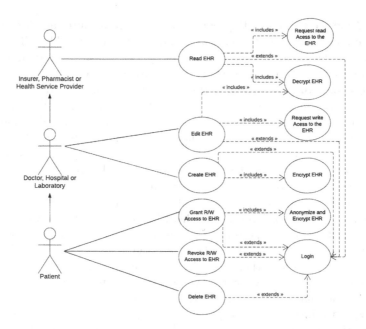

Fig. 2. EHRVault Platform Global Use Case UML Diagram.

Based on the privileges and access rights granted to each user, EHRVault classifies actors into three categories or levels:

- First user level: Represented by insurers, pharmacists and health service providers. Users of this level are only allowed to read EHRs. To do so, they need to initiate a transaction on our Blockchain asking for a read access. This also includes authentication and EHR decryption.
- Second user level: Represented by doctors, hospitals and laboratories. Users of this level have the same access rights of the precedent level as well as two other privileges. They have the possibility to create and edit EHRs. To create a new EHR, they need to encrypt it. To edit an existing EHR, they need to ask for a write access to the EHR and decrypt it.
- Third user level: Represented by patients. Patients have full control over their corresponding EHRs. They have the right to read, create and edit their medical data. In addition, they are responsible for granting or revoking access to the users. To grant read or write access to a user, the patient needs to anonymize a part of or the entire EHR, according to the user profile. They have also the possibility to delete their health data.

In the following, we give a detailed description of each functionality:

Create EHR. As illustrated by Fig. 3, to create an EHR, a user from level 2 or 3 proceeds as follows:

- He encrypts the EHR using AES cryptosystem, stores it in the IPFS and get the hash of the encrypted EHR,
- He encrypts the secret key SK used to encrypt the EHR, with the patient public key $PK_{patient}$ using Crystal Kyber cryptosystem. Then, he initiates a transaction to call the $createEHR$ function, pre-implemented in our Chain-Code (CC), and provides the following parameters: the hash of his encrypted EHR, the encrypted secret key, the corresponding patient ID, his own ID, the version of the EHR and a list, initially empty, to store the public keys of users who have the right to access this EHR with the corresponding access level (read or write). This list is updated when granting access to a new user or revoking access from a user.
- The CC verifies if the data owner has the right to create an EHR as well as the other parameters and decides to validate, or not, the transaction,
- If the transaction is validated by the CC, it passes through the consensus mechanism to be added to the ledger. Elsewhere, an error message is returned back to the data owner.

Read EHR. To read an EHR, stored on our EHRVault platform, a user proceeds as follows (See Fig. 4):

- He starts by initiating a transaction to call the $readEHR$ function and provides his public key as well as the id of the requested EHR,

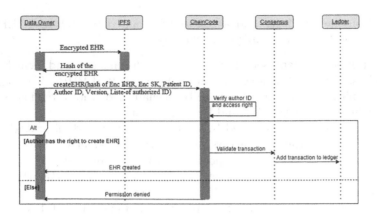

Fig. 3. Create EHR Sequence UML Diagram.

- The CC verifies the existence of the user public key in the list of authorized access to the given EHR,
- If it is the case, the CC sends the user public key to the corresponding patient and asks him for the decryption key of the encrypted and anonymized EHR,
- The patient encrypts the decryption key SK with the user public key PK_{user}, using Crystal Kyber encryption, and returns it back to the CC, which sends it back to the user,
- Then the transaction is validated and added to the ledger,
- The user decrypts SK using his private key, gets the encrypted anonymized EHR from IPFS and decrypts it with SK, using AES cryptosystem,
- If the user doesn't have the right to read the EHR, the CC asks the patient to grant the user a read access,
- If the patient accepts the request, he anonymizes the EHR according to the user profile, encrypts it, uploads it on the IPFS and replies with the encrypted SK as well as the hash of the encrypted and anonymized EHR. The CC updates the list of authorized access, transfers the patient answer to the user and adds the transaction to the ledger,
- Elsewhere, he declined the request.

Edit EHR. As illustrated by Fig. 5, to edit an EHR, a user (from 2nd or 3rd level) proceeds as follows:

- He starts by initiating a transaction to call the *editEHR* function and provides his public key as well as the id of the requested EHR,
- The CC verifies the existence of the user public key in the list of authorized write access to the given EHR,
- If it is the case, the CC sends the user public key to the corresponding patient and asks him for the secret key SK to decrypt the EHR,

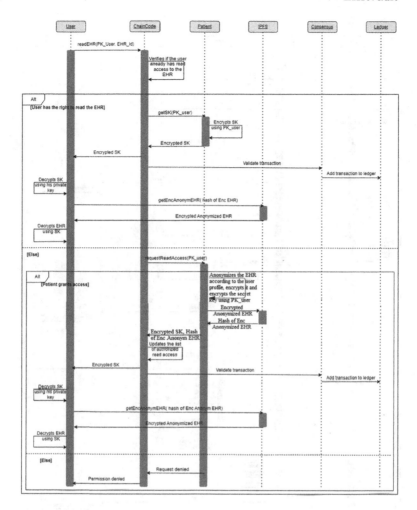

Fig. 4. Read EHR Sequence UML Diagram.

- The patient encrypts SK with the user public key, using Crystal Kyber encryption, and returns it back to the CC, which sends it back to the user. Then the transaction is validated and added to the ledger,
- The user decrypts SK using his private key. He gets the encrypted anonymized EHR from the IPFS. Then, he uses SK to decrypt it. He edits the EHR and generates a new secret key SK' to encrypt the new version of the EHR, using AES cryptosystem. He re-encrypts the anonymized EHR and saves it on IPFS. We encrypt each new version of an EHR with a different secret key to ensure a high level of security and to be immune to known-ciphertext attacks [4]. Finally, he encrypts the new secret key SK' with the corresponding patient public key, using Crystal Kyber cryptosystem, initiates a transaction to call the *updateEHR* function and provides the following

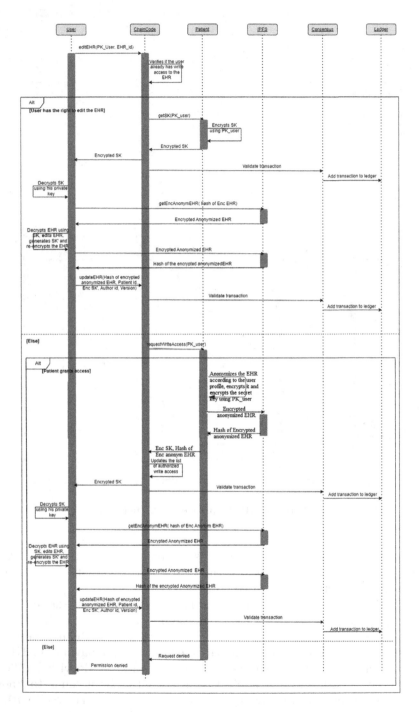

Fig. 5. Edit EHR Sequence UML Diagram.

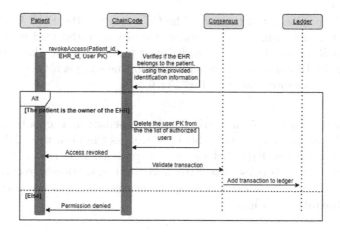

Fig. 6. Revoke Access Sequence UML Diagram.

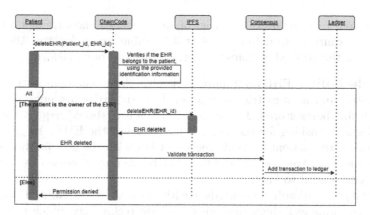

Fig. 7. Delete EHR Sequence UML Diagram.

parameters: hash of the new encrypted anonymized EHR, the corresponding patient id, the new encrypted secret key, his id as well as the version of the document,

- If the user doesn't have the right to edit the EHR, the CC asks the patient to grant the user a write access.
- If the patient accepts the request, he anonymizes the EHR according to the user profile, encrypts it, uploads it on the IPFS and replies with the encrypted SK as well as the hash of the encrypted anonymized EHR. The CC updates the list of authorized access, transfers the patient answer to the user and add the transaction to the ledger. The user executes the step 5,
- Elsewhere, the request is declined.

Revoke Access to EHR. To revoke access to his EHR from a given user, the patient calls the *revokeAcess* function and provides his id, the id of the EHR as well as the public key of the user. The CC verifies if the EHR belongs to the patient. If it is the case, the CC updates the list of authorized users to access the given EHR, by deleting the provided user public key and the transaction is recorded on the Blockchain. Elsewhere, an error message is returned back to the patient. These steps are illustrated by Fig. 6.

Delete EHR. To delete an EHR from our platform, the patient calls the *deleteEHR* function and provides his id as well as the id of the EHR to delete. The CC verifies if the EHR belongs to the patient. If it is the case, the CC interacts with IPFS to delete the EHR and the transaction is recorded on the Blockchain. Elsewhere, an error message is returned back to the patient. These steps are illustrated by Fig. 7.

5   Discussion

In this section, we evaluate the security of our proposed platform against the list of security requirements defined in Sect. 3.1. Table 2 recapitulates the security evaluation of the studied systems in Sect. 2 as well as our platform.

- **Confidentiality:** EHRVault ensures health data confidentiality by using symmetric and asymmetric encryption. Indeed, EHRs are encrypted, using AES, before being stored. To access an EHR, a user should request the patient permission by asking for the secret key to decrypt the EHR. To grant access to the user, the patient encrypts the secret key with the user public key, using Crystal Kyber. Thus, we ensure that EHRs are only accessed by authorized users with a need to know.
- **Integrity:** EHRVault safeguards health data in a distributed way, using IPFS, and manages them through Blokchain technology which is characterized by its immutability. Hence, we guarantee that EHRs are protected from unauthorized alteration or destruction.
- **Accuracy:** Our proposed platform gathers all the pieces of patients' data split across multiple facilities and offers to different healthcare providers a global and complete picture of patients' medical history, reflecting the most up-to-date information available.
- **Privacy:** To ensure health data privacy, EHRVault includes an anonymization layer that anonymizes a part of or the hole EHR, based on the patient directives. EHRs are processed through this layer before being encrypted and stored on IPFS, to protect them from unauthorized disclosure and prevent patient identification.
- **Authentication:** As mentioned in Fig. 2, all users of EHRVault should authenticate themselves before accessing the platform.
- **Authorization:** Using EHRVault system, access to health data is authorized based on the user level. As described in Sect. 4.2, we defined three user-levels with their corresponding privileges and roles.

- **Availability:** EHRVault is immune to cyber attacks that disrupt healthcare services thanks to its fully distributed architecture. In fact, there is no single point of failure since health data are stored and managed in a distributed way, using IPFS and Blockchain technology.
- **Auditability/Traceability:** EHRVault records all EHR-related operations in transactions on Hyperledger Fabric Blockchain, ensuring auditability and traceability.
- **Transparency:** This requirement is ensured thanks to the use of Blockchain technology. In fact, all EHR-related operations (access control, consent management and data sharing) are managed by the chaincode and stored in a transparent way on the Hyperledger Fabric Blockchain.
- **Patient-centric data management:** Our platform is designed to be patient-centric. It allows patients to access and control their EHR. Indeed, they manage access to their EHR by granting or revoking read or write access to users. They also have the possibility to modify or delete their EHRs.
- **Interoperability:** To ensure health data interoperability, EHRVault stores the medical records following Fast Healthcare Interoperability Resources (FHIR)[13] open standard for health data exchange.
- **Explicit Consent:** EHRVault platform ensures that all EHR-related operations are executed with the consent of the corresponding patient. The implemented chaincode interacts with the patient to get his consent when managing access control and data sharing.

Table 2. Evaluation of MedicalChain, PharmaLedger, Ancile, MedChain, MedRec, MediBchain and **EHRVault**; Where "✓" : provided, "X": not provided, "-": no available information, "Dist.": Distributed, "BC": Blockchain, "M. PoA": Modified version of Proof of Authority and "PoW": Proof of Work

	MedicalChain	PharmaLedger	Ancile	MedChain	MedRec	MediBchain	EHRVault
Confidentiality	✓	✓	✓	✓	✓	✓	✓
Integrity	X	X	X	X	X	✓	✓
Accuracy	✓	✓	✓	✓	✓	✓	✓
Privacy	✓	✓	X	X	✓	X	✓
Authentication	✓	✓	✓	✓	✓	✓	✓
Authorization	✓	✓	✓	✓	✓	✓	✓
Availability	X	X	X	X	X	✓	✓
Auditability	✓	✓	✓	✓	✓	✓	✓
Transparency	✓	✓	✓	✓	✓	✓	✓
Patient-centric	X	X	X	X	X	X	✓
Interoperability	✓	✓	✓	✓	✓	X	✓
Explicit Consent	✓	✓	✓	✓	✓	✓	✓
Dist. Storage	X	X	X	X	X	✓	✓
Permissioned BC	Hybrid	✓	✓	✓	X	✓	✓
BC Platform	Hyperledger Fbc Ethereum	Quorum	Ethereum	Ethereum	Ethereum	–	Hyperledger Fbc
Consensus	–	Istanbul	QuorumChain	M. PoA	PoW	–	Raft [20]

---

[13] https://www.hl7.org/fhir/.

6   Conclusion

In this paper, we proposed *EHRVault*, a Blockchain-based platform for EHR management. The system uses Hyperledger Fabric as a permissioned Blockchain for recording all EHR-related transactions and controlling data accessibility and sharing. It is also based on a distributed storage layer, using IPFS, to ensure data availability and integrity. Before being stored on IPFS, health data are anonymized and encrypting using AES-256. This ensures privacy and confidentiality. EHRVault also uses post-quantum cryptography to share the secret encryption key with authorized parties, which makes it immune to quantum attacks. The platform uses a standardized data code, which is FHIR, to ensure interoperability. We evaluated the security of our proposed solution and proved that is secure, trustworthy, patient-centric and compliant with the different PHI standards and regulations. The practical implementation of the platform as well as its performance evaluation are being worked on at the moment.

Future work will be dedicated to formally analyze the security of the proposed system and improve its performance by using cryptographic accumulator [27] to efficiently share the secret decryption key among authorized parties. We also plan to further enhance the functionality of EHRVault platform by adding an emergency case feature, using a threshold version of key escrow mechanism [16]. This feature would allow for the secure sharing of patient EHRs in situations where the patient is unconscious or unable to grant access to their records, which could potentially save lives by ensuring that critical health information is readily available to medical personnel.

References

1. Androulaki, E., et al.: Hyperledger fabric: a distributed operating system for permissioned blockchains. CoRR, abs/1801.10228 (2018)
2. Azaria, A., Ekblaw, A., Vieira, T., Lippman, A.: MEDREC: using blockchain for medical data access and permission management. In: Awan, I., Younas, M. (eds.) 2nd International Conference on Open and Big Data, OBD 2016, Vienna, Austria, August 22–24, 2016, pp. 25–30. IEEE Computer Society (2016)
3. Benet, J.: Ipfs - content addressed, versioned, p2p file system (2014). https://ipfs.io/ipfs/QmR7GSQM93Cx5eAg6a6yRzNde1FQv7uL6X1o4k7zrJa3LX/ipfs.draft3.pdf
4. Biryukov, A.: Chosen ciphertext attack. In: van Tilborg, H.C.A., Jajodia, S. (eds) Encyclopedia of Cryptography and Security, pp. 205–205. Springer, Boston (2011). https://doi.org/10.1007/978-1-4419-5906-5_556
5. Bos, J.W., et al.: CRYSTALS - kyber: a CCA-secure module-lattice-based KEM. In: 2018 IEEE European Symposium on Security and Privacy, EuroS&P 2018, London, United Kingdom, April 24–26, 2018, pp. 353–367. IEEE (2018)
6. Brown, R.G.: Corda: an introduction (2016). https://www.corda.net/whitepaper/
7. Buterin, V.: Ethereum: a next-generation smart contract and decentralized application platform (2014). https://ethereum.org/en/whitepaper/
8. Cavoukian, A.: Understanding how to implement privacy by design, one step at a time. IEEE Consumer Electron. Mag. **9**(2), 78–82 (2020)

9. JPMorgan Chase & Co.: Quorum: a permissioned blockchain platform for financial applications (2018). https://www.jpmorgan.com/global/Quorum

10. Daemen, J., Rijmen, V.: Rijndael for AES. In: The Third Advanced Encryption Standard Candidate Conference, April 13–14, 2000, New York, New York, USA, pp. 343–348. National Institute of Standards and Technology (2000)

11. Daemen, J., Rijmen, V.: The Design of Rijndael: AES - The Advanced Encryption Standard. Information Security and Cryptography, Springer (2002). https://doi.org/10.1007/978-3-662-04722-4

12. Dagher, G.G., Mohler, J., Milojkovic, M., Marella, P.B.: Ancile: privacy-preserving framework for access control and interoperability of electronic health records using blockchain technology. Sustain. Urban Areas **39**, 283–297 (2018)

13. Daraghmi, E.Y., Daraghmi, Y.-A., Yuan, S.-M.: MedChain: a design of blockchain-based system for medical records access and permissions management. IEEE Access **7**, 164595–164613 (2019)

14. Dinh, T.T.A., Wang, J., Chen, G., Liu, R., Ooi, B.C., Tan, K.: BLOCKBENCH: a framework for analyzing private blockchains. CoRR, abs/1703.04057 (2017)

15. Johnson, D.B., Behl, R., Vaughn, M., Wang, C., Meek, C., Gabriel, R.: Hyperledger sawtooth: a modular platform for building, deploying, and running distributed ledgers. Technical report, Hyperledger (2019)

16. Just, M.: Key escrow. In: van Tilborg, H.C.A., Jajodia, S. (eds.) Encyclopedia of Cryptography and Security, 2nd ed., pp. 681–682. Springer, Boston (2011). https://doi.org/10.1007/978-1-4419-5906-5_84

17. Koblitz, N.: Elliptic curve cryptosystems. Math. Comput. **48**(177), 203–209 (1987)

18. Monrat, A.A., Schelén, O., Andersson,K.: Performance evaluation of permissioned blockchain platforms. In: 2020 IEEE Asia-Pacific Conference on Computer Science and Data Engineering (CSDE), pp. 1–8 (2020)

19. Al Omar, A., Rahman, M.S., Basu, A., Kiyomoto, S.: MediBchain: a blockchain based privacy preserving platform for healthcare data. In: Wang, G., Atiquzzaman, M., Yan, Z., Choo, K.-K.R. (eds.) SpaCCS 2017. LNCS, vol. 10658, pp. 534–543. Springer, Cham (2017). https://doi.org/10.1007/978-3-319-72395-2_49

20. Ongaro, D., Ousterhout, J.K.: In search of an understandable consensus algorithm. In: Gibson, G., Zeldovich, N. (eds.) 2014 USENIX Annual Technical Conference, USENIX ATC '14, Philadelphia, PA, USA, June 19–20, 2014, pp. 305–319. USENIX Association (2014)

21. Pongnumkul, S., Siripanpornchana, C., Thajchayapong, S.: Performance analysis of private blockchain platforms in varying workloads. In: 26th International Conference on Computer Communication and Networks, ICCCN 2017, Vancouver, BC, Canada, 31 July–3 Aug. 2017, pp. 1–6. IEEE (2017)

22. Regev, O.: On lattices, learning with errors, random linear codes, and cryptography. J. ACM **56**(6), 34:1-34:40 (2009)

23. Rivest, R.L., Shamir, A., Adleman, L.M.: A method for obtaining digital signatures and public-key cryptosystems (reprint). Commun. ACM **26**(1), 96–99 (1983)

24. Shor, P.W.: Polynomial-time algorithms for prime factorization and discrete logarithms on a quantum computer. SIAM J. Comput. **26**(5), 1484–1509 (1997)

25. Takemiya, M., Sato, T.: Hyperledger iroha: a distributed ledger technology framework (2018). https://iroha.readthedocs.io/en/latest/

26. Ursache, C., Sammeth, M., Alboaie, S.: Opendsu: digital sovereignty in pharmaledger. CoRR, abs/2209.14879 (2022)

27. Vitto, G., Biryukov, A.: Dynamic universal accumulator with batch update over bilinear groups. In: Galbraith, S.D. (ed.) CT-RSA 2022. LNCS, vol. 13161, pp. 395–426. Springer, Cham (2022). https://doi.org/10.1007/978-3-030-95312-6_17

28. Wood, G.: Parity: The fast, secure, and modular blockchain. Technical report, Parity Technologies (2017)
29. Woznica, A., Kedziora, M.: Performance and scalability evaluation of a permissioned blockchain based on the hyperledger fabric, sawtooth and iroha. Comput. Sci. Inf. Syst. **19**(2), 659–678 (2022)

Distributed Transactive Energy Management in Microgrids Based on Blockchain

Leila Douiri[1,3](✉) [iD], Samir Ouchani[2] [iD], Sana Kordoghli[3] [iD], Fethi Zagrouba[3] [iD], and Karim Beddiar[1] [iD]

[1] CESI LINEACT, Nantes, France
douirileila.cand@gmail.com, kbeddiar@cesi.fr
[2] CESI Lineact, 13100 Aix-en-Provence, France
souchani@cesi.fr
[3] RLEST, 1003, 2050 Hammam Lif, Tunisia
sana.kordoghli@enstab.ucar.tn, fethi.zagrouba@isste.rnu.tn

Abstract. While the Internet of Energy (IoE) introduced advanced collaborative management methods through real-time monitoring and demand response programs, smart grids still grapple with challenges related to central governance, ineffective information aggregation, and privacy issues. These problems create significant hurdles in smart grid management, particularly with the high penetration of distributed energy resources (DERs). In this paper, we propose a Distributed Energy Trading Management (**DETM**) framework that combines a blockchain-based peer-to-peer (P2P) energy trading system and an optimal power allocation model, ensuring grid stability. **DETM** focuses on the optimal power flow (OPF) problem for the day-ahead scheduling of dispatchable generators and DERs, taking into account the physical grid constraints. Moreover, the distribution network model interfaces with a prototyped blockchain platform, built using Ethereum Blockchain, to match supply and demand orders via smart contracts and to record transactions. **DETM** enables secure, transparent, and decentralized energy trading, thus overcoming the challenges of central governance and privacy. The experimental results show that our **DETM** framework significantly improves the efficiency of energy management and trading while ensuring the stability and security of the grid. The integration of blockchain technology with the power allocation model effectively eliminates information bottlenecks and promotes higher integration of DERs, demonstrating the substantial potential of **DETM** for future smart grid management.

Keywords: Blockchain · Smart contracts · Smart Microgrids · Energy Trading Management · Distributed Energy Resources · Peer to Peer Trading

Supported by organization x.

A. Ait Wakrime et al. (Eds.): CRiSIS 2023, LNCS 14529, pp. 141–161, 2024.
https://doi.org/10.1007/978-3-031-61231-2_10

1 Introduction

Energy Trading Management (ETM) has evolved into an essential component of the power sector, seeking to balance the aggregated energy injections and withdrawals from various Distributed Energy Resources (DERs) with grid stability and reliability [1,2]. On the one hand, an Energy Trading (ET) system is defined as "a system of economic and control mechanisms that maintains a dynamic equilibrium of demand and supply across the entire electrical infrastructure, with value as a primary operational parameter." This concept, now adopted by the National Institute of Standards and Technology (NIST), was initially proposed in the Transactive Energy Framework by the US Department of Energy's Gridwise Architecture Council [3,4]. On the other hand, Energy Management (EM) is an all-encompassing term referring to the planning, organizing, controlling, and monitoring of the entire energy production, distribution, and consumption process. Predominantly, it is bifurcated into two categories: supplier-side energy management and demand-side energy management [5].

More specifically, the ETM framework serves a crucial role in microgrid (MG) development to facilitate reliable energy trading within a local energy community [3]. Indeed, MGs are envisaged as small-scale networks of distributed energy systems that can operate either in islanded mode or in synergy with the upstream electric grid during emergencies, contingent on the operational requirements [6]. This method of clustering not only benefits the local community of the microgrid by providing small-scale prosumers with equal opportunities to participate in energy markets, but it also enhances the overall smart grid operation by reducing transmission losses and operational costs while promoting sustainable energy utilization [6]. However, the hierarchical organizational trading structure necessitates manual processing by third-party auditors and central authorities (e.g., trading agencies, brokers, and banks) for registration and authentication checks. This process leads to inefficient information aggregation, substantial time complexity, and it complicates dynamic prosumer participation in trading activities.

Moreover, IoT nodes, such as smart meters, are installed within MGs to gather real-time energy data. This information is subsequently utilized by the MG control center for ETM. However, the integration of such technologies exposes the system to a myriad of cyber-physical threats. In the event of a data breach within the MG, the control center's decision-making process could be severely compromised. Therefore, data confidentiality and integrity are paramount in this existing data management system [7]. Confidentiality refers to the protection of data and user's personal information from unauthorized access, while data integrity ensures the accuracy and consistency of data over its lifecycle [8]. Additionally, centralized storage schemes increase the risk of a single-point failure, potentially disrupting the entire system [9,10]. In this context, the application of blockchain technology for ETM in MGs has garnered substantial interest [1,11,12]. This interest is fueled by blockchain's diverse features, including security, privacy, transparency, auditability, and decentralization. These can be detailed as follows:

- **Security and Privacy:** The blockchain network operates trustlessly but safely as nodes do not require a trusted intermediary for interaction and all records and transactions are digitally signed. Unlike traditional systems, blockchain does not necessitate blind trust in certain entities.
- **Transparency:** Nodes on the blockchain network can freely access data on the distributed ledger.
- **Auditability:** Blockchain nodes can verify the authenticity of block data, ensuring its immutability.
- **Decentralization:** The blockchain network is maintained by multiple decentralized nodes employing consensus mechanisms. This network can operate peer-to-peer, negating reliance on a centralized authority for authorization and operation.
- **Secure Script Deployment:** Smart contracts are immutable and can execute instructions autonomously based on predefined parameters, eliminating the need for human intervention or central authorization.

In light of these considerations, this paper proposes a Distributed Energy Trading Management (**DETM**) framework that combines peer-to-peer (P2P) energy trading system with an optimal power allocation model, leveraging blockchain technology. Experimental results demonstrate that our DETM system substantially enhances the efficiency of energy trading and management while ensuring grid stability and security. By effectively eliminating information bottlenecks and encouraging greater integration of distributed energy resources, **DETM** demonstrates significant potential for the future of smart grid management. The main contribution of this paper can be summarized as follows.

1. Developing a distributed transactive microgrid management framework, **DETM**, with three layers (physical layer, information layer, and economic layer).
2. Emulation of peer-to-peer transactive management operation within a 55-bus microgrid using blockchain technology and smart contracts.
3. Exploration of P2P trading effects on the Distribution Network through a comparative analysis with and without the **DETM**.

Table 1 presents the abbreviations and acronyms that will be used throughout this paper for seamless comprehension and ease of reference.

The remainder of this paper is organized as follows. First, we outline in Sect. 2 the addressed problem and motivations behind the introduction of blockchain technology to resolve it. Section 3 identifies previous contributions related to blockchain applications in energy trading and management. Sect. 4 provides a framework for testing the blockchain-based DETM in MGs and describes the ETM's setup. Section 4.1 describes the energy system structure, providing the distribution grid and DERs mathematical models, and also presents the formulation of the OPF problem. Section 4.2 details the blockchain implementation. Subseqyently, Sect. 5 outlines the implementation setup and discusses the numerical results obtained. Finally, Sect. 6 covers the conclusions and future work that can be seen as the next steps in this line of study.

Table 1. Table of Abbreviations.

Abbreviation	Full Form	Abbreviation	Full Form
ADMM	Alternating Direction Method of Multipliers	DERs	Distributed Energy Resources
DETM	Distributed Energy Trading Management	DR	Demand Response
DoS	Denial of Service	DN	Distribution Network
dApps	Decentralized Applications	ECC	Elliptic Curves Cryptography
ET	Energy Trading	EM	Energy Management
ETM	Energy Trading Management	EVM	Ethereum Virtual Machine
EV	Electric Vehicle	IoE	Internet of Energy
IoT	Internet of Things	ID	Identification
MITM	Man In the Middle	MAM	Masked Authentication Messaging
MG	Microgrid	NIST	National Institute of Standards and Technology
OPF	Optimal Power Flow	PBFT	Practical Byzantine Fault Tolerance
P2P	Peer to Peer	PV	Photovoltaic
RE	Renewable Energy	SPOF	Single Point Of Failure
VPP	Virtual Power Plant		

2   Background

As IoE generates a vibrant "grid edge" through bidirectional information between distributed energy nodes, the following section outlines how blockchain's inherited structure overlaps with the integration and management of these distributed nodes in an ever growing and complex electric grid.

2.1   Integration of DERs in Microgrids

The integration of DERs, such as wind turbines, solar panels, storage systems, and IoE devices, is transforming the traditional centralized energy system into a decentralized peer-to-peer (P2P) market. Here, participants can produce and distribute excess energy with other peers. This shift has given rise to 'prosumers', consumers that also produce energy and can act as either sellers or buyers based on their energy profile.

However, the system cannot support limitless energy injections from DERs without certain authorizations or potential modifications to the distribution grid. The large number of DERs connecting to the system may influence power flow, creating phase imbalances and voltage control issues. Traditional distribution networks are designed to accommodate gradually decreasing voltages, with power flowing unidirectionally from the substation to the consumer. Consumer-owned RE installations can increase local voltage by exporting electricity to the grid and/or other peer. This can jeopardize the grid's operational reliability at significant penetration levels. In our study, the microgrid acts as a distribution system operator, maintaining the low-voltage network and delivering power to the end-user as depicted in Fig. 1.

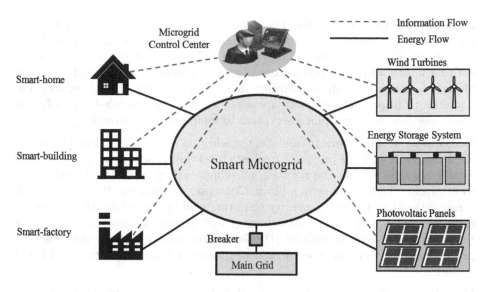

Fig. 1. Microgrid Management Framework.

2.2 Blockchain Structure

Primarily, a blockchain is a distributed computing and storage system [11]. Its operation relies on smart contract-driven infrastructure incorporating a cryptographic scheme, a consensus mechanism, and a distributed ledger (Fig. 2) [13]. It began as a peer-to-peer electronic currency trading system in 2009 with Bitcoin, eliminating the need for third-party intermediaries. The Bitcoin network facilitated reliable transactions through smart contracts among distributed nodes. Later, in 2014, the Ethereum platform developed blockchain-based applications [14]. Now, owing to its increasing success in finance, blockchain is employed in various sectors including healthcare, government services, and energy. The precise mechanisms and technical components may differ depending on the intended application environment however the key components are as follows:

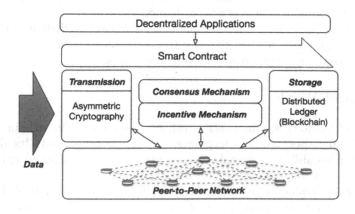

Fig. 2. Blockchain Working Mechanism.

Asymmetric Cryptography: Each node generates a unique pair of keys—a public key and a private key—related through mathematical algorithms. These keys are used for encryption and decryption of data. The public keys are shared with all nodes, while the private key is kept confidential by the node. Present blockchain solutions often use Elliptic Curves Cryptography (ECC) and have the potential to incorporate other technologies such as zero-knowledge proof, ring signatures, and homomorphic encryption to maintain data privacy.

Consensus Mechanism: It validates the addition of newly published blocks to the blockchain. In both public and private blockchains, a consensus mechanism establishes trust within the network, allowing a group of miners or validators to determine the legitimacy of a block. Consensus techniques often involve high computational costs due to security concerns, while private blockchains, with a restricted number of miners/validators, can offer simpler consensus techniques that improve network throughput [11]. Several techniques exist for the consensus process, such as Proof of Work, Practical Byzantine Fault Tolerance, and Proof of Stake.

Data Storage Scheme: In blockchain, data transactions are bundled into cryptographically linked blocks either at regular intervals or when a defined number of transactions is reached. Each block has two sections: the block header, vital for establishing the link with the previous block and validating data, and the block transactions, storing all relevant application data.

Smart Contracts: The implementation of a blockchain system is predicated on smart contracts that connect business logic to the blockchain's technical components. A smart contract is a set of programming instructions that are automatically executed by all nodes in a blockchain system. These contracts manage complex processes automatically based on pre-defined trigger conditions. Due to their transparency, parties can inspect the code and establish trust.

Network: The blockchain network is a peer-to-peer network. Each node in this network creates data locally and uses a protocol to share it with other nodes. Consequently, instead of relying on centralized databases, any node can access the same data. This approach can reduce the maintenance cost of a central node and the risk of a SPOF causing system failure.

In this context, bidirectional communication between DERs and the MG is enabled through blockchain technology to ensure secure, consistent and viable energy transactions in response to system conditions.

3   Related Work

In the era of Industry 4.0, innovative technologies such as Blockchain are being increasingly incorporated in energy trading and management. Its disruptive nature lies in its ability to decentralize, secure and democratize energy transactions.

This section explores existing literature on the application of blockchain technology in energy trading and secure data management, in order to understand the current landscape and identify areas where further research could bring substantial advancements.

3.1   Blockchain in Energy Trading

Blockchain technology has ushered in substantial reforms in the energy trading domain, where it has revolutionized transactional processes, making them more affordable by eliminating intermediaries, and more reliable and auditable through increased transparency. This novel approach has consequently rendered P2P energy trading mutually beneficial and highly efficient for both prosumers and operators.

In this context, Huang et al. [15] proposed a framework demonstrating the application of blockchains for multilateral energy trading, which facilitates fair payments without requiring a centralized aggregator or utility. Their work elucidated the roles of various stakeholders - consumers, producers, speculators, and regulators - in energy trading. Subsequently, they developed and discussed a structure for message and price clearing using smart contracts.

The adoption of smart contracts, as seen in [16], facilitated secure and automated bids and payment transactions between smart homes. Additionally, they outlined the rewards or penalties associated with trading in smart contracts, incentivizing peers who make the most significant contributions to the trade with virtual currency. Mengelkamp et al. [17] also employed a blockchain-based credit system that allows local energy purchases without immediate currency transactions. The credit-based scheme evaluates each node's request for credit tokens, overseen by supervisory nodes, and grants them if the requesting node meets the established criteria.

To enhance operational and supply-side management transparency, [18] introduced blockchain as a consensus mechanism between energy aggregators and DER owners. Thus, automated VPP controls and market settlements, dictated by pre-defined arrangements in smart contracts, were maintained on an immutable distributed data ledger, promoting more reliable DR management. Moreover, [19] developed a distributed method for power dispatching to foster trust between data aggregators and dispatchers using smart contracts. Given the processing power constraints of smart contracts, the dispatching procedure was divided across two smart contracts that cooperated for global adjustments.

Pop et al. [20] explored blockchain-based demand management in energy markets. Their self-enforcing smart contracts compute the expected energy flexibility at the prosumer level for each DR event and adjust it according to the prosumer's baseline energy profile. This method was found effective in fostering confidence among market participants and rectifying energy balance issues, leading to a 7% reduction in the aggregated energy demand profile of all prosumers during peak energy demand.

Lastly, Yang and Wang [16] presented an optimization method for transactive energy systems among smart homes using the ADMM and smart contracts. They distinguished two types of transactions - vertical and horizontal. Smart homes could sell PV energy to the grid and execute demand response events in vertical transactions. They could also exchange energy with peers through horizontal transactions. Their simulations and testing results indicated that blockchain-based transactive energy systems were feasible on practical IoT devices and could reduce total costs by approximately 25%.

3.2   Blockchain for Secure Data Exchange, Aggregation, and Privacy

The development of an adequate, privacy preserving, secure, and reliable data management and storage infrastructure is critical for the power sector [7]. The cryptographic schemes, consensus mechanisms, and inherent data immutability of blockchain technology enable secure communication between system control and physical grid infrastructure. This approach mitigates cyberattacks and data tampering, such as MITM or Denial of Service (DoS) attacks, thereby establishing a secure communication and data management platform [21].

Pradhan et al. [22] employed the MAM protocol. This approach enables energy producers and consumers to communicate data securely within smart grids, ensuring data confidentiality and accessibility. To ensure privacy preservation and reciprocal authentication in vehicle-to-grid trading, Aggarwal, Kumar, and Gope [23] suggested a lightweight cryptographic one-way hash function in order to provide identity privacy protection and mutual authentication between communicating parties. Yang and Wang [16] developed an IoT-based blockchain for smart homes for secure data aggregation, in which they revised the blockchain's structure by adopting a modified PBFT consensus mechanism incorporating a leader selection method. In this innovative approach, validators rotate in assuming the consensus leader role. This strategy eliminates the potential single-point failure inherent in traditional PBFT and ensures rapid transaction finality, which is vital for IoT applications that require quick transaction confirmation times. Furthermore, the resilience of PBFT in asynchronous networks makes it highly robust to message delays and network outages common in IoT networks. The leader collects confirmation messages from other validators and aggregates them into a single confirmation message.

To further enhance user privacy, [8] divided users into multiple groups, each with a dedicated blockchain for recording user data. They utilized a Bloom filter for rapid authentication to swiftly verify the authenticity of a user ID in the system. Users within each community maintain their privacy by adopting pseudonyms. Moreover, Moreover, Gai et al. [24] proposed a blockchain-edge computing method that protects participants' anonymity and resists malicious activity within communication routes and central data centers/clouds. Their blockchain structure includes two primary permissioned entities: super blockchain nodes and edge blockchain nodes. Super nodes, unlike typical nodes represented by edge devices, hold the authority to select specific devices from the edge devices to participate in the consensus and voting process. Prior to authorizing participation in the voting process, super nodes validate the identities of edge nodes using identity authorization and covert channel authorization techniques, thereby ensuring that the voting nodes are not malicious and are less likely to succumb to a 51% attack.

3.3   Learned Lessons

The literature review above illustrates that blockchain technology is compatible with secure and distributed management of either the energy supply side or demand side separately. However, the literature currently lacks a holistic blockchain-based energy trading management system that securely manages power injections and withdrawals within the physical grid's constraints, paving a new way for power market trades and coordinated operations. By formulating an OPF problem [25–27] that interfaces with a blockchain network, we can address various levels of energy trading challenges in a coordinated manner. This integration may fill the existing gap and bring a more nuanced understanding of the interplay between blockchain technology and power grid management.

4   A Distributed Energy Trading Management Framework

The aim of this contribution is to create an integrated transactive energy management system with solutions at the economic, information, and physical levels. To this end, we introduce a Distributed Energy Trading Management framework, called **DETM**, where:

1. The *Physical Layer* optimizes the flow of power in a realistic microgrid configuration with a variety of controlled DERs while taking into account pertinent electrical network constraints such as voltage levels, network branching, and power flow standards.
2. The *Information Layer* provides a high degree of security, privacy, and transparency through blockchain network.
3. The *Economic layer* maximizes social welfare of prosumers through trading and minimizes transmission losses from the upstream grid (*i.e* operational costs) where the highest social welfare is represented by the lowest operational costs and highest prosumer gains.

The coordination between the three layers of **DETM** is made possible through the framework shown in Fig. 3. The input data encompasses 'Prosumer data', which consists of the fixed load profiles for each market participant, in addition to photovoltaic generation profiles. The 'Distribution Network (DN) data' provides the convex OPF problem with the physical structure of the distribution network, including parameters like power line resistance, reactance, and topology. Data exchange between the distribution grid and the blockchain network is facilitated using web3.py Python library. Additionally, the interface is utilized for managing data input/output, as well as providing post-processing and visualization of the trading mechanism and optimal power flow outputs.

4.1   Energy System Structure

DETM is intended to operate on a microgrid network with prosumers having access to EVs, solar PV installations, and battery systems. The management

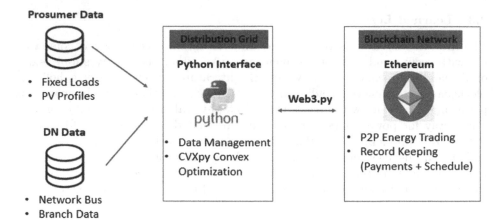

Prosumer Data

- Fixed Loads
- PV Profiles

DN Data

- Network Bus
- Branch Data

Fig. 3. Overview of the Distributed Energy Trading Framework.

system serves as a day-ahead energy scheduling, and each prosumer and MG generator are treated as a separate node on the network. Nodes may exchange surplus or deficit power with one another.

A set of nodes N and a set of edges ε (also known as distribution lines) linking these nodes constitute the distribution network, represented as a radial graph $G(N, \varepsilon)$. Node 0 is the root node (substation) and the remaining nodes in N are branch nodes. An edge in ε is denoted by the pair (i, j) of nodes it connects. We refer to j as the parent of i, represented by $\pi(i)$, and i as the child of j, represented by $\delta(j) = \{i : (i, j) \in \varepsilon\}$.

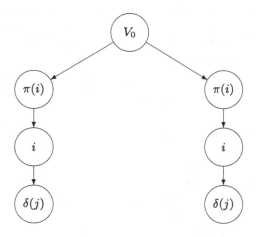

Fig. 4. Radial Distribution Network Graph.

Figure 4 shows an explicative graph of the radial configuration of the distribution network and its notations. Each line $(i, \pi(i))$ is characterized by a complex impedance $Z_i = R_i + iX_i$, a complex apparent power flow $S_i = P_i + iQ_i$, and a complex current I_i, flowing from node i to $\pi(i)$. Each node i is defined by a complex voltage V_i and net complex power injection $s_i = p_i + iq_i$. The complex voltage V_0 at the substation is assumed to be fixed. We denote l_i and v_i as the squared line current and squared nodal voltage respectively, where $l_i = |I_i|^2$ and $v_i = |V_i|^2$. The following branch flow equations represent a single-phase radial power flow in a distribution network.

$$q_i = Q_i - \sum_{k \in \delta(i)} Q_k + X_i l_i \quad \forall\, i = 0, .., n \tag{1}$$

$$p_i = P_i - \sum_{k \in \delta(i)} P_k + R_i l_i \quad \forall\, i = 0, .., n \tag{2}$$

$$l_i \geq \frac{P_i^2 + Q_i^2}{v_i} \quad \forall\, i = 1, .., n \tag{3}$$

$$v_i = v_{\pi(i)} + 2(R_i P_i + X_i Q_i) - (R_i^2 + X_i^2) l_i \quad \forall\, i = 1, .., n \tag{4}$$

Voltage magnitude restrictions on network nodes are considered through the Eq. 5 down below. The minimum and maximum voltage values at each energy node were set at 0.95 and 1.05 pu respectively.

$$v_{i,min} \leq v_i \leq v_{i,max} \tag{5}$$

Additionally, the various types of distributed energy resources are modeled over the microgrid network, as follows:

1. **Dispatchable Generators:** This study considers dispatchable generators that feature a quadratic cost function. Dispatchable production, denoted by $s_{i,t}^g = p_{i,t}^g + jq_{i,t}^g$, is assumed to have quadratic cost functions represented as

$$C_{i,t}(p_i^g(t)) = \alpha_{i,t}\, p_i^{g2}(t) + \beta_{i,t}\, p_i^g(t) + \gamma_{i,t} \tag{6}$$

where $\alpha_{i,t}$, $\beta_{i,t}$, and $\gamma_{i,t}$ are the given coefficients for the cost function of the i-th generator at time t.

2. **Solar Energy Generation:** The injection of renewable energy, specifically solar energy in this context, is considered deterministic and assumed to have no marginal cost, thus:

$$C_{i,t}(p_i^r(t)) = 0 \tag{7}$$

3. **Stationary Batteries:** Stationary batteries are represented as dispatchable loads with the capability to either withdraw or inject electricity. $p_{i,t}^b$ denotes the battery's output power. Here, a power withdrawal is signified by $p_{i,t}^b < 0$ while a power injection is indicated by $p_{i,t}^b > 0$. The operating model for the battery is defined as follows: we assume a charging efficiency of $\eta_{i,in}$ and a discharging efficiency of $\eta_{i,out}$. It is also assumed that the battery will not experience a net drain greater than its capacity throughout the dispatch time.

$$\forall\, t = 1, .., T$$

$$E_i^b(t) = E_i^b(t-1) + c_i^b(t)\,\Delta t\eta_{i,in} - d_i^b(t)\,\Delta t/\eta_{i,out} \tag{8}$$

$$p_i^b(t) = d_i^b(t) - c_i^b(t) \tag{9}$$

$$0 \le c_i^b(t) \le P_{i,charge}^b \tag{10}$$

$$0 \le d_i^b(t) \le P_{i,discharge}^b \tag{11}$$

$$E_{b,min} \le E_b(t) \le E_{b,max} \tag{12}$$

4. **Shapable Loads:** Shapable loads are described as having net energy demand $E_{i,demand}^s$ and charged between the time frames $t_{i,startby}$ and $t_{i,endby}$

$$p_i^s(t) = 0 \quad \forall t = 1, .., t_{i,startby} \tag{13}$$

$$p_i^s(t) \quad = \quad 0 \quad \forall t = t_{i,endby}, .., T \tag{14}$$

$$\sum_{t=1}^{T} p^s(t) \quad = \quad E_{i,demand}^s \tag{15}$$

$$P_{i,min}^s \le p^s(t) \le P_{i,max}^s \quad \forall t = 1, ..., T \tag{16}$$

Finally, the following is the formulation of the optimization problem:

$$min \sum_{t=1}^{T} \sum_{i=1}^{n} C_{i,t}(p_i^g(t)) \tag{17}$$

$$s.t \quad p_i(t) = p_i^g(t) + p_i^r(t) + p_i^b(t) - p_i^u(t) - p_i^s(t), \quad \forall i = 0, ..., n \tag{18}$$

$$s.t \quad (1) - (5) \quad and \quad (8) - (16) \tag{19}$$

4.2   Blockchain Energy System Structure

While optimally scheduling distributed energy resources offers a valuable solution to part of the smart grid management problem, it also introduces certain shortcomings, notably:

- The necessity for secure and privacy-preserving information exchange among energy systems.
- The inability of individual DERs to verify fair billing. Typically, a central utility handles payments and penalties for actual generation/consumption, which could lead to transparency issues.

In light of these challenges, we propose the integration of blockchain technology and smart contracts. With its decentralized, secure, and transparent features, a blockchain-based Distributed Energy Trading Model (**DETM**) provides a promising solution:

– It enables participants to securely exchange energy data through encrypted transactions and records while maintaining their anonymity.
– It ensures direct interaction between energy nodes without the need of central governance.
– It mitigates the risk of monopolistic manipulation by decentralizing the trading process.
– It records planned power dispatch and transactions in an immutable distributed ledger, which enhances transparency and accountability.
– It enables all authenticated nodes to check the legitimacy of the data.

In addition to these advantages, the implementation of smart contracts plays a crucial role by acting as a trusted virtual aggregator for market clearing. In this context, a private blockchain emerges as an ideal platform for implementing the DETM system for two reasons: First, to reduce cybersecurity risks with respect to malicious nodes. Thus, participation of nodes within the system should approved and authenticated by the grid operator. Second, When compared to permissionless blockchain systems, a private blockchain design achieves higher transaction throughput, lower latency, and much less computational burden.

Below, we provide more information about the key steps involved in leveraging blockchain in microgrids:

1. System Initialization: Each energy node becomes a validated entity after registration on the blockchain. An energy node i is characterized by an identification $(ID)_i$ and a pair of public $(PK)_i$ and private keys $(SK)_i$.
2. Market Initialization: The microgrid provides market participants with an economic incentive to trade energy locally and minimize operational costs by setting a threshold on the maximum trading price. In addition, parameters such as StartTimestamp, EndTimestamp, StartDeliveryTimestamp, and EndDeliveryTimestamp are defined to enforce constraints on trading resolution and energy delivery.
3. Role Assignment: Energy nodes, based on their current energy status and future energy demand, determine their roles, i.e., whether they will function as energy buyers or sellers.
4. Matching Offers and Requests: Energy requests and offers, which include the quantity of energy to be traded, price, StartDeliveryTimestamp, and EndDeliveryTimestamp, are submitted to the smart contract. This contract collects all energy offers and broadcasts them to local energy buyers. Subsequently, the smart contract matches energy supply and demand among energy nodes according to the highest bidder.

5 Implementation and Experimental Results

The purpose of this section is to detail the specific methodology employed in our study and to present the results derived from our experimental setup. **DETM** involves two distinct, yet interconnected phases: the implementation of our selected tools, and a focused case study on a 55-bus distribution network.

5.1   Tool's Implementation

The foundation of our implementation scheme, shown in Fig. 5, required a development environment specifically tailored for our Blockchain network. We utilized Truffle, a development tool, to simulate our energy trading scheme on a local Ethereum blockchain network. It is important to highlight that Truffle offers compatibility with all EVM.

We initially performed tests to ensure the reliability and security of our smart contract, which was programmed using Solidity. These tests were facilitated by Truffle's automated contract testing framework and were completed before transitioning to the global **DETM** system. Subsequently, the smart contract was seamlessly deployed throughout the network, taking advantage of Truffle's scriptable migration and deployment features.

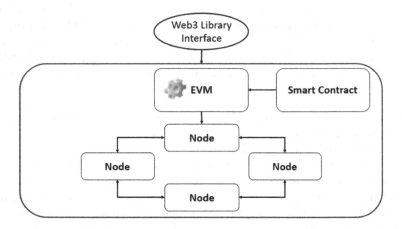

Fig. 5. The Implementation Overview of **DETM** Framework.

Following the development of our smart contract, we required a means to communicate with the blockchain network and other network nodes. This was accomplished through an Ethereum client, and in this experiment, we primarily interacted with the blockchain using a custom Python script in conjunction with the web3.py package. This package is a collection of libraries frequently utilized in dApps to assist with transaction processing, interaction with smart contracts, and reading block data, among other tasks.

Finally, we designed our convex OPF problem using CVXPY, a domain-specific language tailored for formulating optimization problems. Specifically, we modeled a convex optimization problem due to its favorable characteristics, such as global optimality guarantees and the availability of efficient solvers to tackle them [28]. Here are some of CVXPY's key features:

– It is an open-source package with an active community of contributors.

- It provides a variety of solvers, allowing users to select the best one for their problem. It works with common solvers like ECOS, SCS, CVXOPT, and many others.
- It seamlessly integrates with the larger Python ecosystem, making convex optimization easy to combine with other libraries and tools.
- It employs a set of rules and a verification mechanism under the Disciplined Convex Programming (DCP) concept to ensure that the optimization issue is convex. Additionally, DCP limits the model definition to a predefined library of convex base functions and thus confines the model to an adequate range of solution approaches and solvers. This method renders CVXPY package versatile and reliable.

5.2   Case Study on a 55 Bus Distribution Network

We simulate the performance of the **DETM** management system amongst 55 energy nodes (See Fig. 6) over 24 h, adopted from previous management studies on MGs [29–31]. Bus 0 (Substation) serves as the reference bus and is outfitted with higher capacity of dispatchable generator power than other nodes to replicate a utility grid link. Except for bus 0 (substation), each node has its own fixed and shapable load profile as well as stationary battery. While fixed loads are deterministic, shapable loads and batteries are optimally scheduled through the OPF problem. Additionally, shapeable loads are distributed at random on 70 % of the buses. These are supposed to be electric car loads. The time restrictions are established such that they can start self-scheduling as early as 9:00 and continue to consume power until 24:00. We also used a deterministic solar generating profile and randomly installed solar arrays on 60% of the buses.

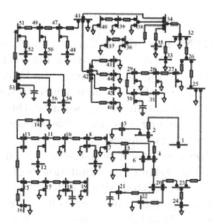

Fig. 6. Distribution network test case – A Layout of 55-bus sample microgrid test network–.

5.3   Results

A comparative study between the trading management system before and after the integration of our **DETM** solution was concluded in this phase of the experiment.

– **Without DETM:** Distribution network simulation is carried out at using the demand profiles (shapeable and fixed demands) with no PV generation and dispatchable generators outputs. Optimal power flow balance was also not included in this scenario
– **With DETM:** Distribution network simulation is carried out using the same input data, and applying the P2P energy trading and optimal power flow balance.

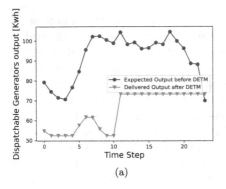
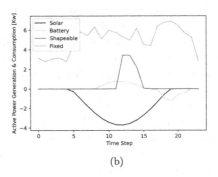

(a)   (b)

Fig. 7. Dispatchable Generators Output: (a) Expected VS Delivered Dispatchable Generators Output; (b) Energy Generation and Consumption Profiles.

After executing **DETM**, it is evident that our solution significantly reduces the dispatchable generators output as shown in Fig. 7a through P2P trading. Furthermore, it's evident from Fig. 7b that the optimal power solution effectively schedules shapable loads, such as EVs, in alignment with the availability of excess solar energy. Moreover, to maintain energy security, the battery charges when the net load is low and solar power is accessible, subsequently discharging its stored energy when consumption surges.

Additionally, no adverse effects of peer-to-peer trading on the distribution network were observed throughout the simulation period. Figure 8 shows the voltage profile for each node, plotted with a different color, at the distribution network. As evidenced in this figure minimal voltage fluctuations in the range of 0.3% were observed, as the minimum and maximum value did not surpass the upper and lower bounds specified in Sect. 4.1 (i.e. 1.05 pu and 0.95 pu).

As expected, voltages at the nodes rises in tandem with PV production from 5 a.m. to 18 p.m., with the maximum value at 15 p.m. matching to peak PV generation. Subsequently, the voltage decreases slightly, with the lowest values between 0 and 5 a.m. as a result of no PV generation at this time and all charging power being imported from the grid.

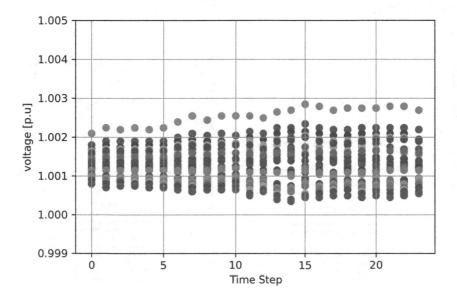

Fig. 8. Daily voltage profiles for all DN nodes.

Moreover, we depicted four samples of active and reactive power import/export captured at different network nodes in Fig. 9. Positive values reflect energy imports at node i, whereas negative values represent peer-to-peer energy tradings and/or energy exports from node to dispatchable generators level. As can be seen in Fig. 9, the imported power (active and reactive) at energy nodes is reduced with the integration of **DETM**.

In fact, in Fig. 9a, we can clearly see that in midday time intervals (between 10 am and 15 pm), the imported power of nodes 1 to 3 significantly drops to negative values up to -13 kwh after the implementation of **DETM**. This can be explained by nodes exporting active power to the grid and/or to other peers, i.e., it sells back the stored power to the grid to attain higher monetary benefits due to the availability of renewable PV generation.

Additionally, Fig. 9b depicts a reduction in reactive power fluctuations after deploying **DETM**. As shown in Fig. 7b, the suggested management system based on the combined energy storage system of the battery, shapeable load, and dispatchable generators were able to reduce reactive power fluctuations from variances ranging from 0.39 to 0.88 kvarh before the integration of **DETM** to variances ranging from 0.02 to 0.04 kvarh after.

In addition to reducing reactive and active power injections, the aggregated reactive and active power are shown to be effectively compensated in Fig. 10. As evidenced by the null orange plot in Fig. 10a and Fig. 10b, all DERs power injections (including dispatchable generators, loads, and RE generators) are balanced out to enable a reliable and balanced power flow in contrast to the expected power injections from the central grid (blue plot) before the integration of **DETM**.

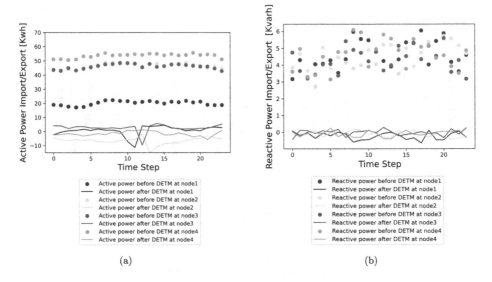

Fig. 9. Power Import/Export (a) Active Power Import/Export; (b) Reactive Power Import/Export.

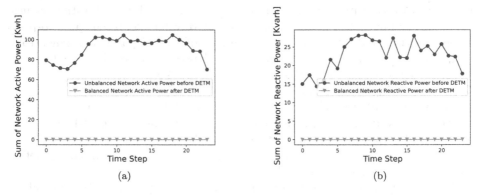

Fig. 10. Power Flow Balance (a) Balanced Network Active Power; (b) Balanced Network Reactive Power.

6   Conclusion

In this paper, we have proposed a Distributed Energy Trading Management (**DETM**) framework, employing blockchain technology to address the common challenges in smart grid management, such as centralized governance, ineffective information aggregation, and privacy issues. **DETM** is designed to tackle the optimal power flow problem, factoring in the scheduling of both dispatchable generators and distributed energy resources while adhering to physical grid limitations. Our Ethereum Blockchain prototype, backed by smart contracts, guarantees secure and transparent supply-demand matching and transaction recording. By doing so, **DETM** not only improves energy management efficiency and grid stability but also enables fair transactions without the necessity of a central authority or a centralized microgrid aggregator. The effective integration of blockchain technology with our power allocation model, corroborated through extensive experimental results, showcases promising prospects for the future of smart grid management.

For our future work, we will focus on the following targets:

- Analyzing workloads with a specific focus on power consumption related to different operations on blockchain platforms [32].
- Conducting comparative studies among various blockchain platforms, with a particular emphasis on energy consumption and its performance trade-offs.
- Shifting the focus from predominantly performance-based evaluations to a more balanced view that also includes energy consumption.
- Profiling the impacts of different workloads on energy consumption.
- Accurately quantifying the energy required for various operations on blockchain platforms like Ethereum and Hyperledger Fabric.

References

1. Miglani, A., et al.: Blockchain for Internet of Energy management: review, solutions, and challenges. Comput. Commun. **151**, 395–418 (2020)
2. Guerrero, J., et al.: Towards a transactive energy system for integration of distributed energy resources: home energy management, distributed optimal power flow, and peer-topeer energy trading. Renew. Sustain. Energy Rev. **132**, 110000 (2020)
3. Orsini, L., et al.: How the Brooklyn Microgrid and TransActive Grid are paving the way to next-gen energy markets. In: The Energy Internet, pp. 223–239. Elsevier (2019)
4. Martins, J.F., et al.: Transactive energy: power electronics challenges. IEEE Power Electron. Mag. **9**(1), 20–32 (2022)
5. Campagna, N., et al.: Energy management concepts for the evolution of smart grids". In: 2020 8th International Conference on Smart Grid (icSmartGrid), pp. 208–213. IEEE (2020)
6. Albarakati, A.J., et al.: Microgrid energy management and monitoring systems: a comprehensive review. Frontiers Energy Res. **10**, 1097858 (2022)

7. Shen, L., et al.: Blockchain-based power grid data asset management architecture. In: 2020 International Conference on Computer Science and Management Technology (ICCSMT), pp. 207–211. IEEE (2020)
8. Guan, Z., et al.: Privacy-preserving and efficient aggregation based on blockchain for power grid communications in smart communities. IEEE Commun. Mag. **56**(7), 82–88 (2018)
9. Wang, S., Zhang, Y., Zhang, Y.: A blockchain-based framework for data sharing with fine-grained access control in decentralized storage systems. IEEE Access **6**, 38437–38450 (2018)
10. Ouchani, S.: A security policy hardening framework for Socio-Cyber-Physical Systems. J. Syst. Arch. **119**, 102259 (2021)
11. Appasani, B., et al.: Blockchain-enabled smart grid applications: architecture, challenges, and solutions. Sustainability **14**(14), 8801 (2022)
12. Borkovcová, A., Černá, M., Sokolová, M.: Blockchain in the Energy Sector- Systematic Review. Sustainability **14**(22), 14793 (2022)
13. Nakamoto, S.: Bitcoin: a peer-to-peer electronic cash system. Decentralized Bus. Rev. 21260 (2008)
14. Wood, G., et al.: Ethereum: a secure decentralised generalised transaction ledger". In: Ethereum Project Yellow Paper **151**, 1–32 (2014)
15. Huang, D., et al.: A framework for decentralized energy trading based on blockchain technology. Appl. Sci. **12**(17), 8410 (2022)
16. Qing Yang and HaoWang: Privacy-preserving transactive energy management for IoT-aided smart homes via blockchain. IEEE Internet Things J. **8**(14), 11463–11475 (2021)
17. Mengelkamp, E., et al.: A blockchain-based smart grid: towards sustainable local energy markets. Comput. Sci.-Res. Dev. **33**(1), 207–214 (2018)
18. Mnatsakanyan, A., et al.: Blockchain-integrated virtual power plant demonstration. In: 2020 2nd International Conference on Smart Power & Internet Energy Systems (SPIES), pp. 172–175. IEEE (2020)
19. Luo, X., et al.: Blockchain based secure data aggregation and distributed power dispatching for microgrids. IEEE Trans. Smart Grid **12**(6), 5268–5279 (2021)
20. Pop, C., et al.: Blockchain based decentralized management of demand response programs in smart energy grids. Sensors **18**(1), 162 (2018)
21. Liu, C., et al.: A survey on blockchain-enabled smart grids: advances, applications and challenges. IET Smart Cities **3**(2), 56–78 (2021)
22. Pradhan, N.R., et al.: A blockchain based lightweight peer-to-peer energy trading framework for secured high throughput micro-transactions. Sci. Rep. **12**(1), 14523 (2022)
23. Aggarwal, S., Kumar, N., Gope, P.: An efficient blockchain-based authentication scheme for energy-trading in V2G networks. IEEE Trans. Ind. Inf. **17**(10), 6971–6980 (2020)
24. Gai, K., et al.: Permissioned blockchain and edge computing empowered privacy-preserving smart grid networks. IEEE Internet Things J. **6**(5), 7992–8004 (2019)
25. Bao, Z., Hu, Z., Mujeeb, A.: DC-based security constraints formulation: a perspective of primal-dual interior point method. arXiv preprint arXiv:2303.01810 (2023)
26. Liu, Z., et al.: Decentralized coordination between economic dispatch and demand response in multi-energy systems. arXiv preprint arXiv:2103.13680 (2021)
27. Strenge, L., et al.: A multiplex, multi-timescale model approach for economic and frequency control in power grids. Chaos Interdiscip. J. Nonlinear Sci. **30**(3) (2020)

28. Sepulveda, S., Garces, A., Mora-Flórez, J.: Sequential convex optimization for the dynamic optimal power flow of active distribution networks. IFACPapersOnLine **55**(9), 268–273 (2022)
29. Pourghasem, P., Seyedi, H., Zare, K.: A new optimal under-voltage load shedding scheme for voltage collapse prevention in a multi-microgrid system. Electric Power Syst. Res. **203**, 107629 (2022)
30. Chakraborty, S., Rana, M.T., Salapaka, M.V.: Active synchronization of islanded microgrid using droop-controlled grid-forming inverters. In: IECON 2022-48th Annual Conference of the IEEE Industrial Electronics Society, pp. 1–6. IEEE (2022)
31. Manousakis, N.M., Korres, G.N.: Application of state estimation in distribution systems with embedded microgrids. Energies **14**(23), 7933 (2021)
32. Dahmane, W.M., Ouchani, S., Bouarfa, H.: Guaranteeing information integrity and access control in smart cities through blockchain. J. Amb. Intell. Hum. Comput. **14**(9), 11419–11428 (2023)

Blockchain-Based Exchange Place: Genericity vs Performance

Salma Bradai[1]([✉]) [ID], Amal Gassara[2] [ID], Khaled Taouil[2,3] [ID], and Badii Louati[1]

[1] Orange Innovation Tunisia, Sofrecom Tunisia, Les Berges du lac 01,
1053 Tunis, Tunisia
salma.bradai@sofrecom.com
[2] Digital Research Center of Sfax, Technopole of Sfax, 3021 Sfax, Tunisia
[3] Laboratory of Signals, systeMs, aRtificial Intelligence and neTworkS,
3038 Sfax, Tunisia
khaled.taouil@enetcom.usf.tn
http://www.crns.rnrt.tn/

Abstract. The traditional exchange places have been overwhelmed by several challenges, including counterparty risk, and lack of consumer trust. Platforms based on blockchain technology have emerged to address these challenges by improving visibility and ensuring the execution of contracts. In this paper, we propose (ODEP), for Orange Decentralized Exchange Place. It allows to pool functionalities for sharing resources of different kinds while preserving the overall performance in terms of Transactions Per Second (TPS) and used gas. For that, we proposed an on-chain/off-chain approach consolidated with ODEPv2 and that consists of limiting the volume of data stored in blockchain. The comparison with ODEPv1, where all data are stored on blockchain, has demonstrated the effectiveness of our approach with an enhancement of 40% on used gas. Moreover, we propose the overall architecture to the simple adaptation of ODEP with different contexts.

Keywords: Blockchain · Generic · Data volume · Gas · TPS

1 Introduction

Today, digitization of society and the push to reduce the environmental impact of human activities have increased the need for exchanges and transactions on physical or digital goods. This is true at many levels: between companies, between individuals, within local ecosystems or much broader systems. The places of these exchanges have become dematerialized and have created digital marketplaces. These marketplaces are based on centralized solutions operated by a single player. This intermediary acts as a trusted third party for the concerned users, which can cause problems and makes it difficult to agree on a solution, especially in a situation of competition between players.

Supported by Orange Innovation and CRNS.

As the whole idea of blockchain relies on the decentralization of processing and storage, we rely on this technology to democratize our exchange place thanks to the collective control that generates confidence in the functioning and sincerity of transactions. Indeed, cryptographic techniques, consensus mechanisms and smart contracts allow to create trust among an untrusted network and they enable direct P2P transactions without any intermediaries. Smart contracts serve as programmed contractual agreement that could handle enforcement, management, or payment transactions whenever conditions are met. They have paved the way to the blockchain to be adapted in many fields beyond cryptocurrency such as healthcare, Internet of Things (IoT) and insurance services.

Several blockchain-based marketplaces have been developed for specific exchange use case such as the exchange of energy [1], IoT data [2], etc. However, being limited to one domain can only be a drawback in many areas because of the development cost, complexity, and implementation time of such solution. With respect to Orange ecosystem, three marketplaces are coexisting together 1) The exchange of connectivity resources between telecom players that aims to enhance user experience in terms of connectivity 2) The exchange of IoT data between the ecosystem actors (territories, building, etc) and 3) The exchange of energy surplus that is not self-consumed with the community. Therefore, the design of a generic marketplace is considered crucial to have the similar marketplace concept and make all business cooperating together. However, designing a generic marketplace that could be instantiated for any use case and that could trade any type of asset could be energy-intensive and pose a lot of question about the marketplace performance. In fact, smart contracts should encapsulate all the exchange process whatever the type of the exchanged asset is.

In this paper, we propose ODEP, a generic exchange marketplace functionality based on blockchain technology, while preserving a good performance in terms of number of transactions per second (TPS) as well as the used gas. Our aim is to generalize functionalities while preserving an acceptable overall performance. For that, we proposed an on-chain/off-chain approach to limit the volume of data stored in the blockchain and reduce execution time of the transaction. To demonstrate the efficiency of the design approach, we make a comparison with ODEPv1 [3], where all treatments are encapsulated as on-chain smart contracts.

The adaptation of ODEP to each use case is done by a simple input parameterization: definition of the actors, the exchanged assets, the use interfaces, etc. This generic exchange marketplace allows the exchange of material or immaterial assets, manages the sale or rental operations and allows the valuation of transactions through a given unit of account. To integrate such generic exchange place to any use case, we firstly separate what could be as common treatments as part of our exchange place. We define specific aspects as recommended module that should be undertaken by the dedicated business application. The key feature of our contribution is:

- The on-chain/off-chain approach that reduces the blockchain environmental impact and enhances the overall performance.

- The genericity of the tool that simplifies the adaptation to each context and reduces the associated development costs.
- The proposed architecture for the simple adaptation of ODEP in different domains.
- The comparison between ODEPv2, with adopted on-chain/off-chain approach, and ODEPv1 where we encapsulate all treatments as part of smart contracts functions.

The remainder of this paper is organized as follows: Sect. 2 introduces the blockchain based marketplaces. We present in Sect. 3 an overview of the ODEP architecture as well as the on-chain/off-chain approach and the configurable data model that paved the way to the genericity of the platform. To highlight the effectiveness of our approach, we present in Sect. 4 the implementation details and an evaluation of ODEP performance in terms of many metrics with a comparison of ODEPv2 vs ODEPv1.

2   Blockchain Based Marketplaces

2.1   Blockchain Background

According to Seebacher & Schüritz [4], "a Blockchain is a distributed database, which is shared among and agreed upon a peer-to-peer network." In fact, it is a technology that enables peer to peer transfer of digital assets without any intermediaries or central authority. Originally, it was a technology created to support the famous cryptocurrency, BitCoin [5]. Then, it has permeated a broad range of applications across many industries, including finance, healthcare, government, manufacturing, and distribution. Its increased interest comes from its auditing capabilities where trust and control are no longer centralized, but rather decentralized and transparent.

Blockchain Structure. Blockhain is a distributed database that stores time stamped transactions and everything of value across a Peer to Peer (P2P) network. Those transactions are secured through cryptography and locked in blocks that are cryptographically linked together forming the chain, so that any involved record cannot be altered retroactively, without the alteration of all subsequent blocks. In fact, each block gets a unique digital signature that corresponds to the hash of all elements in the block header it includes the Merkle Root (256-bit hash based on all of the transactions in the block). If any information inside the block changes, it will get a new signature. Since each block points to its previous one by indicating its hash, if a block is altered, all the succeeded blocks should be modified. As the chain of blocks is replicated among the network, this modification should concern also chains in all peers, making the alteration nearly impossible and creating therefore the trust among an untrusted network.

Blockhain Beyond Cryptocurrency. As it is decentralized and immutable record by design, blockchain makes it possible to transact in a decentralized manner. Transactions could be programmed and regulated in a smart contract, which is a piece of code that serves as programmed contractual agreement. A smart contract could handle enforcement, management, performance and payment transactions whenever conditions are met. For that, it can be used all across the chain from financial services to healthcare, Internet of Things (IoT) and insurance services. Especially, blockchain nowadays becomes strongly recommended to enhance different sector markets, sale and purchase operations and to solve security and transparency issues of traditional marketplaces.

2.2 Current Status of Blockchain-Based Marketplace Solutions

Blockchain based marketplaces use distributed shared ledger, a decentralized consensus mechanism, smart contracts and cryptographic security to enable P2P market platforms that directly connect consumers and producers without any intermediaries. Producers and consumers get an opportunity to sell and buy on a platform that offers a high level of trust even if they don't know each other. It lets them interact by their own rules with no restrictions imposed by third parties. Compared to traditional marketplaces, blockchain based ones are:

- Transparent: The decentralized hosting makes the marketplace always accessible. The immutable records enable to provide information to all market participants and to resolve conflict of interest.
- Flexible: Decentralized design allows removing intermediaries which eliminates the need to accept third-party terms and conditions and allows adopting more flexible terms.
- Secure: Cryptographic techniques, immutable ledger and verification of each single transaction protect customers from frauds and allow offering a secure environment.
- Cheap: Blockchain-based marketplace may offer low fees for transaction validation, or even charges no fees which is incomparable with the fees imposed by intermediaries.
- Competitive nature: Traditional marketplaces exclude a lot of people from global economy as they should have a bank account for payment. Blockchain-based marketplaces engage more people in the economy and then ensure that they got fair compensation. Moreover, smart contracts secure switching of suppliers that mobilize market with increasing competition, which ultimately reduces tariffs.

In literature, those marketplaces are almost all designed for a specific field, making their reuse for different domain an impossible task. Above all, energy exchange between householders has gained particular attention in the last years [1,6,8–10]. In fact, marketplaces were solicited as Renewable Energy Sources (RES) are intrinsically decentralized. These marketplaces depend on supply and demand profiles. They fluctuate according to consumer's preferences, environmental concerns and individual's energy practices. Automated billing for consumers and prosumers is ensured through smart metering and smart contracts.

Christidis et al. [11] are based on a double auction market implemented via a closed order book, with discrete market closing times and price-time precedence. For each time slot, a uniform market clearing is determined according to the lowest bid price that can still be served given the aggregated supply. An order is kept encrypted with public key that correspond to a participant private key for its decryption. However, the marketplace is designed only for the energy use case and its instantiation on different domains is not addressed. The authors in [7] simulate a Go ethereum network and evaluate it against the IEEE Std 1547.3, which provides a guideline for monitoring, information exchange, and control for distributed resources interconnected with electric power systems. However, unlike our work, where we provide real Quorum nodes, authors rely on a simulated blockchain environment and a very basic smart contract that needs face to face meetings to honor exchanges. They also seldom considered the deployed blockchain network architecture. Additionally, the energy exchange process relies on manual and face-to-face meetings, negating one of the key benefits of utilizing smart contracts, i.e automation.

Marketplaces have emerged also for agriculture products. Leduc et al. [12] build a blockchain-based farming marketplace based on three main blocks: The FarMarketchain and Farmarketplace blocks refer to the blockchain, associated smart contracts and also associated database to store long chains of characters. The FarMarketApp refers to the application that allows stakeholders to benefit from and assessing FarMarket services. The paper provides also a comprehensive understanding of blockchain and its interactions with infrastructure related parameters (e.g. implemented network architecture, number of nodes/users) in order to address the QoS requirements. For example, the three parameters: consensus difficulty, hardware and number of nodes inevitably influence the block generation frequency QoS parameter. Moreover, this work presents an in deep evaluation of different parameters such as throughput and latency. However, stakeholder's global satisfaction about finding adequate bids is not discussed.

Electronic blockchain-based marketplace is approached in [13] where some nodes need to perform some computation on other powerful computers. The market stakeholders are publishers. They are the entities who need someone to execute code for them in order to obtain the results of some computation. For that purpose, they publish a description of the task for a financial reward. Farmers are the entities offering computational infrastructure and are willing to complete the publishers. Auditors are a Trusted Third Party (TTP) that is involved in case a publisher suspects the farmer to have not done the computation properly. Different smart contracts are developed using solidity language to execute transactions under different scenarios starting from the standard one where the publisher and farmer behave correctly and up to scenarios with failed reservation. However, we thing that involving auditors as third parties is intrinsically opposite to the blockchain decentralized authority principle. Instead, smart contracts should be fed with external data provided by IoT objects or algorithms that detects computation correctness in this case of resource computation marketplace.

Regarding art marketplaces, to share multimedia content Banerjee and Ruj [14] are based on blockchain peers to maintain listing of all content and the hashes of the chunks held by different peers for each content. However, when dealing with multimedia content, it is the distribution of rights and remuneration in the digital content world that counts. For that, in 2021, the NFT market achieved significant growth and attention. They are widely used to resolve rights problems of digital contents such as art work, game, video or music. Non-fungible tokens (NFTs) are transferrable rights to digital assets. Each NFT has a unique identifier stored in blockchain with a unique value. In other word, a given NFT could not be substituted by another, contrary to bitcoin where 1BC could be substituted with another 1BC. In fact, NFTs serve not as a currency, a commodity or a technology but as an asset. As payment and trading option, NFT marketplaces such as OpenSea or Rarible furthermore use cryptocurrency, most commonly the Ether (ETH). However, the application of these NFT marketplaces is currently limited to digital fantasy artwork, games, intellectual property and patents due to its unique capabilities [15]. Although NFTs have had many applications so far and was associated with the lunch of many new projects, it rarely has been used to solve real-world problems.

Specific marketplaces were also designed for data marketplaces due to its extremely importance nowadays [16–18]. In fact, data becomes subject of multiple analyses to produce insights, such as people's preferences and habitudes for personalized advertisements. However, pushing enormous IoT data directly in blockchain-based marketplace is not feasible for the high amount of transactions and usability impact. For that Özyılmaz et al. [18] proposed an Ethereum-based smart contract that implements data marketplace and Swarm as a distributed data storage platform. Therefore, vendor address and information are registered in blockchain, but data is uploaded from Swarm.

From their hands, Elloumi et al. [16] present a possible architecture for IoT data marketplace. Metadata are presented as fundamental concept to present data. Those metada could be added through the "Data enricher", as an application of algorithms that resells new data sets. However, if we consider data as an asset, we though that it is important that data sellers and buyers share a common understanding of what the asset is about. Reaching this common understanding would only be possible with a standard or agreed asset data model and metadata model. Otherwise, even asset (data in this case) matching will be more and more complex. As extension to these digital assets exchange, blockchain-based physical asset transfer has emerged too. Although tracking physical asset exchange is still challenging, many authors have tackled this field. Kabi and Franqueira [19] developed two Solidity smart contracts hosted on the Ethereum public blockchain. The former concerns the marketplace agent while the latter concerns an escrow agent. The marketplace smart contract enables the logistics of a physical exchange starting from listing and browsing purchasing items until storing exchanging information between buyers and sellers. The escrow smart contract provides the business logic to reduce and mitigate risks for both sellers and buyers. While this work concerns physical assets, how the escrow smart contract is working and what happen if assets never arrives is not well addressed.

In this paper, we introduce ODEP (Orange Decentralized Exchange Protocol), which addresses all the existing limitations. The primary goal of ODEP is to establish a versatile framework that ensures optimal performance in terms of TPS (Transactions Per Second), gas usage, and block size, while enabling the implementation of a generic field.

3   ODEP

In this section, we present the ODEP architecture as well as the off-chain/on-chain approach that paved the way to maintain its performance inspite of its genericity.

3.1   Ecosystem and Architecture

An overview of the ODEP architecture and different stakeholders supporting the ODEP ecosystem is depicted in Fig. 1.

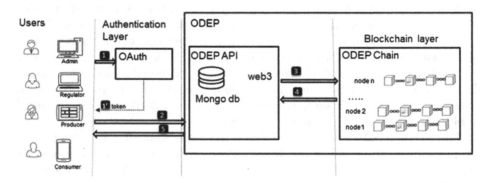

Fig. 1. Overview of the ODEP architecture and associated interactions with its ecosystem

Stakeholders could access the marketplace through a client application. For that, they should firstly authenticate and receive the access token that enables interactions with ODEP services (step 1). Those services are exposed as a Restful API and include all possible interactions with exchange place that are, basically, CRUD operations (step 2). Restful API sérvices call transactions in smart contract which is installed and instantiated in the blockchain (step 3). As an intrinsic characteristic of this technology, all peers will have the same copy of the generated blocks. The exchange place smart contracts provide the business logic which orchestrates the process of offering, requesting, buying of asset, delivery supervision and payment adjustment. It handles therefore, all functionalities needed for asset exchange between stakeholders by providing responses to the Restful layer and hence the client application (step 4 and 5). Indeed, it allows:

- The admin to:
  - Configure different asset types that could be exchanged.
  - Manage ODEP participants.
- The producer to declare what he has to offer as an asset and make it available for sale and notify all matched requesters.
- The consumer to declare what he needs as a request and receive all matched offers ranked per price.
- The regulator to establish a legal basis to regulate an asset, if it is subject of regulation, by attributing a 'regulateId' that mention that all legal aspects of the asset are verified.
- The prosumer (producer and/or consumer) to supervise the delivery. All payments are automatically settled according to the delivery state.

3.2   On-Chain/Off-Chain Approach

In our work in [3], we have encapsulated all treatments of the exchange process on smart contracts side. Having in mind performance optimization, we adopted in this paper an on-chain/off-chain approach to separate what must be processed as digitally executed smart contracts as on-chain modules from what must be processed as off-chain modules at the level of the REST API. We have coupled all services with a mongo db as shown in Fig. 1 so that we stored data that do not require a high level of security in this database. The configuration of the asset types, postulation of offers and requests will be processed as off-chain modules and their data will be stored on mongo database. However, we keep hashes registered with the blockchain to verify the integrity of the data, mainly with payment transactions. This is by comparing the hash stored in the Blockchain with the one calculated from data stored in mongo db. The matching algorithm between offers and requests is fed by mongo data and is performed in an off-chain module as detailed in Fig. 2. However, the management of users and their accounts, payment contracts and all payment transactions will be treated as on-chain module. Following from the on-chain/off-chain approach, designing a blockchain-based generic exchange place that could be instantiated for any use case needs identifying and processing of most relevant common transactions and treatments. A physical asset such as a cell has intrinsically different characteristics from a non-physical one such as energy. In literature, Notheisen et al. [20] have tried to design a generic smart contract inherited by different use cases and implement the specific aspect of the corresponding use case in each smart contract. However, this leads to further implementations and the generic aspect could gradually disappear. Moreover, this makes the marketplace integration a hard task as each specific aspect is treated separately in a specific smart contract.

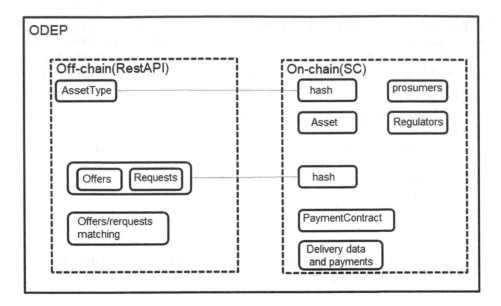

Fig. 2. On-chain/Off-chain approach

To keep the marketplace adaptable to different use cases, we provide a conceptual approach that allows the management of any kind of asset between participants based on a configurable data model. For each entity, we define two parts of attributes. The first is a generic part that is common to all use cases. Whereas the second is a configurable part and it allows to overcome all specificities behind use cases. This part is configured by the admin when defining the Asset Types. In fact, the 'AssetType' is a key feature to tailor the tool for a specific domain and to allow the simple adaptation of the marketplace to different use cases. It is used therefore to define the assets of specific use cases that will be manipulated in the marketplace. An 'AssetType' could be energy, gas, cell (for telecom infrastructure), smartphone, tv, etc.

The generic part of Asset Type attributes includes a name, a description and also the 'AssetType' nature. Intrinsically there is a big difference between the management of energy or gas as "immaterial" assets, and smartphones or tv as identifiable "material" objects. The asset type nature therefore is a baseline property that allows adapting the marketplace, thereafter, to the specificities behind a material or immaterial asset. As a matter of fact, when dealing with immaterial asset, the conditional attribute "unit" should also be indicated, for example KwH for energy or Liter for water. Following from our on-chain/off-chain approach, all of these generic fields will be stored in the blockchain.

The configurable part of AssetType attributes is presented through the 'AssetDataModel' that should include all specific attributes of a given use case. Consequently, this part is different from an 'AssetType' to another and specific to each use case. For each attribute, the admin has to specify its name, its type (string, numeric, list, geographicPoint), whether it is a mandatory attribute or not and whether it has a value list (List of predefined values for doing a choice among it). For example, with energy 'AssetType', we define location as a mandatory specific attribute of type 'geographicPoint' as shown in Table 1. Only a hash of these data is stored in the blockchain side in order to limit the volume of data stored in the blockchain. The real data will be hold by the mongo data base.

Table 1. Asset Type and Asset example in energy exchange use case

Admin: Creation of AssetType "Energy"	Prosumer: Creation of Asset of type "Energy"

Generic part of attributes:
name:energy
description:solar energy
nature:immaterialNotQuantified
unit:KwH
configurablePart
{
attributeName:location
type:geographicPoint
mandatory:true
hasValueList:false
valueList:
}
	Generic part of attributes:
	Id:0
	Name:energyAsset
	Description:Green energy
	assetType:energy
	ownerId:prosumer1
	transactionType:sell
	specificAttributes
	{
	attributeName:location
	value:<10.10>
	}

The 'Asset' represents the exchangeable object between prosumers and it is instantiated with reference to an existing 'AssetType'. With the immaterial asset, we distinguish between immaterial measurable and not measurable assets. In fact, a not measurable asset could be shared among multiple prosumers, such as shared pollution data of a sensor, or a service that could be commonly used. Whereas measurable one can only be used once and it can be 'notQuantified', when offered quantity is based on a future prediction and not on an already host quantity, such as in energy use case. By consistency with the 'AssetDataModel' defined in the 'AssetType', we define also a specific part of attributes instance of the 'AssetDataModel'. In other words, the attributes of the 'AssetDataModel' are displayed with respect to the selected asset type (in case of using an HMI for this) to be fulfilled by the prosumer.

Once created, as shown in the Fig. 3, the assets are subject to one or more offers, according to their asset type's nature. A material asset is subject of one transaction (one posted offer) as it is non-splitable by nature. An immaterial asset is subject of one or many transactions (many posted offers) as it could be split by nature.

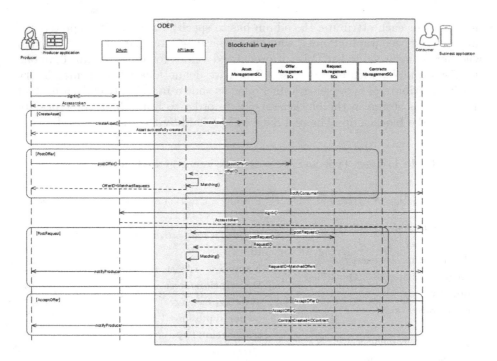

Fig. 3. Exchange protocol supporting ODEP ecosystem

The offerer, therefore, marks the asset as available for other prosumers to acquire. The 'beginTimeSlot' and 'endTimeSlot' indicate the possible delivery period. The offer is considered expired once reaching the 'validityEndTime'. Finally, the prosumer should indicate the offer price and the minimum deposit, as a percentage of the price that should be pre-paid. These offers should be matched against posted requests, using the asset specific attributes for this. Indeed, a Request enables the prosumer to express his desire to acquire assets by indicating either their types or even their offer ids. The maximum price that could be paid, as well as the maximum deposit are specified by the prosumer. The maximum deposit is indicated as the maximum percentage of the offer price accepted to be pre-paid. As depicted in Fig. 2, only a hash of the offer and the request will be stored in the blockhain.

Whenever the prosumer requests for an asset of a desired 'AssetType', it should express the desired specific attribute values while giving a comparison type for this as following:

- ==: search for an exact value, valid for all types of values.
- $>, \geq, <, \leq$: valid only for attributes with a numeric value type. (ex. searching for an apple with a diameter > 5).
- Contains: Valid only for attributes with a string type value. (ex. searching for any mark containing 'xx').

- In(circle), in(rectangle): Valid only with geographic point type value.(ex. Searching for an asset that is localized in a given circle defined by a center and a ray).
- Disj, conj: Valid only with list type value. (ex. Searching for a pollution sensor that measures PM2.5 or PM5, in case of a dis-junction)

Those comparison type will be used for our matching algorithm. In fact, the ability of a marketplace to facilitate multiple parties' trade is a key factor for its prosperity. The sooner a consumer converts a search to a purchase, the happier he will be. Therefore, the marketplace should reduce search costs and allow reaching buyer or seller located anywhere. To best succeed prosumer's experience, we are based on an off-chain matching within the Rest API. The output of the matching process is a list of offers ordered according the matching policy. This list is again ordered through AI-based ranking module according to user preferences (especially when two or more offers have the same price).

Whenever accepting an offer, a payment contract ('PaymentContract') is created as depicted in Fig. 2 and Fig. 3 that contains all necessary data to trigger the delivery (the 'beginTimeSlot'), to end the delivery (the agreed quantity, if the asset is subject of quantity or the 'endTimeSlot') and the agreed price. All of these data are stored in the blockhain as they need a high level of security.

The adopted configurable data model is a bit challenging when designing our smart contracts, as detailed in the next section.

4 Implementation

In this section, we depict details on network configuration and smart contract design.

4.1 Network Configuration

We rely on Raft consensus algorithm that is based on voting system. Each period, an elect node will play the role of the block maker and will be accountable on building the block and broadcast it to the network. The other nodes are called the voters and they are allowed only to vote on the added block. For diversifying architecture, we varied the number of deployed nodes until reaching 7 nodes. All deployments were performed on a VM on the Orange cloud (Flexible engine)[1], 16G RAM with Linux 18.04 as OS.

4.2 Smart Contracts Design

When designing a smart contract, we need to define the terms of agreement by all stakeholders. For that, we brainstormed with all projects leaders of the three use cases: Energy, Connectivity resources and IoT data exchange in order to define different functions as well as trigger events. As a consequence, we made

---

[1] http://90.84.244.69:10010/docs/#/.

an abstraction to define common behavior that could be encapsulated in same functions. Also we define execution conditions for each transaction as well as the expected consequences. As with Quorum platform, similar to Ethereum, each transaction is charged with an amount of gas, whose purpose is to limit the amount of work for its execution, when the EVM executes the transaction, this gas is progressively depleted according to specific rules. Having the gas limit problem in mind, we design smart contracts to manage each manipulated entity x: AssetType, Prosumer, Regulator, Assets, Offers, Requests, Contracts. Firstly, the xManagementSC verifies transaction execution terms, it includes sender and inputs. For example, if the producer tries to deliver the asset before the agreed delivery time, the transaction is reverted with a message: 'beginDeliveryTime is not yet reached'. In fact, verifying payment execution conditions on-chain, offers more security as no one can alter the smart contract code and change the conditions of execution. Indeed, when deployed, a smart contract has a contract address and any little change leads to another deployment and so another address with an initial storage state. Execution terms should be verified first to save computational power, and fees if we use a platform that pays miners, such Ethereum. Taking the example of having a transaction with ten different steps. If it gets through the first eight steps, but then reverted by the EVM because some conditions are not met, we revert back to the initial state before the eight steps were actually executed. In this case, we actually use the computing power of the network to go through step 1 to step 8, but unnecessarily. And, if we deal with Ethereum, there will be no refund, because we actually used computational power of the network.

When the pre-defined terms are met, the xMAnagementSC call the principal transaction to execute agreement per the implemented business logic. This could be an internal transaction (in the same SC) or an external one (accountable on the entity storage). As a consequence, the considered entity state will be updated. For example, if we deal with createAsset transaction in the AssetManagement SC, a new asset will be added to the state of the ledger and of course the transaction is stored in the ledger. Moreover, other consequences on other entities could be coexisted, so that the xManagement SC may call other external SCs to execute these consequences and change also their states. We tried to limit calls to external transaction as they are more expensive in terms of computational power.

So the smart contracts are developed with the Solidity language. We use Truffle[2] for their compilation and deployment on blockchain network. The compilation allows to generate a bytecode value (ABI) which is the machine language and the interface value of the generated smart contract. We use the Web3 models to interact with our smart contracts after defining the smart contract object.

---

[2] https://trufflesuite.com/.

5   Performance Evaluation

We followed the standardization of performance evaluation metrics for blockchains that has been proposed by the Hyperledger Performance and Scale Working Group (PSWG)[3] [21]. Throughput and latency are identified as characterizing metrics to assess the scalability of a blockchain system. We used Chainhammer[4] that allows to measure the number of transactions per second (TPS) by submitting a high load of transactions to an Ethereum based blockchain and produces diagrams of TPS, blocktime, gasUsed and gasLimit, and the blocksize. An overview of the experimental methodology is displayed in Fig. 4.

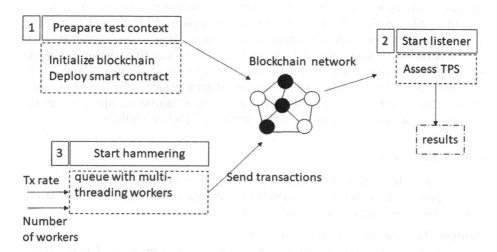

Fig. 4. Experimental methodology

Firstly, we initialize the blockchain by choosing the network topologies for the tests, typically starting with the smallest possible number of nodes. Then, we deployed our smart contracts. The second step is to activate listeners that will listens and provide all needed measurements. At the third step, we vary the number of transactions send rate as the more send rates adopted, the more precise the final insight on performances will be. We vary also the number of workers acting as clients sending transactions through threads. The Fig. 5 shows an example of a chainhammer output, with added columns for more explanation.

For each of evaluated metric, we diversify the transactions: 1) a simple transaction, which is the 'creditAccount' transaction, that allows to the admin to credit the prosumer balances in terms of AU and 2) a complex transaction, which is the 'updateAsset' transaction, that allows to update the state of a created asset. Its complexity comes from the needed terms verification before the

---

[3] https://www.hyperledger.org/blog/2018/03/19/measuring-blockchain-performance-with-hyperledger-caliper.

[4] https://gitlab.com/xshrim/chainhammer.

```
block 338 | new #TX  34 /  400 ms =  85.0 TPS_current | total: #TX  486 /  5.2 s =  93.4 TPS_average
block 346 | new #TX  36 /  400 ms =  90.0 TPS_current | total: #TX  522 /  5.6 s =  93.9 TPS_average
block 353 | new #TX  33 /  351 ms =  94.0 TPS_current | total: #TX  555 /  5.9 s =  94.0 TPS_average
block 360 | new #TX  34 /  349 ms =  97.5 TPS_current | total: #TX  589 /  6.3 s =  94.2 TPS_average
block 367 | new #TX  39 /  350 ms = 111.4 TPS_current | total: #TX  628 /  6.6 s =  95.3 TPS_average
block 374 | new #TX  36 /  350 ms = 102.7 TPS_current | total: #TX  664 /  6.9 s =  95.8 TPS_average
block 380 | new #TX  34 /  300 ms = 113.2 TPS_current | total: #TX  698 /  7.3 s =  96.1 TPS_average
block 387 | new #TX  47 /  350 ms = 134.2 TPS_current | total: #TX  745 /  7.6 s =  97.6 TPS_average
block 395 | new #TX  39 /  399 ms =  97.8 TPS_current | total: #TX  784 /  8.0 s =  98.4 TPS_average
block 401 | new #TX  32 /  300 ms = 106.7 TPS_current | total: #TX  816 /  8.3 s =  98.3 TPS_average
```

Block number	New transactions	blocksktime	TPS current =new TX / blockstime	Total number of transactions	Blocks time	TPS average =total TX / blockstime

Fig. 5. Chainhammer output

update, such as whether the asset is part of a payment contract in a current execution (It hasn't been finished yet). The comparison between the two platforms is undertaken with the 'updateAsset' transaction as its implementation is based on the limitation of data volume stored on the BC (the on-chain/off-chain approach), by storing only the hash of a specific attributes on blockchain side and the real information on the mongo database side. The 'creditAccount' transaction is not concerned with the data volume limitation approach as the balance is stored on the ledger whether with ODEPv1 or ODEPv2.

5.1 Throughput

Transaction throughput is defined as the number of transactions per second (TPS) processed by the blockchain network. We start firstly by the simple transaction, then we evaluate this metric on the complex transaction.

Simple Transaction: 'creditAccount'

As we can vary the number of workers as well as the number of transactions (input rate), we aimed to deduce the best configuration. So, we started with an input rate of 1000 transactions and while varying the number of workers, that are the triggered threads that send transactions. The max obtained TPS was 282 with 100 workers and the max average is 186 TPS with 40 workers. For this, we continue executing tests by increasing the input rate using a configuration of 100 workers. The Table 2 demonstrates that when sending 3000 transactions, the TPS is slightly enhanced. That in fact explains the block size capacity that stills not achieved so that more that we send transactions, more they are gathered in the block and so more the TPS is increased. For that, we decided to increase the number of transactions.

We increased the send rate until reaching 8000 transactions sent by 100 workers and we reached 300 TPS as the max and 227 as the average as shown in Fig. 6.

From those results, we can notice that the adopted consensus algorithm, Raft, provides fast block times (on the order of milliseconds instead of seconds), and fast block times generally means faster transactions. Quorum has tendency to create a new block immediately after a new transaction arrives, but it only creates one after if it's been at least 50 ms since the last block. This is to prevent floods with creating immense amount of blocks.

Table 2. TPS vs Workers

(a) 1000 transactions

workers	maxTPS	AvgTPS
4	112	93
8	134	96
15	177	130
40	255	**186**
100	**282**	184

(b) 3000 transactions

workers	maxTPS	AvgTPS
4	173	119
8	174	109
15	202	153
40	267	**218**
100	**285**	217

Simple vs Complex Transaction: 'updateAsset'

Firstly, we make comparison between the simple and the complex transaction on ODEPv1 to evaluate the impact of transaction complexity on TPS. As shown in Fig. 7, as expected, the TPS average and max TPS are decreased. However, we have noticed that values are starting very similar with 1000 transactions and seem to converge at 8000 transactions. We can deduce therefore that the more we increase transaction rate, the TPS converge vers a constant value.

ODEPv1 vs ODEPv2

In order to evaluate the performance of ODEPv2, we consider the complex transaction ('update asset') to run tests and compare the results with ODEPv1. With ODEPv1, all is treated on smart contract, whereas with ODEP v2, only the generic attributes and the hash of specific attributes are stored on blockchain.

As shown in Fig. 8, the average TPS on ODEPv2 is enhanced compared with ODEPv1. We can deduce therefore that the step of separation of what should be encapsulated at blockchain modules is a salient feature to ensure blockchain-based performance. Of course this distinction should not affect the security of

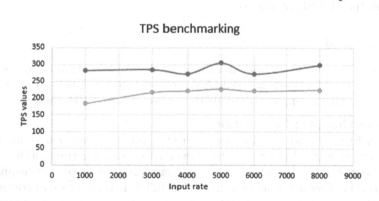

Fig. 6. Increasing transactions rate

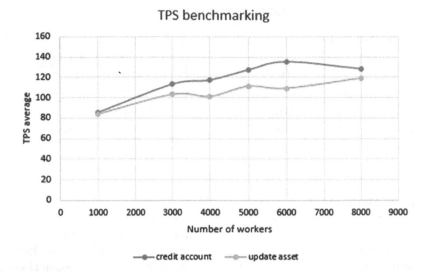

Fig. 7. simple vs complex transaction ODEP v1

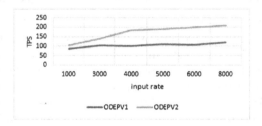

Fig. 8. TPS/complex transaction: ODEPv1 vs ODEPv2

the platform. Only data that doesn't need to a high level of security should be stored on the blockchain side.

5.2 Gas Used

To compare the gas used between a simple and a complex transaction, we measure the gas used for both the 'creditAccount' and the 'updateAsset' transaction on ODEPv1 with an input rate of 1000 transactions and 100 workers.

Simple vs Complex Transaction

A seen in Figs. 9a and 9b, gas used with the simple transaction is around 10^6 Gwei whereas it reaches around 10^7 Gwei with complex transaction. This is obvious as the more the EVM executes iterations the more it consumes gas. Therefore, the direction that we can keep in mind, is taking care of transactions complexity when developing smart contracts. For example, it is important to avoid keccack functions whenever it remains possible. Instead, the hash could be provided by the invoked code.

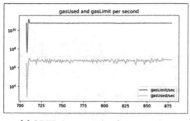

(a) ODEPv1: gas on simple transaction

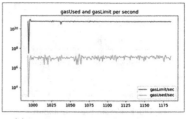

(b) ODEPv1: gas on complex transaction

Fig. 9. ODEPv1: gas used simple vs complex transactions

ODEPv1 vs ODEPv2

We also continue the comparison between the gas used on ODEPv1 and ODEPv2 using the complex transaction 'updateAsset', 1000 transactions and 100 workers (Fig. 10).

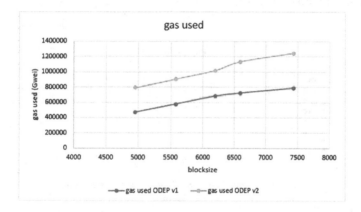

Fig. 10. gas used: ODEPv1 vs ODEPv2

As expected, the used gas is enhanced by 40%. In ODEPv2, the number of iterations is well decreased as we perform off-chain verification of attributes format, for example, and not on security related attributes such as the verification of asset existence.

5.3   Block Size

Simple vs Complex Transaction

The comparison between the two types of transaction is performed with 1000 transactions and 100 workers. With the simple transaction, we reached 172 blocks with an average block size of 1604 bytes with 6.6 tx/block. However, with the

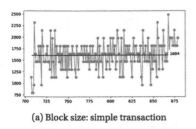

(a) Block size: simple transaction

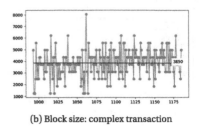

(b) Block size: complex transaction

Fig. 11. Block size: simple vs complex transaction

complex transaction we reached 192 blocks with an average blocksize of 3850 bytes with 5.8 tx/block (Fig. 11).

ODEPv1 vs ODEPv2

Following from other experiences, we made comparison between ODEPv1 and ODEPv2 in terms of block size. The reduced complexity in ODEPv2 enhanced the Block size by 30% (Fig. 12).

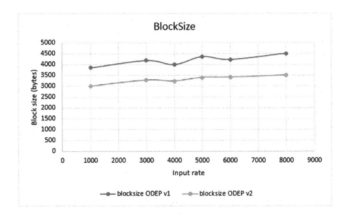

Fig. 12. Block size: ODEPv1 vs ODEPv2

6   Conclusions

In this paper, we addressed the question of research: how to generalize blockchain platforms functionalities while preserving the overall performance? For that, we proposed to limit the data volume stored on blockchain by proposing the on-chain/off-chain approach. We validate our proposal by firstly validating our hypothesis of the more we simplify transactions the more the different metrics will be enhanced. Then, comparison between ODEPv1 and ODEPv2 has demonstrated that the TPS, gas used, and blocks size are getting better values. In the future, we aim to diversify deployment architecture (number of VMs encapsulating nodes and number of nodes per VM) and measure the impact of deployment architecture on different metrics.

References

1. Esmat, A., De Vos, M., Ghiassi-Farrokhfal, Y., Palensky, P., Epema, D.H.J.: A novel decentralized platform for peer-to-peer energy trading market with blockchain technology. Appl. Energy **282**, 1–16 (2021)
2. Sober, M., Scaffino, G., Schulte, S., Schulte, Kanhere, S.S.: A blockchain-based IoT data marketplace. Cluster Comput. 1–23 (2022)
3. Bradai, S., Gassara, A, Ben Ali, A., Genestier, P, Giordani, M.: A generic blockchain-based exchange place. In: Conference on Blockchain Research & Applications for Innovative Networks and Services (BRAINS), Paris, France, pp. 40–44. https://doi.org/10.1109/BRAINS49436.2020.9223273
4. Seebacher, S., Schüritz, R.: Blockchain technology as an enabler of service systems: a structured literature review. Lecture Notes Bus. Inf. Process. **279**, 12–23 (2017)
5. Nakamoto, S.A.: Bitcoin: a peer-to-peer electronic cash system. Decentralized business review (2008)
6. Andoni, M., et al.: Blockchain technology in the energy sector: a systematic review of challenges and opportunities. Renew. Sustain. Energy Rev. **100**, 143–174 (2019)
7. Ilang-Ilang, M.C., Avila, J.M.: Evaluation of a Simulated Blockchain-based P2P Energy Trading System using an Isolated Rural Area Load Profile. Philip. e-J. Appl. Res. Dev. **13**, 10–20 (2023)
8. Mengelkamp, E., Notheisen, B., Beer, C.: A blockchain-based smart grid: towards sustainable local energy markets. Comput. Sci. Res. Dev. **33** (2018)
9. Pop, C., Antal, M., Cioara, T., Anghel, I., Sera, D., Salomie, I., Bertoncini, M.: Blockchain-Based Scalable and Tamper-Evident Solution for Registering Energy Data. Sensors **19** (2019)
10. Dong, Z., Luo, F., Liang, G.: Blockchain: a secure, decentralized, trusted cyber infrastructure solution for future energy systems. J. Mod. Power Syst. Clean Ener. **6** 958–967 (2018)
11. Christidis, K., Sikeridis, D., Wang, Y., Devetsikiotis, M.: A framework for designing and evaluating realistic blockchain-based local energy markets. Appl. Energy **281** (2021)
12. Leduc, G., Kubler, S., Georges, J.P.: Innovative blockchain-based farming marketplace and smart contract performance evaluation. J. Clean. Prod. **306** (2021)
13. Nardini, M., Helmer, S., El Ioini, N., Pahl, C.: A blockchain-based decentralized electronic marketplace for computing resources. SN Comput. Sci. **251** (2020)
14. Banerjee, P., Ruj, S.: Blockchain Enabled Data Marketplace - Design and Challenges; key technologies and challenges. arXiv e-prints (2019)
15. Bamakan, S.M.H., Nezhadsistani, N., Bodaghi, O., Qu, Q., Epema, D.H.J.: Patents and intellectual property assets as non-fungible tokens; key technologies and challenges. Sci. Rep. **12**(2178) (2022)
16. Alliance for IoT and Edge Computing Innovation, https://aioti.eu/white-paper-market-drivers-and-high-level-architecture-for-iot-enabled-data-market-places/. Last accessed 18 Jul 2023
17. Park, J.S., Youn, T.Y, Kim, H.B, Rhee, K.H., Shin, S.U.: Smart contract-based review system for an IoT DataMarketplace. Sensors **18** (2018)

18. Özyilmaz, K.R., Doğan, M., Yurdakul, A.: IDMoB: IoT data marketplace on blockchain. In: Crypto Valley Conference on Blockchain Technology (CVCBT), Zug, Switzerland, pp. 11–19. IEEE Computer Society (2018)
19. Kabi, O.R., Franqueira, V.N.L.: Blockchain-based distributed marketplace. Bus. Inf. Syst. Workshops **339**, 197–210 (2019)
20. Notheisen, B., Cholewa, J.B., Shanmugam, A.P.: Trading real-world assets on blockchain. Bus. Inf. Syst. Eng. **59**, 425–440 (2017)
21. Nasir, Q., Qasse, I.A., Abu Talib, M., Bou Nassif, A.: Performance analysis of hyperledger fabric platforms. Secur. Commun. Networks **59**, 425–440 (2017)

Security Approaches and Infrastructure

A Privacy-Preserving Infrastructure to Monitor Encrypted DNS Logs

Adam Oumar Abdel-Rahman[✉], Olivier Levillain, and Eric Totel

SAMOVAR, Télécom SudParis, Institut Polytechnique de Paris,
91120 Palaiseau, France
{adam_oumar.abdel_rahman,olivier.levillain,eric.totel}@telecom-sudparis.eu

Abstract. In the realm of cybersecurity, logging system and application activity is a crucial technique to detect and understand cyberattacks by identifying Indicators of Compromise (IoCs). Since these logs can take vast amounts of disk space, it can be tempting to delegate their storage to an external service provider. This requires to encrypt the data, so the service provider does not have access to possibly sensitive information. However, this usually makes it impossible to search for relevant information in the encrypted log. To address this predicament, this paper delves into the realm of modern cryptographic tools to reconcile the dual objectives of protecting log data from prying eyes while enabling controlled processing. We propose a comprehensive framework that contextualizes log data and presents several mechanisms to solve the outsourcing problem, allowing searchable encryption, and we apply our approach to DNS logs. Our contributions include the introduction of two novel schemes, namely symmetric and asymmetric, which facilitate efficient and secure retrieval of intrusion detection-related information from encrypted outsourced storage. Furthermore, we conduct extensive experiments on a test bed to evaluate and compare the effectiveness of the different solutions, providing valuable insights into the practical implementation of our proposed infrastructure for monitoring encrypted logs.

Keywords: Forensics · Indicators of Compromise · Searchable Encryption

1 Introduction and Motivation

In the recent years, the amount of encrypted data (either in transit or at rest) has increased drastically. This is *a good thing* from the point of view of the privacy since it significantly reduces the exposition of personal data to cyberattacks. This, however, poses new challenges for information system administrators whose monitoring solutions have become obsolete in the face of user-generated traffic. Should we keep the data relevant to intrusion detection systems (IDSes) in cleartext at the cost of the confidentiality of communications by exposing sensitive information to an external third party? Or should we accept that our detection tools have become blind?

© The Author(s), under exclusive license to Springer Nature Switzerland AG 2024
A. Ait Wakrime et al. (Eds.): CRiSIS 2023, LNCS 14529, pp. 185–199, 2024.
https://doi.org/10.1007/978-3-031-61231-2_12

In the realm of intrusion detection, the necessity to maintain system and application logs often results in the accumulation of extensive data volumes, a scenario that lends itself to potential outsourcing. Moreover, the sheer magnitude of data generated through DNS logs presents a significant predicament for organizations, prompting meticulous deliberation regarding storage solutions. A standard DNS log entry, contingent upon its complexity, consumes between 100 and 1000 bytes of storage. Each operational day, a single machine generates between 1000 and 10,000 DNS requests, each contributing to the accumulation of log data. For an organization comprising 50 machines, operating on the premise of 200 working days annually, the yearly DNS log data volume can oscillate from 1 gigabyte (10^9 bytes) to a staggering 100 gigabytes (10^{11} bytes). This underscores the substantial storage requisites that organizations confront in effectively managing these logs. Notably, this circumstance further accentuates the imperative to reconcile ostensibly conflicting objectives: the imperative to encrypt the data to safeguard it from the service provider handling the logs, while concurrently permitting a certain level of processing to enable the retrieval of information requisite for attack detection. In practical terms, this mandates that the service provider possesses the capability to process the encrypted logs effectively.

DNS is usually central to detect intrusions in retrospect. Indeed, in many cases, malware need to call their Command & Control (or C2) server to get instructions on the action to execute. This communication usually triggers DNS requests at some point. Information about these requests (the requested domain name or the returned IP addresses), which are called Indicators of Compromise (IoCs), can be shared to detect attacks (or even block them sometimes).

By leveraging advanced cryptographic tools, we propose in this paper to encrypt the logs while allowing a partial, controlled and delegatable search capability to the service provider. We thus describe and implement solutions to encrypt DNS logs and allow for specific requests, e.g. to find the DNS queries sent for a given domain name, on them later.

In this paper, our contributions are threefold. First, we describe the DNS context in details, including the logs to store, the relevant requests and the threat model we consider. Then we study and implement several mechanisms, using either symmetric and asymmetric cryptography, to allow for efficient searchable encryption in our precise context. Finally, we design and run a test bed to experiment on the different solutions and compare them.

2   DNS Use Case

2.1   Description

Every usual operation (such as accessing a website, checking an e-mail, or logging into a user account via an application) starts with a name resolution. This task is handled by the DNS resolver. Since cyberattacks usually trigger DNS requests, one of the ways to deal with these incidents is to identify traces of Indicators of Compromise in DNS logs (such as domain names or IP addresses corresponding to a malicious server).

To illustrate our use case shown on Fig. 1, we consider a company with one or several internal DNS resolvers and employees using these resolvers. The company wants to delegate storage and monitoring of its DNS logs to an external service provider. Since DNS logs contain sensitive information, they require encryption to guarantee confidentiality. Additional guarantees such as search capabilities are required. As the goal is to reconcile privacy-preserving storage with the ability to search for IoCs in an efficient and outsourced manner, we need a suitable cryptographic scheme. We describe such schemes in Sect. 3.

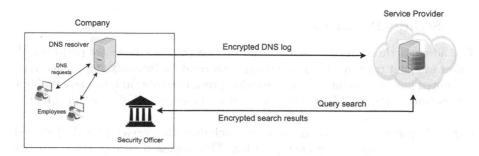

Fig. 1. Platform Illustration

In our reference scenario, when an employee sends a query for a domain name, the DNS resolver responds and generates the corresponding DNS log entry. This entry is then encrypted and transmitted to a designated service provider in charge of storing and monitoring the encrypted logs. While we assume the service provider to be honest in performing their assigned tasks, they may possess a level of curiosity and attempt to extract sensitive information from the logs. To facilitate Indicators of Compromise (IoC) detection, the company's security officer, responsible for IT security, has the authority to grant search capabilities for specific IoCs to the service provider. This enables the service provider to conduct searches over the encrypted logs. It is important to define searchable attributes within the logs to facilitate these search operations accurately.

Each log entry associated to a DNS query, that we call a DNS log, is a record containing the following information:

- the timestamp of the query;
- the DNS resolver identifier (in case the company has several resolvers);
- the IP address of the employee who makes the request;
- the domain name queried;
- the type of the query (A, AAAA, MX etc.);
- the response code (which describes the result/status of the request, e.g. NOERROR, NXDOMAIN);
- the list (possibly empty) of IP addresses returned to the employee.

To allow for future IoC lookup, each DNS log entry is linked with both the requested domain name and all the IP addresses provided in response to that specific request. We refer to these attributes, whether it's the domain name or the IP addresses, as *keywords*. On average, a log entry is associated with approximately 5 keywords. When a *keyword* is later used during a query search, because it is supposedly related to malicious activity, we talk about an *IoC*.

As described above, we need to share DNS logs that contain sensitive information with a service provider that is supposed to be honest but curious. We therefore need a threat model to define the required security properties.

2.2   Security Properties

The adopted threat model assumes the service provider honestly performs all their tasks, but tries to obtain confidential information by analyzing the received encrypted logs, search queries, and matching results to obtain information about the content of the logs. Moreover, we assume the existence of external threats.

Log Unforgeability. Unauthorized party (including the service provider) should not be able to forge a valid encrypted log. This means that only DNS requests sent to a legitimate resolver should be present in the logs.

Predicate Privacy. In order to analyze the stored encrypted logs, the security officer must provide the search capability to the service provider which we refer to as a *trapdoor*. A *trapdoor* is generated using a secret key owned by the security officer and an IoC. We expect the service provider to extract all encrypted logs relevant to this IoC. In this scenario the IoC is considered sensitive, thus a trapdoor should not reveal any information on the encapsulated IoC. This requirement is known as *Predicate Privacy* [10].

Correlation Privacy. Finally the search results of the analysis should not reveal any information to the service provider except the number of matching entries. In particular, the knowledge of a trapdoor and an encrypted entry matching the IoC represented by the trapdoor should not reveal any information about the plaintext log associated with this entry.

3   Searchable Encryption

To reconcile data encryption and the ability to search for IoCs in the logs, a trivial but naive solution is to download the complete logs from the server, decrypt them, and search for IoCs in the plaintext data. Obviously, this is an inefficient and costly approach due to the expense of downloading large amounts of data on the client side. Thus, it is desirable to support search functionality at the server level without having to decrypt all the data. To address this issue, *Searchable Encryption* (SE) has been proposed as a mechanism to encrypt data while supporting keyword search over the encrypted data, without requiring access to plaintext. Searchable encryption was first introduced and defined formally by Song et al. [12].

As described by Bösch et al. [7], SE can be used either for data outsourcing or sharing. In the first case, outsourcing, also known as *Symmetric Searchable Encryption* (SSE), the secret key holder both produces ciphertexts and search queries using symmetric primitives. The first SSE was proposed by Song et al. [12]. In the second case, which corresponds to data sharing, we use a public key setting called *Asymmetric Searchable Encryption* (ASE). Such a scheme allows multiple users (in possession of the public key) to generate searchable ciphertexts, and only the private key holder controls the ability to perform encrypted search. The first ASE is due to Boneh et al. [4] who proposed a *Public key Encryption with Keyword Search* (PEKS) scheme.

Informally, in searchable encryption schemes, there is a message and a set of associated keywords. During encryption, the user encrypts the message with a symmetric key encryption, then, generates *searchable encrypted indexes* from these keywords, which we call *tokens*. In the SSE, a *token* may be generated by using a one-way function as a hash function or pseudo-random function (PRF) [6, 8], while in the ASE, a *token* may be a ciphertext corresponding to a keyword. Let M be a message with associated keywords $kw_1, \ldots, kw_n$. We denote the searchable ciphertext as $\{Enc_K(M), TK_1, \ldots, TK_n\}$ where each TK_i is a *token* corresponding to the keyword kw_i.

In our formalism, an SE scheme is defined by five algorithms: The `Setup` algorithm generates the cryptographic setting. It takes a security level and generates the public and private parameters. The `Encryption` algorithm takes a message M, a set of keywords $kw_1, \ldots, kw_n$ associated to M and the public parameters (for an ASE scheme) or the secret key (for an SSE scheme). Then this algorithm produces a searchable ciphertext output. The `TrapdoorGen` algorithm takes a keyword kw and private parameters and then produces a *trapdoor* $T(kw)$ for that keyword. The trapdoor $T(kw)$ is a search capability who authorizes the service provider to only process encrypted entries relevant to the keyword kw. When a trapdoor $T(kw)$ is sent to the service provider, it runs the `Search` algorithm to extract all encrypted entries that match the keyword kw. Finally, the `FinalDecryption` algorithm is required to decrypt the plaintext logs from the search results. The complete cinematics is represented in Fig. 2 in Sect. 4.2.

SE schemes are mostly used to secure sensitive data outsourcing or sharing. It is thus important to consider the privacy and security requirements, which include the confidentiality protection of the data, the privacy of the search queries, the prevention of unauthorized access either to the data or search results, and the guarantee that the search process does not reveal any information about the data (Correlation Privacy) or the search queries (Predicate Privacy) [4,10].

Additionally, the SE scheme should be efficient and scalable to support practical applications.

4   Application of Searchable Encryption to DNS Logs

4.1   Studied Schemes

In this section, we present three cryptographic schemes to create encrypted and searchable entries. We first present the symmetric scheme proposed by Waters et al. [13] and a new symmetric solution based on PRFs. The third scheme is an ASE based on Identity-Based Encryption.

All the schemes rely on symmetric primitives, namely an authenticated encryption scheme E_k and a pseudo-random function PRF.

WBDS–SSE Scheme. We now present an SSE proposed by Waters et al. in [13].

Setup. The security officer generates a random secret K_R and shares it with the DNS resolver R.

Encryption. We assume the security officer and the resolver R share the K_R secret to encrypt log entries. Let record be a DNS log along with keywords $kw_1, \ldots, kw_n$. Let flag be a constant bitstring of length l^1. The resolver executes the following steps

1. Choose a random symmetric key K and compute $E_K(\text{record})$.
2. Choose a random bitstring r of some fixed length[2].
3. For each keyword kw_i, compute

$$a_i = \text{PRF}_{K_R}(kw_i), \quad b_i = \text{PRF}_{a_i}(r), \quad c_i = b_i \oplus (\text{flag}|K).$$

4. Return the encrypted DNS log $\{E_K(\text{record}), r, c_1, \ldots, c_n\}$.

The output will be sent to the service provider.

TrapdoorGen. When the company wants to look for an IoC, the security officer generates the search capability by evaluating a PRF keyed by the secret key K_R on the IoC denoted by $K_{IoC} := \text{PRF}_{K_R}(IoC)$, and sends it to the service provider.

Search. When the service provider receives K_{IoC}, it executes the following algorithm:

1. For each entry $\{E_K(\text{record}), r, c_1, \ldots, c_n\}$
   (a) Compute $p = \text{PRF}_{K_{IoC}}(r)$.
   (b) For each c_i in the entry, compute $p \oplus c_i$. If the first l bits of the result matches flag, extract K as the remainder of the result; otherwise, the computation is disregarded. If none of the results starts with flag, move to the next query (the query is not a keyword match).

---

[1] The flag can have a length significantly less than that of an encryption key K [13].
[2] The length of r does not affect the security properties of the scheme with regards to the expected security properties since it is the input to a PRF. The impact of the size of r on other properties is discussed in Sect. 5.3.

(c) If one of the results matches, use the computed K to decrypt E_K(record) to obtain the record in clear text form.
2. Send the (possibly empty) list of gathered records to the security officer.

Note that this steps directly produces the plaintext entries, letting the service provider have access to them. It also makes the `FinalDecryption` step trivial.

An Indexable, PRF-Based SSE Scheme. We propose a different approach from the previous scheme. The idea is to deterministically derive tokens from the keywords and a truncated version of the timestamp[3]. A trapdoor for our scheme is simply the corresponding token, which allows to efficiently retrieve the relevant lines, e.g. by using database indexes. The rest of the record (and the search results) are encrypted to preserve the confidentiality of logs.

The `Setup` algorithm is the same as the WBDS–SSE scheme and suppose that the security officer share the secret key K_R with the resolver R.

Encryption. Let record be a DNS log along with keywords $kw_1, \ldots, kw_n$ and a timestamp TS. We run the following steps to generate the encrypted entry.

1. For each keyword kw_i, compute the associated token TK_i by evaluating the PRF $TK_i = \mathrm{PRF}_{K_R}(kw_i \| \overline{TS})$ where $\overline{TS}$ is the truncated version of TS.
2. Generate the symmetric key $K = \mathrm{PRF}_{K_R}(TK_1 \| \ldots \| TK_n)$.
3. Compute the encryption E_K(record).
4. Return the encrypted DNS log $\{E_K(\text{record}), TK_1, \ldots, TK_n\}$.

The resolver sends $\{E_K(\text{record}), TK_1, \ldots, TK_n\}$ to the service provider who stores it in its database.

TrapdoorGen. In case one wants to recover all the queries associated with an IoC within some time frame $[T_A, T_B]$, the security officer executes the following steps to generate the trapdoor corresponding.

1. Generate $K_{IoC} = \mathrm{PRF}_{K_R}(IoC)$.
2. Find the minimal set of truncated timestamps $\overline{TS_1}, \ldots, \overline{TS_m}$ covering the time frame $[T_A, T_B]$.
3. For each t_i generate the corresponding token $tk_i = \mathrm{PRF}_{K_R}(IoC \| \overline{t_i})$.
4. Return the trapdoor $T(IoC) = \{tk_1, \ldots, tk_m\}$.

Search. Suppose that the service provider receives a query search (a trapdoor $T(IoC) := \{tk_1, \ldots, tk_m\}$) from the security officer. The service provider works as follows to retrieve all queries matching the encrypted IoC. For each entry $\{E_K(\text{record}), TK_1, \ldots, TK_n\}$ in the encrypted database, check the intersection of token sets $\{TK_1, \ldots, TK_n\} \cap \{tk_1, \ldots, tk_m\}$. If this intersection is non-empty set, i.e., there exist $i \in \{1, \ldots, n\}$ and $j \in \{1, \ldots, m\}$ such that $TK_i = tk_j$, the

---

[3] A typical value for the truncation windows would be 1 h or 1 day. Small windows will lead to the multiplication of trapdoors, whereas big windows will make token collision more probable (see Sect. 5.3 for a discussion on the matter).

entry match, then add the entire entry (encrypted record with all its tokens) to the search results. Finally, send the search results to the security officer.

FinalDecryption. When the security officer receives the search results, it can derive, for each entry $\{E_K(\text{record}), TK_1, \ldots, TK_n\}$ the decryption key $K = \text{PRF}_{K_R}(TK_1 || \ldots || TK_n)$, and finally decrypt $E_K(\text{record})$ to recover the plaintext record.

Asymmetric Searchable Encryption (ASE) Using IBE. We propose a solution based on an asymmetric approach. We first present the Identity-Based Encryption (IBE) scheme of Boneh and Franklin [5], and then the ASE scheme built on it.

Identity-Based Encryption. IBE is a public key scheme where any arbitrary string is a valid public key. The corresponding private key is generated by a trusted third-party from the public key. The canonical example of IBE is to use one's identity (e.g. an email address) as the public key, hence the name of the scheme.

In our use case, we use the keywords associated to the DNS logs as public keys (or identities); the third party generating private keys is the security officer.

Boneh and Franklin proposed the FullIdent IBE protocol [5], which is proven to be IND-CCA under *BDH* assumption[4]. This scheme, on which we build the ASE scheme, defines the following operations.

IBE.Setup. Choose a large prime number q, two groups $\mathbb{G}_1$ and $\mathbb{G}_2$ of order q and choose an admissible bilinear map e : $\mathbb{G}_1 \times \mathbb{G}_2 \to \mathbb{G}_T$. Choose a random generator P of $\mathbb{G}_1$, a random master key $s \in \mathbb{Z}_q^*$. We also need four hash functions $H_1 : \{0,1\}^* \to \mathbb{G}_2^*$, $H_2 : \mathbb{G}_T \to \{0,1\}^n$, $H_3 : \{0,1\}^n \times \{0,1\}^n \to \mathbb{Z}_q^*$ and $H_4 : \{0,1\}^n \to \{0,1\}^n$. Finally the authority publish the public parameters **params** $= \langle q, \mathbb{G}_1, \mathbb{G}_2, \mathbb{G}_T, e, n, P, P_{pub}, H_1, H_2, H_3, H_4 \rangle$ where $P_{pub} = sP \in \mathbb{G}_1$ and keep secret the master key s.

IBE.Extract. Given an $ID \in \{0,1\}^*$ as a public key, this algorithm computes the corresponding private key $SK_{ID} = sH_1(ID) \in \mathbb{G}_2$ where s is the master key.

IBE.Encrypt. To encrypt a message $M \in \{0,1\}^n$ under the public key ID:

1. Compute $Q_{ID} = H_1(ID) \in \mathbb{G}_2$.
2. Choose a random bitstring $\sigma \in \{0,1\}^n$ and set $r = H_3(\sigma, M) \in \mathbb{Z}_q^*$.
3. The ciphertext is $C = \langle rP, \sigma \oplus H_2(e(P_{pub}, Q_{ID})^r), M \oplus H_4(\sigma) \rangle$.

IBE.Decrypt. Let $C = \langle U, V, W \rangle$ a ciphertext encrypted using the public key ID. If $U \notin \mathbb{G}_1$, reject the ciphertext. To decrypt C using the private key SK_{ID}:

---

[4] Assuming the *Bilinear Diffie-Hellman Problem (BDH)* is hard (i.e. all polynomial time algorithms have a negligible advantage in solving BDH), FullIdent is semantically secure against an adaptive chosen ciphertext attack (IND-CCA) [5].

1. Compute $\sigma = V \oplus H_2(e(U, SK_{ID}))$ and $M = W \oplus H_4(\sigma)$.
2. Set $r = H_3(\sigma, M)$. Test that $U = rP$. If not, reject the ciphertext.
3. Return M as the decryption of C.

The decryption function is a kind of try-decrypt, which is particularly interesting for our use case. Let $C = $ IBE.Encrypt(params, ID, M) be a ciphertext and SK_{ID^*} a private key (corresponding to the public key ID^*) generated by the IBE.Extract algorithm. The decryption of C success if and only if C is well formed and $ID^* = ID$.

ASE Scheme The IBE-based ASE scheme relies on the following algorithms.

Setup. First, run the IBE.Setup algorithm to generate public parameters params and the master key s. Then, draw a random secret key K_R which is shared with the resolver. Public parameters are shared with the different actors.

Encryption. Let record be a DNS log along with keywords $kw_1, \ldots, kw_m$, the DNS resolver executes the following steps to generate the encrypted and searchable entry:

1. Choose a random secret key K.
2. For each keyword kw_i, compute $C_i = $ IBE.Encrypt(K, kw_i) i.e. we encrypt K using the keywords kw_i as public keys.
3. Compute the encryption $E_{K'}(\text{record})$ where $K' = \text{PRF}_{K_R}(K)$.
4. Return the encrypted DNS log $\{E_{K'}(\text{record}), C_1, \ldots, C_m\}$.

The resolver sends the result of this algorithm with a timestamp TS which can be stored by the service provider in form $\{E_{K'}(\text{record}), \text{TS}, C_1, \ldots, C_m\}$.

TrapdoorGen. When the security officer wants to search for an *IoC*, it runs IBE.Extract algorithm to generate SK_{IoC} the private key corresponding to the public key *IoC*, which is trapdoor. It sends the trapdoor with the time frame of interest $\{SK_{IoC}, [T_A, T_B]\}$ to the service provider which processes encrypted logs received in the $[T_A, T_B]$ period.

Search. Let SK_{IoC} a trapdoor and $[T_A, T_B]$ the time frame sent to the service provider. For each encrypted record $\{E_{K'}(\text{record}), TS, C_1, \ldots, C_m\}$ within the given time frame, the service provider executes the following steps.

1. For each C_i, it tries to decrypt C_i with IBE.Decrypt using the private key SK_{IoC}. If the decryption succeeds, C_i corresponds to *IoC* and the secret $K := $ IBE.Decrypt(C_i, SK_{IoC}) is recovered. It thus adds $\{E_{K'}(\text{record}), K\}$ to the search results and moves to the next log entry.
2. If none of the C_i can be decrypted, the entry does not match the *IoC* and it moves to the next entry.

In the end, the service provider sends all the relevant search results to the security officer.

FinalDecryption. For each entry $\{E_{K'}(\text{record}), K\}$, the security officer can derive the decryption key $K' = \text{PRF}_{K_R}(K)$, and finally decrypt $E_{K'}(\text{record})$ to recover the plaintext record.

4.2   Platform Implementation

Our proposed infrastructure for monitoring DNS logs using searchable encryption is designed to provide secure and efficient monitoring of DNS logs. As shown in Fig. 2, the infrastructure consists of several actors that work together to achieve this goal. We describe in detail in this section the main task of these actors.

Step 1–2 (initialization and sharing secret key). At the beginning, the security officer runs the `Setup` algorithm to initialize cryptographic materials for the considered scheme (SSE or ASE) and shares the secret key K_R with the DNS resolver. The public parameters, including cryptographic primitives and public key (in case of ASE) are shared with the resolver and the service provider.

Step 3 (processing log). At the core of the infrastructure is a DNS resolver, which generates DNS logs. For each DNS query, the resolver extracts the keywords from the DNS log, constructs the `record` and encrypts it using `Encryption` algorithm. The `Encryption` takes as input the `record` and a set of keywords and produces a searchable ciphertext as described in Sect. 3. The resolver sends the `Encryption` output (including the tokens), to the service provider who stores them in its database.

Step 4 (searching over encrypted logs). To perform a search query on the encrypted logs, the security officer generates the search capabilities for an IoC by running the `TrapdoorGen` algorithm and sends them to the service provider. When the service provider receives a query from the security officer, it runs the `Search` algorithm which takes as input a search capability. It retrieves all matching records from the encrypted logs stored in the database and sends results to the security officer.

Step 5 (decrypting search results). When the security officer receives the search results for its query search, it runs the `FinalDecryption` algorithm to decrypt them and recover the plaintext records.

Implementation Details. We implemented our test bed in C. Symmetric primitives come from OpenSSL. For the indexable PRF-based scheme, the database is SQLite. Finally, for the asymmetric primitives, we use the RELIC library, a modern, research-oriented, cryptographic meta-toolkit with emphasis on efficiency and flexibility [1]. The IBE scheme we use indeed requires an asymmetric pairing-friendly setting $(q, \mathbb{G}_1, \mathbb{G}_2, \mathbb{G}_T, e, P, P_{pub})$. RELIC implements several elliptic curves; it also implements hash functions on elliptic curves and asymmetric pairings.

For our implementation parameters, we use the BLS12-381 elliptic curve [3]. In terms of symmetric primitives, we have employed $E = $ AES-256-GCM for encryption and $PRF = $ HMAC-SHA-2 for PRF. The selection of the BLS12-381 curve for our IBE-based ASE scheme is underpinned by a comprehensive assessment that considers established standards and practical suitability. This particular curve has gained widespread recognition and adoption in prominent

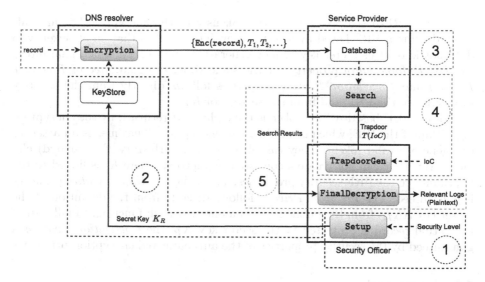

Fig. 2. Platform Architecture

blockchain projects such as Zcash and Ethereum 2.0, a testament to its resilience and its alignment with the stringent requirements of security-sensitive applications. Furthermore, our choice aligns with the recommendations outlined by the IETF [9], which emphasize the merits of the BLS12-381 curve. This alignment with industry best practices, particularly for achieving a 128-bit security level, underscores the curve's status as both *widely used* and *efficient*. These attributes collectively reinforce its credibility as a secure and pragmatic choice for our cryptographic setup.

5   Evaluation

5.1   Security

In the WBDS–SSE scheme, the log is encrypted using a random key, which means anyone can generate valid encryption. Only the generation of the tokens requires the knowledge of the secret key K_R. However, knowing a trapdoor is sufficient to forge a valid token (for the corresponding keyword), which means the *Log Unforgeability* property is not completely satisfied, especially w.r.t. the service provider which is supposed to eventually learn trapdoors. In this scheme, the trapdoor for a keyword results from a PRF keyed by the secret key K_R. The *Predicate Privacy* property is a direct result of the PRF properties.

Finally, by construction, the original scheme described by Waters et al. does not provide *Correlation Privacy*. A simple way to add this property would be to encrypt the record with a key shared only between the resolver and the security officer before running the scheme. Adding this encryption step would also guarantee *Log Unforgeability*.

In our PRF-based SSE scheme the tokens and the encryption key are calculated using a PRF keyed by a secrete key. This implies that an attacker who does not know this secret key cannot generate a valid entry, which guarantees the *Log Unforgeability* property. At the same time, the guarantee of *Predicate Privacy* and *Correlation Privacy* properties follows directly from the security properties of the PRF and from the secrecy of K_R.

For our IBE-based ASE, a token is the ciphertext returned by the encryption algorithm of the IBE, which is a public key encryption. That means an attacker can generate valid tokens. They can also create an arbitrary $E_{K'}(\texttt{record})$ element. Yet, they can not create a consistent ciphertext where K' is linked to the C_i, thanks to the PRF security properties. Thus, the *Log Unforgeability* property is guaranteed. The *Predicate Privacy* follows directly from the definition of the secret key SK_{ID} from the public key, via a one-way hash function. Finally, since the actual record is protected by the secret key K_R, the *Correlation Privacy* is guaranteed by the security properties of the authenticated encryption primitive.

5.2   Benchmarking

We evaluate the effectiveness and scalability of our proposed infrastructure using a realistic DNS log dataset [11]. We compare the performance of our infrastructure with a baseline approach that uses plaintext log data and a conventional search function. Since the plaintext and the PRF-based schemes are compatible with database indexes, we also provide figures for a variant thereof using a database back-end.

We evaluated the studied with 21 PCAP files (each files corresponds to 1-h long captures form) of size 6.29 GB from [11]. Among these files, the DNS response packets of interest amounted to 3.45 GB. We preprocess these PCAP files to generate the corresponding record files (according to the records format described in Sect. 2.1). These record files make a total of $14,816,004$ records and a size of 763 MB. For our experiments, we ran the whole cinematics (from Setup to Search and FinalDecryption with different IoCs) on those files. The experiments were run on a computer running Linux with a 32-core Intel Xeon Gold 5218R CPU, 2.10 GHz and 64 GB of RAM memory.

The results in Table 1 clearly show that the IBE cost are orders of magnitude bigger in terms of processing time. For the schemes which are compatible with database indexes, using an SQLite back-end leads to bigger storage requirements, and slows down significantly the encryption time, but it allows for drastic improvements in the search time. This is indeed expected since these schemes allow to retrieve the relevant lines using an index, without the need for testing each line, which can be a game changer when looking at a handful of records in huge logs.

5.3   Discussion About Token Collision

In the PRF-based SSE, the tokens are directly derived from keywords and a truncated timestamp, therefore, within a truncation interval, the token for a

Table 1. Comparison of different schemes using a public DNS data set [11]. Schemes with a "+ DB" annotation correspond to variants which allows for indexable search and where the data is stored in an SQLite back-end. The Encryption Time is per DNS log. The Size of Searchable Ciphertext is given relative to the plaintext baseline, which averages around 102 bytes. The Search Time corresponds to the processing time of one IoC in 705,524 encrypted lines logs (1-h long capture).

	Encryption Time (μs/log)	Size of Searchable Ciphertext (in bytes)	Search Time (s/IoC)
Plaintext (baseline)	2.7	1.0 (102)	0.4
Plaintext + DB	130.0	2.4 (248)	< 0.01
WBDS–SSE [13]	22.4	2.3 (236)	2.2
PRF-based SSE	28.9	1.3 (129)	9.97
PRF-based SSE + DB	134.4	3.3 (343)	0.02
IBE-based ASE	5569.0	4.7 (480)	2189.28

given keyword is deterministic. Such leakage allow the service provider to derive statistics on the encrypted logs, including those unrelated to IoCs.

With WBDS–SSE, the collision are subtler. As discussed earlier, a collision on the masked `flag` (of length l) may arise by accident, with probability 2^{-l}. However, two logs pertaining to the same keyword can be encrypted with the same random r, which will lead to the same b_i. This will happen with probability $2^{-|r|/2}$. So, if $|r|$ is small and significantly less than l, collisions may reveal the presence of a common keyword between two records.

We believe this leakage is small and should not be problematic for the studied use cases. This might however require further analysis. In the meantime, a conservative measure would be to choose parameters reducing the collision probability (long enough random bitstring r for WBDS–SSE or small truncation windows for the PRF-based scheme).

5.4   Summary

	Log Unforgeability	Predicate Privacy	Correlation Privacy	Token Collisions	Search Efficiency
WBDS–SSE [13]	✗	✓	✗	if $|r| \ll l$	+
PRF-based SSE	✓	✓	✓	Within the truncation window	++
IBE-based ASE	✓	✓	✓	No	--

6   Related Work

In recent years, there has been a growing interest in the use of searchable encryption techniques for secure and efficient searching of encrypted data. One of the earliest works in this area was published in 2000. In this paper, Song et al. [12] proposed a symmetric key-based scheme. In their scheme, the message to be encrypted is seen as a sequence of keywords. The main idea is to achieve, for each keyword, a special two-layered encryption construct. Thus, given a trapdoor, the server can strip the outer layer and check if the inner layer is in the correct form. This scheme works on text content and allow to filter ciphertexts containing a given keyword. Since the schemes we study take advantage of the underlying data structure (domain names, IP addresses, etc.), our results are more efficient, both in terms of processing time and encrypted data volume.

Boneh et al. [4] introduced the idea of using public key encryption to enable search over encrypted data. They provide a precise definition of what they call *Public key Encryption with Keyword Search (PEKS)* along with several constructions that are provably secure in their model under suitable cryptographic assumptions. Our work proposes a suitable construction using a hybrid symmetric scheme for monitoring DNS logs securely.

Building on these foundational works, several research efforts have explored the use of searchable encryption for secure logging. Waters et al. [13] proposed an encrypted and searchable audit log. They proposed two approaches: an SSE, which we introduced in Sect. 4.1 and an ASE similar to the construction presented in this paper. Our work proposes a new symmetric scheme, which is compatible with database indexes. We validate the performance of this scheme with regards to schemes proposed by Waters et al. [13].

More recently, Araújo and Pinto [2] proposed a system for secure remote storage of logs while maintaining its confidentiality and server-side search capabilities. This work uses symmetric and asymmetric encryption algorithms to enable secure and efficient search over encrypted log data. The system provides very expressive queries, however, their experiments were only run on small datasets (they target logs from web servers, with 30,000 lines), which makes it difficult to assess the scalability in use cases as ours.

7   Conclusion

In this work, we design an architecture for monitor encrypted DNS logs while ensuring the privacy preserving of the DNS logs. To do so, we leverage the use of searchable encryption. We have proposed two solutions which are symmetric and asymmetric approaches. We also studied the SSE scheme proposed by Waters et al. [13]. We set up a platform with the different actors and implemented the studied schemes.

Our symmetric approach allows for efficient and secure searching of encrypted DNS logs, while preserving the privacy of sensitive information. We evaluate our approach using real-world DNS log data and demonstrate its effectiveness in terms of performance and security. By using our infrastructure, companies could outsource and monitor their DNS logs while ensuring the privacy and security of the logged data.

Beyond DNS logs, we believe our work can be extended as future work to more complex and more sensitive data, such as system logs or mail-related logs. However, this extension would raise interesting questions to accommodate the constraints related to these logs, e.g. mail logs contain both structured and non-structured (textual) data which might be hard to reconcile.

Acknowledgment. This work was supported by the French ANR Project ANR-19-CE39-0011 PRESTO.

References

1. Aranha, D.F., Gouvêa, C.P.L., Markmann, T., Wahby, R.S., Liao, K.: RELIC is an Efficient LIbrary for Cryptography. https://github.com/relic-toolkit/relic
2. Araújo, R., Pinto, A.: Secure remote storage of logs with search capabilities. J. Cybersecu. Privacy **1**(2), 340–364 (2021)
3. Barreto, P.S.L.M., Lynn, B., Scott, M.: Constructing elliptic curves with prescribed embedding degrees. In: Cimato, S., Persiano, G., Galdi, C. (eds.) SCN 2002. LNCS, vol. 2576, pp. 257–267. Springer, Heidelberg (2003). https://doi.org/10.1007/3-540-36413-7_19
4. Boneh, D., Di Crescenzo, G., Ostrovsky, R., Persiano, G.: Public key encryption with keyword search. In: Cachin, C., Camenisch, J.L. (eds.) EUROCRYPT 2004. LNCS, vol. 3027, pp. 506–522. Springer, Heidelberg (2004). https://doi.org/10.1007/978-3-540-24676-3_30
5. Boneh, D., Franklin, M.: Identity-based encryption from the Weil pairing. In: Kilian, J. (ed.) CRYPTO 2001. LNCS, vol. 2139, pp. 213–229. Springer, Heidelberg (2001). https://doi.org/10.1007/3-540-44647-8_13
6. Boneh, D., Waters, B.: Constrained pseudorandom functions and their applications. In: Sako, K., Sarkar, P. (eds.) ASIACRYPT 2013, Part II. LNCS, vol. 8270, pp. 280–300. Springer, Heidelberg (2013). https://doi.org/10.1007/978-3-642-42045-0_15
7. Bösch, C., Hartel, P., Jonker, W., Peter, A.: A survey of provably secure searchable encryption. ACM Comput. Surv. (CSUR) **47**(2), 1–51 (2014)
8. Goldreich, O., Goldwasser, S., Micali, S.: How to construct random functions. J. ACM (JACM) **33**(4), 792–807 (1986)
9. Sakemi, Y., Kobayashi, T., Saito, T., Wahby, R.: Pairing-friendly curves. IETF draft (2021)
10. Shen, E., Shi, E., Waters, B.: Predicate privacy in encryption systems. In: Reingold, O. (ed.) TCC 2009. LNCS, vol. 5444, pp. 457–473. Springer, Heidelberg (2009). https://doi.org/10.1007/978-3-642-00457-5_27
11. Singh, M., Singh, M., Kaur, S.: TI-2016 DNS dataset (2019)
12. Song, D.X., Wagner, D., Perrig, A.: Practical techniques for searches on encrypted data. In: Proceeding 2000 IEEE Symposium on Security and Privacy. S P 2000, pp. 44–55 (2000)
13. Waters, B., Balfanz, D., Durfee, G., Smetters, D.K.: Building an encrypted and searchable audit log. In: NDSS (2004)

VAE-GAN for Robust IoT Malware Detection and Classification in Intelligent Urban Environments: An Image Analysis Approach

Huiyao Dong[1] 🔟 and Igor Kotenko[2](✉) 🔟

[1] ITMO University, Saint Petersburg, Russia
[2] SPC RAS, Saint Petersburg, Russia
ivkote@comsec.spb.ru

Abstract. The Internet of Things (IoT) has revolutionised technology in intelligent urban environments. Meanwhile, security and privacy risks have emerged, including the presence of various malware, resulting in detrimental consequences. Generative attack networks (GAN) can not only build superior representations for complex and multi-dimensional data but also maximise prediction performance due to their min-max optimisation manner. This paper proposes a GAN approach, utilising an autoencoder (AE) as the generator and a transfer learning for the discriminator, to identify various types of malware threats that exploit the IoT network using RGB images collected directly from malware samples. The generator is built for effective data reconstruction, with different AE structures and denoising manner; the discriminator utilises a pre-trained MobileNet for maximised performance. Two well-known image classification models, VGG19 and Xception, are used for performance comparison. The experiment proves that the Variational AE-GAN is highly implementable and scalable for the malware classification task, in both detection performance and generalizability.

Keywords: Internet of Things · malware detection · autoencoder · generative attack networks

1 Introduction

The Internet of Things (IoT) is a network of devices that includes wireless sensors, software, actuators, and computer systems that operate over the Internet. Its purpose is to facilitate the automated exchange of data between various things or systems. The IoT has fundamentally transformed our interactions with technology, particularly in the anticipated context of intelligent urban environments. The IoT is revolutionising the approach to the planning and development of intelligent urban areas. The implementation of IoT applications in urban environments has the potential to enhance efficiency, promote environmental sustainability, and establish interconnectivity. These applications encompass a wide range of functions, including but not limited to waste management, intelligent lighting systems, and traffic control. Nevertheless, with the proliferation of

IoT applications, new issues such as security and privacy risks have surfaced [1]. Organisations are implementing diverse protection strategies to address these concerns, including encrypted communication protocols, secure data storage, access management, and detection and prevention mechanisms based on different machine learning methods [2]. The identification of anomalies in network traffic and the prediction of potential security breaches can be achieved through the application of various probabilistic models such as Bayesian networks. Additionally, the utilisation of deep learning models, such as convolutional neural networks (CNN), can facilitate real-time sequential data analysis and pattern recognition, thereby enabling the detection and prevention of cyber attacks [3].

Malware is a significant security challenge for the IoT in smart city contexts. The presence of malware in IoT-based smart cities can result in a range of detrimental consequences, including but not limited to unauthorised access, data theft, system disruption, botnet creation, and ransomware attacks. These outcomes can lead to a host of additional threats to information security and privacy, such as identity theft and DDoS attacks. There exist two distinct methodologies for conducting malware analysis: static methods for detecting malware rely on attributes extracted from executable artefacts, while dynamic techniques depend on behavioural features. In any case, the current trend in research is shifting from traditional approaches to more sophisticated and robust ones, and solutions based on deep learning (DL) are deemed to be dependable and efficacious. The utilisation of deep learning models such as LSTM, bidirectional LSTM, and one-dimensional CNN in analysis and detection mechanisms has been shown to provide prompt and precise detection in both approaches [4, 5].

While DL-based malware analysis approaches are unquestionably important, certain deep learning models, like autoencoders (AEs), have the capacity to build superior representations for complex and multi-dimensional data. As a result, when compared to one-dimensional sequential data, they can provide a more thorough insight of virus activities. Typically, sequential data refers to distinct events that occur in an ordered manner. Multidimensional data, on the other hand, includes a wide range of data kinds, including system logs, time series-based network traffic, grayscale images created straight from executables, and control flow graphs. Furthermore, the high-dimensional data can be transferred into visualisation representation, which can not only extract patterns and anomalies that may not be obvious from sequential data alone, but also provide visualisation features for a better understanding of the malware characteristics and behaviours. Generative attack networks (GAN), a combination of generative models and discriminator models, are another approach that can increase detection performance by generating synthetic data for model training. While unbalanced datasets are common for malware analysis-related research since there are more examples of benign files than malware, GANs may create varied but realistic samples that are comparable to the original represented class to prevent bias and increase performance. Furthermore, GANs can generate samples that are difficult for models to detect; as malware has been manipulated to avoid easily detectable patterns or signatures, generating simulated samples that are similar but not identical to known malware can significantly improve models' detection ability.

This paper proposes an approach to address the security challenges posed by malware threats exploiting IoT networks using RGB (red, green, blue) images directly collected from malware samples.

The novelty of our approach lies in leveraging autoencoders to learn underlying behavioural patterns of benign and malicious software, enabling the generation of anomalous network traffic data to enhance detection effectiveness. The ease of feature extraction and the rapid performance of autoencoders make our technique highly implementable and scalable in production environments.

This study contributes to the field in three significant ways.

- Firstly, we explore the use of generative adversarial networks (GANs) for malware detection, comparing their performance against state-of-the-art deep networks developed for image categorization.
- Secondly, we conduct experiments with different autoencoder architectures, including general convolutional autoencoders and variational autoencoders, evaluating their capabilities for reconstruction and malware detection. This comprehensive comparison allows us to identify the most effective solution.
- Thirdly, we employ transfer learning techniques for the discriminator model, resulting in improved detection performance and reduced training time.

Additionally, we introduce data augmentation techniques such as image rotation and shuffling to increase the variation of training data, enhancing the generalizability and robustness of our proposed technique across different input shapes. These measures ensure that our autoencoder-based solutions are highly adaptable and applicable in various contexts.

The paper is structured as follows. Section 2 provides an overview of related works. Section 3 discusses the theoretical foundations of the proposed approach. Section 4 describes the experimental results and their discussion. Section 5 contains conclusions and directions for further research.

2 Related Work

CNN, as one of the most widely used models in high-resolution image processing, can obtain representative characteristics from high-dimensional inputs containing insufficient information. As for malware analysis, CNN's deep convolutional layers can capture malware samples' unique visual patterns and structural qualities, allowing the model to detect subtle indicators of dangerous behaviour that traditional analytic approaches may miss. Due to CNN's great security potential, researchers have been applying CNN-based DL models in malware detection and classification. Vasan et al. [6] employed a security-focused approach by utilising and combining different CNN architectures to study various semantic representations of input data. The ensemble CNN architecture demonstrated superior feature extraction capabilities, leading to high accuracy in classifying both unpacked and packed malware samples. Building upon their work, Vasan et al. [7] proposed a fine-tuned CNN architecture specifically designed for malware imagery classification, further enhancing the security aspect of malware analysis. Kim [8] introduced a CNN-based approach that effectively identified different types of malwares, surpassing the performance of traditional multilayer perceptron (MLP) models in terms of detection accuracy and generalizability. Notably, it has been emphasized [9] that image-based malware classification should consider the challenges posed by malware obfuscation techniques; researchers applied the gist descriptor method to extract general features, which exhibited robustness and outperformed CNN-based approaches in handling obfuscated malware samples. In recent years, the increasing numerosity and variety of software has necessitated the exploration of transfer learning techniques for malware image analysis. Awan et al. [10] adopted the transfer learning approach using the pre-trained VGG19 model as a base and incorporated additional CNN layers and spatial attention mechanisms for classification. Similarly, Prajapati et al. [11] implemented transfer learning with two base models, ResNet152 and VGG-19, demonstrating that transfer learning approaches could achieve accuracies of around 91%–92%, outperforming traditional deep learning approaches with different model architectures, with VGG-19 yielding the best performance. Furthermore, Bhodia et al. [12] proposed a practical method that utilized pre-trained models for image classification tasks, showcasing its effectiveness in identifying zero-day attacks, an essential security requirement in malware analysis.

On the other hand, the emergence of GANs has introduced new possibilities for security-related analysis. One of the significant challenges in employing DL techniques for security analysis is the scarcity of sufficiently labelled datasets. However, GANs offer a solution by synthesizing labelled datasets, even for minor classes such as malwares and network intrusions, thus enabling improved classifier training. To leverage the strengths of GANs in the context of security, Su et al. [13] proposed a GAN-based malware classification model explicitly incorporating prior domain knowledge obtained from the input into the training process. Dovom et al. [14] created an image dataset from executables and utilized auxiliary classifier GANs (AC-GAN) to generate synthetic malware images; multiple classification models were then employed to evaluate performance. In a similar vein, Zhang et al. [15] proposed a GAN-based approach for mobile malware detection by implementing GAN-based data augmentation after converting malware features into image representations. Comparing conventional methods with GAN-based techniques, it was observed that while both approaches increased classification accuracy, GANs demonstrated greater efficiency in recognizing malware samples, particularly in highly imbalanced datasets.

These works highlight the growing spectrum of malware analysis security approaches. Even with insufficient information, CNN can extract representative qualities from sophisticated, high-dimensional inputs. Using pre-trained models learned on large datasets can assist researchers in significantly improving performance, training time, and generalisation. GANs can handle dataset scarcity and imbalanced data distribution issues, and the capacity to generate synthetic data that matches the features of real malware can potentially increase classifier performance. In our paper we are trying to boost the defence against ever-evolving malware attacks by embracing and integrating these strategies by a GAN based approach, utilising an autoencoder and a transfer learning.

3 Methods

3.1 Visualisation of Software Characteristics

To begin, we visualise the binary information as image matrices and compare the similarities of various types of software samples. The binary information is collected from binary files and contains easily accessible representative features, based on the premise that the headers of each block of opcode might indicate the malware files' characteristics. As a result, the first three letters of each malware opcode block are retrieved and concatenated into string-format sequential data. The hash function first transfers the sequences into a one-dimensional numeric matrix, which computes the numeric value of each data point and defines the RGB colour; the one-dimensional data is then reshaped into RGB-coloured (size: width*hight*3 channels) matrices.

Figure 1 displays the visualisation results of random software samples, as well as grayscale picture matrices containing solely constant values for comparison. The samples were chosen from our experiment dataset that exclusively contained RGB image matrices [16]. As the figures show, while benign and malicious wares have distinct variances, there is no discernible difference between malware and hackwares. Meanwhile, based on the samples, the pixel value of benignware appears to have a broader dynamic range.

To quantify the similarities, we employ three metrics that can measure the pixel-wise differences between software visualization, the quality of reconstructions and the structural similarities of the matrices, respectively: (1) mean squared error (MSE) to calculate the mean of pixel-wise differences; (2) peak signal-to-noise ratio (PSNR) to calculate the MSE in relation to the highest potential pixel value; (3) structural similarity index (SSIM) to compare the structural similarities of two matrices. With two image matrices $I = \{i_{(1,1)}, ..., i_{(m,n)}\}$ and $J = \{j_{(1,1)}, ..., j_{(m,n)}\}$, , the calculation of three metrics is listed as (1), (2), and (3), respectively:

$$MSE = \frac{1}{m}\frac{1}{n}\sum_{x=1}^{m}\sum_{y=1}^{n}(i_{(x,y)} - j_{(x,y)})^2, x \in [1, m], y \in [1, n] \tag{1}$$

$$PSNR = 10 * log_{10}\left(\frac{MAX_I^2}{MSE}\right) = 20 * log_{10}MAX_I - 20 * log_{10}MSE \tag{2}$$

$$SSIM(i, j) = \frac{(2\mu_i\mu_j + c_1)(2\sigma_{ij} + c_2)}{(\mu_i^2 + \mu_{ij}^2 + c_1)(\sigma_i^2 + \sigma_j^2 + c_2)}, c_1 = (k_1L)^2, c_2 = (k_2L)^2 \tag{3}$$

The $i_{(x,y)}$ and $j_{(x,y)}$ in Eq. (1) represent data points at the same location in two distinct matrices. While the MSE in (2) corresponds to the *MSE* calculated in (1), the MAX_I represents the utmost pixel within the matrix; in our case, as all images use 8-bit pixels, the maximum pixel value is 255. As SSIM is calculated based on sliding, square-shaped windows on different images. Formula (3) displays the computation with mean μ and variance σ of two windows $i \in I, j \in J$, with L stands for the dynamic range of pixel values, while $\mu_i, \mu_j, \sigma_i, \sigma_j$ stands for the pixel sample mean and variance of windows i and j respectively, the σ_{ij} represents the covariance of i and j. c_1 and c_2 are designed for division stabilisation, while L is the dynamic range of pixel values, k_1, k_2 are set to constants of 0.01 and 0.03 [17].

Table 1 compares the degree of image similarity between pairs of software; the samples used for the calculation are selected at random from each category.

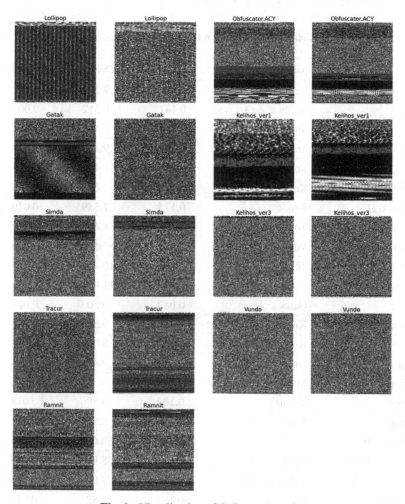

Fig. 1. Visualization of Software Samples

The following is observed based on the results of the sampling and calculations. Most software pairs have a larger MSE, implying a significant difference in pixel-based comparisons. Kelihos_ver3 and Vundo have the lowest MSE score, indicating that their images are comparatively similar. Kelihos_ver1 and Simda have the maximum MSE score, indicating that the differences are evident. The corresponding PSNR values indicate the same observations, and the highest SSIM score indicates the high similarity between Kelihos_ver3 and Vundo compared with the other pairings. Obfuscator.ACY and Kelihos_ver1 have the highest PSNR score, indicating they are the combination of software with the closest relationship. Overall, the results indicate that various software pairs can have varying degrees of similarity, with some pairs possessing relatively similar images and most software types demonstrating distinct visual characteristics. This also demonstrates the viability of image analysis-based malware detection solutions.

Table 1. Statistics of Software Similarity based on Random Sampling.

pair_1	pair_2	MSE	PSNR	SSIM
Gatak	Kelihos_ver1	0.118	9.297	0.017
Gatak	Kelihos_ver3	0.141	8.512	0.007
Gatak	Simda	0.142	8.486	0.005
Gatak	Tracur	0.116	9.342	0.005
Gatak	Vundo	0.143	8.443	0.008
Kelihos_ver1	Kelihos_ver3	0.174	7.604	0.009
Kelihos_ver1	Simda	**0.175**	**7.559**	0.019
Kelihos_ver1	Tracur	0.144	8.416	0.006
Kelihos_ver1	Vundo	0.175	7.579	0.010
Kelihos_ver3	Tracur	0.091	10.425	0.015
Kelihos_ver3	Vundo	**0.079**	**11.023**	0.013
Lollipop	Gatak	0.089	10.503	0.008
Lollipop	Kelihos_ver1	0.111	9.543	0.014
Lollipop	Kelihos_ver3	0.127	8.953	0.013
Lollipop	Obfuscator.ACY	0.114	9.416	0.008
Lollipop	Simda	0.117	9.311	0.016
Lollipop	Tracur	0.102	9.896	0.018
Lollipop	Vundo	0.129	8.891	0.011
Obfuscator.ACY	Gatak	0.137	8.635	0.010
Obfuscator.ACY	Kelihos_ver1	0.129	8.895	**0.049**
Obfuscator.ACY	Kelihos_ver3	0.124	9.082	0.008
Obfuscator.ACY	Simda	0.131	8.823	0.013
Obfuscator.ACY	Tracur	0.116	9.340	0.010
Obfuscator.ACY	Vundo	0.125	9.041	**0.003**
Simda	Kelihos_ver3	0.091	10.404	0.021
Simda	Tracur	0.098	10.077	0.011
Simda	Vundo	0.094	10.271	0.013
Tracur	Vundo	0.091	10.416	0.008

3.2 Generative Attack Network

GAN is a hybrid model that simultaneously uses two models performing antagonistic tasks: the generative model G to represent the data distribution and the discriminative model D to assess the likelihood that a sample came from the training data rather than the model G. For model optimisation, the objective of G is to generate synthetic data as similar as possible to the origin, while the objective of D is to perform at its best at label prediction. Hence, the two models perform contradictive tasks and are trained in a competing manner with the max-min optimization. Due to G's capacity to learn the data distribution and calculate simulated samples, this hybrid technique can be utilised for oversampling or performance boosting for challenging classification tasks. In our specified GAN framework, G attempts to perplex the D network by creating samples that are analogous to the real ones, while D works to categorise them precisely.

The suggested method involves feeding a random noise vector into the generator network prior to training in order to increase G's capacity for denoising the original data. Denoising will help generate synthetic data that is as close to the actual data as feasible. With a random noise vector z of the same size as original input X, the structure of GAN can be expressed with (4) and (5).

The basic mathematics of a GAN can be expressed using the following formulas:

$$X' = G(X + z) \tag{4}$$

$$p(X) = D(X') = D(G(X + z)) \tag{5}$$

For the random noise vector, we apply the random data following Gaussian distribution, for which the standard deviation is set to 0.1. The Gaussian noise can be modelled as the addition of a random variable derived from a normal distribution with mean 0 and standard deviation 0.1, where the noise added to each input sample is independent from the others and can regularise the model and minimise overfitting. The added Gaussian noise z can be written as follows, in which $\sigma = 0.1$:

$$z \sim N(0, \sigma^2). \tag{6}$$

The generator and discriminator networks are trained with a loss function that computes the difference between input and output. For G, we use mean square error to evaluate the reconstruction error between X and X'; for D, we use binary cross entropy to evaluate the label prediction performance.

3.3 Generative Models: AE and Variations

For generator model, AE can learn an informative representation of the origin by minimising the difference between the input and output. To learn and reconstruct the input data with little error, the AE is trained to learn the most representative characteristics of original data. The proposed model consists of an encoder, bottleneck, and decoder. The encoder consists of three blocks for convolutional and pooling operations: each block begins with convolutional layers with (3,3) size filters, followed by an activation layer with LeakyReLU function as shown in (7) and a batch normalisation layer:

$$\text{LeakyReLU}(x) = f(x) = \begin{cases} alpha * x, x < 0 \\ x, x \geq 0 \end{cases}, alpha < 0. \tag{7}$$

These three layers are executed with two cycles, and a pooling layer with (2,2) size is then implemented. The bottleneck is a fully connected layer that flattens and compresses the convolutional result's feature representation into a reduced dimensional space. The decoder replicates the structure of the encoder, substituting upsampling layers for pooling layers. Last but not least, the output layer employs batch normalisation and a dropout rate of 0.5 to prevent overfitting.

While utilising normal AE as the generator of GAN framework can be effective, it can also be practical to use the variance like a variational autoencoder (VAE). The concept of VAE-GAN was first introduced by Larsen et al. [18], in which work they proposed to use a learned similarity metric to represent data in an autoencoder. Since this probabilistic and statistic-based metric can capture higher-level features and relationships between the data points, it can produce more meaningful encoding than simply rely on the raw pixel values.

The original high-dimensional data is transformed into a low-dimensional representation, typically the bottleneck layer of every autoencoder architecture. Next, in contrast to standard autoencoders that utilize a single fully connected layer for the bottleneck representation, VAEs incorporate a regularization term known as Kullback-Leibler (KL) divergence [19]. This term ensures that the hidden representation follows a normal distribution, providing additional control over the encoding process. In VAEs, the bottleneck layer encodes data into two small-dimensional spaces representing the mean and variance distributions. After convolutional encoding, the data is flattened to a one-dimensional format. Subsequently, two fully connected layers with significantly smaller output units process the input and calculate the mean μ_z and log variance σ_z, and a sampling process operation as (8) is performed.

$$z = \mu_z + \sigma_z * \varepsilon, \varepsilon \sim N(0,1) \tag{8}$$

Equation (8) utilises the two latent layers, the mean μ_z and log variance σ_z, and incorporates a random number vector ε following the standard normal distribution $N(0,1)$ to calculate the sampling result z. After the computation of μ_z and σ_z and sampling, the decoder takes the sampled result and reshapes the one-dimensional latent representations for data reconstruction.

VAE's loss function consists of two components: the reconstruction loss and the KL divergence. The reconstruction loss quantifies the difference between the original samples and their reconstructed counterparts using MSE. The KL divergence measures the dissimilarity between the encoded Gaussian distribution $q(z|x)$ and the standard normal distribution $p(z)$, providing an assessment of the loss of significant information. Assuming a defined latent space with latent representations in D dimensions, denoted by mean μ_d and standard deviation σ_d for each dimension, the KL divergence is calculated as shown in Eq. (9):

$$KL_{loss} = KL[q(z|x)||p(z)] = -0.5 * \sum_{d=1}^{D}\left[1 + \log(\sigma_d)^2 - \mu^2_d - (\sigma_d)^2\right]. \tag{9}$$

Here, $(q(z|x))$ represents the encoding distribution, while $p(z)$ denotes the prior distribution. It captures the information loss when using the entire conditional distribution $(q(z|x))$ instead of solely relying on the prior distribution $(p(z))$. A KL divergence close to zero indicates that crucial information is not being compromised.

For model implementation, apart from similar structure of encoder and decoder, we create a custom layer, Variational Layer, to implement the sampling process and loss functions. It computes the binary cross-entropy between the original inputs and the reconstructed ones. The sampling process uses the mean and variance, namely the encoder's two outputs, to create the output following the random normal distribution.

3.4 Transfer Learning-Based Discriminator

Whereas CNN's feature extraction capability can decrease when the dimension arises, it is highly conceivable to use transfer learning with those models highly trained with massive datasets. Since transfer learning enables the discriminator to employ pre-trained weights from an effective image classification model, it is advantageous for the image-based software classification task. By utilising the information and feature representations learnt from the pre-trained model, the discriminator is able to dramatically increase the model's accuracy and shorten the training process. Since the model is trained on a huge and diverse dataset, transfer learning can also reduce overfitting and aid the model's ability to generalise better on fresh data.

In the proposed method, the model architecture is based on MobileNet [20], a pre-trained neural network model for image classification with deep but training-efficient

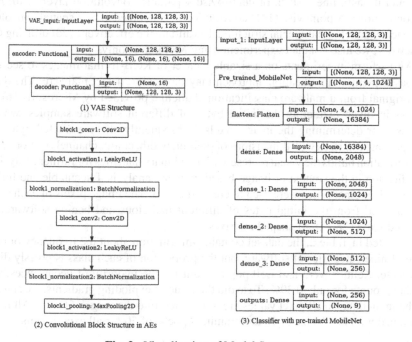

Fig. 2. Visualization of Model Structure

structure, and the weights pre-trained with "imagenet" dataset is loaded. Utilising the MobileNet as base model, the output of base model is flattened and processed by four Dense layers with 2056, 1028, 512, and 256 units, respectively, with ReLU activation. The last Dense layer has output units of label number with SoftMax activation, since the discriminator is used for a multi-class classification problem. Figure 2 displays key components of our approach, providing visual representations of the model structures.

Figure 2 (1) depicts the general AE architecture, using VAE as an example; the three low-dimensional layers represents the mean, variance, and sampling layers. Figure 2(2) visualizes a convolutional block within the AEs, while both the decoder and encoder consist of multiple blocks with varying output units (the pooling layers are modified to upsampling layers in decoder's blocks). Lastly, Fig. 2(3) illustrates the structure of the transfer-learning based classifier.

4 Experiment and Discussion

4.1 Baselines

We selected two well-known, deep, and successful image classification models to evaluate their performance in contrast to other cutting-edge approaches. The first one is the VGG19 [21], which increased the performance by pushing the depth of a CNN-based model to 16–19 weight layers deep with identical (3*3) unit convolution filters in each CNN layer. They show that adding depth can considerably boost performance, but occasionally the added time cost makes this model unfeasible. The second one is Xception [22], and it has a linear stack of depth-wise separable convolution layers with residual connections. A pointwise (1*1) convolution is conducted after a spatial convolution over each channel in the special structure. To validate the effectiveness of utilising GAN framework, we also conduct experiment using MobileNet only.

We perform experiments on a sizable dataset of RGB-format images to see if the AE-based picture classification approach may be used to detect malware. The dataset was original from a malware classification challenge provided by Microsoft [16]. The process involved extracting the initial bytes of different software samples, which is the basis for determining the image pixels. Subsequently, these extracted bytes were reshaped into matrices with dimensions of (height, width, colour channels of 1 or 3). This transformation builds the visual representation of binary data files for further analysis and classification in the context of image-based malware analysis. Executable and linkable format (ELF) binary files were used to create the data. The image pixels of each sample were derived from the initial bytes of different malicious and benign software, then reshaped into (128,128,3)-shaped matrixes.

As stated in Table 2, the dataset contains information about the frequency of occurrence of nine categories of software, but the proportion of each class is grossly disproportionate. Kelihos_ver3 and Lollipop account for the majority of occurrences, while Simda accounts for only 0.39%. To avoid the issue of exploding gradients, we standardize the input data, so all pixel values are transferred into the range of 0 to 1. All models are trained with batch size of 16 and training epochs of 50 for all experiments.

Table 2. Statistics of Software Samples.

Software	Percentage
Lollipop	22.82%
Obfuscator.ACY	11.31%
Gatak	9.33%
Kelihos_ver1	3.66%
Simda	0.39%
Kelihos_ver3	27.09%
Tracur	6.92%
Vundo	4.37%
Ramnit	14.12%

4.2 Reconstruction Results

Although the classification task is the most crucial, the ability to accurately reconstruct data is also of utmost importance. Reconstruction serves as the foundation for various sophisticated tasks, including the generation of synthetic samples, intricate image modifications, and the reliable detection of abnormal data in network security analysis. When only normal behaviours or software are available for analysis, autoencoders can be trained on negative examples and the reconstruction error can be computed to identify anomalous samples, thus aiding in the identification of malware.

To improve and evaluate the effectiveness of denoising techniques, we conduct experiments with varying settings of noising vectors. The introduction of noise is a technique that plays a significant role in enhancing the overall performance of generative models, specifically in terms of reconstruction loss. By incorporating noise into the original data, AEs are encouraged to learn more accurate and reliable data representations. The primary advantage of introducing noise is to ensure that the models do not excessively rely on noise or irrelevant features during reconstruction. This process helps in cultivating a more comprehensive understanding of the underlying patterns and features, resulting in improved reconstruction performance. In the case of "without noise," the noise vector contained only zeros, while other settings introduced noise to input data matrices.

Table 3 illustrates the reconstruction error for different models. The results demonstrate that adding noise to the original data improves the performance of generative models in terms of reconstruction loss. Specifically, the AE with noise exhibits slightly lower reconstruction loss compared to the original VAE. This improvement can be attributed to the comprehensive evaluation of the VAE, which quantifies not only the mean squared error (MSE)-based reconstruction error but also the KL loss. On the other hand, the VAE with denoising techniques shows a significantly lower reconstruction loss compared to the original VAE.

By introducing noise, the models are encouraged to learn more reliable representations of the data that are not overly dependent on noise or irrelevant features. This enhancement in capacity leads to improved reconstruction performance as the models

Table 3. Reconstruction Error.

Reconstruction	Loss
AE_without_noise	0.2384
AE_with_noise	0.2373
VAE_without_noise	0.3834
VAE_with_noise	0.2686

acquire more universal patterns and features. Moreover, in the case of VAEs, increasing noise can also contribute to the creation of a smoother latent space, which facilitates sampling and enhances the quality of generated samples.

4.3 Classification Results

Table 4 displays the overall performance of different models for malware classification. The results clearly indicate that MobileNet, particularly when using as a pretrained model, outperforms VGG16 and Xception in terms of both accuracy and detection rate. Meanwhile, the VAE-GAN utilising MobileNet model achieves the best performance in all the metrics. Interestingly, when employing normal AE as the generator, the performance decreased than using MobileNet alone, indicating the inadequate feature extraction and data reconstruction capabilities of a regular AE for malware imagery. Meanwhile, using VAE not only enhances the detection ability but also reduces false alarms compared to using MobileNet alone. Based on these experiment results, the VAE-GAN approach incorporating transfer learning based on MobileNet emerges as the most effective model for malware classification.

Table 4. Overall Performance.

Model	Accuracy	Precision	Recall	F1-score	False Alarm
GAN_AE	**0.9334**	**0.9549**	**0.9150**	**0.9345**	**0.0054**
GAN_VAE	0.9619	0.9627	0.9609	0.9618	0.0047
MobileNet	0.9494	0.9537	0.9476	0.9507	0.0057
VGG16	0.9030	0.9125	0.9007	0.9066	0.0108
Xception	0.7583	0.8730	0.6728	0.7599	0.0122

Table 5 presents the detection rates of various software. Among the most prevalent software, such as Lollipop and Kelihos_ver3, all models exhibit excellent detection rates surpassing 90%. Notably, the VAE-GAN model outperforms the others and achieves a perfect detection rate of 100% for Kelihos_ver3. In contrast, for the rarest software, namely Simda, VGG16 underperforms slightly and Xception fails to detect any instances. Nevertheless, MobileNet-based approaches still manage to detect the majority of cases. Though GAN_VAE outperforms other models in the majority of instances, MobileNet alone outperforms GAN for Tracur and Vundo, which are also relatively minor among the datasets.

However, despite the improvements achieved with the GAN approach, further enhancements should be explored and evaluated. It is plausible that certain types of software share similarities with others, making it challenging for the generator to learn and for the discriminator to identify, especially given the limited training data. One potential approach to address this issue is to configure the generator as a conditional model, enabling the generation of minority data based on specific conditions to balance the data classes before training the discriminator.

Table 5. Detection Performance.

Recall	GAN_AE	GAN_VAE	MobileNet	VGG16	Xception
Lollipop	**0.95**	0.97	0.97	0.95	0.86
Obfuscator.ACY	**0.87**	0.92	0.87	0.86	0.72
Gatak	**0.95**	0.97	0.95	0.92	0.61
Kelihos_ver1	**0.99**	0.99	0.98	0.97	0.85
Simda	**0.89**	0.89	0.88	0.70	0.00
Kelihos_ver3	**0.99**	1.00	0.99	0.97	0.92
Tracur	**0.81**	**0.88**	0.93	0.82	0.70
Ramnit	**0.91**	0.96	0.95	0.90	0.60
Vundo	**0.83**	**0.89**	0.90	0.84	0.27

4.4 Discussion: Practicality and Applicability

The results of the experiments offer significant new insights into a number of components of image-based malware analysis.

First off, the denoising VAE performs better for malware imagery reconstruction than the standard AE, and adding noise to the original data seems to improve both the AE and VAE generative models' performance for reconstruction loss. This suggests that the most valuable representations of malware imagery can be successfully captured by incorporating demystifying generative models.

Second, the use of transfer learning illustrates its potential advantages in malware analysis using images. The classifier can perform better by using pre-trained models with a light structure as the foundation for the malware classification task, such as MobileNet. In the context of malware analysis, this emphasises the significance of knowledge transfer from previously trained models in enhancing detection performance and generalizability.

Additional research might investigate the use of conditional models to create minority data for the discriminator's training and evaluate the efficacy of other lightweight models for improved analysis.

Finally, GANs may be able to help with the analysis of malware that is polymorphic or obfuscated by producing a variety of malicious code representations. This provides possibilities for more effective and flexible malware analysis techniques.

5 Conclusion

This paper proposes VAE-GAN classification methods for malware. Using the image-based malware approach, this method can capture the most valuable representation of high-dimensional inputs and conduct effective malware detection and classification.

The conducted experiments yield valuable findings: (1) Adding noise to the original data proves to be a critical factor in enhancing the reconstruction loss performance of both AE and VAE generative models. (2) Among the models evaluated, MobileNet emerges as the top performer for malware classification, while the VAE-GAN approach demonstrates superior performance across all evaluated metrics. Moreover, it is evident that the use of a standard AE results in decreased efficacy compared to employing MobileNet alone.

The proposed method employs denoise VAE-GAN and transfer learning to improve detection performance and generalizability and is highly implementable and scalable in a production setting.

In addition, additional enhancements, such as using a conditional model to generate minority data prior to training the discriminator and examining other light-weighted models, should be tested, and evaluated.

Acknowledgements. This research is being supported by the grant of RSF #21-71-20078 in SPC RAS.

References

1. Ruiz, J.F., Harjani, R., Maña, A., Desnitsky, V., Kotenko, I., Chechulin, A.: A methodology for the analysis and modeling of security threats and attacks for systems of embedded components. In: Proceedings of 20th Euromicro International Conference on Parallel, Distributed and Network-Based Processing, PDP 2012, pp. 261–268 (2012)
2. Branitskiy, A., Kotenko, I.: Hybridization of computational intelligence methods for attack detection in computer networks. J. Comput. Sci. **23**, 145–156 (2017)
3. Ucci, D., Aniello, L., Baldoni, R.: Survey of machine learning techniques for malware analysis. Comput. Secur. **81**(1), 123–147 (2019)
4. Darabian, H., Homayounoot, S., Dehghantanha, A.: Detecting cryptomining malware: a deep learning approach for static and dynamic analysis. J. Grid Comput. **18**, 293–303 (2020)
5. Ijaz, M., Durad, M.H., Ismail, M.: Static and dynamic malware analysis using machine learning. In: Proceedings of the 16th International Bhurban Conference on Applied Sciences and Technology (IBCAST), pp. 687–691. Islamabad, Pakistan (2019)
6. Vasan, D., Alazab, M., Wassan, S., Safaei, B., Zheng, Q.: Image-Based malware classification using ensemble of CNN architectures. Comput. Secur. **92**(1), 101748 (2020)
7. Vasan, D., Alazab, M., Wassan, S., Naeem, H., Safaei, B., Zheng, Q.: IMCFN: image-based malware classification using fine-tuned convolutional neural network architecture. Comput. Netw. **171**(1), 107138 (2020)

8. Kim, H.-J.: Image-based malware classification using convolutional neural network. In: Park, J.J., Loia, V., Yi, G., Sung, Y. (eds.) CUTE/CSA -2017. LNEE, vol. 474, pp. 1352–1357. Springer, Singapore (2018). https://doi.org/10.1007/978-981-10-7605-3_215

9. Tran, K., Di Troia, F., Stamp, M.: Robustness of image-based malware analysis. In: Silicon Valley Cybersecurity Conference, pp. 3–21. Silicon Valley, USA (2022)

10. Awan, M.J., et al.: Image-based malware classification using VGG19 network and spatial convolutional attention. Electronics 10, 2444 (2021)

11. Prajapati, P., Stamp, M.: An empirical analysis of image-based learning techniques for malware classification. In: Malware Analysis Using Artificial Intelligence and Deep Learning (2021)

12. Bhodia, N., Prajapati, P., Di Troia, F., Stamp, M.: Transfer learning for image-based malware classification. arXiv preprint (arXiv:1903.11551) (2019)

13. Su, J., Vasconcellos, D.V., Prasad, S., Sgandurra, D., Feng, Y., Sakurai, K.: Lightweight classification of IoT malware based on image recognition. In: 2018 IEEE 42nd Annual Computer Software and Applications Conference, pp. 664–669. Tokyo, Japan (2018)

14. Dovom, E.M., Azmoodeh, A., Dehghantanha, A., Newton, D.E., Parizi, R.M., Karimi-pour, H.: Fuzzy pattern tree for edge malware detection and categorization in IoT. J. Syst. Architect. 97, 1–7 (2019)

15. Zhang, X., Wang, J., Sun, M., Feng, Y.: AndrOpGAN: an opcode GAN for android malware obfuscations. In: Chen, X., Yan, H., Yan, Q., Zhang, X. (eds.) ML4CS 2020. LNCS, vol. 12486, pp. 12–25. Springer, Cham (2020). https://doi.org/10.1007/978-3-030-62223-7_2

16. Ronen, R., Radu, M., Feuerstein, C., Yom-Tov, E., Ahmadi, M.: Microsoft malware classification challenge. arXiv preprint (2018)

17. Wang, Z., Simoncelli, E.P., Bovik, A.C.: Multiscale structural similarity for image quality assessment. In: Conference Record of the Thirty-Seventh Asilomar Conference on Signals, Systems and Computers, vol. 2, pp. 1398–1402 (2004)

18. Larsen, A., Sønderby, S., Winther, O.: Autoencoding beyond pixels using a learned similarity metric. arXiv preprint (2015)

19. Cinelli, L.P., Marins, M.A., Barros, E.A., da Silva, S., Netto, L.: Variational autoencoder. In: Cinelli, L.P., Marins, M.A., Barros, E.A., da Silva, S., Netto, L. (eds.) Variational Methods for Machine Learning with Applications to Deep Networks, pp. 111–149. Springer International Publishing, Cham (2021). https://doi.org/10.1007/978-3-030-70679-1_5

20. Howard, A., et al.: Searching for MobileNetV3. In: Proceedings of the IEEE/CVF International Conference on Computer Vision (ICCV), pp. 1314–1324. Seoul, Korea (2019)

21. Simonyan K., Zisserman A.: Very deep convolutional networks for large-scale image recognition. In: Proceedings of the IEEE Conference on Computer Vision and Pattern Recognition. pp. 1–9. Boston, MA, USA (2015)

22. Francois, C.: Xception: deep learning with depthwise separable convolutions. In: Proceedings of the IEEE Conference on Computer Vision and Pattern Recognition, pp. 1800–1807. Honolulu, USA (2017)

A Novel Software Defined Security Framework for SDN

Srijita Basu[1]([✉]) [iD], Neha Firdaush Raun[1], Avishek Ghosal[1], Debanjan Chatterjee[1], Debarghya Maitra[2], and Chandan Mazumdar[1] [iD]

[1] Centre for Distributed Computing, Jadavpur University, Kolkata, India
srijitab.cse.rs@jadavpuruniversity.in
[2] Jadavpur University, Kolkata, India

Abstract. Software Defined Security (SDS) entails the security implementation of a network, based on certain applications. It can be portrayed as a virtualized abstraction of the essential security features into a single software layer. SDS can be designed for traditional physical, virtualized, NFVs (Network Function Virtualization) and SDN (Software Defined Networking) based networks. This paper aims at developing an SDS framework for ONOS based SDN systems. Though most of the existing controllers like RYU, Floodlight, POX and ODL provide a framework for designing SDN applications and REST APIs, ONOS (Open Network Operating System) is comparatively more flexible. The novelty in considering the "SDS on SDN" design lies in the uniformity and scalability of the system. Moreover, a data plane device can now act in a polymorphic manner. The required security rules are provided into the SDS framework that in turn modifies the corresponding flow rules and the control plane forwards the same to the dataplane devices. Thus, a data plane device can have the functionalities of a firewall, IDS, IPS, AAA, etc. depending upon the triggered flow rule. Dependency on a particular security appliance or VNF and the necessity of maintaining multiple instances of the same is eliminated in the proposed system. The experimental setup comprises of a hybrid network topology of virtual mininet switches and HP Aruba switches. The performance analysis of the system in terms of throughput, bandwidth, and RTT latency shows a considerably low overhead thereby proving the effectiveness of the scheme.

Keywords: Application · Controller · Firewall · Security

1 Introduction

Software Defined Security (SDS) refers to the software based instantiation and management of different security functionalities and events responsible for implementing, updating, viewing and deleting the concerned security rules for a given network topology. The concept of SDS eliminates the dependency on traditional hardware based security systems and adds a layer of abstraction that administers the behavior of different security applications like firewall, Intrusion Detection System (IDS), Intrusion Prevention System (IPS), Authentication, Authorization and Accounting (AAA) Services, etc.

A. Ait Wakrime et al. (Eds.): CRiSIS 2023, LNCS 14529, pp. 216–230, 2024.
https://doi.org/10.1007/978-3-031-61231-2_14

A SDS framework can work in four different flavors.

(i) *SDS in Traditional Network*: In traditional networking models, devices make traffic forwarding decisions using routing tables installed within them. Each network device acts as an individual agent capable of controlling its own communication. This scenario becomes quite complicated for large and complex networks. In such a case, the SDS framework acts as a centralized unit for controlling and monitoring the organization's security parameters by interacting with each of the individual network devices as in a Security Operations Centre.

(ii) *SDS for NFV*: Virtual Network Functions (VNFs) are created to implement different functionalities between virtual machines over a CMS (Cloud Management System) platform or virtualization layer [1]. An SDS framework can be designed to instantiate different security functionalities for the VNFs. Even in this scenario, SDS needs to interact with each VNF individually in order to modify the activities of the connected VMs

(iii) *SDS for Virtualized Network*: A Physical Network can be mapped to a corresponding virtual one with all the network elements being logically tagged to its physical counterpart [3]. An SDS can be designed over this virtual network layer to instantiate the various security rules for the virtual elements which would finally make its physical counterparts act accordingly.

(iv) *SDS for SDN*: Software Defined Networking (SDN) based network comprises the data plane (e.g. Openflow enabled switch, router, etc.), control plane and the application plane [2]. Here, the SDS framework (Fig. 1) interacts with the application plane using REST APIs to instantiate the required security rules. The advantage of this design lies in the fact that a dataplane device itself can act as a security device (Firewall, DDoS Handler, etc.) depending upon the rules that have been communicated by the control plane.

In this paper the "SDS for SDN" architecture has been used to design a SDS framework over an ONOS controller with an underlying hybrid topology consisting of physical HP Aruba Openflow switches and mininet-virtual network. Different security applications like Firewall, Distributed Denial of Service (DDoS management), AAA configuration, NAT (Network Address Translation), etc. have been implemented as part of the proposed methodology. The selection of ONOS over other SDN controllers was preferred because ONOS presents better fault management in the control plane and higher throughput and lower latency in the data plane compared to ODL, RYU, Floodlight, NOX, POX etc. [4, 5].

Rest of the paper has been organized as follows. Section 2 presents a short literature survey of different SDS systems. The proposed SDS framework containing the detailed architecture and implementation has been depicted in Sect. 3. Section 4 presents the results and performance analysis of the proposed system. Finally, the paper is concluded in Sect. 5.

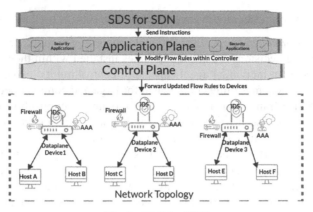

Fig. 1. SDS for SDN

2 Related Work

A good amount of research work has been carried out in the field of SDS. A few of them, relevant to our work, have been discussed in the following.

A Security Controller-based Software Defined Security (SC-SDS) architecture has been presented in [6]. A modularized security controller is defined in the architecture which interacts with other components through APIs. Based on the SC-SDS architecture, security service orchestration is achieved, which combines independent security services to enhance the overall security of the system.

A novel virtualized testbed environment (SDSecurity) has been presented in [7]. The paper has divided the SDSec into three parts: SDSec Host, SDSec Switch and SDSec Controller. This framework is built on the SDN Mininet simulator. The authors intend to extend SDSecurity to build a distributed controller to reduce its overhead and to improve its performance. Adding more security controls inside each controller and creating more tests to analyze its performance was also pointed out as one of the possible future works.

In [8] a survey on SDN security has been depicted. The security loopholes and strengths of SDN have been highlighted in this paper. In doing so, different security vulnerabilities in application, control, and data planes of SDN and their corresponding countermeasures have been discussed. Security recommendations of ITU-T and their associated costs have been briefly described. Some of the probable solutions like DDoS (DDOS framework), SE-Floodlight (Apps Authorization), VeriFlow (Fault flowrules) etc. were conceptually explained in this paper.

A SNORT based early DDoS detection system using Opendaylight and ONOS controllers has been depicted in [9]. Huge traffic was generated by using some penetration testing tools and later the same was captured in order to detect a DDoS attack. The authors intend to develop a DDoS prevention framework as a future work.

The scheme presented in [10] builds a firewall application to filter the packets based on their headers and matches them against different predefined policies. It detects different packets like TCP, UDP, ICMP and blocks them depending upon the induced policy. The authors plan to add more functionalities in order to facilitate different routing mechanisms.

In [11] a Certificate-Based AAA (C-BAS) for SDN environment has been proposed. This paper also serves as a guide for a seamless migration path for existing SDN experimental facilities which employ username-and-password authentication mechanisms.

The above mentioned papers give a brief overview of the research advancements in the field of SDS for SDN. Though most of the schemes have independently tried to cover different aspects of SDN security, they fail to provide a uniform framework to address the concerned security issues as a whole. Moreover, most of the works try to provide conceptual solutions rather than actual implementation. The main contributions of our scheme are as follows.

1. Designing and implementing an end-to-end SDS system based on Python-Django framework.
2. Using a hybrid network consisting of physical data plane devices and mininet based virtual network for proving that the concept works for both physical and virtual networks.
3. Achieving a considerably low performance overhead for both the type of networks.
4. Achieving a uniform architecture where the SDS framework needs to communicate with the application plane of the controller layer for implementing the concerned security features in the dataplane devices. Multiple communication points can therefore be avoided. In other proposals [6, 9, 11] this kind of uniformity is missing. Though the security policies are implemented no single point of communication exists.
5. Here, the same data plane device can have different security functionalities depending on the configuration and flow rules forwarded by the controller.

3 Proposed SDS Framework

3.1 Architecture

The generic architecture of the SDN based SDS framework has already been depicted in Fig. 1. The user authentication at this level is handled by the SDS framework itself. The framework considers three user roles viz. *Admin*, *Manager* and *Operator* where *Admin* has the highest set of privileges followed by the *Manager* and *Operator* in a decreasing order of access privileges. The SDS framework receives the security policies or configuration inputs from the user (Network Security Administrators). These inputs are passed as parameters to the REST APIs [2] of SDN controllers. The REST APIs on receiving the required input values trigger the concerned security applications in the Application plane. Next, the target application executes and modifies the flow rules or other related functionalities of the controller (control plane). Finally, these updated rules and functionalities are forwarded to the dataplane devices through a suitable southbound protocol. An overview of the architecture for the developed framework has been presented in Fig. 2. The entities depicted in the figure are presented as follows:

1. *SDS Framework:* Initially, the framework establishes its connection with the intended SDN controller. Later, it instantiates different security applications for the underlying network topology, depending upon the provided user inputs. The detailed process has been depicted in the upcoming sub-section.

2. *SDN REST API:* The SDS framework communicates with the SDN REST APIs. The main links that have been added in the REST API page in context of the security applications include GET, POST and DELETE.

3. *SDN Applications:* In general, this layer contains all the applications that are built on the controller. Here, some specific SDN applications have been designed in this layer for adding the required security functionalities

4. *Core Networking Layer:* The basic SDN controller kernel [2] lies in this layer. It contains the required set of network controls and configuration abstraction. This is the base minimum required to run the controller. In order to extend different existing functionalities of the core networking layer various extensions exist in the form of applications. Again, in order to communicate to the external environment different adapters (UI, REST API, gRPC, RESTCONF) come into action. In this framework the REST API adapter has been used for the purpose.

5. *Distributed Application Platform:* At the base of the SDN controller architecture lies the Distributed Application Platform layer required for ensuring high availability, scalability and performance of the system.

6. *Network Topology:* The data plane devices i.e. the openflow [3] enabled switch and routers of the underlying physical/virtual network are connected to the controller (generally done using the set-controller command at the device end). Multiple end hosts are connected to these devices. These openflow enabled devices along with the end hosts form the network topology layer.

The implementation of each of these architectural entities have been elaborated in the next subsection.

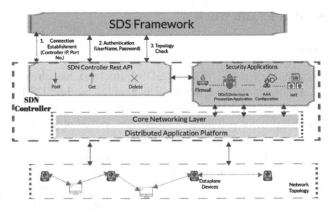

Fig. 2. A Detailed SDS Framework

3.2 Implementation

The ONOS SDN controller has been integrated with the SDS framework in order to implement the intended security modules. The different phases of the actions between the SDS framework and ONOS controller are depicted as follows:

1. *Connection Establishment*: The Python-Django based SDS framework connects and authenticates with the ONOS controller instance. Three types of connections, Single ONOS instance, Multiple ONOS instance and ONOS controller cluster [7] (handles controller fault tolerance) are possible here. After entering a valid IP address and port number for the ONOS controller, some standard authentication methods (password-based, public key-based password-less mechanism) are next used to complete the connection and authentication phase. Next, a topology check is executed by the SDS framework in order to ensure that some network topology is associated with the concerned ONOS controllers. If no network is detected, then the SDS framework displays an error. Otherwise, upon successful detection of a topology, the SDS framework can now interact with the controller for implementing different security functionalities.

2. *API Design*: The ONOS REST API page is available at http://<ONOSIP>:8181/onos/v1/docs/. The REST APIs that have been designed for the implementation of different security applications provide an interface for instantiating (POST), extracting (GET) and removing (DELETE) the required security rules and configurations. The POST API is used to instantiate some configuration or rule into the ONOS controller. Generally, rules can be instantiated as JSON (JavaScript Object Notation) format or normal text inputs depending upon the design of the REST API for the application. For example, firewall rules can be pushed into the controller using the POST /firewalladd/{sourceMAC}/{destMAC}/{protocol} API. The GET API returns different details of the ONOS controller and its underlying network topology. For example, GET /firewall returns the firewall rules that have been added. The DELETE API is used to delete some configuration or rules from the ONOS controller. For example, the added firewall rules can be deleted using the DELETE /firewall/{sourceMAC}/{destMAC}/{protocol} API.

3. *Application Design*: A few security applications have been implemented in the ONOS application layer. These applications include a separate module for REST API creation. An ONOS application can't interact directly with the SDS framework and therefore the REST APIs act as an intermediary channel. Once an application is installed and activated in the ONOS environment (along with its REST API module), the same is reflected in the REST API page of the ONOS controller. Next, whenever a user sends any instruction through the SDS framework, it is communicated to the ONOS Application layer via the REST API adapter. The application executes the intended task which is manifested by modifications in the behavior of the dataplane layer.

4. *Rule Forwarding:* The ONOS controller forwards Openflow messages to send any kind of information to the dataplane devices. In a nutshell, any input provided by the user at the SDS framework layer passes through the ONOS controller and gets translated into required configuration item or flow rule. Finally, these items are sent to the dataplane devices to modify their functionalities or activities accordingly.

Security Application Implementation: The logic and implementation of three of the security applications that have been designed as part of the SDS framework are detailed here.

Table 1. Methods used in Firewall Application

Sl. No.	Method name	Utility
1	processPacket(PacketContext context, Ethernet eth, Byte protocol)	a. Processes a specified packet to extract its source and destination MAC address and protocol b. Retrieves the rules given by the user (by REST API) c. Matches the packet against these rules d. If the rule suggests a packet drop then call the method *banpings()*
2	dropPacket(DeviceId deviceId, MacAddress src, MacAddress dst, Byte protocol)	Installs a drop flow rule between the source and destination hosts by adding or modifying ingress rules of the flow table
3	PingPacketProcessor()	Checks the Protocol Type of a packet
4	setRule(String source, String dest, Byte protocol	Set the firewall rules
5	removeRule(String source, String dest, Byte protocol)	Remove the firewall rules
6	getRules()	Return the list of firewall rules
7	matches(String source, String dest)	Matches a packet against the firewall rules. This method is invoked from *processPing()*
8	allowPings(DeviceId deviceId, MacAddress src, MacAddress dst, Byte protocol)	Installs a forward rule between the source and destination hosts by adding or modifying ingress rules of the flow table
11	BlockPort(DeviceId deviceId, PortNumber port)	Blocks a particular port of a device

Firewall Application: Two separate modules have been designed for the ONOS firewall application. The first module concentrates on the design of the REST API for the application. The second module contains the main logic of the firewall.

i) The REST API module is implemented in the *AppWebResource.java* file. The methods *setRule()*, *getRules()*, and *deleteRule()* are used for the POST, GET and DELETE REST APIs respectively. The return type of these methods is a *Response* which denotes a json object body.

ii) The main logic module is implemented in the *AppComponent.java* file. Table 1 presents a few of the significant methods and their utility for implementing the firewall policy. The firewall policies implemented in this paper are based on two broad rule types. According to the first type, the application can allow or deny a packet based on source and destination MAC address and the protocol involved (ICMP, TCP, etc.). There is also a provision for allowing as well as blocking all the packets from all the end hosts at a time. The second type specifies a particular dataplane device i.e. a switch and its port number which can be either blocked or opened. Here again, a user can allow as well as block all the ports of all the devices in the topology at a time.

Therefore, the SDS user interacts with this firewall application to instantiate required firewall rules in order to deny/accept packets from intended hosts for a particular protocol or even to block/allow a particular port of a dataplane device according to the requirement. It is to be noted that the firewall rules provided by the SDS user is ultimately converted into an equivalent flow rule at the application layer which in turn gets forwarded to the dataplane devices. The translation logic has been included in the *App-Component.java* file. The firewall rules are added as flow rules with particular match fields, action being: *NO ACTION* for dropping, and *OUTPUT* for forwarding and priorities lower than default flow rules. In the present implementation, in case any conflicting rule is added by the user, the previous ones are overridden so that the latest rule prevails.

The user can also view as well as remove all these rules. The SDS user interface for providing the firewall rules is presented in Fig. 3.

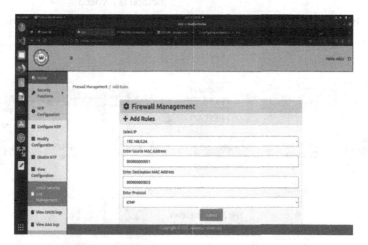

Fig. 3. SNAPSHOT of SDS framework

DDoS Detection and Prevention Application: Table 2 depicts the different methods and their significance for implementing the DDoS detection and prevention application. The core logic of the application assumes that the increase in the value of *bandwidth* of a particular port and/or *CPU usage* of a host beyond a particular threshold indicates DDoS attack. A suitable threshold value is set for both the parameters. Whenever an observed value exceeds this threshold, DDoS is flagged in the system. Upon this detection, the corresponding port of the device is turned down by pushing necessary SDS instructions, thereby attempting to prevent the attack.

The SDS user can view a list of hosts where DDoS was detected. Upon selecting a particular instance, the bandwidth and CPU utilization graph for the same is displayed.

Table 2. Methods used in DDoS Application

Sl. No.	Method	Utility
1	BandwidthCheck(DeviceId deviceId, PortNumber port)	This method retrieves the bandwidth of a particular port. Checks the same against a given threshold value (~20 Gbits/s). If the current value of bandwidth is more than this threshold then the CPUCheck() method is invoked
2	CPUCheck(HostMacID host)	This method checks the CPU utilization of a Host. If the value goes beyond a given threshold (~90%) then the BlockPort() method is invoked
3	BlockPort(DeviceId deviceId, PortNumber port)	Blocks a particular port of a device

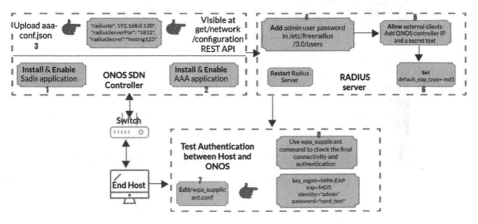

Fig. 4. Detailed workflow of AAA Application

AAA Application: The AAA (Authentication, Authorization, and Accounting) [11] application using MD5 signature is configured from the SDS framework by providing the RADIUS server [12] IP address, port number and secret-text. The same hits the ONOS */network/configuration* API and is stored accordingly. Next, whenever an end host tries to check its authenticity with the ONOS controller a series of EAP (Extensible Authentication Protocol) [12] messages and finally a success message is displayed as presented in Fig. 5. The detailed workflow is presented in Fig. 4.

Fig. 5. Successful Completion of EAP authentication

4 Results and Discussion

The Experimental test bed depicted in Fig. 6 contains three LINUX PCs (PC1- ONOS Controller, PC2- Mininet virtual network and PC3- SDS software) and three HP Aruba-2930M-24G OpenFlow switches [16]. A hybrid network consisting of HP Aruba hardware switches and Mininet based software switches has been considered for the experiment. The framework is quite scalable as it directly interacts with the ONOS controller for implementing the policies. So as long as ONOS can handle an increase in network size, the performance of the SDS framework remains unaffected.

Hardware Specifications: I) PC1: Ubuntu v.20.04.5 LTS (64 bit) OS, Intel Core i3-4130 CPU @ 3.40 GHz 4, 8 GB RAM. *ii) PC2*: Ubuntu v.20.04.6 LTS (64 bit) OS, Intel Core i5-8265U CPU @ 1.60 GHz 8, 16 GB RAM. *iii) PC3*: Ubuntu v.20.04.5 LTS (64 bit) OS, Intel Core i5-8265U CPU @ 1.60 GHz 8, 16 GB RAM.

Software Specifications: The experimental setup required different software installations on the three different PCs.

1. PC1: **ONOS** (VERSION 2.7) is an open source project widely used as an SDN controller. As a prerequisite of ONOS we need ***curl 7.68.0*** and ***openjdk-11-jre-headless_11.0.14***
2. PC2: **MININET** (Version 2.3.1b1) is a virtual network emulator, **IPERF** (Version 2.0.13) is a tool for network performance measurement and tuning. **WIRESHARK** (Version 3.2.3) is an open source packet analyzer tool. **HPING3** (Version 3.0.0-alpha-2) is an open source packet generator. It is generally used for launching DoS/DDoS attacks (TCP SYN, TCP ACK, flood, etc.) [15]. **NMON** and **NMON VISUALIZER** [13] for measuring system performance.
3. PC3: **DJANGO** (Version 4.1.3) - Python web framework, **PYCHARM** (Version 2022.2.2) - Software Development IDE, PYTHON (Version 3.8.6), **MYSQL** (Version 3.31.1) - Use to store user data and configuration.

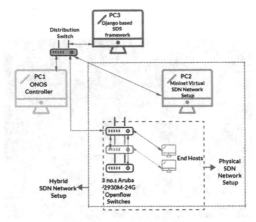

Fig. 6. Experimental Setup

We have implemented different security applications (password manager, NAT, logic based firewall that drops packets for a pre-defined amount of time, etc.) as a part of the SDS framework. Due to paucity of space we present the results and corresponding performance analysis in the context of the firewall and DDoS manager applications only. We have tested our framework in terms of three parameters viz., Bandwidth, Throughput and RTT Latency [14].

4.1 Firewall Application

Figure 7 (i and ii) plots the bandwidth (Mbps) of the TCP packets against time (seconds) for both the mininet virtual network and physical network (connected to Aruba switch) respectively. Iperf has been used to measure the same. Bandwidth is measured both before and after the firewall application was enabled. It is quite clear from the graph that for a mininet network the average bandwidth without a firewall is 48.2 Mbps whereas the value changes to 47.2 Mbps after enabling the firewall. The same for a physical

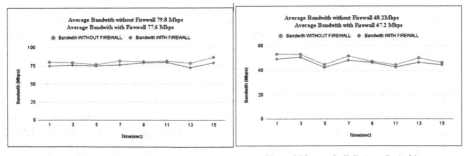

Physical Network (Aruba Switch)   Virtual Network (Mininet Switch)

Fig. 7. Bandwidth v/s Time (i. Physical Network ii. Virtual Network)

network turns out to be 79.8 Mbps and 77.6 Mbps respectively. In both cases, the bandwidth slightly decreases (1–2.2 Mpbs) after the firewall is enabled, thus proving that the SDS implementation does not have an adverse effect on the performance of the system irrespective of the nature of the underlying network.

Figure 8 (i and ii) plots the throughput (bits/second) of the TCP packets against time (seconds) for both the mininet virtual network and physical network (connected to Aruba switch). Wireshark has been used to capture the same. Average throughput measured for mininet network without firewall is 44 Mbits/s and that with firewall is 43 Mbits/s. Similarly, for the Aruba network the values turn out to be 78 Mbits/s and 77 Mbits/s respectively. In both the cases, the throughput slightly decreases (1 Mbits/s) after the firewall is enabled. This again proves that the proposed framework has a very low performance overhead.

Similarly, Fig. 9 (i and ii) plots the RTT Latency (milliseconds) of the TCP packets against time (seconds) for both the mininet virtual network and physical network (connected to Aruba switch). The RTT latency shows an average growth of 7.75 ms in case of Aruba network and 7.87 ms for mininet network when the firewall is enabled. The growth being subtle and uniform proves the efficiency of the system.

The detailed values of bandwidth (BW), throughput (TH) and RTT latency have been given in Table 3. +F and −F signifies the reading with firewall enabled and firewall disabled respectively.

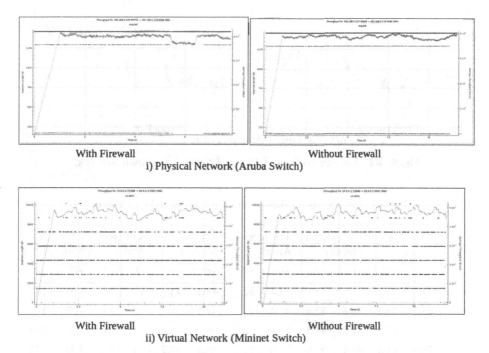

With Firewall   Without Firewall

i) Physical Network (Aruba Switch)

With Firewall   Without Firewall

ii) Virtual Network (Mininet Switch)

Fig. 8. Throughput v/s Time (i. Physical Network ii. Virtual Network)

4.2 DDoS Detection and Prevention Application

In our experimental testbed we have initially started a TCP communication between two end hosts. After a certain time (~30 s) a DDoS attack has been launched using *hping3* on one of the hosts. Next, *Nmon* has been used to measure the CPU utilization. It is quite evident from Fig. 10 that when the attack was launched, the CPU utilization went up at 94%. Once the attack is stopped by turning down the concerned port using the DDoS application, the CPU utilization goes down to 0–15% depending upon the utilization of the core.

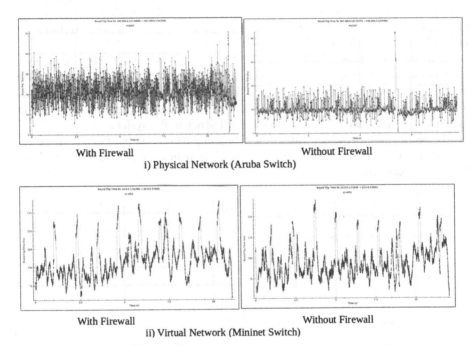

  With Firewall   Without Firewall
i) Physical Network (Aruba Switch)

  With Firewall   Without Firewall
ii) Virtual Network (Mininet Switch)

Fig. 9. RTT Latency v/s Time (i. Physical Network ii. Virtual Network)

Table 3. Data points for Bandwidth, Throughput and RTT Latency

Time	BW (Mbps) Aruba		BW (Mbps) Mininet		TH (Mbps) Aruba		TH (Mbps) Mininet		RTT (ms) Aruba		RTT(ms) Mininet	
	+F	−F	+F	−F	+F	−F	+F	−F	+F	−F	+F	−F
1	74.8	80.2	49.1	53.1	73.4	82	43.1	44.1	40	34	160	151
3	75.8	79.3	50.6	52.9	75.4	78.3	47.2	48.3	42	39	120	111
5	74.8	76.6	42.2	44.5	73.8	76.5	49.1	51.4	29	23	110	105
7	76.3	81.5	48.1	51.6	75.6	81	46.5	47.2	30	24	160	145

(continued)

Table 3. (*continued*)

Time	BW (Mbps) Aruba		BW (Mbps) Mininet		TH (Mbps) Aruba		TH (Mbps) Mininet		RTT (ms) Aruba		RTT(ms) Mininet	
	+F	−F	+F	−F	+F	−F	+F	−F	+F	−F	+F	−F
9	78.9	80.3	46.2	47.1	77.2	79.1	46.2	47.6	40	30	100	97
11	79.4	81.1	42.5	44.3	78.2	81	41.2	43.3	50	34	130	125
13	72.3	78.4	46.3	49.9	82.3	85.4	43.4	45.6	45	38	134	129
15	78.8	86.3	44.3	46.1	79.8	82.1	45.2	43.7	37	29	150	138

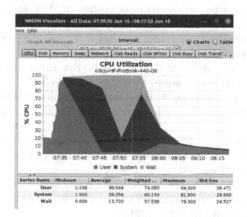

Fig. 10. CPU Utilization v/s Time (DDoS attack)

5 Conclusion

In this paper, a SDS framework based on the ONOS SDN controller has been described. The underlying network topology considered here is hybrid in nature consisting of Mininet-virtual network and Aruba-physical network. Various security applications like firewall, DDoS manager, AAA, NAT etc. have been developed as a part of the SDS framework. The proposed framework communicates with the ONOS controller using REST APIs and the controller implements the required security policies into the dataplane devices in terms of flow rules. The scheme introduces an effective means of securing the network using a minimum number of messages and eliminating the need of separate security appliances/applications with a very low performance overhead. The paper in its current form lacks the feature for mutual authentication between the SDS framework and controller, and the ability to handle runtime topological changes in the network that might affect some security functionalities.

The future work is geared towards adding more features, optimizing and fine tuning the existing security applications. Some more security applications (Stateful Firewall, Access Control for ONOS Applications, Secured Device Authorization etc.) need to be designed for the framework. We also intend to explore the possibility of implementing the SDS architecture on other controllers like Floodlight, ODL, RYU etc. and testing the framework with other physical data plane devices (other make and model than Aruba). We are already into the process of testing the framework with an ONOS controller cluster. Standard mutual authentication protocols will be implemented between SDS framework and ONOS controller in future.

References

1. Kavre, M.S., Sunnapwar, V.K., Gardas, B.B.: Cloud manufacturing adoption: a comprehensive review. Inf. Syst. E-Bus. Manage. (2023). https://doi.org/10.1007/s10257-023-00638-y
2. Tupakula, U., Karmakar, K.K., Varadharajan, V., Collins, B.: Implementation of techniques for enhancing security of southbound infrastructure in SDN. In: 2022 13th International Conference on Network of the Future (NoF), pp. 1–5. IEEE (2022)
3. Liatifis, A., Sarigiannidis, P., Argyriou, V., Lagkas, T.: Advancing SDN from Openflow to P4: a survey. ACM Comput. Surv. **55**(9), 1–37 (2023)
4. Ruchel, L.V., Turchetti, R.C., de Camargo, E.T.: Evaluation of the robustness of SDN controllers ONOS and ODL. Comput. Netw. **219**, 109403 (2022)
5. Amiri, E., Alizadeh, E., Rezvani, M.H.: Controller selection in software defined networks using best-worst multi-criteria decision-making. Bull. Electr. Eng. Inform. **9**(4), 1506–1517 (2020)
6. Qiu, X., Cheng, F., Wang, W., Zhang, G., Qiu, Y.: A security controller-based software defined security architecture. In: 20th Conference on Innovations in Clouds, Internet and Networks (ICIN), pp. 191–195. IEEE (2017)
7. Darabseh, A., et al.: A software defined security experimental framework. In: IEEE International Conference on Communication Workshop (ICCW), London, pp. 1871–1876 (2015). https://doi.org/10.1109/ICCW.2015.7247453
8. Ahmad, I., Namal, S., Ylianttila, M., Gurtov, A.: Security in software defined networks: a survey. IEEE Commun. Surv. Tut. **17**(4), 2317–2346 (2015). Fourth Quarter
9. Badotra, S., Panda, S.N.: SNORT based early DDoS detection system using Opendaylight and open networking operating system in software defined networking. Cluster Comput. **24**, 501–513 (2021)
10. Othman, W.M., Chen, H., Al-Moalmi, A., Hadi, A.N.: Implementation and performance analysis of SDN firewall on POX controller. In 2017 IEEE 9th International Conference on Communication Software and Networks (ICCSN), pp. 1461–1466. IEEE (2017)
11. Toseef, U., Zaalouk, A., Rothe, T., Broadbent, M., Pentikousis, K.: C-BAS: certificate-based AAA for SDN experimental facilities. In: 2014 Third European Workshop on Software Defined Networks, pp. 91–96. IEEE (2014)
12. What is radius server? https://www.cisco.com/c/en/us/support/docs/security-vpn/remote-aut hentication-dial-user-service-radius/12433-32.html. Accessed 20 Jun 2023
13. NMON Documentation. https://nmon.sourceforge.io/pmwiki.php?n=Site. Accessed 20 Jun 2023
14. Suh, M., Park, S.H., Lee, B., Yang, S.: Building firewall over the software-defined network controller. In: 16th International Conference on Advanced Communication Technology, pp. 744–748. IEEE (2014)
15. Bawany, N.Z., Shamsi, J.A., Salah, K.: DDoS attack detection and mitigation using SDN: methods, practices, and solutions. Arab. J. Sci. Eng. **42**, 425–441 (2017)
16. HP Aruba Manual: Aruba 2930 M/F Management and Configuration Guide for AOS-S Switch 16.10. Accessed 20 Jun 2023

A Process-Centric Approach to Insider Threats Identification in Information Systems

Akram Idani(✉)📷, Yves Ledru, and German Vega

Univ. Grenoble Alpes, CNRS, Grenoble INP, LIG, 38000 Grenoble, France
{akram.idani,yves.ledru,german.vega}@univ-grenoble-alpes.fr

Abstract. The development of complex software systems as done today generates countless security vulnerabilities that are difficult to detect. In this context, several research works have adopted the Model Driven Security (MDS) approach, which investigates software models rather than implementations. However, although these works provide useful techniques for security modeling and validation, they do not address the impact of functional behavior on the security context of the system, which can be cause for several flaws, specially insider threats. In order to address this challenge, we propose a dynamic analysis based on the B method for both functional and security concerns. Our contribution extends the **B4MSecure** platform that we developed in our previous works, by introducing a workflow-centric layer to model expected business processes, as well as possible malicious activities. This new layer is built on CSP||B and brings new validation possibilities to B4MSecure.

Keywords: B Method · CSP · Verification · RBAC · Access Control

1 Introduction

Computer security often refers to hackers or intruders, who are persons with high technical skills and whose intention is to exploit security breaches in order to get an illegal access to a system. However, in reality the greatest threats come from inside the system, *i.e.* from trusted users who are already granted a legal access. This kind of threat is called "insider attack" in cyber-security and it is known to be difficult to tackle [14]. Studies done by IBM X-Force Research in the cyber-security landscape state that: "*In 2015, 60 percent of all attacks were carried out by insiders [...] and they resulted in substantial financial and reputational losses*". The problem is beyond the access control frontier since it includes unpredictable human behaviours. To deal with these threats, existing industrial, academic and government studies [6,7,10] elaborate human profiles and advocate for the use of surveillance systems. Without being exhaustive, some of these profiles are:

© The Author(s), under exclusive license to Springer Nature Switzerland AG 2024
A. Ait Wakrime et al. (Eds.): CRiSIS 2023, LNCS 14529, pp. 231–247, 2024.
https://doi.org/10.1007/978-3-031-61231-2_15

- Curious persons who, without a malicious intention but without self-control too, get access to sensitive data or do some actions that are in contradiction with the company rules.
- Super-heroes who, in order to fix a problem or help someone, bypass the company policies believing that it may be useful or simply be approved.

Other profiles are established in the literature, like audacious, greedy, disgruntled, opportunistic, etc. Unfortunately, the eventuality of a breach of trust is difficult to predict in advance based on human-centric factors. On the one hand there is no certainty about a possible acting out, and on the other hand people surveillance must comply with privacy legislation, which makes it almost ineffective. Nonetheless, Information Systems (IS) together with their business logic and processes, provide useful knowledge allowing one to deal with the insider threat problem. In fact, based on the aforementioned studies it can be observed that insiders often do not have high computer skills (contrary to intruders), but they have a fine-grained knowledge about the IS procedures. The latter are mostly well-established and already protected via access control mechanisms. Hence, by being able to answer the question *"who has access to sensitive data and what kind of access is given?"*, one cannot claim that the system is secure enough. The good question should be: *"is the user able to run a sequence of actions that may bring him from a prohibition to an authorization?"*.

The first question refers to static concerns, and it is widely addressed in Model-Driven Security (MDS) thanks to several access control models (*e.g.* SecureUML, UMLSec). However, the second question remains open in MDS because it refers to behavioural features and the reachability of unwanted situations granting to the user misappropriated privileges. In [11], we applied the B method and its composition mechanism, to provide a way to take into account the intertwining of security policies and functional concerns of the IS. The underlying analysis technique builds on a forward search approach that is intended to verify whether a given targeted functional state is reachable, and eliminate threats by proving that a given unwanted state is unreachable. Forward search is a classical approach that is often done thanks to model-checking techniques, but it is more efficient for relatively small applications. As this is not always possible in the case of IS, a model-checker may require some guidance. This paper contributes towards our previous works by taking into account business processes. We propose to extend our approach and its tool support with a process-based search applying CSP||B [4], which would exhibit malicious behaviours more efficiently.

Section 2 provides a formal framework to MDS, which allows us to apply automated reasoning tools in order to verify the correctness of the IS concerns. Section 3 gives the contribution of this paper and describes how business processes can be taken into account when dealing with insider attacks. Section 4 discusses related works and Sect. 5 draws the conclusions and the perspectives.

2   Separation of Concerns

This work applies B4MSecure [8], a tool that we developed in order to model the IS as a whole by covering its functional description, and its security policy. The tool generates from these models a formal B specification, allowing one to formally reason about their correctness: functional and security models can be first proved separately, and then integrated in order to verify their interactions.

B4MSecure is built on an MDE architecture in which the input models are UML class diagrams that are extended with the SecureUML profile. The extraction of B specifications from these input models applies transformation rules that are defined at a meta-level. The ideas behind the tool are inspired by existing software products, such as popular commercial database management systems (*e.g.* Oracle, Sybase) or webservers (*e.g.* JBoss, Tomcat). The available implementations of RBAC act like a filter which intercepts a user request to a resource in order to permit or deny the access to associated functional actions (*e.g.* transactions on databases, file operations, etc.). The tool is based on the same principles, but at a modeling level. Each functional operation is encapsulated in a secure operation checking that the current user has the required authorizations.

2.1   Functional Modeling

To illustrate our approach, we consider the UML class diagram of Fig. 1. This model is inspired by [1], and represents functional concerns of a banking IS: it deals with customers (class *Customer*) and their accounts (class *Account*).

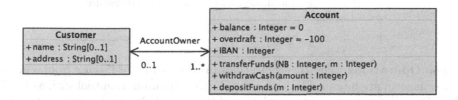

Fig. 1. UML Class Diagram − Functional Model

A bank account is characterized by its balance (attribute *balance*), the authorized overdraft (attribute *overdraft*) and a unique identifier (attribute *IBAN*). Operation *transferFunds* allows one to transfer an amount of money (parameter *m*) from the current account to any account defined with an *IBAN* number (parameter *NB*). Operations *withdrawCash* and *depositFunds* allow respectively to withdraw or to deposit money.

Translation into B. The translation of this diagram into B follows well-established UML-to-B rules. First, a UML class (*e.g. Customer*) produces: (*i*) an abstract set[1] ($CUSTOMER$) defining the set of possible instances; (ii) a variable[2] ($Customer$) defining existing instances; and (iii) an invariant[3] meaning that the set of existing instances is a subset of the set of possible instances ($Customer \subseteq CUSTOMER$). Regarding class attributes, they are translated into B functions relating the set of existing instances to the type of the attribute. The resulting functions depend on the attribute character: mandatory or optional, unique or not unique, single or multi-valued. For example, attribute $IBAN$ of class $Account$ is single-valued, mandatory and unique; it is translated as a total injection function. The translation of associations follows the same principle. Indeed, each association leads to a functional relation that depends on the multiplicities of the two ends of the association. For example, association $AccountOwner$ is translated into a partial surjective function since its multiplicities are 0..1 and 1..*. Figure 2 presents the typing invariants that are automatically produced by B4MSecure from Fig. 1.

$$
\begin{array}{l}
\textbf{INVARIANT} \\
Account \subseteq ACCOUNT \\
\wedge\ Customer \subseteq CUSTOMER \\
\wedge\ AccountOwner \in Account \twoheadrightarrow Customer \\
\wedge\ Account\_\_balance \in Account \rightarrow \mathbb{Z} \\
\wedge\ Account\_\_overdraft \in Account \rightarrow \mathbb{Z} \\
\wedge\ Customer\_\_name \in Customer \nrightarrow STRING \\
\wedge\ Customer\_\_address \in Customer \nrightarrow STRING \\
\wedge\ Account\_\_IBAN \in Account \rightarrowtail \mathbb{N}
\end{array}
$$

Fig. 2. Structural invariants produced by B4MSecure

Basic Operations. The B specifications produced by B4MSecure from a given class diagram are intended to be animated using an animation tool such as ProB [12]. This allows one to see the evolution of the IS and observe the impact that an execution scenario could have on the functional state. Thus, B4MSecure generates all basic operations such as creation/deletion of class instances, creation/deletion of links between these instances, getters/setters of attributes and links, etc. In general, these operations are correct by construction, meaning that they do not violate the generated typing invariants. In fact, the proof of correctness of the functional model means that basic operations preserve the multiplicities of the associations as well as the character of attributes. Figure 3 gives an example of a basic operation that is generated by B4MSecure. It is a creation operation of class $Account$. This operation preserves, on the one hand, the mandatory character of attribute $IBAN$ because a value is assigned to the attribute when the object is

---

[1] Clause SETS.
[2] Clause VARIABLES.
[3] Clause INVARIANT.

created, and on the other hand, the uniqueness of this attribute. The operation also takes into account the default values of attributes *balance* and *overdraft*; they are respectively initialized to 0 and -100.

Account__NEW(*Instance, Account__IBANValue*) ==
PRE
   Instance $\in$ *ACCOUNT* $\wedge$ *Instance* $\notin$ *Account*
    $\wedge$ *Account__IBANValue* $\in \mathbb{N}$
    $\wedge$ *Account__IBANValue* $\notin$ **ran**(*Account__IBAN*)
THEN
   Account := *Account* $\cup$ {*Instance*}
   || *Account__balance* := *Account__balance* $\cup$ {(*Instance* $\mapsto$ 0)}
   || *Account__overdraft* := *Account__overdraft* $\cup$ {(*Instance* $\mapsto$ -100)}
   || *Account__IBAN*   :=   *Account__IBAN* $\cup$ {(*Instance* $\mapsto$ *Account__IBANValue*)}
END;

Fig. 3. Basic creator generated by B4MSecure

Account___transferFunds(*Instance, N, m*) ==
PRE
   Instance $\in$ *Account* $\wedge$ $N \in \mathbb{N}$ $\wedge$ $m \in \mathbb{N}_1$
    $\wedge$ *AccountOwner*[{*Instance*}] $\neq \emptyset$
    $\wedge$ $N \in$ **ran**({*Instance*} $\lhd$ *Account__IBAN*)
    $\wedge$ *AccountOwner*[{*Account__IBAN* $^{-1}$ (*N*)}] $\neq \emptyset$
    $\wedge$ *Account__balance*(*Instance*) $- m \geq$ *Account__overdraft*(*Instance*)
THEN
   Account__balance :=
      {(*Instance* $\mapsto$ (*Account__balance*(*Instance*) $- m$))}
      $\cup$ {(*Account__IBAN*$^{-1}$(*N*) $\mapsto$ (*Account__balance*(*Account__IBAN*$^{-1}$(*N*)) + *m*))}
      $\cup$ ({*Instance, Account__IBAN* $^{-1}$ (*N*)} $\lhd$ *Account__balance*)
END ;

Fig. 4. Operation transferFunds of class *Account*

User-Defined Concerns. The user may introduce within the resulting formal specification invariant properties and the underlying preconditions in order to keep correct the basic operations. The user-defined operations, such as operations *transferFunds* and *withdrawCash* of class *Account*, must also be defined. Figure 4 presents the B specification of operation *transferFunds*. It takes an account number (parameter *N*) and a positive amount (parameter *m*) and performs the transfer of funds if the following conditions are met: the current account and the beneficiary account are held by customers, *N* corresponds to an existing account other than the current account, and the authorized overdraft will not be exceeded by this transfer.

2.2   Security Modeling

SecureUML is an extension to UML Class Diagrams whose concrete syntax is based on UML stereotypes. In the version we consider, the main ones used are Role and Permission, where Permission is an association class between roles and functional classes, and can be further annotated with Authorization Constraints. The latter are logical predicates denoting the conditions under which a given permission holds. Figure 5 is a SecureUML model associated to the class diagram of Fig. 1. This model defines two roles: *CustomerUser* and *AccountManager*. They respectively represent the customer of the system and the financial manager in charge of the bank's customers. Customers can read their personal data (permission *CustomerUserPerm1*), transfer money, deposit and withdraw cash (permission *CustomerUserPerm2*). The account manager has a full access (read and write) on class *Customer* (permission *AccountManagerPerm1*). He/She can thus create customers, read or modify their data. However, his/her rights on class *Account* are limited to the creation of new accounts (permission *AccountManagerPerm2*). Furthermore, an authorization constraint is associated to permissions *CustomerUserPerm1* and *CustomerUserPerm2* in order to grant the corresponding actions to the sole holder of the account on which they are invoked. In this security policy, the account manager has no access, neither read nor write, to the attributes of class *Account*.

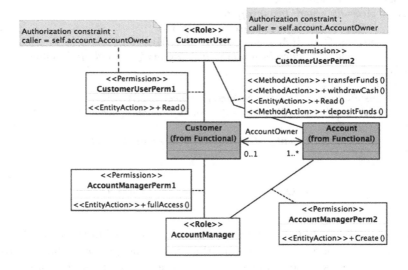

Fig. 5. Security modeling with SecureUML

Translation into B. Given a SecureUML model, B4MSecure produces a B machine that grants permission or forbids functional operations based on the set of roles that are activated by a user. For example, if *Paul* is a *CustomerUser*, he can only read his personal data by calling getters of class *Customer*. The other operations (modification, creation, etc.) are forbidden to him. In order to translate the security model, our approach follows two steps: (i) propose a "stable" formalization of the SecureUML meta-model, then (ii) translate a given security model and inject it into the formalization of the meta-model. Each operation of the functional model is encapsulated in a secure operation checking that the current user is allowed (or not) to call this operation. Figure 6 presents an excerpt of the resulting B machine that is dedicated to user assignments. It refers to: *ROLES, USERS* and *SESSIONS*. The assignment of roles to users is defined with relation *roleOf*. Contrary to users and roles, which are explicitly represented by sets, sessions are defined by means of a relation between users and roles. We consider that a user cannot open several sessions in the system. When a user u belongs to the domain of relation *Session*, thus a session is created for him and $Session[\{u\}]$ gives the set of roles that are activated by u. Variable *currentUser* is useful during the animation of the model because it allows us to identify the user who is running a given operation. Machine *SecureUML* provides also several utility operations that are useful during the animation. For example, Fig. 7 gives the B specifications of operations *Connect* and *setCurrentUser*. Operation *Connect* creates a session to a given user in which a set of roles is activated. This operation is done under two conditions: (i) the user is not concerned by any existing session, (ii) if a role r_1 is a super-role of a role r_2, therefore the user can activate r_1 or r_2 but not both of them $\{r_1, r_2\}$. Operation *setCurrentUser* selects the user who is currently concerned with the animation.

MACHINE *SecureUML* **INCLUDES** *Functional_Model*
SETS *ROLES* ; *USERS*
VARIABLES *roleOf, Roles_Hierarchy, currentUser, Session*
INVARIANT
```
/* Typing invariants */
```
   $currentUser \in USERS$
   $\wedge\ roleOf \in USERS \rightarrow \mathbb{P}\,(ROLES)$
   $\wedge\ Roles\_Hierarchy \in ROLES \leftrightarrow ROLES$
   $\wedge\ Session \in USERS \leftrightarrow ROLES$
```
/* No cycles in role hierarchy */
```
   $\wedge\ (Roles\_Hierarchy)^{+} \cap \mathbf{id}(ROLES) = \emptyset$
```
/* Conformance of role assignments and role activation */
```
   $\wedge\ \forall\,(uu).(uu \in USERS \wedge uu \in \mathbf{dom}(Session) \Rightarrow Session[\{uu\}] \subseteq roleOf(uu))$

Fig. 6. Excerpt of the SecureUML meta-model dedicated to user assignments

B4MSecure produces for every functional operation, a secured operation that verifies (using a security guard) whether the current user is allowed to call the functional operation. The secure operation also verifies the authorization

Connect(*user*, *roleSet*) =
PRE
  user ∈ *USERS* ∧ *user* ∉ **dom**(*Session*)
  ∧ *roleSet* ∈ ℙ₁(*ROLES*) ∧ *roleSet* ⊆ *roleOf*(*user*)
  /* avoid hierarchical redundancy in the roleSet */
  ∧ ∀ (*r1,r2*).(*r1* ∈ *roleSet* ∧ *r2* ∈ *roleSet* ∧ *r1* ≠ *r2* ⇒ *r2* ∉ (*Roles_Hierarchy*)⁺[{*r1*}])
THEN
  Session := *Session* ∪ ({*user*} × *roleSet*)
END;

setCurrentUser(*user*) =
  PRE
    user ∈ *USERS* ∧ *user* ≠ *currentUser* ∧ *user* ∈ **dom**(*Session*)
  THEN
    currentUser := *user*
  END ;

Fig. 7. Utility operations

constraints, if they are defined in the underlying permissions, and updates the assignment of roles when required. Figure 8 shows the secure operations associated to *Account_transferFunds*. The security guard is defined in clause *SELECT*. It verifies that the functional operation belongs to set *isPermitted* [*currentRoles*], where definition *currentRoles* refers to the roles activated by *currentUser* (in a session) as well as their super-roles: *currentRoles* == *Session* [{*currentUser* }] ∪ **ran** (*Session* [{*currentUser* }] ◁ (*Roles_Hierarchy*)⁺).

secure_Account_transferFunds(*aAccount*, *NB*, *m*) =
  SELECT
    *Account_transferFunds_* ∈ *isPermitted*[*currentRoles*]
    ∧ (*CustomerUser* ∈ *currentRoles* ⇒ *AccountOwner*(*aAccount*) = *currentUser*)
  THEN
    Account_transferFunds(*aAccount*, *NB*, *m*)
  END;

Fig. 8. Operation *secure_Account_transferFunds*

3   Dealing with Business Processes

3.1   Animation in B4MSecure

In order to validate the model, B4MSecure uses ProB Java API as presented in Fig. 9.

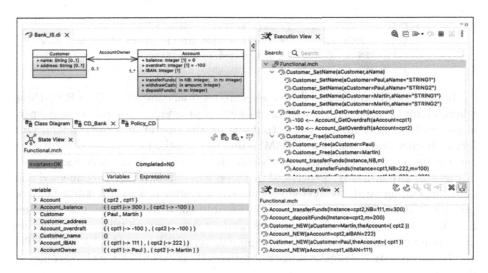

Fig. 9. Animation in B4MSecure

The State View (bottom-left) gives the values of the B variables in the current state, *i.e.* after animating the sequence of the History View (bottom-right). The Execution View (top-right) shows the B operations that can be triggered in the current state. The content of these views is computed by the Java API of ProB; B4MSecure just provides some convenient actions to ensure animation and/or model-checking via the API. Figure 9 shows a sequence of functional operations that creates customers Paul and Martin, as well as their respective accounts cpt_1 and cpt_2. An amount of 200€ is added to Martin's account and then 300€ are transferred from this account to Paul's account. This scenario corresponds to a normal use case of the IS without considering security concerns. Playing with functional scenarios shows that use cases are feasible with the current specification, and helps identifying missing steps in the use cases or the specification. A similar animation can be performed by calling the secured version of the use case. This eases the understanding and validation of the security policy and shows that the security policy does not prevent the execution of functional use cases.

3.2 A CSP||B Approach

One facility supported by ProB is the use of CSP||B, that is, a CSP layer that guides the animation of the B machine. This guidance restricts the execution space to relevant traces with respect to pre-established processes, which would make verification potentially faster. In CSP, a process refers to a sequence of events and the communication between processes is ensured via channels. A channel ch may transmit data d, which is denoted as ch?d for inputs, and ch!d for outputs. Note that by convention, processes are named in uppercase and channels in lowercase. Some of the used CSP constructs are:

```
PROCESS ::= SKIP                    /* terminating process */
          | ch -> PROCESS           /* simple action prefix where ch is a channel */
          | PROCESS ; PROCESS       /* sequential composition */
          | PROCESS [] PROCESS /* external choice */
```

In the CSP||B approach [4] processes are used as controllers for a B machine where channels correspond to B operations, and events to a call to the operation, with channel inputs and outputs being the operation's parameters. Our formal framework, ensured with B4MSecure, favours the integration of a process-centric approach for animation. Let's consider for example the business process of Fig. 10 written in CSP. Process UI is a loop where first a user is connected and next, depending on the activated role, he/she executes process MANAGER_FUNC or process CLIENT_FUNC. For space reason we only show the former. The manager has the choice between creating a new account or a new customer, or updating an existing customer record. The SKIP process terminates process MANAGER_FUNC and hence operation disconnecUser of process UI is executed, which disconnects the user.

Having this CSP model, ProB can be used to animate the operational formal model of the security policy, by following traces allowed by the CSP processes. The sequence of operations given in Fig. 11 corresponds to a normal use case where users execute permitted operations after they activate the right role and such that they satisfy functional preconditions as well as authorization constraints. In this trace, we show for every step the CSP process that is considered by the animator. The resulting state is represented with the object diagram of Fig. 12. In this sequence, the account manager Bob creates two customers (Paul and Martin) and two accounts (cpt_1 and cpt_2) and then Paul deposits money into his own account.

3.3   Insider Threats Identification

One major advantage of B is theorem proving, which refers to the demonstration of logical formulas (called proof obligations, POs) to ensure a correctness claim for a given property (such as an invariant property). For example, the correctness of an operation guarantees that the invariant is true before and after the execution of the operation. For our example, we proved the correctness of our B specifications. The advantage is that when looking for threats, the security analyst has the guarantee that flaws are not issued from invariant violations, but rather from the functional or the security logic. In this sense, the identification of attack scenarios is mainly a validation task, which can be done by animation and/or model-checking. Indeed, an exhaustive model exploration may exhibit a malicious sequence of operations leading to a state (where a property holds) that represents an unwanted situation.

To exhibit a malicious scenario based on our simple example, we start the exploration from a normal state, that of Fig. 12. In this state *Paul* is a customer and owns account cpt_1 whose balance is equal to 500. *Bob* as *AccountManager* cannot execute operations *transferFunds* or *withdrawCash* on cpt_1. The answer

```
MAIN = UI

UI = (Connect?user!{AccountManager} -> setCurrentUser(user) -> MANAGER_FUNC
   [] Connect?user!{CustomerUser} -> setCurrentUser(user) -> CLIENT_FUNC)
   ; disconnectUser -> UI

MANAGER_FUNC =
      CREATE_ACCOUNT [] CREATE_CUSTOMER [] UPDATE_CUSTOMER [] SKIP

CREATE_ACCOUNT =
      secure_Account_NEW -> (CREATE_ACCOUNT [] MANAGER_FUNC)

CREATE_CUSTOMER =
      secure_Customer_NEW?customer -> secure_Customer__SetName!customer
      -> (ADD_CUSTOMER_ACCOUNT(customer) [] CREATE_CUSTOMER [] MANAGER_FUNC)

ADD_CUSTOMER_ACCOUNT(customer) =
      secure_Customer__AddAccountOwner!customer
      -> (ADD_CUSTOMER_ACCOUNT(customer) [] MANAGER_FUNC)

UPDATE_CUSTOMER =
      secure_Customer__GetName?customer -> UPDATE(customer)

UPDATE(customer) =
      secure_Customer__SetName?customer -> UPDATE(customer)
      [] secure_Customer__SetAddress?customer -> UPDATE(customer)
      [] secure_Customer__RemoveAccountOwner?customer -> UPDATE(customer)
      [] ADD_CUSTOMER_ACCOUNT(customer)
      [] MANAGER_FUNC
```

Fig. 10. Business process in CSP

to a static query such as "Is Bob able to transfer funds from Paul's account?" would be NO, since the permission given to a manager on class *Account* only allows instance creation. In fact, the good question should be "Is there a sequence of operations that can be executed by Bob in order to become able to transfer funds from Paul's account?". To answer the question, one naive solution is to use the model-checking feature of ProB to exhaustively explore the state space and find states that satisfy property: $AccountOwner(cpt_1) = $ Bob. We are therefore looking for a sequence of operations executed by Bob allowing him to become the owner of cpt_1 meaning that he may reach a state granting him the permission to execute an action that initially he cannot do. Without considering the CSP guidance, ProB reached a time out after exploring millions of transitions, meaning that the state space is too big to be explored efficiently.

To solve this issue we propose to describe insider threats using a CSP model and take benefit of the CSP||B approach of ProB to check if the business process contains traces that are conformant to this attack model. Figure 13 shows

```
-> Process: MAIN -> UI
       Connect(Bob, {AccountManager}) ;
       setCurrentUser(Bob) ;
-> Process: MANAGER_FUNCTIONS -> CREATE_ACCOUNT
       secure_Account_NEW(cpt₁, 111) ;
       secure_Account_NEW(cpt₂, 222) ;
-> Process: MANAGER_FUNCTIONS -> CREATE_CUSTOMER
       secure_Customer_NEW(Paul,{cpt₁}) ;
       secure_Customer_SetName(Paul,"Paul Durand") ;
       secure_Customer_NEW(Martin,{cpt₂})
       secure_Customer_SetName(Martin,"Martin Favier") ;
-> Process: MANAGER_FUNCTIONS -> SKIP
       disconnectUser
-> Process: UI
       Connect(Paul, {CustomerUser}) ;
       setCurrentUser(Paul) ;
-> Process: CLIENT_FUNCTIONS -> DEPOSIT
       secure_Account__depositFunds(cpt₁,500)
-> Process: CLIENT_FUNCTIONS -> SKIP
       disconnectUser
```

Fig. 11. Execution trace

Fig. 12. Resulting state represented with an object diagram

the proposed insider threat model for the example discussed above. Statement
[]x:Set(S)@P used in process ATTACKER is a replicated external choice. This
statement evaluates process P for each value of set S and composes the resulting processes together using external choice. Hence, process ATTACKER means
that Bob is trying to connect to the system by varying his roles. Statement
P|||Q used in process ATTACK is an interleaving, which runs P and Q in parallel
without any synchronisation. In fact, the goal of the attack is to run operation
secure_ transferFunds on account cpt_1 by the attacker who abuses his/her roles.

The synchronisation of process UI with the attack model is done in the MAIN
process. The latter applies a generalized parallel composition with synchroni-
sation on critical actions. In fact, statement P[|A|]Q runs processes P and Q
in parallel forcing them to synchronise on events in A; any event not in A may
be performed by either process. In other words, if event goal is produced by
ATTACK therefore the critical operation has been also executed by process UI ;
which means that a flaw conformant to the attack model is detected.

Based on this model, ProB explored about 70000 states and 200000 transitions and was able to exhibit sequence of Fig. 14. We structure it in three steps.

```
MAIN = UI [|{| Connect, secure_Account_transferFunds |}|] ATTACK

ATTACK = ATTACKER ||| secure_Account_transferFunds!cpt1 -> goal -> SKIP

ATTACKER = []role:Set(ROLES) @ Connect!Bob!role -> ATTACKER
```

Fig. 13. Insider threat model

In **step** 1 *Bob* adds himself to the system as a customer. As the creation of a customer requires at least one account, *Bob* creates a fictive account cpt_3 and then he calls operation *secure_ Customer_ NEW*. In **step** 2, the attacker becomes the owner of cpt_1. To this purpose he must first remove the link between *Paul* and cpt_1. But, in the functional model a customer must have at least one account, consequently operation *secure_ Customer_ RemoveAccount(Paul, {cpt_1})* is possible only if *Paul* has another account. For this reason, *Bob* creates another fictive account cpt_4 and adds it to *Paul's* accounts. The last action of **step** 2 reaches the malicious state where *Bob* is the owner of cpt_1. Finally, **step** 3 realizes the attack.

```
/* step 1: create customer Bob */
    Connect(Bob, {AccountManager}) ;
    setCurrentUser(Bob) ;
    secure_Account_NEW(cpt3, 333) ;
    secure_Customer_NEW(Bob,{cpt3}) ;
    secure_Customer_SetName(Bob,"…") ;

/* step 2: get the ownership of Paul's Account */
    secure_Account_NEW(cpt4, 444) ;
    secure_Customer_AddAccount(Paul,{cpt4}) ;
    secure_Customer_RemoveAccount(Paul,{cpt1}) ;
    secure_Customer_AddAccount(Bob,{cpt1}) ;

/* step 3: attack */
    disConnect(Bob) ;
    Connect(Bob, {CustomerUser}) ;
    secure_Account_transferFunds(cpt1, 333, 500) ;
```

Fig. 14. Malicious scenario

This malicious scenario can be countered by enhancing the functional model and/or the security model. If the analyst assumes that the flaw is favored by the functional logic, one possible solution would be to introduce the following invariant: *Account_ _ balanceValue* $\neq$ 0 $\Rightarrow$ *AccountOwner* [{*Instance*}] $\neq \varnothing$. In fact, operation *secure_ Customer_ RemoveAccount(Paul, {cpt_1})* is the dangerous operation. This invariant means that accounts whose balance is not equal to zero must be owned by a customer. By introducing this invariant, several functional operations must be corrected and proved, such as: *Customer_RemoveAccount* and *Account_SetBalance*. In other words, to remove the ownership relation between cpt_1 and *Paul*, the account of *Paul* must be empty. If the analyst assumes that the flow is favored by the security logic, a possible solution would be to limit the scope of permission *AccountManagerPerm1* because it currently grants a full access to role *AccountManager* on customer's data, including the deletion of his accounts.

4 Related Works

Model-Driven Security [3] advocates for the separation of concerns principle and suggests the validation of functional and security models in isolation. Hence, most existing works [5] in MDS are stateless and they mostly validate security policies statically without taking into account the dynamic evolution of the IS. A major contribution of our proposal in MDS is that it favours dynamic analyses, using animation and model-checking, of the interactions between the IS concerns.

As far as we know, works that addressed access control together with a formal method, did not deal with the insider threat problem, such as discussed in this paper. However, we can assume that this kind of threat is a typical reachability problem. In [16], the authors proposed a plain model-checking approach, built on security strategies, in order to check specifications written in the RW (Read-Write) language. However, the proposed algorithm faces scalability issues because the RW language is poor compared to B. A similar approach is proposed in [9] in order to validate access control in web-based collaborative systems. Even though their experiments show that they achieve better results compared to [16], the approach still has a partial coverage of realistic policies.

In [13], the authors proposed two approaches to prove reachability properties in a B formal information system modelling. In the first one, they used substitution refinement techniques based on Morgan's specification statement, and in the second one, they proposed an algorithm that produces a proof obligation in order to prove whether a given sequence of operations reaches (or not) a defined state. However, unlike our approach, they don't search sequences leading to a goal state from an initial one. Their approach starts from a given sequence of operations, and tries to prove its reachability.

Existing works, including our previous work [11,15] in the field, do not deal with business processes, which is indeed a limitation because, in IS, the three concerns (functional models, security policies and business processes) are important. This work introduced the business process dimension via CSP‖B, which brings the ability to limit the state space exploration during model-checking.

This work led to the development of an extension of B4MSecure that is used to exhibit execution paths from a B modelling of an IS. The approach has been experimented with several case studies such as the meeting scheduler example discussed in [2], the medical IS studied in [11] and the conference review IS inspired by [16]. For each example, the tool aimed to reach the same malicious goal as handled in the article which addressed the same example, and it was able to extract all reported attacks. Some metrics about these experiments are given in Table 1.

Table 1. Summary table of experiments

Case study	Operations	Variables	Permissions	Roles	Users	scenarios
Library	13	4	3	2	3	8
Medical IS [11]	15	9	3	4	3	10
Meeting scheduler [2]	23	7	5	3	3	8
Bank IS [1]	31	11	4	2	3	9
Conference Review [16]	48	24	8	3	4	14

Several research works have been devoted to the validation of access control policies. They are mainly focused on detecting external intrusion. Recently, the interest to insider attacks grew leading to two categories of validation: stateless and dynamic access control validation. Stateless access control validation is dedicated to validate security policies in a given state without taking into account the dynamic evolution of the IS states. Among these works we can cite the SecureMova tool [2] which models security policies using SecureUML and OCL expressions. In this paper we proposed to take into account business processes in order to identify these attacks. A business process model represents a set of steps in which intrinsically operations concerning the IS data (like reading, modification, etc.) and responsibilities for performing tasks are defined.

5 Conclusion

Authorized actions often lead to evolutions of the functional state, which may favour insider threats. A well known attack that was possible due to evolutions of the functional state is that of 'Société Générale'. This attack resulted in a net loss of $7.2 billion to the bank[4]. The insider circumvented internal security mechanisms to place more than $70 billion in secret, unauthorized derivatives trades. Through authorized actions, he was able to cover up operations he has made on the market by introducing into the functional system fictive offsetting inverse operations, so that the unauthorized trades were not detected. Dynamic analysis is therefore crucial because it would establish that a system evolves as expected and that unwanted situations are not possible.

---

[4] The New York Times. French Bank Says Rogue Trader Lost $7 Billion. January 2008.

Perspectives. One major perspective of this work is to identify inconsistencies between functional models, security policies and business processes. Indeed, insider threats may also come from a bad alignment of these models, such as when the access control policy gives more permissions than the actions required by the business process. In this case following the process may hide several authorizations giving the impression that some bad actions are not possible while they can still be done from outside the process, which is a typical example of insider attacks. We also plan to extend the notion of attack models. A security expert, when faced with the challenge of finding a way of performing a malicious operation, will often try to break down the requirements for performing this operation and try to find how to achieve them, one by one. We may translate this problem solving technique with "checkpoints", that is, intermediate steps necessary for the attack to take place, similarly to how a privilege escalation attack is composed of various steps that must be climbed.

B4MSecure addresses the modeling activities and is based on Platform Independent Models (PIM), described using UML models and their associated formal B specifications. However, in addition to modeling notions, MDS also promotes the transformation of the PIM into a PSM. One interesting perspective is to translate the models into concrete security mechanisms of a target infrastructure. In practice, this transformation usually includes manual coding activities. The challenge is therefore to guarantee that security models, graphically designed and formally validated, correspond to a deployed security policy.

References

1. Bandara, A., et al.: Security Patterns: Comparing Modeling Approaches. IGI Global, Hershey (2010)
2. Basin, D., Clavel, M., Doser, J., Egea, M.: Automated analysis of security-design models. Inf. Softw. Technol. **51** (2009). http://dblp.uni-trier.de/db/journals/infsof/infsof51.html#BasinCDE09
3. Basin, D., Doser, J., Lodderstedt, T.: Model driven security: from UML models to access control infrastructures. ACM Trans. Softw. Eng. Methodol. **15**(1) (2006). https://doi.org/10.1145/1125808.1125810
4. Butler, M., Leuschel, M.: Combining CSP and B for specification and property verification. In: Fitzgerald, J., Hayes, I.J., Tarlecki, A. (eds.) FM 2005. LNCS, vol. 3582, pp. 221–236. Springer, Heidelberg (2005). https://doi.org/10.1007/11526841_16
5. Geismann, J., Bodden, E.: A systematic literature review of model-driven security engineering for cyber-physical systems. J. Syst. Softw. **169**, 110697 (2020). https://doi.org/10.1016/j.jss.2020.110697
6. Greitzer, F.L.: Insider threats: it's the HUMAN, Stupid! In: Proceedings of the Northwest Cybersecurity Symposium. NCS '19. Association for Computing Machinery, New York, NY, USA (2019). https://doi.org/10.1145/3332448.3332458
7. Homoliak, I., Toffalini, F., Guarnizo, J., Elovici, Y., Ochoa, M.: Insight into insiders and IT: a survey of insider threat taxonomies, analysis, modeling, and countermeasures. ACM Comput. Surv. **52**(2) (2019)

8. Idani, A., Ledru, Y.: B for modeling secure information systems - the b4msecure platform. In: Butler, M., Conchon, S., Zaïdi, F. (eds.) ICFEM 2015. LNCS, vol. 9407, pp. 312–318. Springer, Cham (2015). https://doi.org/10.1007/978-3-319-25423-4_20

9. Koleini, M., Ryan, M.: A knowledge-based verification method for dynamic access control policies. In: Qin, S., Qiu, Z. (eds.) ICFEM 2011. LNCS, vol. 6991, pp. 243–258. Springer, Heidelberg (2011). https://doi.org/10.1007/978-3-642-24559-6_18

10. Kont, M., Pihelgas, M., Wojtkowiak, J., Trinberg, L., Osula, A.M.: Insider threat detection study. The NATO Cooperative Cyber Defence Centre of Excellence (2018)

11. Ledru, Y., et al.: Validation of IS security policies featuring authorisation constraints. Int. J. Inf. Syst. Modeli. Des. (IJISMD) (2014)

12. Leuschel, M., Butler, M.: ProB: a model checker for B. In: Araki, K., Gnesi, S., Mandrioli, D. (eds.) FME 2003. LNCS, vol. 2805, pp. 855–874. Springer, Heidelberg (2003)

13. Mammar, A., Frappier, M.: Proof-based verification approaches for dynamic properties: application to the information system domain. Formal Asp. Comput. 27(2), 335–374 (2015). https://doi.org/10.1007/s00165-014-0323-x

14. Probst, C.W., Hunker, J., Gollmann, D., Bishop, M. (eds.): Insider Threats in Cyber Security. AIS, vol. 49. Springer, Heidelberg (2010). https://doi.org/10.1007/978-1-4419-7133-3

15. Radhouani, A., Idani, A., Ledru, Y., Rajeb, N.B.: Symbolic search of insider attack scenarios from a formal information system modeling. LNCS Trans. Petri Nets Other Models Concurr. 10, 131–152 (2015)

16. Zhang, N., Ryan, M., Guelev, D.P.: Synthesising verified access control systems through model checking. J. Comput. Secur. 16(1), 1–61 (2008)

Machine Learning and Security

Deep Learning-Based Outliers Detection in Compressed Trajectories

Yousra Chabchoub[1]([⊠]) [iD] and Michele Luca Puzzo[2]

[1] ISEP - Institut Supérieur d'Électronique de Paris,
10 rue de Vanves, 92130 Issy les Moulineaux, France
Yousra.Chabchoub@isep.fr
[2] University of Rome (Sapienza),
Piazzale Aldo Moro, 5, 00185 Rome, RM, Italy
puzzo.1783133@studenti.uniroma1.it

Abstract. Nowadays anomalous trajectory detection has a prominent place in many real-world applications. In this paper, firstly, we have proposed a comparison between two Deep Learning models, Gaussian Mixture Variational Sequence Auto-Encode (GM-VSAE) and Anomalous Trajectory Detection using Recurrent Neural Network (ATD-RNN) using a public taxi service dataset. The goal is to compare the performances of these two recent models which have addressed the problem differently, but which have already overcome traditional anomalous trajectory detection methods. Furthermore, we have dealt with trajectories compression which allows to reduce the size of data, to cut down the memory space and to improve the efficiency of transmission, storage and processing. Compression of trajectory data is crucial since currently there is an exponential increase of the amount of spatial and temporal information that trace a moving object's path. Therefore, we focused on the GM-VSAE model, which gave the best performance, and applied several compression algorithms to our trajectories data to evaluate the impact of the compression on the performance's metrics, such as the AUC and the execution time of GM-VSAE. Results show the superiority of Uniform Sampling compared to the other compression algorithms. Moreover, compressing data trajectories significantly reduced the training, and the evaluation time while keeping a relatively high value of the AUC (close to 1).

Keywords: Trajectories · Anomalies detection · Data compression · ATD-RNN · GM-VSAE

1 Introduction

Nowadays it is possible to track a large volume of moving objects (e.g., people, vehicles, animals, ...), due to the emergence of wireless communication, satellites and GPS positioning. Therefore, a huge amount of spatial trajectory data is generated at an unprecedented speed since there are so many scenarios where

© The Author(s), under exclusive license to Springer Nature Switzerland AG 2024
A. Ait Wakrime et al. (Eds.): CRiSIS 2023, LNCS 14529, pp. 251–262, 2024.
https://doi.org/10.1007/978-3-031-61231-2_16

moving objects are traced for various purposes. Hence Analyzing and extracting knowledge from these data is a major issue, but since the fields of application are pretty different, the possible tasks of trajectory mining are very various. We focus in this paper on the trajectory outlier detection which can be applied in many real-world domains such as event detection and taxi fraud. This latter has been chosen as application to delve into the trajectory outlier detection since taxis play a critical role in public traffic systems providing convenient and available services for a myriad of urban passengers every day. However, many people, mostly tourists, are victims of taxi driving frauds committed by greedy taxi drivers who overcharge passengers by deliberately taking unnecessary detours. So it is crucial to be able to spot an abnormal driving behavior during a journey, but it is not a trivial task. In fact, before understanding what an anomalous trajectory is, normal routes have to be defined, but due to the complexity of transportation systems, they cannot be defined a priori. Furthermore, to allow actions to be promptly taken when anomalies occur, it is more desirable to support efficient online detection of anomalous trajectories, but trajectories are often generated at a very high speed and in a massive scale, so efficient online detection is really challenging [1]. In the next sections we briefly introduce two recent deep learning methods which have tried to face these issues, make a comparison between them using a public real-world dataset and finally we focus on compression trajectory algorithms which will turn out to speed up the execution time of the model and to deal with the large number of trajectories.

2   Anomalies Detection and Trajectories Compression Algorithms

2.1   Anomalies Detection: GM-VSAE and ATD-RNN

No single universally applicable or generic outlier detection approach exists; thus, it is very critical to select an appropriate one. Several outlier detection algorithms which belong to different approaches (statistical-based, clustering-based, pattern-based, distance-based, density-based, ...) have been developed during the last years to tackle the trajectory outlier detection. Currently, through the development of the neural network, deep learning methods have been used to discover anomalies, in particular generative models were widely employed to discover anomalous trajectories. So, we have chosen to compare two very recent deep-learning based models: the GM-VSAE, explained in [1], and the ATD-RNN illustrated in [2]. Both models gave already promising results on the Porto Service Trajectory dataset and outperformed the baseline outlier detection algorithms.

The GM-VSAE is a deep generative model which can effectively capture complex sequential information of trajectories and model normal route in a latent embedding space. Furthermore, it can efficiently detect anomalous trajectories using detection-via-generation scheme. The architecture of the GM-VSAE consists of three components: *route inference network*, *probability distribution of the routes* and *generative network*. Route inference network converts the trajectory information into a vector in a latent space. A RNN is used to capture the sequential information of the trajectory and handles the input in the form of a vector. The probability distribution is used to measure the likelihood of the route to be considered as normal. It is a difficult task in the real-world scenario as the routes can be of different types, such as highway, street, ramps and so on. The generative network is designed with the ability of generating trajectories from a given route [1].

The ATD-RNN learns the trajectory embeddings through a delicately designed recurrent neural network and it can capture and detect anomalous trajectory in the embedded space. Also, this method mainly consists of three steps: *trajectory data preprocessing, trajectory embedding* and *anomalous detection.* In trajectory data preprocessing step, it discretes the trajectory points so that the continuous numerical variables could be fed into the trajectory embedding step. After that, a stacked RNN is applied to learn the trajectory embedding which can capture the sequential information and the internal characteristics of the trajectories. Then, the multilayer perceptron and the softmax layer are used to detect anomaly from the trajectory embeddings [2].

2.2   Trajectories Compression Algorithms

After having briefly analyzed the two more recent models for anomalies detection in trajectories, we address the challenging problem of the compression of trajectory data. This is motivated by the fact that the time to run the two models, in particular the training time, will be quite high and this could give some difficulties for their usage. From a high point of view, location-based services and applications built from GPS-equipped mobile devices represent a rapidly expanding consumer market [4]. The consequence of this is that nowadays there is an exponential increase in the amount of spatial and temporal information that traces a moving object's path and as technology advances, the generation speed of trajectory data gets faster and faster. This process entails three major issues:

- Transmission of large amounts of data is expensive and time-consuming. According to [5], the cost of sending a volume of data over remote networks can be prohibitively expensive, typically ranging from $5 to $7 per Mb. Thus, tracking a fleet of 4000 vehicles for a single day would incur a cost of $5,000 to $7,000, or approximately $1,825,000 to $2,555,000 annually.
- Queries on large amounts of trajectory data require computationally expensive operations to extract useful patterns and information.
- GPS trajectories often contain a large amount of redundant data that wastes storage and causes increased disk I/O time. Furthermore, if data is collected without compression at 10 s intervals, 1 Gb of storage capacity is required to store just over 4,000 objects for a single day [5]. Another example could be the NASA's Earth Observing System which produces 1 TB of data per day or the Hubble Telescope which generates 140 GB of raw spatial data every week [6].

For these reasons moving object trajectory compression is becoming one of the major issues in moving object data mining. The data compression is a method that reduces the size of data to cut down the memory space and improve the efficiency of transmission, storage, and processing [5].

Several trajectory compression strategies have been proposed, in fact it is possible to address the issues previously listed following different approaches, which are based on distinct compression theories. An initial distinction can be done classifying compression algorithms into two categories: *lossless* and *lossy* compression. Lossless compression enables exact reconstruction of the original data without any loss of information. On the other hand, in lossy compression there is a certain loss of information aiming to reduce the size of a trajectory. However at the same time, the goal is not compromising much precision in its new data representation, although knowing that the new trajectory shows inaccuracies when compared to the original one [4]. Since lossy compression algorithm can remarkably reduce the size of trajectories while maintaining an acceptable degree of error (information loss is known as error and is measured through different metrics that calculate the applied error over a trajectory if a certain point is discarded), they are largely studied and all the compression algorithms that are used in this paper belong to this category.

Compression algorithms can also be classified as *online* or *offline* depending on the moment the compression procedure is performed. Offline algorithms compress a trajectory after it has been fully generated so they are able to obtain more accurate results. On the other hand, online algorithms compress the trajectory during the point collection process so they can remove redundant data from trajectories as they occur, avoiding the unnecessary transfer of data over the network, improving data storage, and reducing the memory space [6].

Another classification can be considered based on the manner to partition the trajectories [5]:

- *Top-Down Approach.* The trajectories are recursively subdivided until some stopping condition is met.
- *Bottom-Up Approach.* Starting from the finest possible representation for the trajectory, successive data points are merged until some stopping condition is met.
- *Sliding Window Approach.* A window of fixed size is moved over the data points and compression takes place only on the data points inside the window.
- *Opening Window Approach.* Unlike the previous approach, here the window size is not constant while compressing. Compression takes place on the data points inside the window which size is decided by the number of points to be processed. Its process will not end until some halting condition is met.

Now, after having a clearer view of the existing compression algorithms, it is important to define a way to compare the performance of trajectory compression algorithms. One common metric that is largely used is the *compression time* which refers to the amount of time that it takes to compress a trajectory. Another crucial metric is the *Compression ratio (R)* which is defined as:

$$R = \left(1 - \frac{n}{m}\right) \times 100\% \tag{1}$$

where m represents the size of the original trajectory, while n is the size of the compressed representation of that trajectory [5].

We focus in this paper on the following compression algorithms as they are the most commonly used in the literature:

Uniform Sampling. Uniform Sampling is an online simple compression algorithm very efficient to reduce massive data streams. It down samples a trajectory at fixed time intervals in order to achieve a desired compression ratio. The main advantage of this algorithm is that it is very fast: its computational complexity is just $\mathcal{O}(n)$ where n is the size of the trajectory.

Douglas-Peucker. Douglas-Peucker algorithm is a recursive compression algorithm which was described for the first time in 1973 [8] and then it has been improved through the years indeed it has been widely used in many fields. It is one of the most popular top-down compression methods (see Fig. 1). It works according to the following steps [8]:

a. It defines the first point of the trajectory as the *starting point* and the last point as the *floating point.*
b. It computes the perpendicular distance from all other trajectory points to the line connecting the starting point and the floating point and identifies the point with the largest distance.
c. If the maximum distance is greater than the given threshold, the original line segment is divided into two parts, and the maximum distance point becomes the front. The floating point of a line segment is also the starting point of the next line segment, and the maximum distance point is stored.
d. Return to step b.

The cycle is repeated until all distances are less than the threshold, then the trajectory formed by the stored points is the compressed trajectory. Unlike the uniform sampling where all the points of the trajectory have the same probability to be sampled, the selected points of the trajectory, using Douglas-Peucker algorithm, correspond to the major direction changes. It is an offline algorithm because it needs the starting and the ending point of the trajectory. The original running time of the algorithm was $\mathcal{O}(n^2)$, but it was improved up to $\mathcal{O}(n \log n)$. Its major drawbacks are that it ignores temporal data and that it does not allow users to set the desired compression ratio.

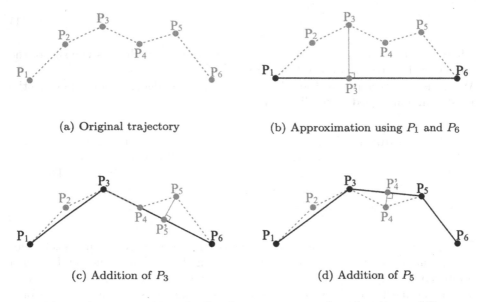

(a) Original trajectory   (b) Approximation using P_1 and P_6

(c) Addition of P_3 (d) Addition of P_5

Fig. 1. Execution of Douglas-Peucker compression algorithm (source [4])

Scikit-Mobility. It is a python library for the analysis, generation, and risk assessment of mobility data. It is well explained in [7]. We focus on the method *compress*, a bottom-up approach in the *compression* module. It allows to merge all the points in a trajectory that are closer than a certain threshold from each other. In other words, all points within a certain radius from a given initial point are compressed into a single point that has the median coordinates of all points and the time of the initial point. The main disadvantage of this method is that it requires in input a trajectory in the *TrajDataFrame* format, and the output is in the same format.

Opening Window. It is a compression iterative algorithm introduced in [10] in 2001. There are several variations of this algorithm. We have used the Normal Opening Window Algorithm or NOWA (see Fig. 2). It works according to the following steps [8]:

a. Select the first point in the trajectory as the starting point, the third point is set as a floating point.
b. Establish a connection between the starting point and the floating point. The points between the starting point and the floating point are regarded as the inspection points, and then the distance between the inspection points and this connecting line are calculated point by point.
c. If all distances in step b are less than the given threshold, the next point of the floating point is regarded as a new floating point, and return to step b.
d. If the distance of a certain point is greater than the threshold, then this point becomes a new starting point. Both the initial starting point and the new

starting point are stored. The third point after the new starting point is used as a floating point, and return to step b.

Fig. 2. Opening Window algorithm. Original data points are represented by closed circles (source [9])

Although this algorithm is computationally expensive, since its time complexity is $\mathcal{O}(n^2)$ it is very popular. This is because it can work reasonably well in presence of noise, and it only needs to know just the starting point of the trajectory and does not need to determine the end point of the trajectory. Therefore, this algorithm can calculate the dynamically added data and is well adapted to an online execution.

3   Experimental Setup

To evaluate the two deep-learning models and the data compression algorithms, we considered the public dataset *Taxi Service Trajectory*[1] which describes one-year trajectories performed by 442 taxis running in the city of Porto, from 01/07/2013 to 01/07/2014. It contains 1,710,670 data samples and each one corresponds to a completed trip. Each trip is characterized by 9 features. For each trip the GPS coordinates of the taxi are given every 15 s. We focused on the following important four features:

- **TRIP_ID**: a unique identifier for each trip.
- **TIMESTAMP**: the start time of the trip.
- **MISSING_DATA**: it is *False* when the GPS data stream is complete and *True* whenever at least one location a missing.
- **POLYLINE**: trajectory of the trip in the form of a list of GPS coordinates (WGS84 format) in which each pair [longitude, latitude] is taken each 15 s of the trip.

As in [2], we generated several anomalies for evaluation since the dataset is unlabeled. The number of injected anomalies is around 5% of the size of the entire dataset. An anomalous trajectory has the same starting and ending point, as a real normal trajectory, but is much longer. Our objective is to compare the performance of two deep learning methods (GM-VSAE and ATD-RNN) for the detection of these anomalous trajectories.

---

[1] https://www.kaggle.com/datasets/crailtap/taxi-trajectory.

4   Results

The objective of outlier detection techniques is to achieve a high detection rate (rate of correctly predicted anomalous trajectories among all real anomalies) while keeping the false alarm rate (proportion of normal trajectories that are predicted as anomalous) low. *ROC-AUC* [3] is an adapted classical metric to take handle this trade-off. *F1-score*, defined as the harmonic mean of the precision and recall, is also a commonly used metric in the anomalies detection context. In addition to these two main metrics, we computed the *Training Time* of the two models which is relatively long.

Table 1. Performance evaluation of the two models

	GM-VSAE	ATD-RNN
AUC	0.989	0.949
Training time	3248 s	3175 s
Precision	0.987	0.986
Recall	0.829	0.890
F1-Score	0.901	0.932

Table 1 shows that both algorithms accomplish outstanding results, but GM-VSAE model achieves better performances in terms of AUC, which is the meaningful evaluation criterion to assess an outlier detection method. The execution time of both algorithms is high: it is slightly larger than 50 min and ATD-RNN is about one minute faster. In the next section, through compression of the data, this execution time will be significantly reduced. The precision of both algorithms is basically identical, while ATD-RNN has a recall, or detection rate, a bit higher: it means it can correctly predict anomalous trajectories among all real anomalies better than GM-VSAE model.

We have applied the algorithms previously explained to compress the trajectories of *Taxi Service Trajectory*. We have used the Uniform Sampling algorithm

Table 2. Performance metrics of compression algorithms

	Execution Time	Computational Complexity	Compression Ratio
Uniform Sampling (SR = 30 s)	411 s	$\mathcal{O}(n)$	50.0%
Uniform Sampling (SR = 45 s)	362 s	$\mathcal{O}(n)$	65%
Uniform Sampling (SR = 60 s)	272 s	$\mathcal{O}(n)$	73%
Uniform Sampling (SR = 90 s)	210 s	$\mathcal{O}(n)$	81%
Uniform Sampling (SR = 120 s)	180 s	$\mathcal{O}(n)$	85%
Douglas-Peucker	2269 s	$\mathcal{O}(n \log n)$	81.4%
sk-mobility	10001 s	$\mathcal{O}(n \log n)$	53.9%
Opening window	3522 s	$\mathcal{O}(n^2)$	85.0%

with a varying compression ratio. In the Table 2 we have summarized the performance metrics of the used compression ratio.

As expected, the Uniform Sampling algorithm is the fastest one, and the higher the compression ratio, the lower is the time required to compress the trajectories. The sk-mobility method is the slowest one since it requires a trajectory in the *TrajDataFrame* format, both for the input and output, but in any case, the compression ratio achieved is just over the 50%. On the contrary, through the Douglas-Peucker and Opening Window algorithms a compression ratio greater than 80% is reached. Specifically, the Opening window can reach a compression ratio a bit higher, although its computational complexity is higher and therefore it is slower than Douglas-Peucker algorithm.

We focus on the GM-VSAE model since it gave the best AUC, and we applied it to new the compressed trajectories to detect the anomalies. In the Table 3 we have displayed the execution time for the three steps of the model: preprocessing, training, and evaluation, for each distinct compression of the trajectories.

In the Table 3, it is noteworthy to notice that compression significantly reduces the Training time. It drops from 3248 s in uncompressed trajectories (Table 1) to only 19 s with a compression ratio of 85%. Moreover, the required time to complete the preprocessing, the training or the evaluation, is strongly dependent on the compression ratio. As the intuition suggests, the longer the trajectories are, the greater is the time needed. In fact, the processes which are more time consuming are the ones which have used compressed trajectories by Uniform Sampling with SR equals to 30 s and the sk-mobility method: both of them are the only ones that have the compression ratio just around the 50%. The size of trajectory has an impact on all the different phases, but since the training is the heaviest one, we can notice larger difference in the training time. For example, the training using compressed trajectories by Opening window algorithm just takes 11 s, while using compressed trajectories by Uniform Sampling, with SR equals to 30 s, takes almost half an hour. Also, the ratio between their evaluation time is big (62 times larger).

Table 3. Execution time of the GM-VSAE model using compressed trajectories

	Prep. Time	Train. Time	Eval. Time
Uniform Sampling (SR = 30 s)	396 s	1607 s	62 s
Uniform Sampling (SR = 45 s)	289 s	430 s	16 s
Uniform Sampling (SR = 60 s)	273 s	22 s	2 s
Uniform Sampling (SR = 90 s)	221 s	25 s	1.8 s
Uniform Sampling (SR = 120 s)	236 s	19 s	1.4 s
Douglas-Peucker	250 s	20 s	1.2 s
sk-mobility	387 s	1272 s	34 s
Opening window	230 s	11 s	1 s

After having analyzed the performances of GM-VSAE model in terms of execution time, we evaluate the AUC, which is the main evaluation criterion to assess an outlier detection method. We also evaluate the impact of compression algorithm on the other performance's metrics (F1-score, precision and recall) of GM-VSAE. Results are presented in the Table 4.

Table 4. Perfomance's metrics of the GM-VSAE model using the compressed trajectories

	AUC	Precision	Recall	F1-score
Uniform Sampling (SR = 30 s)	0.986	0.956	0.906	0.930
Uniform Sampling (SR = 45 s)	0.984	0.951	0.942	0.947
Uniform Sampling (SR = 60 s)	0.977	0.954	0.877	0.914
Uniform Sampling (SR = 90 s)	0.970	0.950	0.886	0.917
Uniform Sampling (SR = 120 s)	0.951	0.960	0.868	0.912
Douglas-Peucker	0.969	0.960	0.878	0.917
sk-mobility	0.983	0.960	0.882	0.919
Opening window	0.944	0.955	0.554	0.701

According to Table 4, the highest value of the AUC is reached when the trajectories have been compressed through the Uniform Sampling with SR = 30 s. This can be explained noticing that in this case we have the lowest compression ratio. It is clear that the higher the compression ratio, the lower the AUC. This behaviour is predictable because, increasing the compression ratio means losing some information about the trajectory, so we have less accurate trajectories and for the model it is harder to detect outliers. However, looking at the AUC values, they are not decreased that much, on the contrary they have dropped by less than 0.05. As an example, with a compression ratio of 85% (SR = 120 s) uniform sampling, the obtained AUC is still high (0.951). Also, regarding the precision and recall values, they are remained pretty the same. The only exception concerns the recall value after the Opening window compression which is dropped up to 0.55.

The previous tables showed that the compression ratio is a crucial metric that has a heavy impact on the execution time. The distinct strategies to compress trajectories, when they have the same compression ratio, have not led to significant differences in the model's performances. For example, the AUC reached having compressed the trajectories using Douglas-Peucker algorithm is 0.969 while the one obtained using Uniform Sampling with SR equals to 90 s (same compression ratio of Douglas-Peucker) algorithm is 0.970, basically the same. So, the best compression algorithm is the simplest one, the Uniform Sampling, which has the lower computational complexity and it allows to choose a desired compression ratio.

In the Fig. 3 we have represented how the AUC and *total time*, defined as the sum of compression, preprocessing, training and evaluation time, varies in function of the compression ratio, using uniform sampling. A compression ratio of 0 corresponds to uncompressed trajectories, to highlight the effectiveness of the compression. With a compression ratio of just 0.5, the total time is almost halved while the AUC is decreased of just 0.003.

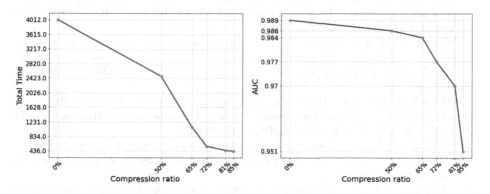

Fig. 3. Impact of the compression ratio of Uniform Sampling on AUC and execution time of GM-VSAE

5 Conclusion

In this paper, we carried out two main studies: firstly we have performed a comparison between two deep-learning models, GM-VSAE and ATD-RNN for anomalies detection using a public real-world taxi service dataset. The obtained results showed the superiority of GM-VSAE in terms of AUC. So we chose to focus on this model to study the impact of trajectories compression on both the execution time and the performance of anomalies detection using GM-VSAE. For this purpose, we introduced and compared four well known trajectories compression algorithms: uniform sampling, Douglas-Peucker, sk-mobility and opening window. We then trained and evaluated the GM-VSAE model using compressed trajectories with these four algorithms. Results show that sampling significantly reduces the execution time of GM-VSAE while keeping a good performance for anomalies detection (AUC near 1). Moreover, Uniform Sampling, which is the simplest approach, is the most convenient one because it allows to choose the compression ratio, which is the metric that significantly reduces the execution time of all the phases of the model (preprocessing, training and evaluation). Uniform Sampling is also the fastest compression approach, as its complexity is relatively low ($\mathcal{O}(n)$).

References

1. Song, L., Wang, R., Xiao, D., Han, X., Cai, Y., Shi, C.: Anomalous trajectory detection using recurrent neural network. In: Gan, G., Li, B., Li, X., Wang, S. (eds.) ADMA 2018. LNCS (LNAI), vol. 11323, pp. 263–277. Springer, Cham (2018). https://doi.org/10.1007/978-3-030-05090-0_23
2. Liu, Y., Zhao, K., Cong, G., Bao, Z.: Online anomalous trajectory detection with deep generative sequence modeling. In: 2020 IEEE 36th International Conference on Data Engineering (ICDE), Dallas, TX, USA, pp. 949–960 (2020). https://doi.org/10.1109/ICDE48307.2020.00087
3. Shahid, N., Naqvi, I.H., Qaisar, S.B.: Characteristics and classification of outlier detection techniques for wireless sensor networks in harsh environments: a survey. Artif. Intell. Rev. **43**(2), 193–228 (2015). https://doi.org/10.1007/s10462-012-9370-y
4. Muckell, J., Olsen Jr., P., Hwang, J., Lawson, C., Ravi, S.: Compression of trajectory data: a comprehensive evaluation and new approach. GeoInformatica. **18** (2014). https://doi.org/10.1007/s10707-013-0184-0
5. Penghui, S., Xia, S., Yuan, G., Li, D.: An overview of moving object trajectory compression algorithms. Math. Probl. Eng. **2016**, 1–13 (2016). https://doi.org/10.1155/2016/6587309
6. Makris, A., Silva, C.L.d., Bogorny, V., et al.: Evaluating the effect of compressing algorithms for trajectory similarity and classification problems. Geoinformatica **25**, 679–711 (2021). https://doi.org/10.1007/s10707-021-00434-1
7. Pappalardo, L., Simini, F., Barlacchi, G., Pellegrini, R.: scikit-mobility: A Python library for the analysis, generation, and risk assessment of mobility data. J. Stat. Softw. **103** (2022). https://doi.org/10.18637/jss.v103.i04
8. Zhong, Y., Kong, J., Zhang, J., Jiang, Y., Fan, X., Wang, Z.: A trajectory data compression algorithm based on spatio-temporal characteristics. PeerJ Comput. Sci. **3**(8), e1112 (2022). https://doi.org/10.7717/peerj-cs.1112
9. Frentzos, E., Theodoridis, Y.: On the effect of trajectory compression in spatiotemporal querying. In: Ioannidis, Y., Novikov, B., Rachev, B. (eds.) ADBIS 2007. LNCS, vol. 4690, pp. 217–233. Springer, Heidelberg (2007). https://doi.org/10.1007/978-3-540-75185-4_17
10. Keogh, E., Chu, S., Hart, D., Pazzani, M.: An online algorithm for segmenting time series. In: Proceedings IEEE International Conference on Data Mining, pp. 289–296. IEEE, San Jose, USA, Piscataway (2001)

Experimental Toolkit for Manipulating Executable Packing

Alexandre D'Hondt$^{(\boxtimes)}$ (ID), Charles Henry Bertrand Van Ouytsel$^{(\boxtimes)}$ (ID), and Axel Legay$^{(\boxtimes)}$ (ID)

Université Catholique de Louvain, Rue Archimede 1, Louvain-la-Neuve, Belgium
{alexandre.dhondt,charles-henry.bertrand,axel.legay}@uclouvain.be

Abstract. Executable packing is a well-known problematic especially in the field of malware analysis. It often consists in applying compression or encryption to a binary file and embedding a stub for reversing these transformations at runtime. This way, the packed executable is more difficult to reverse-engineer and/or is obfuscated, which is effective for evading static detection techniques. Many detection approaches, including machine learning, have been proposed in the literature so far, but most studies rely on questionable ground truths and do not provide any open implementation, making the comparison of state-of-the-art solutions tedious. We thus think that first solving the issue of repeatability shall help to compare existing executable packing static detection techniques. Given this challenge, we propose an experimental toolkit, named Packing Box, that leverages automation and containerization in an open source platform that brings a unified solution to the research community. We present our engineering approach for designing and implementing our solution. We then showcase it with a few basic experiments, including a performance evaluation of open source static packing detectors and training a model with machine learning pipeline automation. This introduces the toolset that will be used in further studies.

Keywords: executable packing · packer detection · packed classification · toolkit · machine learning · static analysis

1 Introduction

Executable packing can be seen as a set of transformations on a binary file (including compression or encryption) that modifies it so that it recovers its logic at runtime. It can be applied to many executable formats but is particularly diversified for the Windows Portable Executable (PE) format. Its use dates from the 1990's already, especially with malicious software for evading detection by antivirus software that typically use signatures and ad hoc heuristics. Packing detection has already been addressed in many researches since the early 2000's. Its main challenge is *performance*, involving static and dynamic analysis. While dynamic techniques can collect more information, they require executing the target binary, which incurs an additional cost. Static techniques, on the other hand, are faster as the binary is not executed. Many static techniques were presented in the past, relying on entropy [15], signatures [12,18,23], control flow graphs [5,6] or even ad hoc heuristics [8,13,14,25]. Many researches [1,4,7,19] have been published, often bringing excellent results to the forefront but never sharing a solution to repeat experiments and compare methods with each other. A recent survey [17] highlights the different works regarding packing detection and the wide variety of datasets (often custom-made) used in literature, only providing a qualitative analysis of state-of-the-art detection techniques. In this context, it is not easy to compare the results from several studies based on a same dataset. *Repeatability* is thus a major concern. To do this, we need to standardize the process of creating and formatting datasets but also provide a single operations pipeline so that each researcher can reproduce results from other studies for comparison. Moreover, machine learning has become the emerging trend for gaining in accuracy while keeping execution fast enough. Its optimal use, considering supervised learning, involves datasets of collected packed and not packed executables, but also capturing their most relevant characteristics in a trade-off between the number of features and their quality while maintaining sufficient accuracy. *Feature engineering* is thus yet another concern. Furthermore, addressing machine learning requires making datasets that can be considered generalized enough, otherwise the resulting model will not be relevant for every target executable. A major concern then lies in the *relevance of* the available *datasets* and the *correctness* in the establishment of a ground truth considered for training models.

The above considerations show that there is still room for improvement in packing detection, including tools to find and prove the best ways to do this. While *performance* and underlyingly *feature engineering* in the use of machine learning are the ultimate goals of our research, the primary focus of this work is on designing a toolkit that can ensure *repeatability* and help us build accurate and shareable ground truths and automate the entire machine learning pipeline, in preparation for further experiments to find the best features and models. Therefore, this work does not yet aim to make a scientific contribution, but rather proposes a framework that will constitute the reference toolbox for future studies. Given our focus, the design questions hereafter arise.

Q1. How can we enhance *repeatability* of the experiments of packing detection?
Q2. How can we build *accurate ground truths*?
Q3. How can we measure the *performance of state-of-the-art static detectors*?

To date, as far as we know, there exists no framework that gathers packing techniques and tools yet. For this purpose and in order to address the issue of *repeatability*, our contribution is to propose an experimental toolkit aptly named the Packing Box [11] that automates dataset generation for building accurate ground truths in a shareable format and provides tools for training machine learning models in a convenient and repeatable way. This toolset also includes data visualization utilities and allows to assess the performance of open detectors (e.g. PEiD or DIE).

The remainder of this paper first presents, in Sect. 2, some background on the topic of packing detection, including general considerations about packing, common static detection techniques and machine learning, together with requirements for our experimental toolkit that we could deduce. In Sect. 3, it then outlines our solution, including its design and implementation, its capabilities and how it can help us solve our questions. Then in Sect. 4, we showcase our solution with some experiments focused on the evaluation of the performance of some open static detectors and model training with our automated machine learning pipeline. We finally conclude in Sect. 5 on what we have achieved and what remains to be further developed and studied.

2   Background

This section aims to present the most important concepts that will be the source material of our toolkit. All along those, we deduce the requirements (REQ) for our design and implementation explained in Sect. 3.

Packing can be defined as a set of transformations that modify the layout of a binary file (an image file, typically .exe, or an object file, e.g. a DLL) without affecting its logic, adding a stub that allows either to revert these transformations when executing the binary for restoring its original logic in memory or to execute an equivalent one. In particular, this allows to hide the logic when the binary resides on the disk, therefore preventing certain static detection systems like antiviruses from viewing the real payload (i.e. causing evasion from detection). But it can also be used to reduce size or even to protect the target binary against piracy (e.g. by adding a prompt at startup to require a license key). By nature, packing is thus not limited to malware.

We distinguish seven types of distinct transformations used jointly by packers. *Bundling* makes a single executable with multiple files and is the typical behavior for portable versions of executables produced by tools like Cameyo, ThinApp or even Enigma Virtual Box. *Compression* allows to reduce the binary's size, sometimes for obfuscating some of its regions. Most packers are compressors, including some very popular ones like UPX and UPack, typically using LZMA, LZ77 or Deflate as compression algorithms. *Encoding* is a reversible operation that changes a given character set to another, possibly of different size. Base64 and a simple XOR with a 1-byte key of value 1 are examples of encodings that could be used. *Encryption* allows to obfuscate parts of the binary and to protect the binary from piracy. It is reversible and requires a key, either embedded or requested at runtime. *Mutation* alters the executable's code so that it uses a modified instruction set and architecture, e.g. using metamorphism (that is, the executable mutates its code at each execution). *Protection* makes reverse engineering harder by using anti-debugging, anti-tampering or other tricks that prevent analysis tools to properly do their job (e.g. Themida). *Virtualization* involves embedding a virtual machine that allows to virtualize executable's instructions for the sake of isolating it from the underlying operating system. This can be used for portability (e.g. BoxedApp Packer and Enigma Virtual Box) but for obfuscation as well (e.g. Molebox). While the aforementioned taxonomy is not the primary focus of this work, it shows the variety of packing operations and the potential for classifying packers per *categories*.

(REQ01) Our experimental toolkit should allow to deal with the categories from the aforementioned taxonomy. This involves supporting multi-label classification.

Many previous researches focused on telling whether a binary is packed or not (binary classification) [13,15] while others aimed to go further and classify packers according to their names (e.g. UPX or Themida) or *families* (as of the term used by Biondi *et al.* [4]) [7,23]. This term of *family* is used as a single product may yield variants in function of the version and point in time it was released. Moreover, a packer may have input options that can shape the layout of the packed executable differently. This is also a challenge if we want to be able to train models that can detect a whole family or a category (e.g. compressors) while the packer has very dissimilar versions and a panel of available options.

(REQ02) Our toolkit should handle different packer versions and configurations.

(REQ03) It should also allow to handle either binary or multi-class classification.

Among the techniques for packing detection, static ones consist of actions performed without ever executing the binary (on the contrary of dynamic techniques). Some of them rely on characteristics of the executable formats and others on computed values. In the current literature, we find various methods relying on entropy (such as Bintropy [15] or REMINDer [13]), signatures (based on opcodes [23], byte sequences [18] or metadata [12]), control flow graphs (relying on similarity [5] and decompilation [6]) or heuristics (based on a vector of structural or header features and using a distance metric [8] or a risk score [14,25]). Most of the aforementioned studies focused on malware analysis and Windows Portable Executables, often considering a single static technique. Most of them achieved good results on specific datasets and showed few or no comparison of performance with other approaches, often relying on popular signature-based open tools like PEiD[1], i.e. using them to validate a reference ground truth.

(REQ04) Our toolkit shall handle more than simply Portable Executables (PE) from Windows, i.e. Executable and Linking Format (ELF) from Unix and if possible Mach Objects from MacOS.

(REQ05) It should implement as many readily available static detection tools and techniques as possible. This will allow for further comparison of the state-of-the-art tools and techniques and it could also greatly help analyze weaker techniques like those based on entropy as shown by Mantovani *et al.* [16].

---

[1] http://www.secretashell.com/codomain/peid.

Even though many researches exhaustively detail the functioning of their approaches, it is rare that an open implementation is provided, therefore making the task of comparing approaches very tedious and time-consuming as it is necessary to re-implement tools relying on these approaches.

(REQ06) Our toolkit shall be open and transparent to other researchers.

Various sources of executables can be found in the wild, especially related to malware, but few provides packer labels or they have their labels determined based on proprietary or unpublished detection algorithms. It appears from many studies that some open datasets do not survive over time, making performance testing even more tedious with approaches from studies using more recent datasets. Among the interesting works for offering datasets, we note EMBER [2] (2018, large collection of features from PE files), PackingData[2] (2019, small collection of native PE files from Windows packed with 19 packers – reference dataset of Choi *et al.* [7]) and its extension [10] (2021, 6 more packers added) but also a new similar set with ELF samples[3] (2022, native Linux files packed with 6 different packers). There are also older datasets that were used in some studies and that are now unmaintained like Malfease[4] (2008), VX Heaven[5] (from 2010 to 2017) or even ViruSign[6] (stopped in 2020). Some more recent datasets are still actively maintained and usable, like Malware Bazaar[7] and VirusShare[8].

(REQ07) Our toolkit shall allow easy ingestion of items from external data sources for replicating datasets from related studies.

Given these data sources, it is frequent that labels are not standardized and even not accurate or verifiable. This issue can be addressed by building a superdetector [4,12,24] gathering multiple detectors and aggregating their results through a decision heuristic handling their normalized outputs. Based on ad hoc heuristics (e.g. a majority vote), we can then filter out labels that are not considered fully reliable and obtain a ground truth that is assumed to be of good quality. Another approach for building an accurate ground truth is to manually pack native binaries [7]. This is de facto the most reliable way to build a dataset but also the most time-consuming. Presently, as far as we know, there does not exist any solution yet that automates this process.

(REQ08) Our toolkit shall include as many detectors as possible and define a superdetector for reproducing experiments based on sets of detectors.

(REQ09) Our experimental toolkit shall automate packers to allow for bulk-creation of datasets of packed samples.

---

[2] https://github.com/chesvectain/PackingData.
[3] https://github.com/packing-box/dataset-packed-elf.
[4] https://web.archive.org/web/20141221153307/http://malfease.oarci.net.
[5] https://web.archive.org/web/20170817143838/http://vxheaven.org.
[6] https://www.virusign.com.
[7] https://bazaar.abuse.ch/browse.
[8] https://virusshare.com.

Machine learning tends to become the best way to tie multiple techniques together, using their results as features to improve the models. While simpler techniques like custom heuristics use feature vectors with simple distance metrics [8], machine learning algorithms offer far more possibilities in shaping models and leveraging features. Currently, *Supervised learning* is the area most covered by the literature, which exploits feature sets of different sizes [1, 3, 4, 20, 22]. *Semi-supervised learning* is relatively few covered [21, 26] and *Unsupervised learning* is even less so and has only recently been addressed [19]. Today, it appears that supervised learning was already extensively tackled while not identifying best features yet, except in the study of Betrand Van Ouytsel *et al.* [3]. It should also be noted that no implementation to automate the learning pipeline and compare model results has yet been provided.

(REQ10) Our toolkit shall automate the ML pipeline and cover supervised, semi-supervised and unsupervised learning as well.

3   Toolkit

This section explains the design and implementation choices with regard to the requirements mentioned in Sect. 2.

Given our requirements, our toolkit needs to rely on many existing libraries. While the framework could be designed upon several host operating systems, our objective is to provide a single platform and not a set of toolkits for different executable formats. Moreover, given the nature of some of the required libraries, i.e. for dealing with the different formats, and the fact that we may be working with malware samples, it involves, as a good practice, isolation from the host. Therefore, as virtualization may be too heavy for our needs in terms of performance and maintenance, containerization can provide an elegant solution. We thus plan our design starting with a container with several layers: its operating system, the libraries for handling our scope (at a minimum including the machinery for running Windows PE and Unix ELF formats) and our toolset.

Given our design, we choose Docker[9] as the containerization technology and we host our project on GitHub (REQ06). Figure 1 depicts our layered architecture. At the lower layer, we rely on Ubuntu 22.04 with no desktop interface, thus only relying on a command-line interface. We choose this OS as it is particularly convenient for adding libraries that can extend our scope. Furthermore, for our intermediate layer, this OS supports the well-known frameworks Wine[10] for executing PE binaries and Mono[11] for .NET executables. Of course, it natively supports running ELF binaries and can also run Mach Objects with Darling[12], a translation layer to run MacOS software on Linux (REQ04). For our upper layer, we select Python as our programming language as it is shipped with Ubuntu and

---

[9] https://www.docker.com.
[10] https://www.winehq.org.
[11] https://www.mono-project.com.
[12] https://www.darlinghq.org.

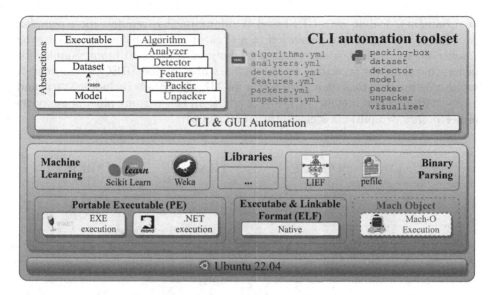

Fig. 1. Packing Box's architecture

it has a large support for libraries that can parse binaries and that implement ML algorithms. For building our toolset, we use LIEF[13] as our binary parsing library and select Scikit Learn[14] as our primary ML framework. We also support Weka[15] (Java-based) via Python with a dedicated package that provides a wrapper for its execution. We call our resulting Docker image "*Packing Box*" [11].

Since our goal is to provide researchers with a convenient interface for using our toolkit, we pay attention to the integration of new elements that should not require profound changes to the container. To this end, we abstract the raw material from our toolkit, considering elements that require no tunability and others that do. For the first type, we define *Executable* to be handled in a *Dataset* that can itself be processed by a *Model*. For tunable items that should provide the extensibility of our toolkit (REQ05), i.e. packers or detectors, we define an abstraction that holds attributes that we can customize through YAML[16] configuration files. This way, one dictionary per abstraction (see the above layer in Fig. 1) is defined. Among the attributes, we define metadata including the item's source, applicable executable formats and packing categories (REQ01), interesting references and status. We also define the installation and execution steps and also variants (REQ02). Thanks to these, our toolset can include custom libraries that will contain the logic to handle simple but also more complex items. For instance, as our container is headless (using Ubuntu with no desktop

---

[13] https://lief-project.github.io.

[14] https://scikit-learn.org.

[15] https://waikato.github.io/weka-site.

[16] Yet Another Markup Language.

environment), dealing with GUI-based Windows packers requires more complex processing relying on the emulation of a desktop environment. Thanks to the *Packer* abstraction, it is easy to apply plenty of packers to input samples for generating datasets according to the *Dataset* abstraction (REQ09). Moreover, we also define the *Algorithm* abstraction for ML algorithms including static and cross-validation parameters (REQ10). In addition, the learning pipeline supports either binary or multi-class classification (REQ03).

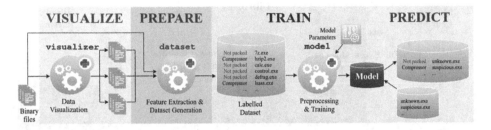

Fig. 2. Machine Learning pipeline and the automation toolset

While running the Docker image, the user ends up in a terminal that makes all the necessary tools available. It includes **packing-box**, an administrative utility for setting up and testing new items. **detector** is the tool that relies on the *Detector* abstraction and allows to use multiple detectors at once as a superdetector (REQ08) or even to apply mass detection and to output statistics for a given dataset. **packer** and **unpacker** are the tools that rely on the *Packer* and *Unpacker* abstractions and allow to test the packing and unpacking processes or also allows to apply bulk packing/unpacking. Other tools are readily available to start with experiments, including **visualizer**, **dataset** and **model** that automate the steps of the machine learning pipeline (REQ10) as depicted on Fig. 2. At the *VISUALIZE* step, **visualizer** helps sort the input samples or even complete packer labels or discard outliers. At the *PREPARE* step, **dataset** provides commands for creating, merging or splitting all kinds of datasets or even ingesting samples from a data source (REQ07) and simplify the preparation for model training. Then at the *TRAIN* step, **model** allows to train models and select the best parameters with a grid search based on the selected algorithm as defined in the related YAML file. At the *PREDICT* step, **model** also allows to further test the trained model on other datasets to evaluate its performance.

   dataset is the tool that relies on the *Dataset* abstraction to apply mass packing based on the packers defined in the related YAML configuration. Currently, it considers samples as successfully packed if and only if the hash of the original version has been changed in the packed version and is not known as a failure hash (e.g. hash of an empty binary file, with only headers and no section). As we only aim to work statically at this time, we do not use dynamic techniques to verify that the packed binary still runs as intended, hence the importance of studying the behavior of a packer when integrating it through its YAML definition. Attention shall be paid to reviewing the packer's documentation (if any) and testing edge cases to see if there exists failure hashes. With mass packing automated (REQ09), we can build accurate ground truths (Q2) as we make them based on prior knowledge because we know how we pack the binaries.

Data aims to be easily exported and shared with other users. This is ensured by setting a workspace folder that sorts datasets and models in separate subfolders, enforcing their structure. A dataset folder consists of its metadata, its features dictionary of descriptions, its data and, if relevant, its sample files. In the case when a dataset is converted to its fileless version, features are computed and stored with the dataset's data and the file samples are then dropped to save space. A model folder contains its model dumped in the JobLib[17] format. The **experiment** tool can be used to set up a dedicated workspace for a particular experiment. This way, specific datasets and models can be saved in the experiment's folder but configuration files can also be tuned in this specific context, without affecting the base configurations from the main workspace. It is worth being noted that the **dataset** tool can also export a dataset folder to multiple formats including ARFF (dataset format used in Weka – this allows for interoperability with Weka while using the same interface as Scikit Learn), CSV and a custom-made format relying on XSLX called DataSet File Format (DSFF) [9].

The Packing Box [11], thanks to the aforementioned functionalities, solves the issue of *repeatability* (Q1), bringing clarity in the conditions that lead to the best models but also allowing for portability of research results.

4   Experiments

For this paper, we focus our experiments on two aspects: performance evaluation of the integrated detectors and training machine learning models. The part related to feature engineering will be addressed in a further study. In the remainder of this section, we use the list of commands from Table 1 aimed to execute the experiments of this study. "DS" is our target dataset for the sake of conciseness but, in our scope, it is in particular **dataset-packed-pe** [10].

Our reference dataset is **dataset-packed-pe** [10], which is a sanitized (from outliers found via visualization) and augmented (with 5 new packers) fork of PackingData [7] consisting of 432 not packed samples, and ~130 samples for each of the following packers: Alienyze, Amber, ASPack, BeroEXEPacker, Enigma VirtualBox, Eronana's Packer, Exe32pack, EXpressor, FSG, JDPack, MEW, Molebox, MPRESS, Neolite, NSPack, Packman, PECompact, PEtite, RLPack, Telock, Themida, UPX, WinUPack, Yoda's Crypter and Yoda's Protector.

---

[17] https://joblib.readthedocs.io.

Table 1. Commands used during the experiments

ID	Phase	Command	Purpose

CMD01	Setup	`git clone`
		https://github.com/packing-box/
		docker-packing-box
		`cd docker-packing-box`
		`docker build -t packing-box.`
		`docker run -it -h packing-box -v`
		`` `pwd`:/mnt/share packing-box ``
			From the host, clone the Git repository, change the directory to it, build the box and then run it

CMD02	/	`detector ds -d die -m [-b] [-w]`	Test DIE against DS, using binary classification and/or weak mode
CMD03	*PREPARE*	`dataset update test-upx -s` `DS/not-packed -l DS/labels.json`	Update the target dataset (creating it if not existing) with the not-packed samples from the given source
CMD04	*PREPARE*	`dataset update test-upx -s` `DS/packed/UPX -l DS/labels.json`	Same as above but for UPX-packed samples
CMD05	*PREPARE*	`dataset make test-upx -n 300 -f` `PE -p upx --pack-all`	Make 300 UPX-packed PE samples to be added to the target dataset
CMD06	/	`dataset show test-upx`	Show the metadata and statistics of the given dataset
CMD07	*TRAIN*	`model train test-upx -a rf`	Train a Random Forest on a dataset
CMD08	/	`model show test-upx_pe_854_rf_f138`	Show the metadata and statistics of the given model, including a ranking of the best features
CMD09	*TEST*	`model test test-upx_pe_854_rf_f138` `test-mix`	Test the newly trained model on another dataset

4.1 Detectors Performance

For this experiment, it is worth being noted that many studies do not provide an open implementation (as addressed in Sect. 2, leading to REQ06). Therefore, it is difficult at this point to compare the performance of those techniques. However, our design allows to easily integrate these but this is currently a work in progress. At this time, we could already include various open source static detectors that can be found on the Web. Most of them rely on simple but yet relevant heuristics based on entropy or structural features of executable formats (mostly PE), including DIE[18], Manalyze[19], PEFrame[20] and RetDec[21]. We also reimplemented one open source detector (which is unmaintained), PyPackerDetect[22], and a few techniques addressed in the literature, including Bintropy[23] [15], PEiD[24] (used in almost all studies for building ground truths) and REMINDer[25] [13]. The characteristics of these detectors are presented in Table 2. This shows the supported

---

[18] https://github.com/horsicq/DIE-engine.
[19] https://github.com/JusticeRage/Manalyze.
[20] https://github.com/guelfoweb/peframe.
[21] https://github.com/avast/retdec.
[22] https://github.com/packing-box/pypackerdetect.
[23] https://github.com/packing-box/bintropy.
[24] https://github.com/packing-box/peid.
[25] https://github.com/packing-box/reminder.

Table 2. Base characteristics of in-scope detectors

Detector	Formats	Multiclass	Weak Mode	Superdetector	Comments
Bintropy	PE, ELF, MSDOS	N	N	N	Python CLI version of the tool of Lyda et al. [15] that integrates a plot capability
DIE	All	Y	N	Y	Most diversified detector we could find, supporting PE, ELF and Mach-O; it contains many fine-grained signatures and heuristics and is used in many studies
Manalyze	PE, MSDOS	Y	Y	N	Open source tool relying on PEiD's signatures DB, Yara rules and some heuristics (e.g. pattern matching on some packer names), sometimes used in studies
PEFrame	PE, MSDOS	Y	Y	N	Open source tool that relies on PEiD's signatures DB and some heuristics, found in only one study
PEiD	PE, MSDOS	Y	N	Y	Python CLI version of the original tool holding a sanitized database (aggregating many sources from GitHub repositories with signatures unrelated to packing removed) that we implemented for use with the Packing Box
PyPacker-Detect	PE, MSDOS	Y	Y	Y	Fork of the unmaintained open source tool that relies on PEiD's signatures DB and a few simple heuristics
REMINDer	PE, ELF, MSDOS	N	N	N	Python CLI version of the tool of Han et al. [13], using a simple heuristic relying on the writable property and the entropy of the EP section
RetDec	All	Y	N	Y	Open source retargetable machine-code decompiler supporting many executable file format and using custom signatures and header-based heuristics

Table 3. Performance test results for in-scope detectors

Detector	Accuracy	Time	Complexity	Observations
Bintropy	58,71%	0,5–10,5 s	$\mathcal{O}(n)$	Solely relies on entropy (i.e. block entropy)
DIE	84,25%–85,81%	~450 ms	$\mathcal{O}(log(n))$	Narrow detection rate interval (<2%), null FPR, strong signatures combined with some heuristics
Manalyze	45,17%–94,83%	~350 ms	$\mathcal{O}(log(n))$	Very broad detection rate interval (~50%), high FPR, relying on a short list of known section names and some simplistic heuristics
PEFrame	57,42%–87,52%	1,39–27,6 s	$\mathcal{O}(n)$	Flawed; only relies on signatures and entropy
PEiD	69,29%–71,63%	1,69–2,37 s	$\mathcal{O}(n)$	Narrow detection rate interval (<3%), low FPR, many signatures are missing from the database
PyPacker-Detect	79,69%–94,65%	0,71–1,36 s	$\mathcal{O}(n)$	Decent FPR, provides good results and its heuristics cover cases not covered by the PEiD signatures
REMINDer	47,55%	72–190 ms	$\mathcal{O}(n)$	Poor detection rate, only relies on the writable property of the EP section and its entropy
RetDec	70,71%–75,76%	0,32–0,84 s	$\mathcal{O}(n)$	Narrow detection rate interval (~5%), low FPR, relying on custom signatures and some heuristics covering unmatched cases

formats for each detector and whether it supports multi-class classification (that is, either it only output whether the target is packed or not, or the name of the packer used), weak mode (meaning that the detector outputs formal detection decisions but also suspicions that are used in a simple plurality vote; when using this mode, we also consider for instance section names of the binary found as an indication of packing) and if it is selected in our superdetector (resulting from the analysis of Table 3).

In order to measure accuracy, we divided our experiments into 4 classes, taking 2 parameters into account: whether classification is binary (packed or not) or multi-class (per packer name) and if detection is strong (the detector outputs a formal decision) or weak (the output provides detection traces but also suspicions that may yield a decision that is less robust). Accuracy metrics were collected based on the execution of each detector on all the subsets (not packed and 25 packers) from our dataset [10]. With the detections rates of the 4 classes, considering weighted averages per class, we then considered the lower and upper bounds among the four resulting metrics. We used the `detector` tool from the Packing Box for bulk detection. CMD02 illustrates how to get the accuracy for a given dataset with a single detector. This command takes the following arguments: the target folder of the input dataset, `-d` is used to specify the integrated detector to be selected, `-m` enables metrics acquisition (i.e. accuracy), `-b` enables binary classification and `-w` enables the weak mode. While using a Bash script to run every detector on each subset of our reference dataset [10], we obtain the accuracy for the 4 different classes.

Processing time and complexity were evaluated by running the detectors (using a script relying on the `detector` tool) against samples from our dataset [10], only keeping the results for file sizes from 0 to 10 megabytes and then considering the lower and upper bounds. Taking the results of this evaluation, we applied curve fitting to get the best fit among constant, logarithmic, linear, linear-algorithmic and quadratic complexities. Results are shown in Table 3.

For the performance evaluation (Q3), Table 3 shows the collected metrics and our related observations. We note that a few detectors have a stable detection (including DIE, PEiD and RetDec) while others do not (i.e. Manalyze, PEFrame and PyPackerDetect). We also see that only a few ones perform in less than 1 s (the best performers being DIE, Manalyze and PEPack and the worst ones being PEFrame, REMINDer and Bintropy). Moreover, we point out that most of the detectors have a complexity in $\mathcal{O}(n)$ which means they parse the entire binary. While this result is logical for Bintropy (as it requires to compute the entropy of the whole binary), for some others it is not. PEiD, which was used for matching signatures from the Entry Point (EP), surprisingly holds this complexity while we expect it to perform in $\mathcal{O}(1)$ because it should only require a constant calculation to find the EP and a pattern matching that is bounded to a constant maximum length. However, this result comes from the underlying library that systematically parses the entire file. The same issue applies to REMINDer too. It is also worth being noted that even the best detector, DIE, only performs at around 86%. This is due to the specificity of the dataset in use, which contains multiple recent custom packers found on GitHub like Alienyze (which relocates the EP but does not actually perform packing in its demo version), Amber and Eronana's Packer. From these results, we see that DIE is the best performer in terms of accuracy, followed by PyPackerDetect. It shall be noted however that PyPackerDetect holds a non-negligible False Positives Rate (FPR). Regarding time complexities, DIE remains the best. In terms of processing time, also considering the FPR and accuracy range, DIE stays at the top.

In terms of candidates for the superdetector, Bintropy and Manalyze can be excluded due to their accuracy. Moreover, PeFrame has a particularly high cost in processing time and can then be discarded. Among the best performers, we thus keep DIE, PEiD, PyPackerDetect and RetDec.

4.2 Model Training

This experiment aims to briefly showcase learning pipeline automation. Other experiments for identifying categories, best features and models are left for future works. Following the learning pipeline of Fig. 2, we address dataset generation and model training, that is, the *PREPARE, TRAIN* and *TEST* phases.

For data preparation, CMD03 and CMD04 are used to respectively create and update the dataset with input samples and take the following arguments: a dataset name (e.g. `test-upx`), `-s` specifies the source folder to get samples from and `-l` specifies the JSON file containing the labels to be used. Note that, if no labels dictionary (with file hashes as keys and labels as values) is provided, samples will be considered not labelled. CMD05 shows the `make` command that takes the following arguments: `-n` gives the maximum number of samples, `-f` specifies the executable format to be selected from the source folder, `-p` specifies the packer to be used and `--pack-all` enables packing every sample (otherwise, samples are packed or not randomly so that the dataset gets balanced). Creating a second dataset with CMD03 and CMD04, we can reuse this last command to add for instance Neolite and Packman samples. This set of commands completes the *PREPARE* phase. For our experiment, we end up with two datasets: one consisting of 854 samples whose 422 are UPX-packed (this can be inspected using CMD06) and the second consisting of 785 samples including 116 Neolite, 115 Packman and 122 UPX-packed samples. We can then train our model.

CMD07 aims to train a model using the Random Forest algorithm based on the first dataset we just made. The `model` tool takes the following arguments: the target dataset is specified to train the model on and `-a` specifies the algorithm to be selected. The result of this command displays evaluation metrics as shown in Table 4, including the accuracy, precision, recall, F-measure, Matthews Correlation Coefficient (MCC) and Area Under the Curve (AUC)[26]. Note that the default for the train set split is 80%, hence we get both train and test metrics in the training results. We obtain a perfectly fitted model that gets automatically named "`test-upx_pe_854_rf_f138`" according to the reference dataset and its related size, the learning algorithm's short name and the number of applicable

---

[26] https://scikit-learn.org/stable/modules/model_evaluation.html.

features (that is, excluding the features with a null variance). We can inspect our new model with CMD08, i.e. for getting the ranking of the best features according to their importance. At this point, we completed the *TRAIN* phase.

CMD09 shows how to address the *TEST* phase by applying our new model to our second dataset. The `model` tool takes the following positional arguments: the automatically generated name of the trained model (shown after training it) and the name of the dataset to test the model on. We get 83.18% accuracy on our new dataset, meaning the model trained based on UPX samples cannot fully explain samples packed with Neolite and Packman. As the precision is 100%, it means that our model does not yield False Positives. However, the recall shows that it yields many False Negatives, which means that it does not use relevant information for detecting samples packed with another packer than UPX. In a few commands, we thus followed the complete learning pipeline. By playing with input datasets, it is now easy to study other classifications, i.e. packer categories.

Table 4. Metric values for training and testing a simple model based on a dataset consisting of not packed and UPX-packed samples, then tested on a separate dataset including UPX, Neolite and Packman samples

	Accuracy	Precision	Recall	F-Measure	MCC	AUC
Train (test-upx)	100%	100%	100%	100%	100%	100%
Test (test-upx)	100%	100%	100%	100%	100%	100%
Test (test-mix)	83.18%	100%	62.61%	77%	69.25%	100%

5 Conclusion

In this paper, we first stated the problem of executable packing and emphasized the need for *repeatability* in experiments for its detection. We set the background for this topic, enumerated techniques of static detection as currently presented in the literature and parsed some aspects that could help us deduce requirements for our experimental toolkit. We then described our design and implementation of the Packing Box, including the capabilities it offers especially for making experiments repeatable, promoting results sharing (Q1) and building accurate ground truths (Q2). Finally, we conducted some experiments to showcase the functionalities and how the entire machine learning pipeline could be traversed in just a few terminal commands thanks to our toolset. We took advantage of our toolkit to study the performance (Q3) of open source static detectors, as well as a number of detectors proposed in the literature which we have re-implemented.

We designed a platform for studying executable packing, not especially focused on malware analysis but well on packing in general and not limited to only Windows PE but also applicable to other executable formats like ELF. This brings an open source unified solution to the research community that addresses the many related practical challenges, including the need for a solution that allows to compare results from multiple studies in a quantitative way (unlike qualitative such as the survey of Muralidharan *et al.* [17]), allowing to compare approaches based on common data. With the Packing Box, we showed that it significantly enhances experiment *repeatability* as it fully integrates assets (i.e. detectors and packers) and it automates the complete learning pipeline (from dataset generation to model training, testing and comparison). Through packers integration, we showed how it allows to generate accurate ground truths starting from a set of cleanware samples. Through detectors integration, we demonstrated how to mass-process a dataset we created to evaluate the performance of state-of-the-art detectors, allowing us to select the best ones for a superdetector. With this experimental toolkit in hand, we propose a complete solution for creating and sharing datasets, comparing, improving and sharing machine learning models for static packing detection and even managing and sharing our experiments.

We already planned a few enhancements in terms of functionalities but also in our experiments as well;

- *Packer categories:* We mentioned categories at the beginning of Sect. 2 but we did not present any experiment focused on detecting them as this is still a work in progress. We plan to train many models based on many datasets of our own in the hope of identifying sets of features that could better apply to one category or another.
- *Feature engineering:* We already enhanced our toolkit to support custom features handling through another declarative YAML configuration file. Furthermore, we added the logic to compose new features from the ones currently extracted (e.g. for PE files, via `pefeats` [4]). Throughout our review of the literature, we gathered state-of-the-art features and established our own set in what we called the *Feature Book*. We thus plan to implement this to further refine our features set for our next experiments.
- *State-of-the-art techniques:* Among the techniques mentioned in Sect. 2, we plan to implement a few more to extend our scope and provide a comparison to measure how much better our ML approach could be.

Acknowledgements. Charles-Henry Bertrand Van Ouytsel is FRIA grantee of the Belgian Fund for Scientific Research (FNRS-F.R.S.). The authors are funded by the CyberExcellence project (RW, Convention 2110186).

References

1. Aghakhani, H., et al.: When malware is Packin' heat; limits of machine learning classifiers based on static analysis features, p. 20 (2020)
2. Anderson, H.S., Roth, P.: EMBER: an open dataset for training static PE malware machine learning models (2018)
3. Bertrand Van Ouytsel, C.H., Given-Wilson, T., Minet, J., Roussieau, J., Legay, A.: Analysis of machine learning approaches to packing detection (2021)
4. Biondi, F., Enescu, M.A., Given-Wilson, T., Legay, A., Noureddine, L., Verma, V.: Effective, efficient, and robust packing detection and classification (2019)

5. Cesare, S., Xiang, Y.: A fast flowgraph based classification system for packed and polymorphic malware on the endhost. In: 24th International Conference on Advanced Information Networking and Applications. IEEE (2010)

6. Cesare, S., Xiang, Y., Zhou, W.: Malwise - an effective and efficient classification system for packed and polymorphic malware (2013)

7. Choi, M.J., Bang, J., Kim, J., Kim, H., Moon, Y.S., Díaz-Verdejo, J.: All-in-one framework for detection, unpacking, and verification for malware analysis (2019)

8. Choi, Y.S., Kim, I.K., Oh, J.T., Ryou, J.C.: PE file header analysis-based packed PE file detection technique (PHAD). In: International Symposium on Computer Science and Its Applications, pp. 28–31. IEEE (2008)

9. D'Hondt, A.: Dataset file format (DSFF) (2022). https://github.com/packing-box/python-dsff

10. D'Hondt, A.: Dataset of packed PE files (2022). https://github.com/packing-box/dataset-packed-pe

11. D'Hondt, A.: Packing box – study executable packing easy (2022). https://github.com/packing-box/docker-packing-box

12. Hai, N.M., Ogawa, M., Tho, Q.T.: Packer identification based on metadata signature. In: Proceedings of the 7th Software Security, Protection, and Reverse Engineering. SSPREW-7, p. 11. ACM (2017)

13. Han, S., Lee, K., Lee, S.: Packed PE file detection for malware forensics. In: 2nd International Conference on Computer Science and Its Applications. IEEE (2009)

14. Lim, C., Nicsen: Mal-EVE: static detection model for evasive malware. In: 10th International Conference on Communications and Networking in China. IEEE (2015)

15. Lyda, R., Hamrock, J.: Using entropy analysis to find encrypted and packed malware (2007)

16. Mantovani, A., Aonzo, S., Ugarte-Pedrero, X., Merlo, A., Balzarotti, D.: Prevalence and impact of low-entropy packing schemes in the malware ecosystem. In: Network and Distributed Systems Security Symposium. NDSS (2020)

17. Muralidharan, T., Cohen, A., Gerson, N., Nissim, N.: File packing from the malware perspective: Techniques, analysis approaches, and directions for enhancements. ACM Comput. Surv. (2022)

18. Naval, S., Laxmi, V., Gaur, M.S., Vinod, P.: SPADE: signature based PAcker DEtection. In: Proceedings of the First International Conference on Security of Internet of Things. SecurIT '12, pp. 96–101. ACM (2012)

19. Noureddine, L., Heuser, A., Puodzius, C., Zendra, O.: SE-PAC: a self-evolving PAcker classifier against rapid packers evolution. In: Proceedings of the 11th ACM Conference on Data and Application Security and Privacy. CODASPY '21, pp. 281–292. ACM (2021)

20. Perdisci, R., Lanzi, A., Lee, W.: McBoost: boosting scalability in malware collection and analysis using statistical classification of executables. In: 2008 Annual Computer Security Applications Conference (ACSAC), pp. 301–310 (2008)

21. Santos, I., Nieves, J., Bringas, P.G.: Semi-supervised learning for unknown malware detection. In: Abraham, A., Corchado, J.M., González, S.R., De Paz Santana, J.F. (eds.) International Symposium on Distributed Computing and Artificial Intelligence. AISC, vol. 91, pp. 415–422. Springer, Heidelberg (2011). https://doi.org/10.1007/978-3-642-19934-9_53

22. Shafiq, M.Z., Tabish, S.M., Farooq, M.: PE-probe: leveraging packer detection and structural information to detect malicious portable executables. In: Proceedings of the Virus Bulletin Conference (2009)

23. Shin, D., Im, C., Jeong, H., Kim, J., Won, D.: The new signature generation method based on an unpacking algorithm and procedure for a packer detection. Int. J. Adv. Sci. Technol. IJAST (2011)
24. Sun, L., Versteeg, S., Boztaş, S., Yann, T.: Pattern recognition techniques for the classification of malware packers. In: Steinfeld, R., Hawkes, P. (eds.) ACISP 2010. LNCS, vol. 6168, pp. 370–390. Springer, Heidelberg (2010). https://doi.org/10.1007/978-3-642-14081-5_23
25. Treadwell, S., Zhou, M.: A heuristic approach for detection of obfuscated malware. In: International Conference on Intelligence and Security Informatics. IEEE (2009)
26. Ugarte-Pedrero, X., Santos, I., Bringas, P.G., Gastesi, M., Esparza, J.M.: Semi-supervised learning for packed executable detection. In: 5th International Conference on Network and System Security. IEEE (2011)

A Collaborative Real-Time Object Detection and Data Association Framework for Autonomous Robots Using Federated Graph Neural Network

Feryal Batoul Talbi[1,2], Samir Ouchani[2(✉)], Yohan Dupuis[3], and Mimoun Malki[1]

[1] École Supérieure en Informatique, Sidi Bel-abbes, Algeria
[2] CESI LINEACT, Aix-en-Provence, France
souchani@cesi.fr
[3] CESI LINEACT, Paris La Défense, France

Abstract. Autonomous robotics require secure and decentralized decision-making systems that ensure data privacy and computational efficiency, especially in critical areas. Current centralized models or human input are associated with data breaches and security vulnerabilities. To counter these, we propose **CoRODDA**, a dedicated framework combining federated learning and graph neural networks. **CoRODDA** enhances object detection and data association in autonomous robots, enabling them to learn from local data while preserving privacy and interpreting graph-structured associated data to understand the surrounding environments. The experiments showed the effectiveness of **CoRODDA** compared to the state-of-the-art, particularly in non-detected objects, improving data privacy and decision-making capabilities.

Keywords: Federated Learning · Graph Neural Network · Autonomous Robots · Data Association · Object Detection · Security

1 Introduction

Motivation. Although significant advancements have been made in robotic systems, a key challenge that persists is the execution of complex tasks during censorious situations in critical environments. These tasks, based on object detection and data association, need to be performed in a decentralized manner while ensuring data privacy [1]. Conventional approaches often fall short in situations where centralized data aggregation is either unfeasible or poses a threat to privacy [2]. However, in the current era of rapid technological evolution, autonomous robotic systems are recognized as a driving force behind numerous industry transformations [3,4]. Yet, a global challenge remains to ensure these robotic systems not only carry out complex tasks (such as object detection and data association) but also maintain data privacy, especially in outdoor environments [5,6].

Related Work. Existing solutions often grapple with challenges when centralized data processing becomes infeasible, or as data privacy takes center stage [7]. Recognizing these challenges, the adoption of Graph Neural Networks (GNNs) and Federated Learning (FL) has significant advancements in autonomous robotic systems, notably in intricate tasks like object detection and data association [8]. GNNs, renowned for their adeptness in managing graph-structured data, have revolutionized robotic interactions and understanding of their surroundings [9]. In parallel, FL has ushered in transformative methodologies, allowing robots to harness local data insights while upholding rigorous data privacy and refining computational efficiency [10].

The field of Fed and GNN has seen extensive research, covering areas such as privacy preservation, non-IID data challenges, decentralization, and FL personalization [11]. Though innovative techniques such as local differential privacy and homomorphic encryption have been seminal, they also underscore computational and model convergence dilemmas. Persistent challenges revolve around data heterogeneity and the nuances of managing non-IID data. Decentralization, despite its merits in distributed control, contends with obstacles in real-time responsiveness and model scalability [12]. While numerous strategies address spatial-temporal dependencies, aligning them with the dynamic needs of stakeholders is a complex endeavor [13]. Striking an equilibrium between instantaneous adaptability and stringent data privacy remains a significant hurdle [14].

Contributions. In the realm of autonomous robotics, the integration of GNN and FL (FedGNN) holds great promise. GNNs are pivotal for handling graph-structured data, empowering robots to understand better and navigate their environment. Concurrently, FL ensures efficient decentralized learning, emphasizing data privacy. We develop a Collaborative Real-Time Object Detection and Data Association (**CoRODDA**) framework for autonomous robots using FedGNN that synergistically leverages the capabilities of both FL and GNNs, specially tailored for object detection and data association tasks. Emphasizing real-world critical applications, **CoRODDA** stands out, marking a new frontier in data privacy and decision-making. Drawing from an extensive review of the related literature and building on the state-of-the-art, this work presents the following contributions:

1. Suggest **CoRODDA**, an amalgamation of FL and GNN strengths, optimized for object detection Section 2.
2. An in-depth assessment of **CoRODDA**, highlighting its preeminence in maintaining data privacy and decision-making Sect. 3.

2   CoRODDA Framework

In this section, we present a detailed overview of our proposed framework, highlighting the significance and operation of each component. Figure 1 depicts the structure of **CoRODDA**. It progresses through a series of local and centralized stages, with each stage serving a pivotal role in realizing the overarching objective of detecting objects with low scores or those missed by object detection algorithms.

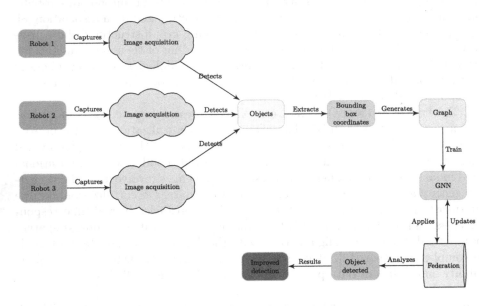

Fig. 1. Detailed Object Detection Process in **CoRODDA**.

1. **Local Operations:**
   (a) **Data Acquisition and Preprocessing:** Robots capture images, serving as the primary input for **CoRODDA**. All raw image data remains localized to each robot, ensuring the confidentiality of the initial dataset.
   (b) **Object Detection and Extraction:** Advanced object detection techniques and pre-defined models are utilized to identify objects within the processed images. This step also meticulously extracts the spatial boundaries of identified objects.
   (c) **Graph Generation and Training:** A graph that represents detected objects and their spatial relationships is produced. FedGNN model is then fed with this data. Robots individually refine their models without transmitting any data elsewhere.
2. **Centralized Operations:**
   (a) **Model Aggregation:** The server accumulates updates from all participating robots, refining a global model to improve object detection capabilities and confidence scores. The strength of the federated learning approach is evident here, as only model updates, devoid of any raw or derivative data, are shared.
   (b) **Real-time Analysis:** The global model is employed for real-time object analysis. Feedback is dispatched to the robots, amplifying their ability to recognize not just common objects but also those that might be minute or situated closely - objects previously undetected by initial techniques.

3   Experimental Results

In this section, we analyze **CoRODDA**'s performance in object detection with YOLOv5 across 80 classes, using the Stanford Drone Dataset[1]. **CoRODDA** uses a spatial approximation to segment insights across a federated network. By incorporating the GNN model, GraphSAGE, **CoRODDA** interprets graph-structured data, emphasizing cooperative learning and data privacy.

3.1   GNN Model Architecture

Central to **CoRODDA** is the GraphSAGE GNN model, known for its ability to generalize larger unseen graphs. Its selection is based on attributes apt for our application. Below, we detail the model's architecture and features.

- **Node Features:** Nodes are defined by features forming the base for further analysis. These features capture the essential attributes and characteristics of the nodes,
- **Network Depth:** The 16-layer deep model emphasizes critical data patterns through multiple nonlinear transformations.
- **Optimization:** We use the Adam optimizer with a 0.01 learning rate, known for its adaptive properties, to strike a balance between convergence speed and precision.
- **Dropout:** A 0.5 dropout rate is applied to reduce overfitting by randomly deactivating neurons during training.
- **Training Duration:** The model is trained over 10 epochs to optimize learning without risking overfitting.
- **Metrics:** Post-training, the model achieves a 73% accuracy rate for the training dataset, demonstrating its proficiency in handling graph data.

This intricate architecture, characterized by its depth, underscores our commitment to achieving unparalleled results in graph data processing and analysis. The model is adept at capturing contextual information and relational dependencies, as illustrated in Fig. 2. Over the span of 10 epochs, the training accuracy begins at 70.31% and peaks at 73.09%, while the validation accuracy commences at 71.31% and culminates at 74.09%. In tandem, the F1 Score for training initiates at 65.18% and reaches 69.00%, and for validation, it starts at 66.18% and ascends to 70.00%.

3.2   Enhancements via FL

In his approach, we have married the strengths of GNNs with the decentralization and privacy preservation features of FL. Key attributes and advantages of this federated model are:

---

[1] https://cvgl.stanford.edu/projects/uav_data/.

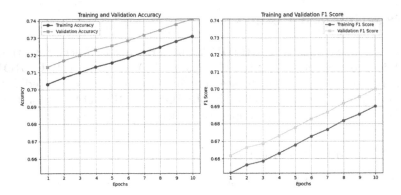

Fig. 2. Accuracy and F1 Score achieved by the GNN Model.

- **Decentralized Training:** Our approach empowers each robot with its own GNN model, promoting learning from real-time interactions. This reduces communication needs, optimizes bandwidth, and notably bolsters data privacy by retaining data locally.
- **Genetic Algorithms:** We utilize GAs in the FL workflow, refining model weights by mimicking biological evolution. As a result, models are iteratively optimized based on performance with local datasets.
- **Federated Genetic Algorithm** [15–17]: Our advanced FedGA method amalgamates weights from all robot models, crafting a holistic global model that benefits from the entire network's collective intelligence.
- **Collaborative Data Utilization:** Robots contribute unique insights, and when combined, these diverse updates form a global model that's adaptable and represents various environments.
- **Accuracy Gains:** Post a 50-epoch training, our federated and genetically enhanced approach achieved a significant 78% rise in accuracy.

The trajectory of accuracy over training epochs is illustrated in Fig. 3 which shows the distinct improvements brought by FedGA. Table 1 methodically contrasts the standalone GNN model with the enhanced FedGA and FedAVG models. The most notable observations from this table are:

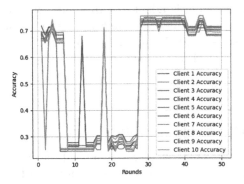

Fig. 3. Accuracy improvement over epochs in the federated GNN Model.

- FedGA has undergone a significant increase in training epochs compared to the 10 epochs of the standalone GNN model.
- In terms of accuracy, FedGA achieved a notable 5% improvement over the GNN model, registering at 78% for the validation training. Meanwhile, FedAVG slightly underperformed with an accuracy of 70.8% training dataset.
- Furthermore, the F1 Score for FedGA outshines both the GNN model and the FedAVG, boasting a score of 80%, a marked increase from the GNN model's 69% and a substantial leap from FedAVG's 0.59%.

3.3   Integration with YOLOv5 and Performance Insights

In **CoRODDA**, we combine the real-time object detection capabilities of YOLOv5 with the sophisticated data interpretation potential of FedGNN, resulting in significant performance enhancements.

3.3.1   YOLOv5 Object Detection. YOLOv5 efficiently detects objects in images using confidence scores; while high scores signify precise detection, low scores can result in missed objects, represented by empty brackets.

- **Predefined Classes in YOLOv5.** YOLOv5 is trained in specific classes. Objects outside these classes, may be present but remain undetected due to the predefined scope.
- **FedGNN's Role in Refinement.** FedGNN adopts a graph-based approach that leverages spatial relationships between objects for a deeper understanding. It refines YOLOv5's initial detections and improves accuracy.
- **Performance Indicators. CoRODDA** provides the following performance indicators:

Table 1. Comparative Summary of Performance Metrics and Model Features.

Metrics/Features	GNN Model	FedGa	FedAVG
Input features per node	3	3 (Unchanged)	3 (Unchanged)
Hidden layers	16	16 (Unchanged)	16 (Unchanged)
Optimizer's learning rate	0.01	0.01 (Unchanged)	0.01 (Unchanged)
Dropout rate	0.5	0.5 (Unchanged)	0.5 (Unchanged)
Training epochs	10	50	50
Achieved accuracy	73%	78%	70.8%
F1 Score	69%	80%	0.59%
Inference time	Real-time	Real-time	Real-time
Machine Specifications	MacBook Pro M1 chip, 16GB RAM		

1. **Detection Accuracy.** It evaluates the correctness compared to ground truth annotations. Collaboration between YOLOv5 and FedGNN enhances the accuracy.

2. **F1 Score.** An harmonic mean of precision and recall, providing a balanced detection performance measure.

3.3.2   Results. To shed light on the confidence differences between the YOLOv5 and **CoRODDA** object detection algorithms, Fig. 4 was charted. In this figure, the x-axis represents different object regions (or images), while the y-axis quantifies their corresponding scores. Blue bars denote YOLO's confidence, whereas green bars depict the scores from **CoRODDA** for images overlooked by YOLOv5.

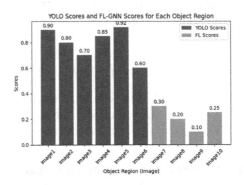

Fig. 4. Comparison of YOLO and FL-GNN Scores for Object Regions. Green bars correspond to objects missed by YoloV5. (Color figure online)

The notable drop in confidence scores for **CoRODDA**, evident from the green bars, suggests that while it identifies objects YOLOv5 misses, it is often less confident in its detections. Objects may be missed by YOLOv5 due to factors like subtle variations in lighting, orientation, or occlusions, which might be more perceptible to **CoRODDA**. However, the framework's lower confidence could also arise from the challenges in dealing with such nuances. This comparison emphasizes the unique strengths and potential gaps of both algorithms, underscoring their combined potential in providing a holistic object detection system.

4   Conclusion

This paper has highlighted the significance of enhancing robotic responsiveness in dynamic settings. Our research journey began with an in-depth examination of the complexities of decision-making, which subsequently uncovered distributed object detection as a pivotal solution. Through **CoRODDA**, we illustrated the mechanism of robots capturing images, detecting objects, and systematically representing the detected object's coordinates on a graph. Intriguingly, the subsequent processing by FedGNN, which updates a central server in real-time, offers insights into potential optimizations in the realm of object detection. As the server meticulously analyzes the derived data, the prospects of enhancing object detection precision emerge more clearly, aligning seamlessly with the overarching goals we set out with. This work underscores the potential for refining robotic actions, adaptability, and interactions, especially in dynamic contexts. As we continue to push the boundaries of automated capabilities, the findings from this study provide a roadmap for future endeavors in this domain and we target to improve the federation process and apply **CoRODDA** on more benchmarks.

Acknowledgements. This work is partially funded under the ANR-21-ASRO-0005-01 agreement attached to the SCOPES project (ASTRID ASRO 2021 scheme funded by the Agence de l'Innovation de Défense (AID)).

References

1. Ouchani, S., Lenzini, G.: Generating attacks in SysML activity diagrams by detecting attack surfaces. J. Ambient. Intell. Humaniz. Comput. **6**, 361–373 (2015)
2. Bonawitz, K., et al.: Towards federated learning at scale: System design. In: Proceedings of the 2nd SysML Conference (2019)
3. Guizzo, E.: The rise of the robot worker. IEEE Spectr. **48**(10), 34–41 (2011)
4. Zerrouki, F., Ouchani, S., Bouarfa, H.: Quantifying security and performance of physical unclonable functions. In: 2020 7th International Conference on Internet of Things: Systems, Management and Security (IOTSMS), pp. 1–4. IEEE (2020)
5. Zhou, Y., Tuzel, O.: Towards safe autonomous driving: capture uncertainty in the deep neural network for lidar 3d vehicle detection. arXiv preprint arXiv:1804.05132 (2018)
6. Ouchani, S.: A security policy hardening framework for socio-cyber-physical systems. J. Syst. Architect. **119**, 102259 (2021)
7. Howard, P.N., Hussain, M.M.: Big data and the future of business. Manag. Inf. Syst. Q. **38**(2), 625–638 (2014)
8. Zhou, J.: Convolutional neural networks explained. Towards Data Science (2018). https://towardsdatascience.com/convolutional-neural-networks-explained-9cc5188c4939
9. Zhou, J., et al.: Graph neural networks: a review of methods and applications. AI Open **1**, 57–81 (2018)
10. Li, T., Sahu, A.K., Talwalkar, A., Smith, V.: Federated learning: challenges, methods, and future directions. IEEE Sig. Process. Mag. **37**(3), 50–60 (2020)
11. Tan, Y., Liu, Y., Long, G., Jiang, J., Lu, Q., Zhang, C.: Federated learning on non-IID graphs via structural knowledge sharing (2022)
12. Kai, H., Jiasheng, W., Li, Y., Meixia, L., Weng, L., Xia, M.: FedGCN: federated learning-based graph convolutional networks for non-EUCLIDEAN spatial data. Mathematics **10**(6), 1000 (2022)
13. Meng, C., Rambhatla, S., Liu, Y.: Cross-node federated graph neural network for spatio-temporal data modeling. In: Proceedings of the 27th ACM SIGKDD Conference on Knowledge Discovery and Data Mining, pp. 1202–1211 (2021)
14. Ouchani, S., Jarraya, Y., Mohamed, O.A., Debbabi, M.: Probabilistic attack scenarios to evaluate policies over communication protocols. J. Softw. **7**(7), 1488–1495 (2012)
15. Guendouzi, S.B., Ouchani, S., Malki, M.: Genetic algorithm based aggregation for federated learning in industrial cyber physical systems. In: García Bringas, P., et al. (eds.) CISIS ICEUTE 2022. LNNS, vol. 532, pp. 12–21. Springer, Cham (2022). https://doi.org/10.1007/978-3-031-18409-3_2

16. Guendouzi, S.B., Ouchani, S., Malki, M.: Aggregation using genetic algorithms for federated learning in industrial cyber-physical systems. In: 2022 International Conference on INnovations in Intelligent SysTems and Applications (INISTA), pp. 1–6. IEEE (2022)
17. Guendouzi, S.B., Ouchani, S., Malki, M.: Enhancing the aggregation of the federated learning for the industrial cyber physical systems. In: 2022 IEEE International Conference on Cyber Security and Resilience (CSR), pp. 197–202. IEEE (2022)

Author Index

A. Ait Wakrime et al. (Eds.): CRiSIS 2023, LNCS 14529, pp. 289–290, 2024.
https://doi.org/10.1007/978-3-031-61231-2

Printed in the United States
by Baker & Taylor Publisher Services